HER MAJESTY'S DOG

1

STORY AND ART BY
MICK TAKEUCHI

LOVE
BEAST

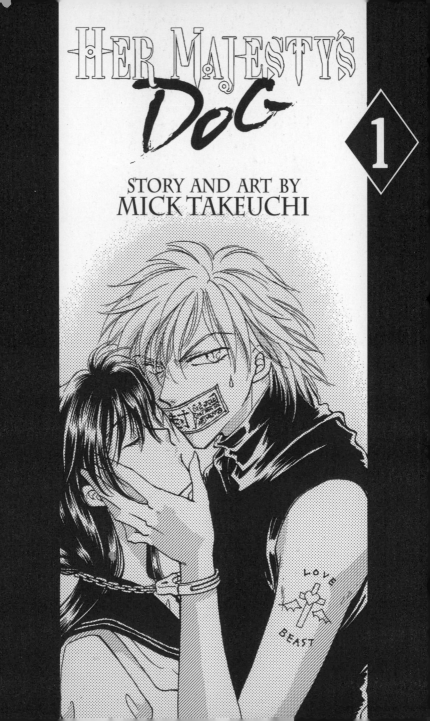

Translation – Akira Tsubasa
Lettering – Jake Forbes
Cover Design – MediaSlam

Editor – Jake Forbes

A Go! Comi manga

Published by Go! Media Entertainment, LLC

Jo-ousama no Inu Volume 1 © 2001 Mick Takeuchi/ Akitashoten.
Originally published in Japan in 2001 by AKITA SHOTEN CO, LTD., Tokyo.
English translation rights arranged with AKITA SHOTEN CO., LTD.
through TOHAN CORPORATION, Tokyo.

Visit us online at www.gocomi.com
e-mail: info@gocomi.com

ISBN 0-9768957-3-0

First printed in October 2005

1 2 3 4 5 6 7 8 9

Manufactured in the United States of America.

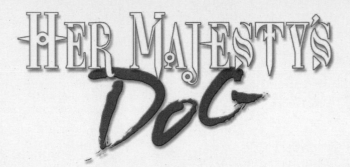

STORY AND ART BY
MICK TAKEUCHI

VOLUME 1

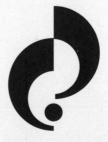

go!comi

Concerning Honorifics

At Go! Comi, we do our best to ensure that our translations read seamlessly in English while respecting the original Japanese language and culture. To this end, the original honorifics (the suffixes found at the end of characters' names) remain intact. In Japan, where politeness and formality are more integrated into every aspect of the language, honorifics give a better understanding of character relationships. They can be used to indicate both respect and affection. Whether a person addresses someone by first name or last name also indicates how close their relationship is.

Here are some of the honorifics you might encounter in this book:

-san: This is the most common and neutral of honorifics. The polite way to address someone you're not on close terms with is to use "-san." It's kind of like Mr. or Ms., except you can use "-san" with first names as easily as family names.

-chan: Used for friendly familiarity, mostly applied towards young women and girls.

-kun: Like "-chan," it's an informal suffix for friends and classmates, only "-kun" is usually associated with boys. It can also be used in a professional environment by someone addressing a subordinate.

-sama: Indicates a great deal of respect or admiration.

Sempai: In school, "sempai" is used to refer to an upperclassman or club leader. It can also be used in the workplace by a new employee to address a mentor or staff member with seniority.

Sensei: Teachers, doctors, writers or any master of a trade are referred to as "sensei." When addressing a manga creator, the polite thing to do is attach "-sensei" to the manga-ka's name (as in Takeuchi-sensei).

[blank]: Not using an honorific when addressing someone indicates that the speaker has permission to speak intimately with the other person. This relationship is usually reserved for close friends and family.

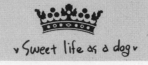

♥ Sweet life as a dog ♥

CONTENTS

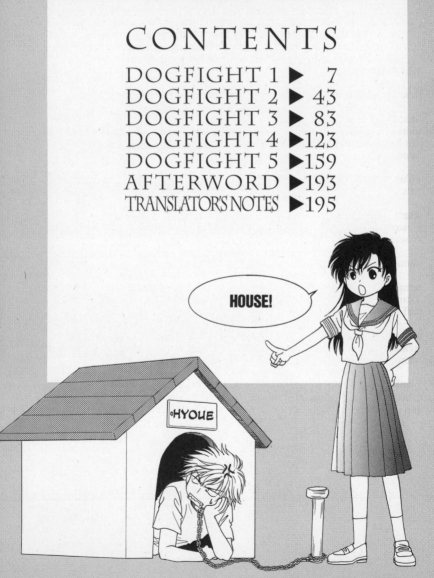

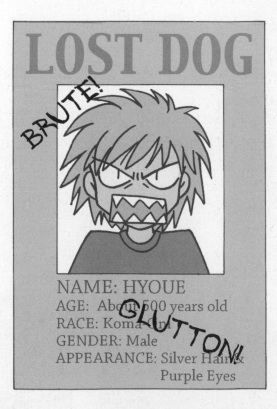

LOST DOG

BRUTE!

GLUTTON!

NAME: HYOUE
AGE: About 500 years old
RACE: Koma Inu
GENDER: Male
APPEARANCE: Silver Hair &
                           Purple Eyes

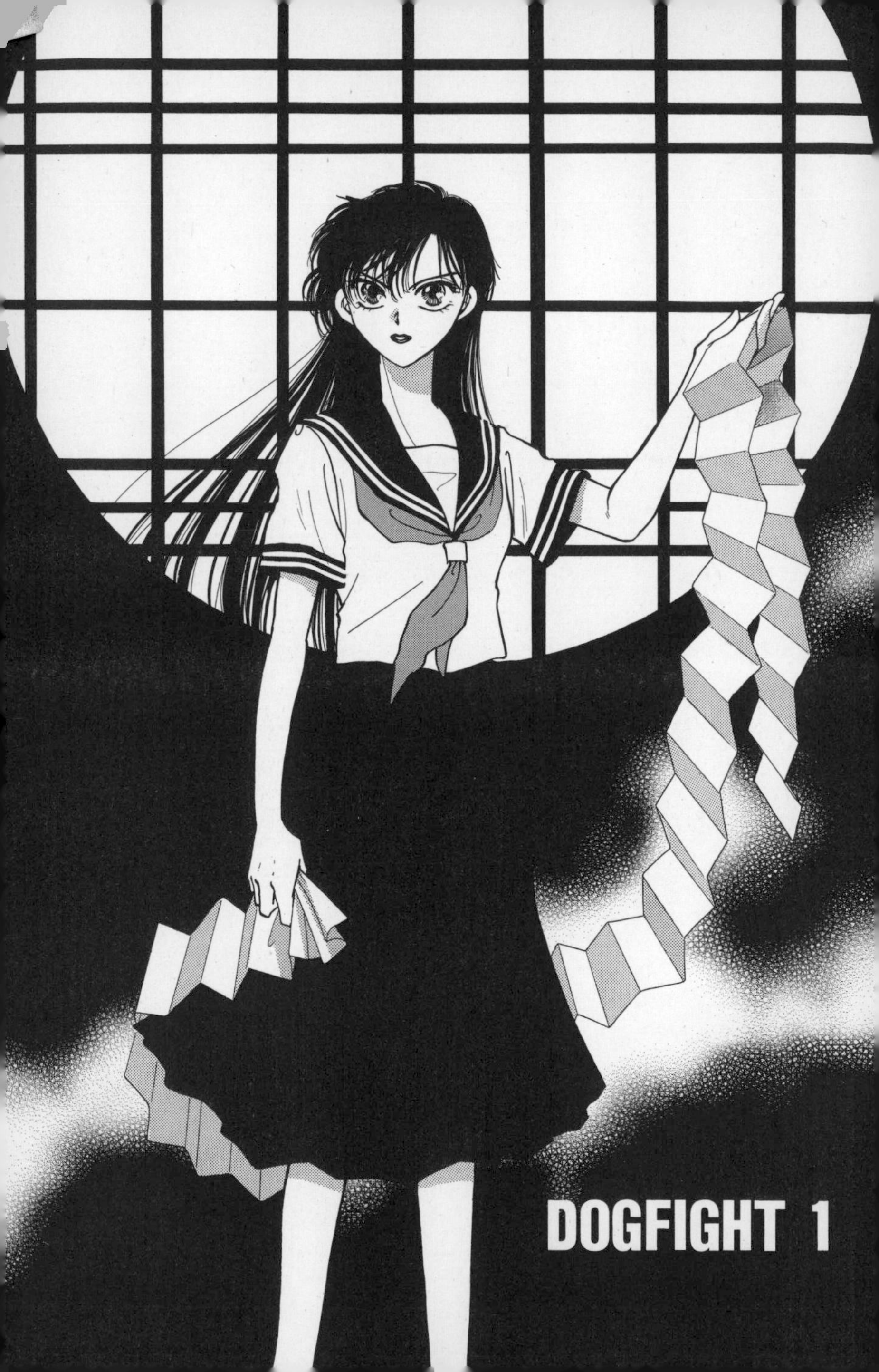
DOGFIGHT 1

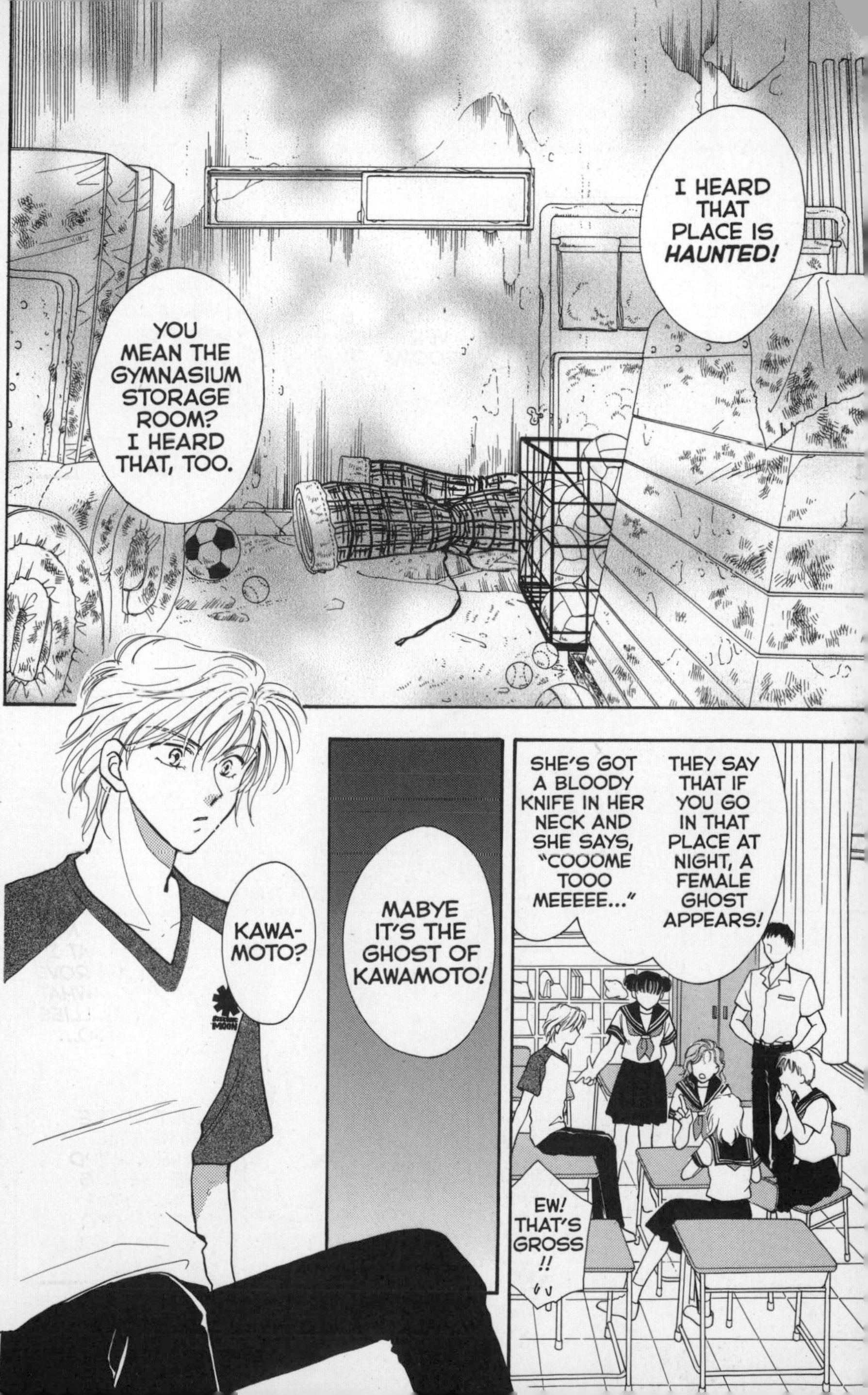
I HEARD THAT PLACE IS *HAUNTED!*
YOU MEAN THE GYMNASIUM STORAGE ROOM? I HEARD THAT, TOO.
THEY SAY THAT IF YOU GO IN THAT PLACE AT NIGHT, A FEMALE GHOST APPEARS!
SHE'S GOT A BLOODY KNIFE IN HER NECK AND SHE SAYS, "COOOME TOOO MEEEEE..."
EW! THAT'S GROSS!!
MABYE IT'S THE GHOST OF KAWAMOTO!
KAWA-MOTO?

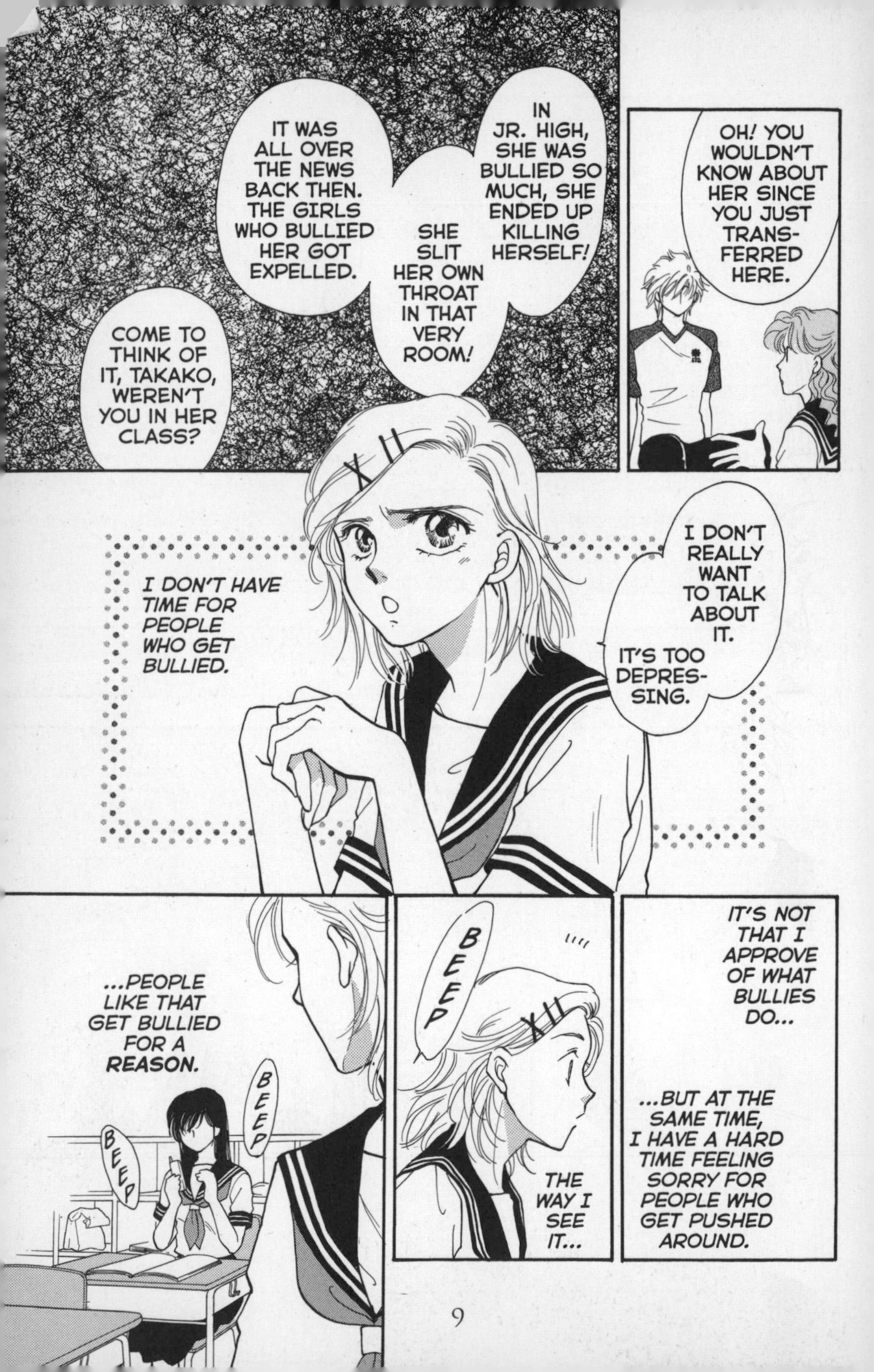

OH! YOU WOULDN'T KNOW ABOUT HER SINCE YOU JUST TRANS-FERRED HERE.
IN JR. HIGH, SHE WAS BULLIED SO MUCH, SHE ENDED UP KILLING HERSELF!
SHE SLIT HER OWN THROAT IN THAT VERY ROOM!
IT WAS ALL OVER THE NEWS BACK THEN. THE GIRLS WHO BULLIED HER GOT EXPELLED.
COME TO THINK OF IT, TAKAKO, WEREN'T YOU IN HER CLASS?
I DON'T REALLY WANT TO TALK ABOUT IT.
IT'S TOO DEPRES-SING.
I DON'T HAVE TIME FOR PEOPLE WHO GET BULLIED.
IT'S NOT THAT I APPROVE OF WHAT BULLIES DO...
...BUT AT THE SAME TIME, I HAVE A HARD TIME FEELING SORRY FOR PEOPLE WHO GET PUSHED AROUND.
BEEP
THE WAY I SEE IT...
...PEOPLE LIKE THAT GET BULLIED FOR A REASON.
BEEP
BEEP

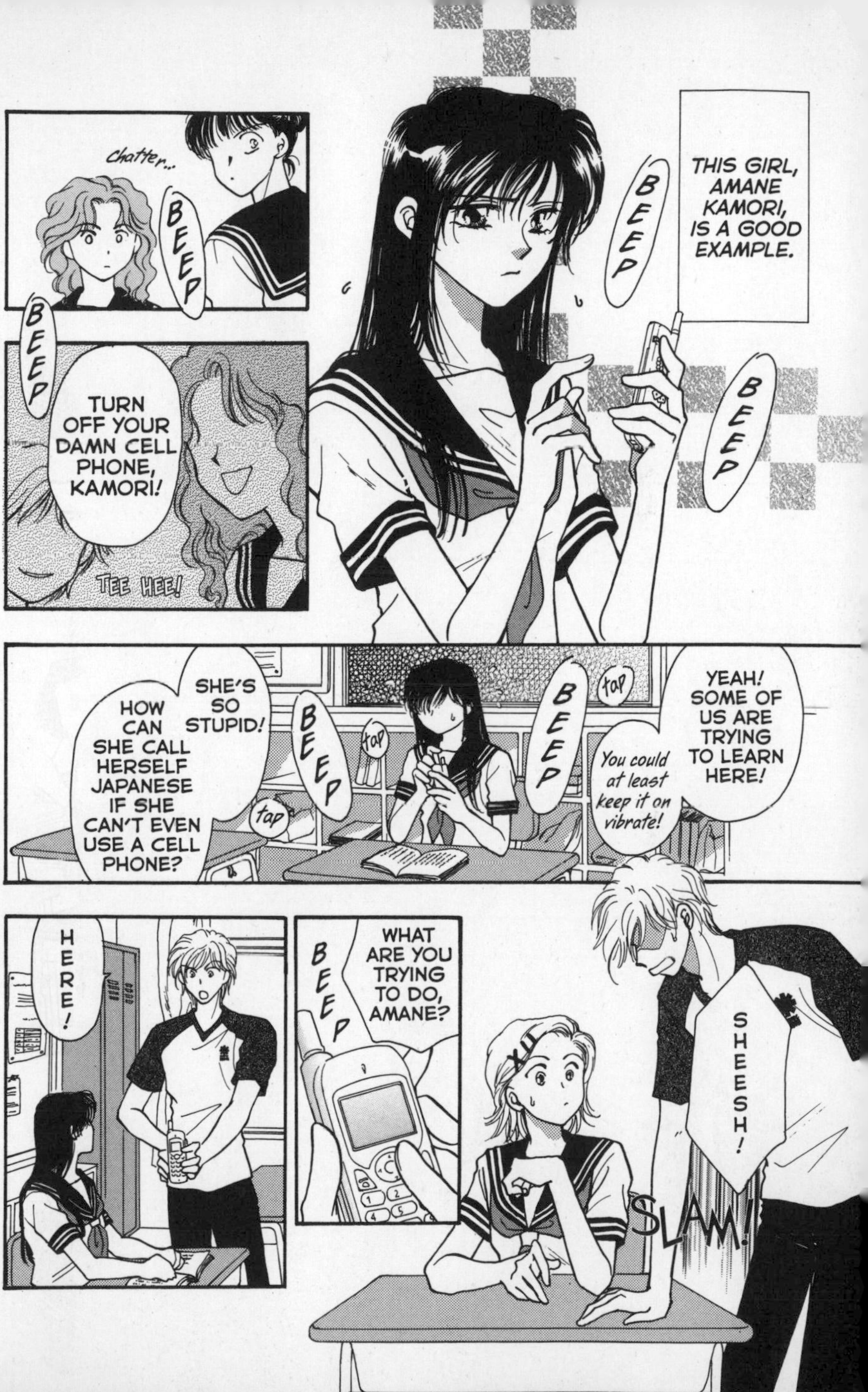
THIS GIRL, AMANE KAMORI, IS A GOOD EXAMPLE.
BEEP
BEEP
Chatter...
BEEP
BEEP
TURN OFF YOUR DAMN CELL PHONE, KAMORI!
TEE HEE!
YEAH! SOME OF US ARE TRYING TO LEARN HERE!
You could at least keep it on vibrate!
tap
BEEP
tap
BEEP
SHE'S SO STUPID!
HOW CAN SHE CALL HERSELF JAPANESE IF SHE CAN'T EVEN USE A CELL PHONE?
tap
SHEESH!
SLAM!
WHAT ARE YOU TRYING TO DO, AMANE?
BEEP
HERE!

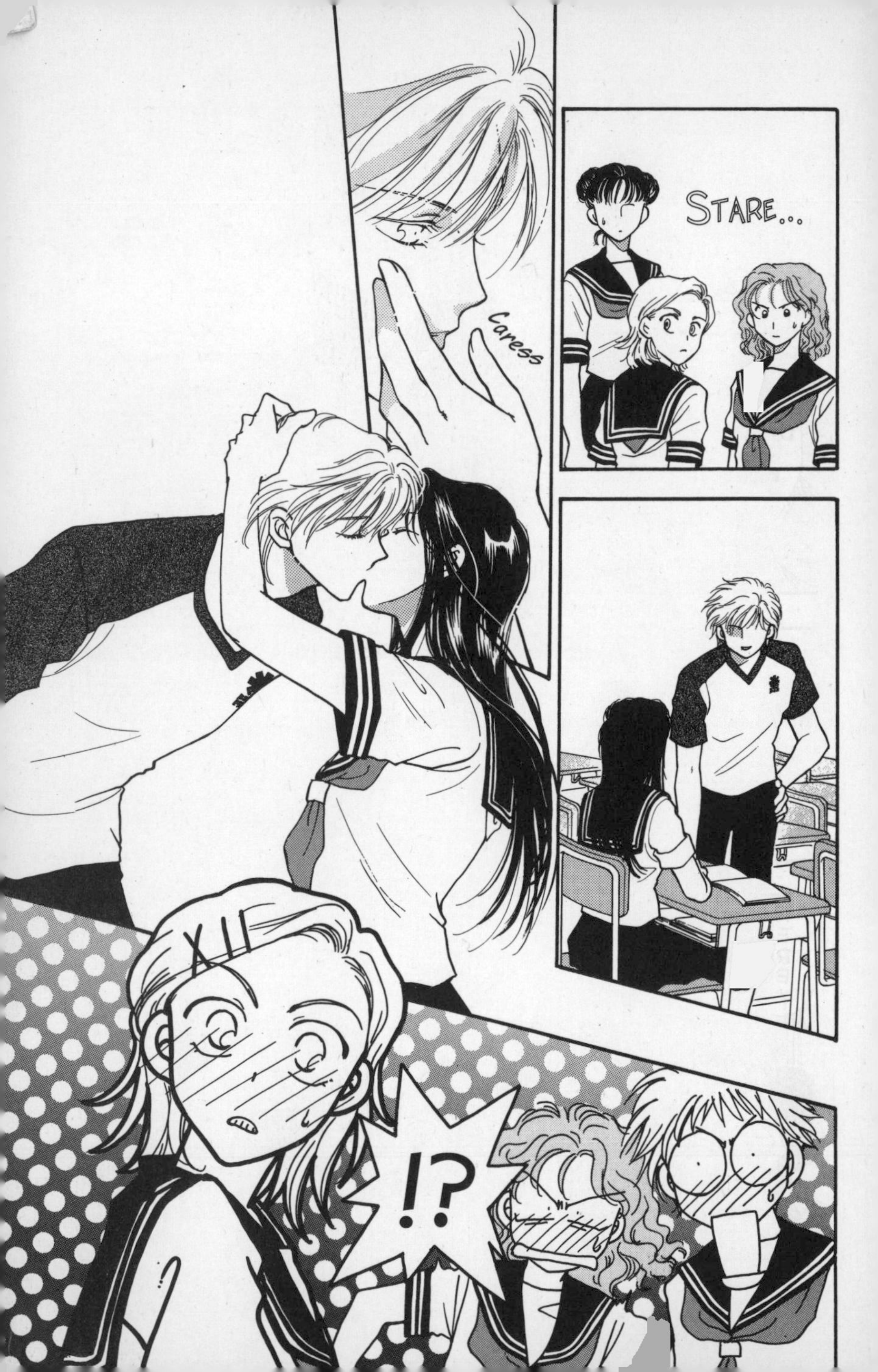
STARE...
Caress
!?

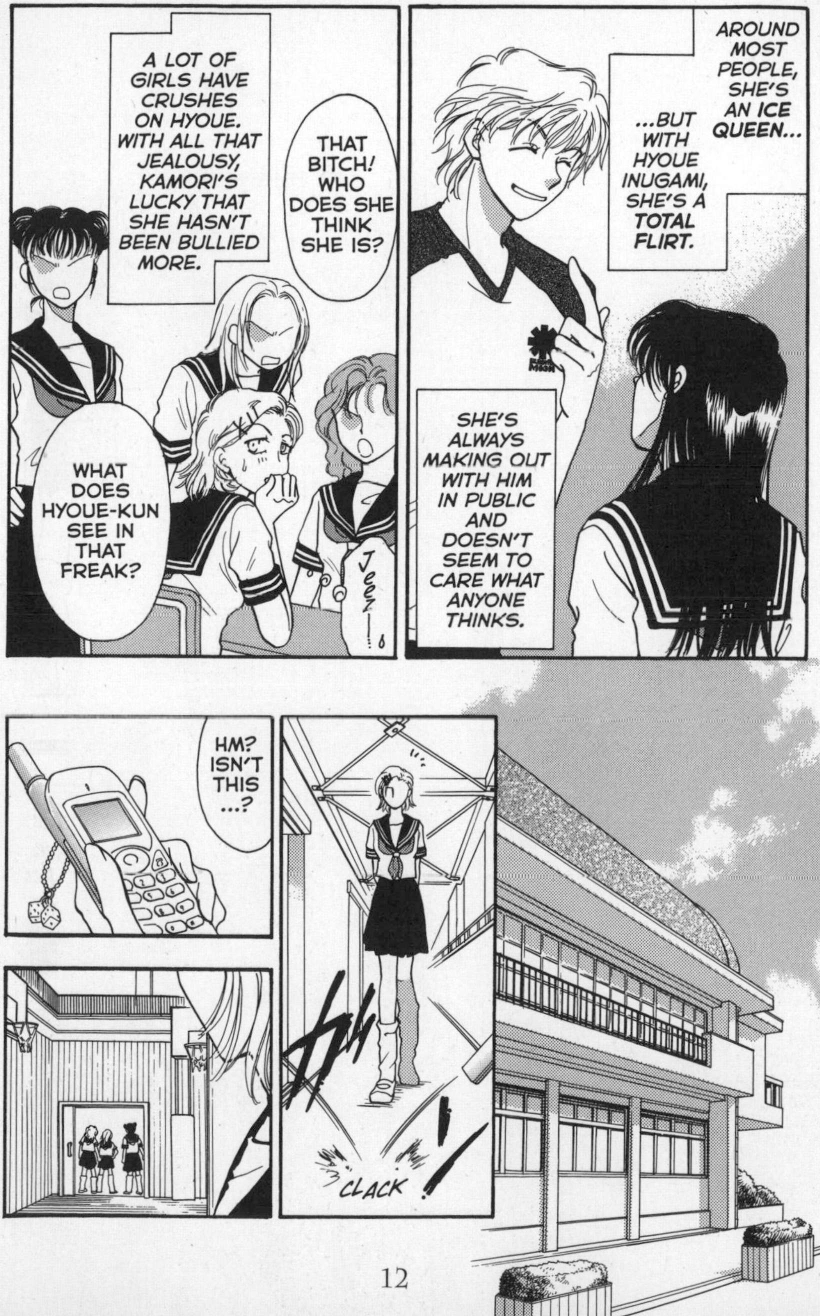
AROUND MOST PEOPLE, SHE'S AN ICE QUEEN...
...BUT WITH HYOUE INUGAMI, SHE'S A TOTAL FLIRT.
SHE'S ALWAYS MAKING OUT WITH HIM IN PUBLIC AND DOESN'T SEEM TO CARE WHAT ANYONE THINKS.
A LOT OF GIRLS HAVE CRUSHES ON HYOUE. WITH ALL THAT JEALOUSY, KAMORI'S LUCKY THAT SHE HASN'T BEEN BULLIED MORE.
THAT BITCH! WHO DOES SHE THINK SHE IS?
WHAT DOES HYOUE-KUN SEE IN THAT FREAK?
Jeez...!
CLACK
HM? ISN'T THIS ...?

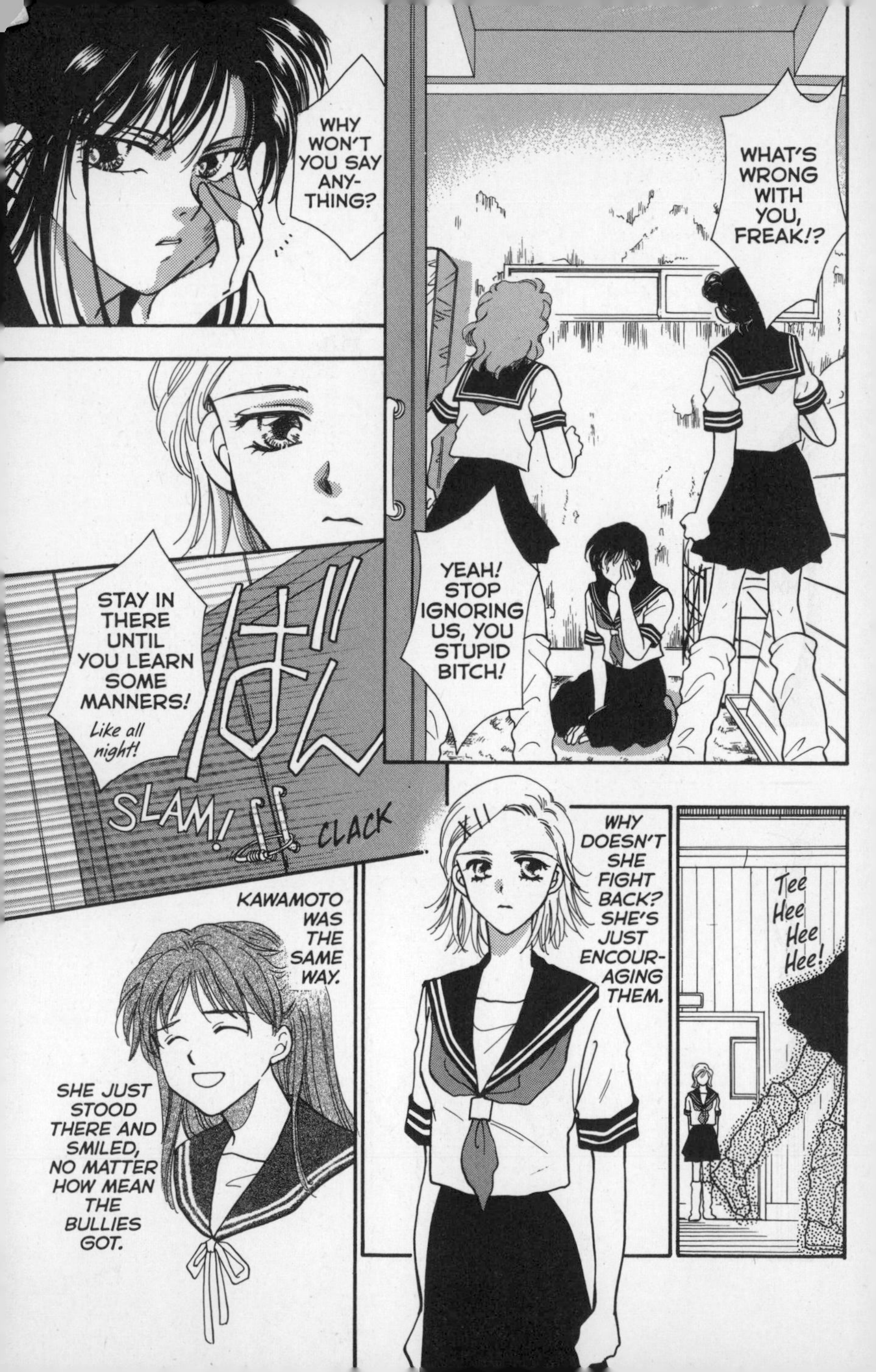
WHAT'S WRONG WITH YOU, FREAK!?
YEAH! STOP IGNORING US, YOU STUPID BITCH!
WHY WON'T YOU SAY ANY-THING?
...
STAY IN THERE UNTIL YOU LEARN SOME MANNERS!
Like all night!
ばん
SLAM!
CLACK
Tee Hee Hee Hee!
WHY DOESN'T SHE FIGHT BACK? SHE'S JUST ENCOUR-AGING THEM.
KAWAMOTO WAS THE SAME WAY.
SHE JUST STOOD THERE AND SMILED, NO MATTER HOW MEAN THE BULLIES GOT.

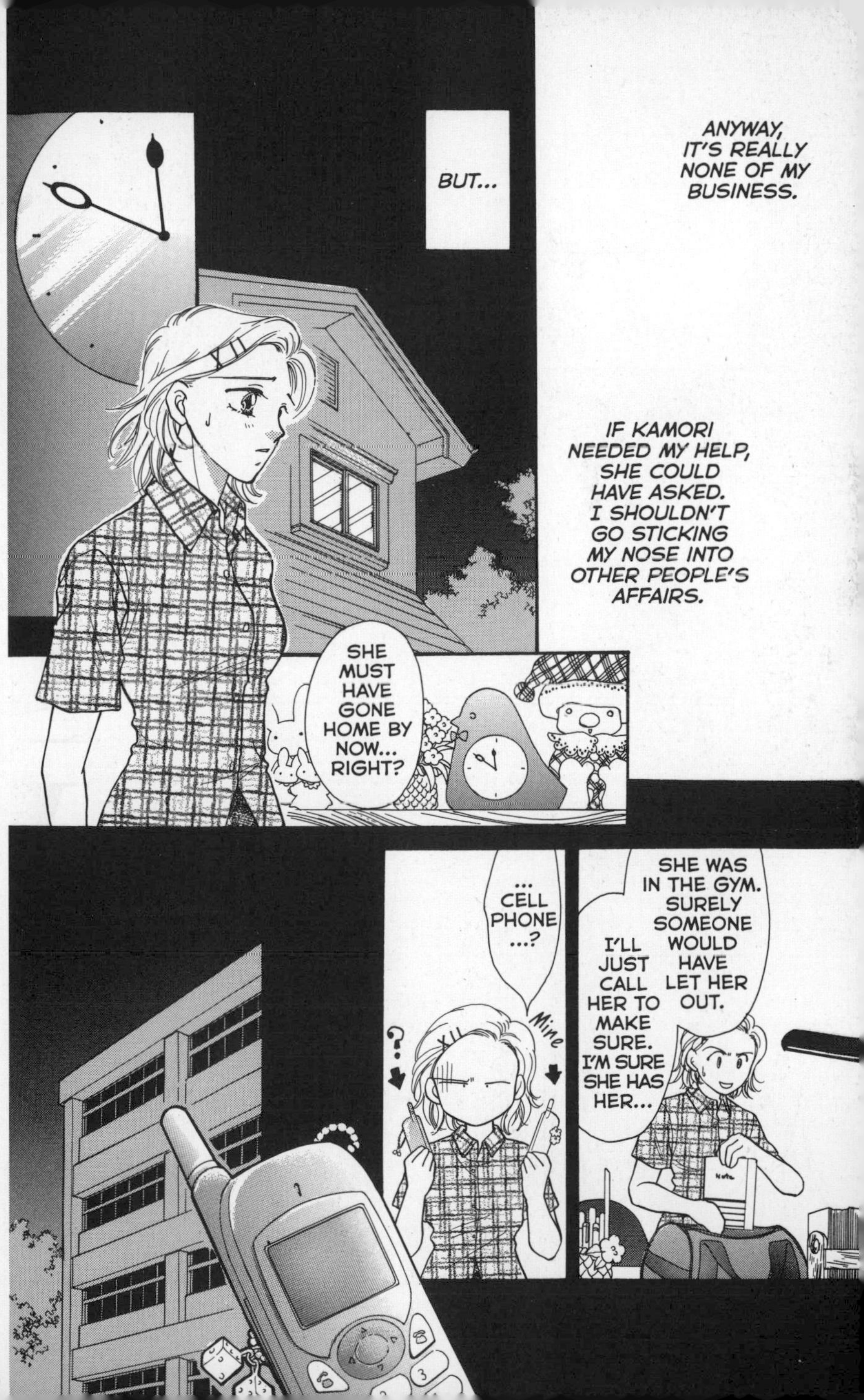
ANYWAY, IT'S REALLY NONE OF MY BUSINESS.
IF KAMORI NEEDED MY HELP, SHE COULD HAVE ASKED. I SHOULDN'T GO STICKING MY NOSE INTO OTHER PEOPLE'S AFFAIRS.
BUT...
SHE MUST HAVE GONE HOME BY NOW... RIGHT?
SHE WAS IN THE GYM. SURELY SOMEONE WOULD HAVE LET HER OUT.
I'LL JUST CALL HER TO MAKE SURE. I'M SURE SHE HAS HER...
...CELL PHONE ...?
Mine
?

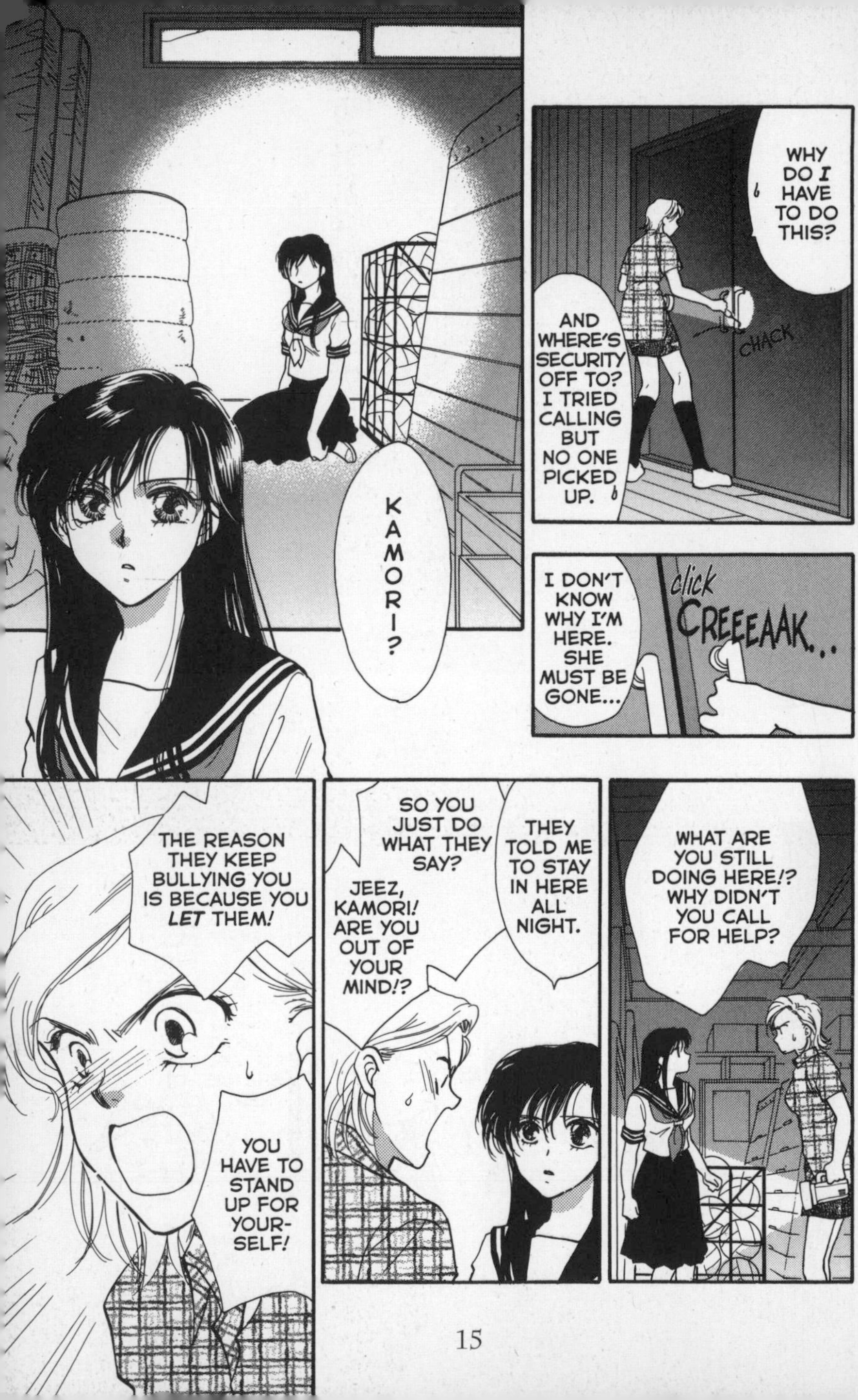
WHY DO *I* HAVE TO DO THIS?
AND WHERE'S SECURITY OFF TO? I TRIED CALLING BUT NO ONE PICKED UP.
CHACK
I DON'T KNOW WHY I'M HERE. SHE MUST BE GONE...
click
CREEEAAK...
KAMORI!?
WHAT ARE YOU STILL DOING HERE!? WHY DIDN'T YOU CALL FOR HELP?
THEY TOLD ME TO STAY IN HERE ALL NIGHT.
SO YOU JUST DO WHAT THEY SAY?
JEEZ, KAMORI! ARE YOU OUT OF YOUR MIND!?
THE REASON THEY KEEP BULLYING YOU IS BECAUSE YOU *LET* THEM!
YOU HAVE TO STAND UP FOR YOUR-SELF!

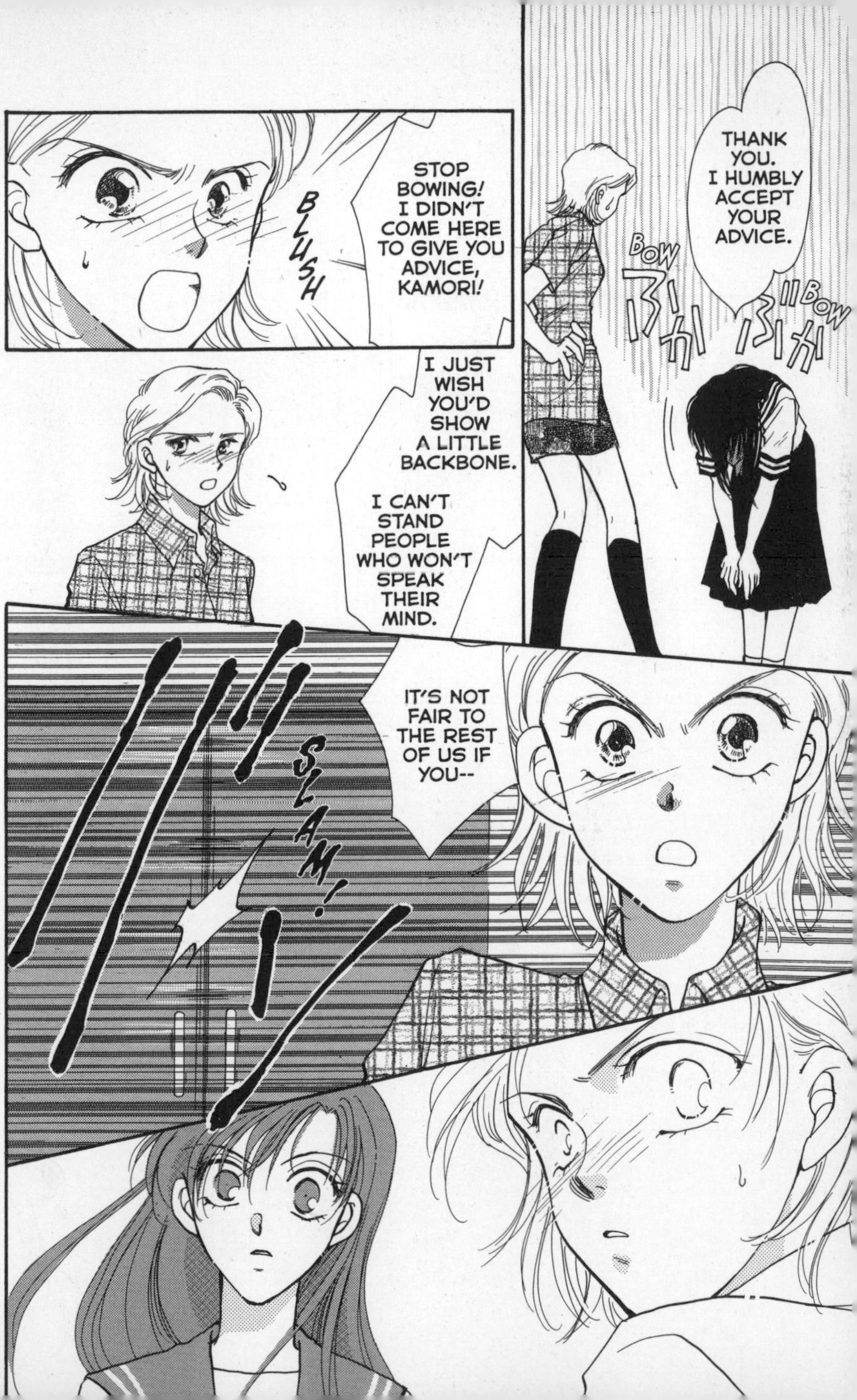
THANK YOU. I HUMBLY ACCEPT YOUR ADVICE.
BOW
BOW
BLUSH
STOP BOWING! I DIDN'T COME HERE TO GIVE YOU ADVICE, KAMORI!
I JUST WISH YOU'D SHOW A LITTLE BACKBONE.
I CAN'T STAND PEOPLE WHO WON'T SPEAK THEIR MIND.
IT'S NOT FAIR TO THE REST OF US IF YOU--
SLAM!

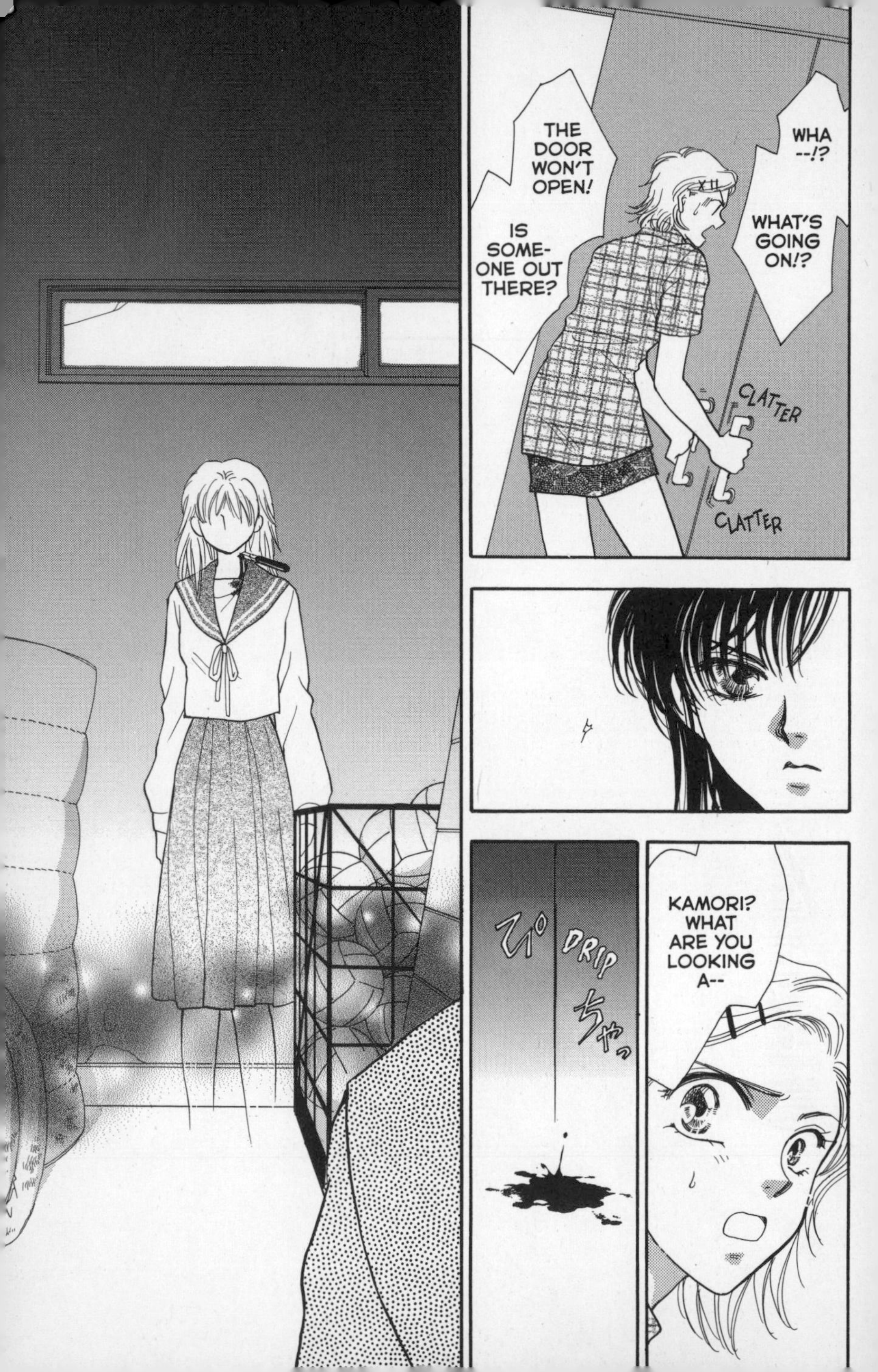
WHA --!?
WHAT'S GOING ON!?
THE DOOR WON'T OPEN!
IS SOME-ONE OUT THERE?
CLATTER
CLATTER
KAMORI? WHAT ARE YOU LOOKING A--
ぴちゃっ
DRIP

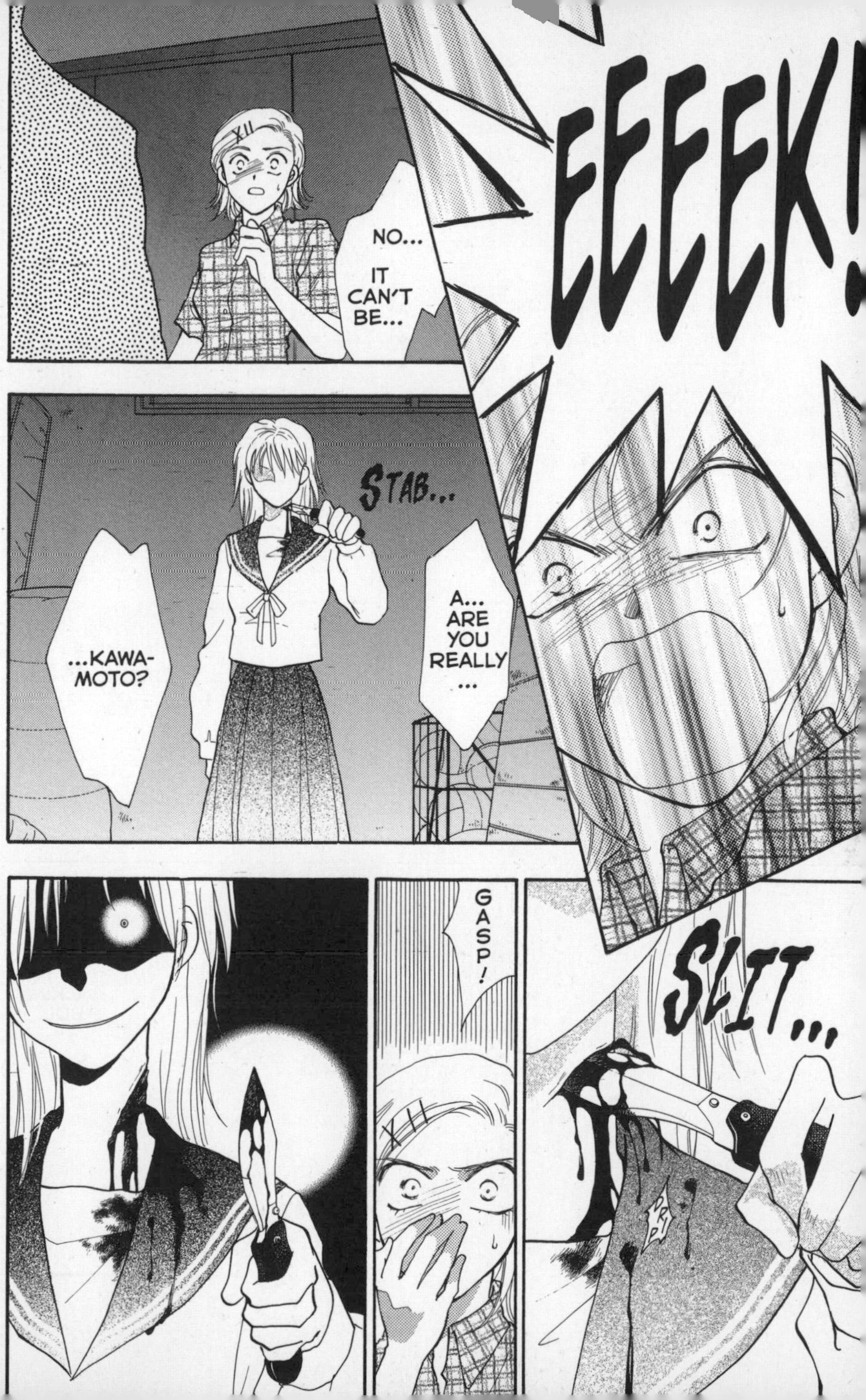
EEEEK!
NO...
IT CAN'T BE...
STAB...
A... ARE YOU REALLY ...
...KAWA-MOTO?
SLIT...
DRIP
GASP!

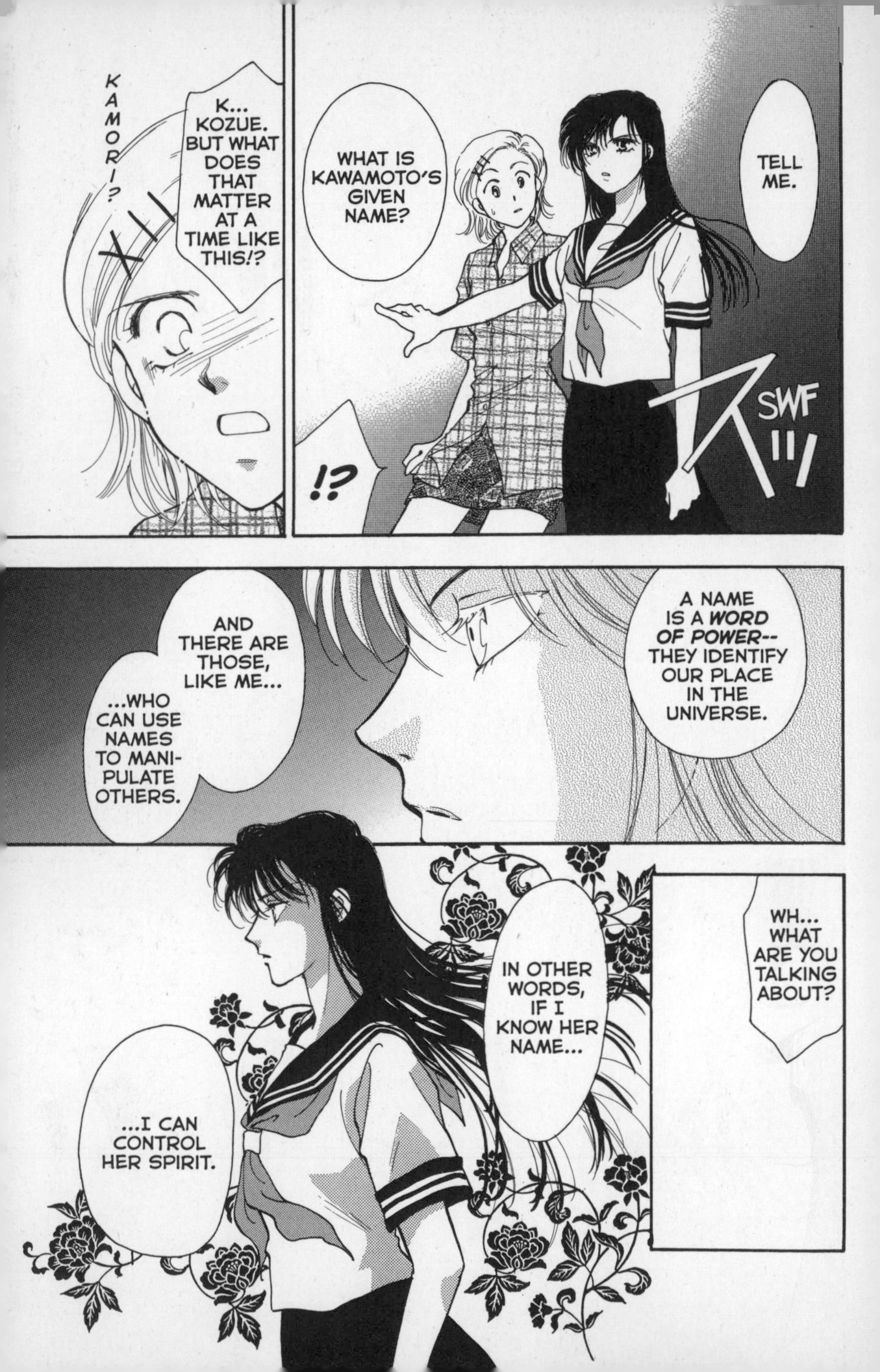
TELL ME.
WHAT IS KAWAMOTO'S GIVEN NAME?
SWF
!?
K... KOZUE. BUT WHAT DOES THAT MATTER AT A TIME LIKE THIS!?
KAMORI?
A NAME IS A *WORD OF POWER*-- THEY IDENTIFY OUR PLACE IN THE UNIVERSE.
AND THERE ARE THOSE, LIKE ME...
...WHO CAN USE NAMES TO MANI-PULATE OTHERS.
WH... WHAT ARE YOU TALKING ABOUT?
IN OTHER WORDS, IF I KNOW HER NAME...
...I CAN CONTROL HER SPIRIT.

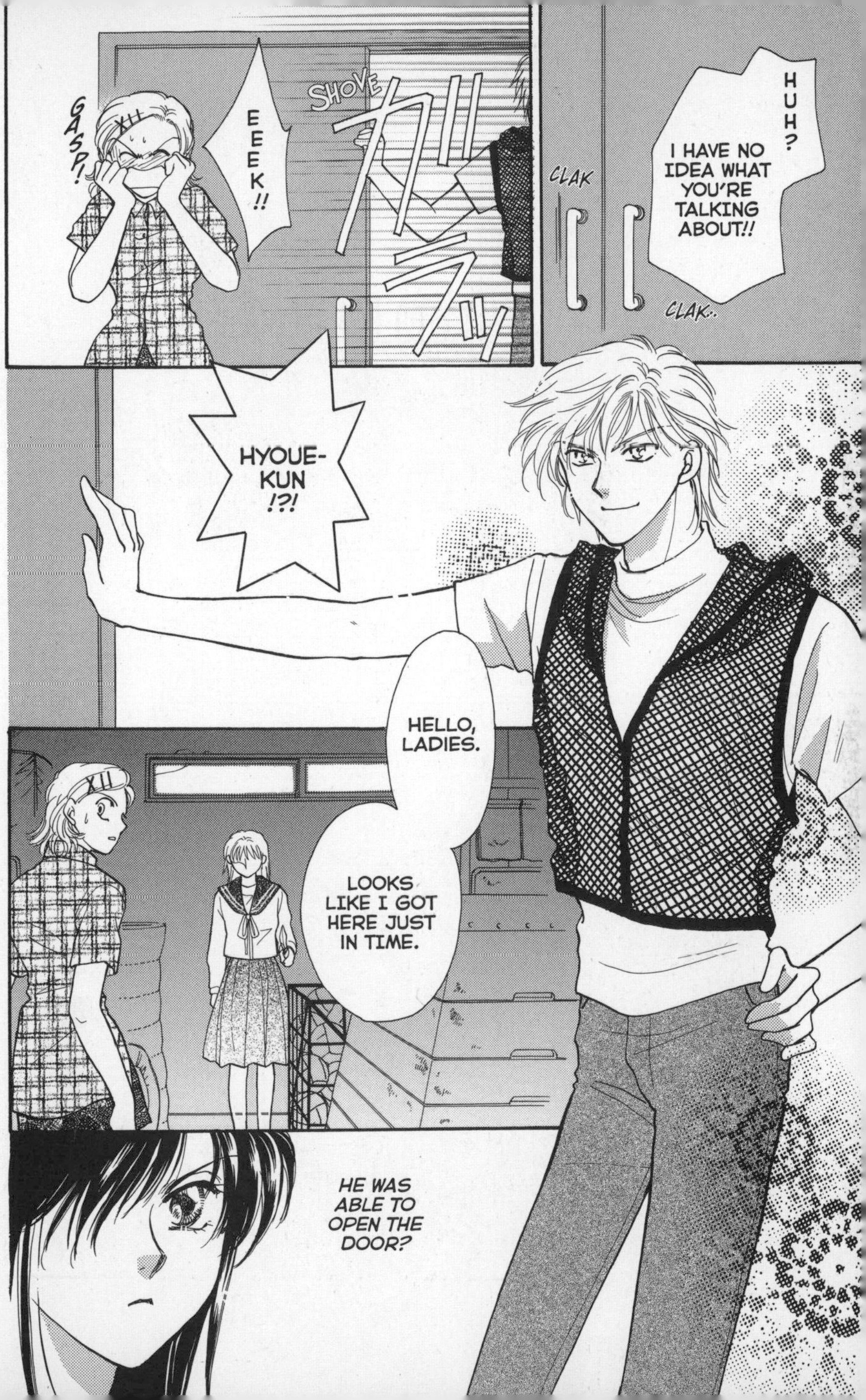
HUH?
I HAVE NO IDEA WHAT YOU'RE TALKING ABOUT!!
CLAK
CLAK..
SHOVE
EEEK!!
GASP!
HELLO, LADIES.
LOOKS LIKE I GOT HERE JUST IN TIME.
HYOUE-KUN !?!
HE WAS ABLE TO OPEN THE DOOR?

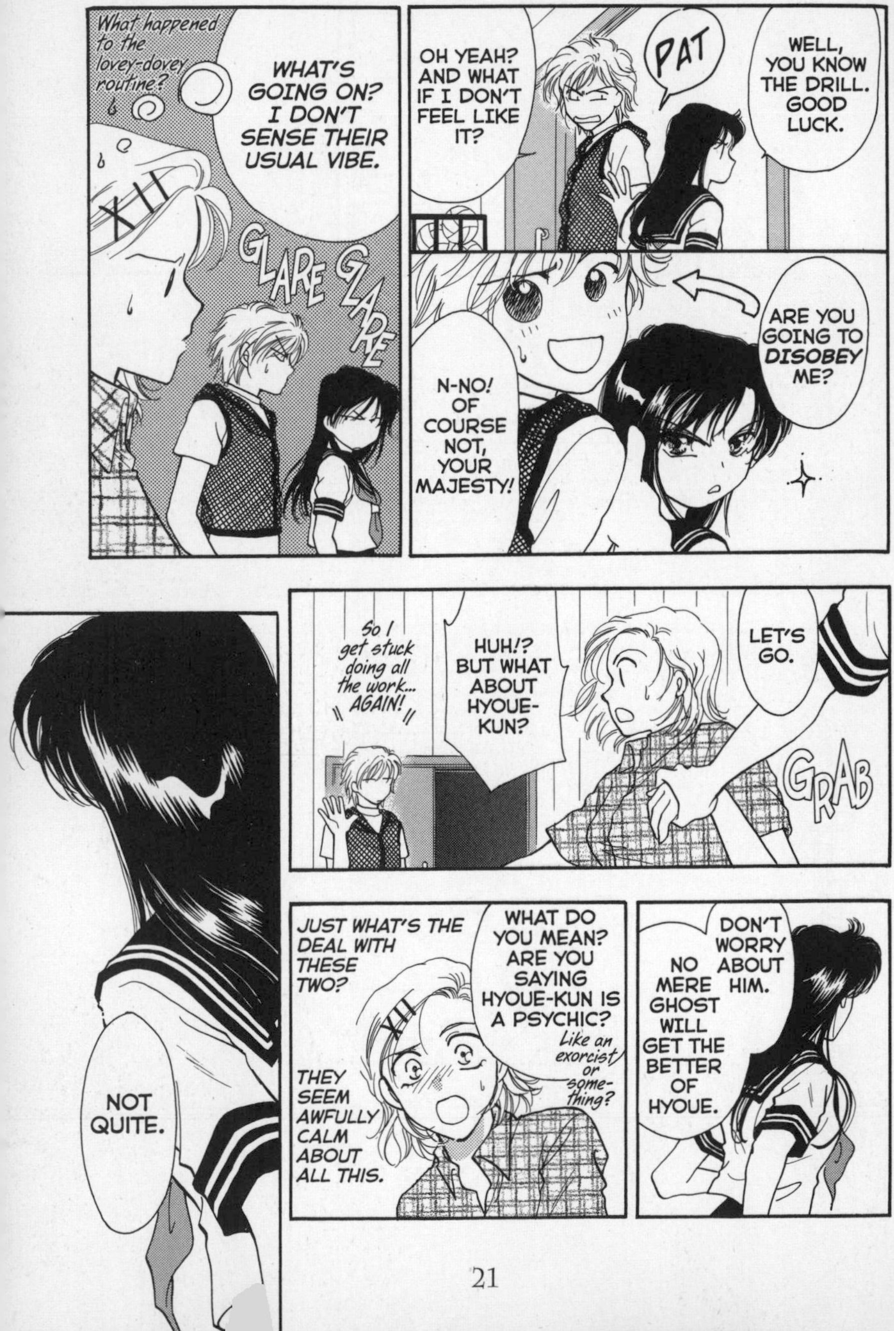
WELL, YOU KNOW THE DRILL. GOOD LUCK.
PAT
OH YEAH? AND WHAT IF I DON'T FEEL LIKE IT?
ARE YOU GOING TO DISOBEY ME?
N-NO! OF COURSE NOT, YOUR MAJESTY!
WHAT'S GOING ON? I DON'T SENSE THEIR USUAL VIBE.
What happened to the lovey-dovey routine?
GLARE GLARE
LET'S GO.
HUH!? BUT WHAT ABOUT HYOUE-KUN?
GRAB
So I get stuck doing all the work... AGAIN!
DON'T WORRY ABOUT HIM.
NO MERE GHOST WILL GET THE BETTER OF HYOUE.
WHAT DO YOU MEAN? ARE YOU SAYING HYOUE-KUN IS A PSYCHIC?
Like an exorcist or some-thing?
JUST WHAT'S THE DEAL WITH THESE TWO?
THEY SEEM AWFULLY CALM ABOUT ALL THIS.
NOT QUITE.

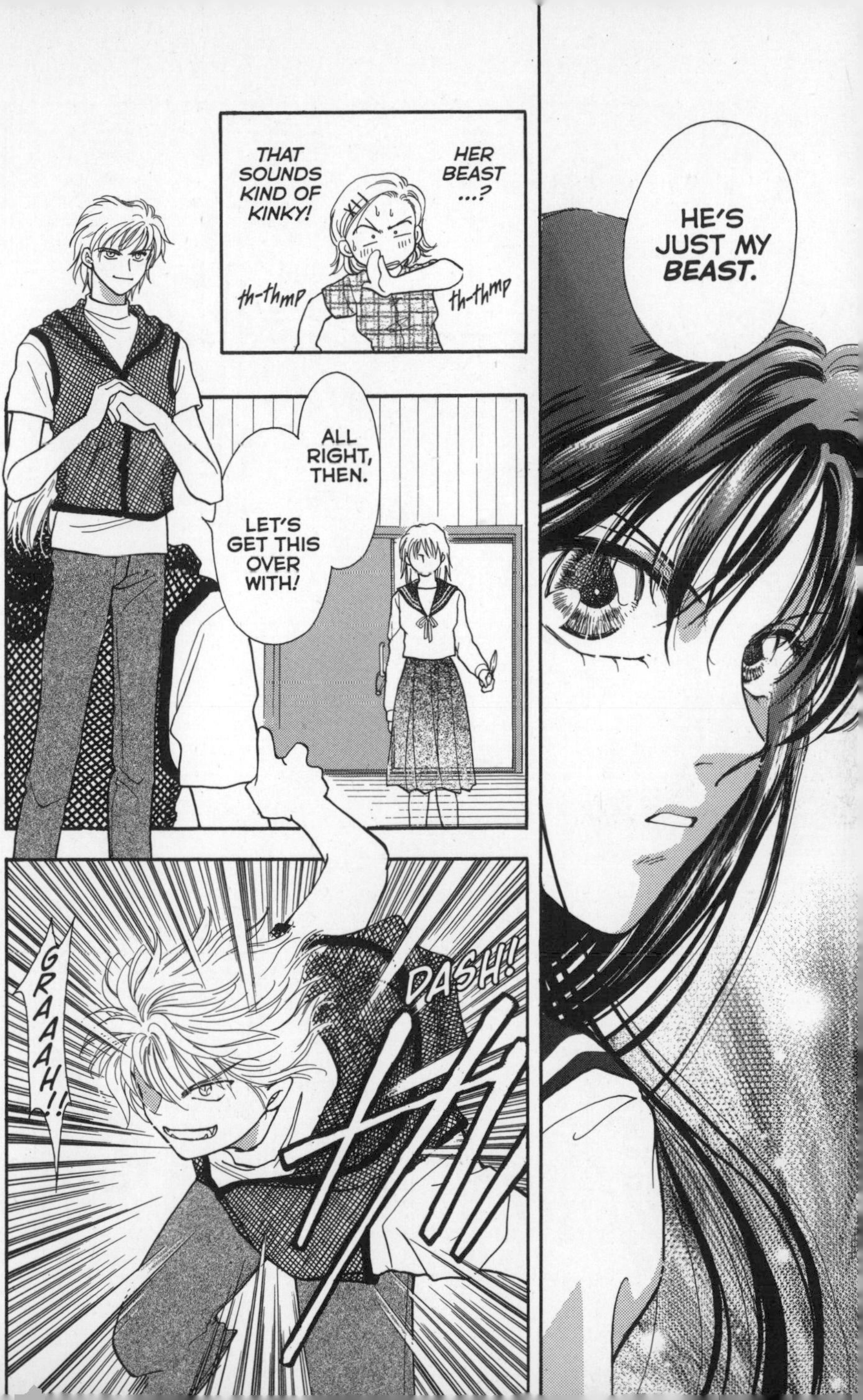
HE'S JUST MY BEAST.
HER BEAST ...?
THAT SOUNDS KIND OF KINKY!
th-thump
th-thump
ALL RIGHT, THEN.
LET'S GET THIS OVER WITH!
DASH!
GRAAAH!!

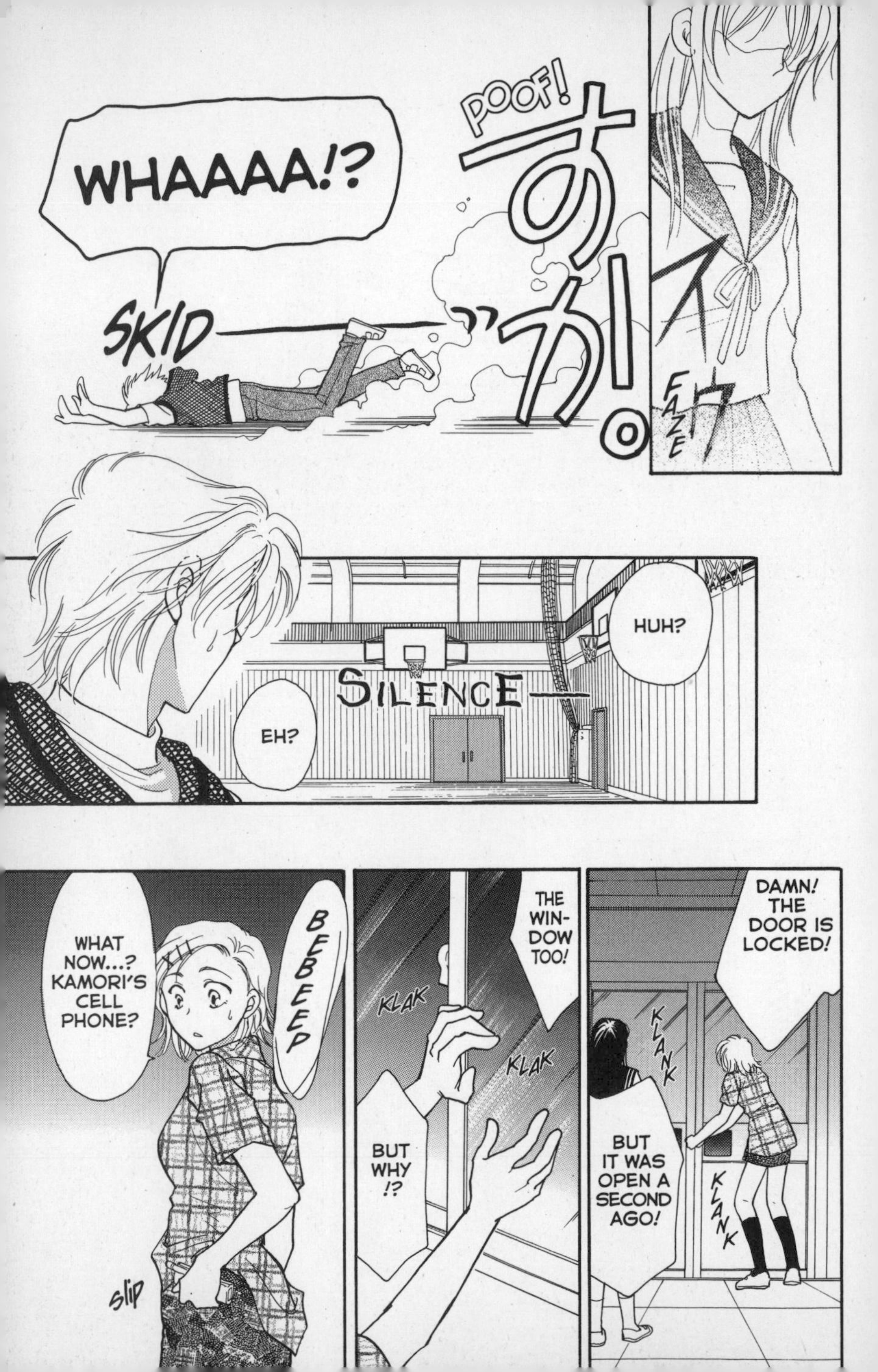
FAZE
POOF!
あわ!
WHAAAA!?
SKID
HUH?
SILENCE
EH?
DAMN! THE DOOR IS LOCKED!
KLANK
BUT IT WAS OPEN A SECOND AGO!
KLANK
THE WIN-DOW TOO!
KLAK
KLAK
BUT WHY!?
BEBEEP
WHAT NOW...? KAMORI'S CELL PHONE?
slip

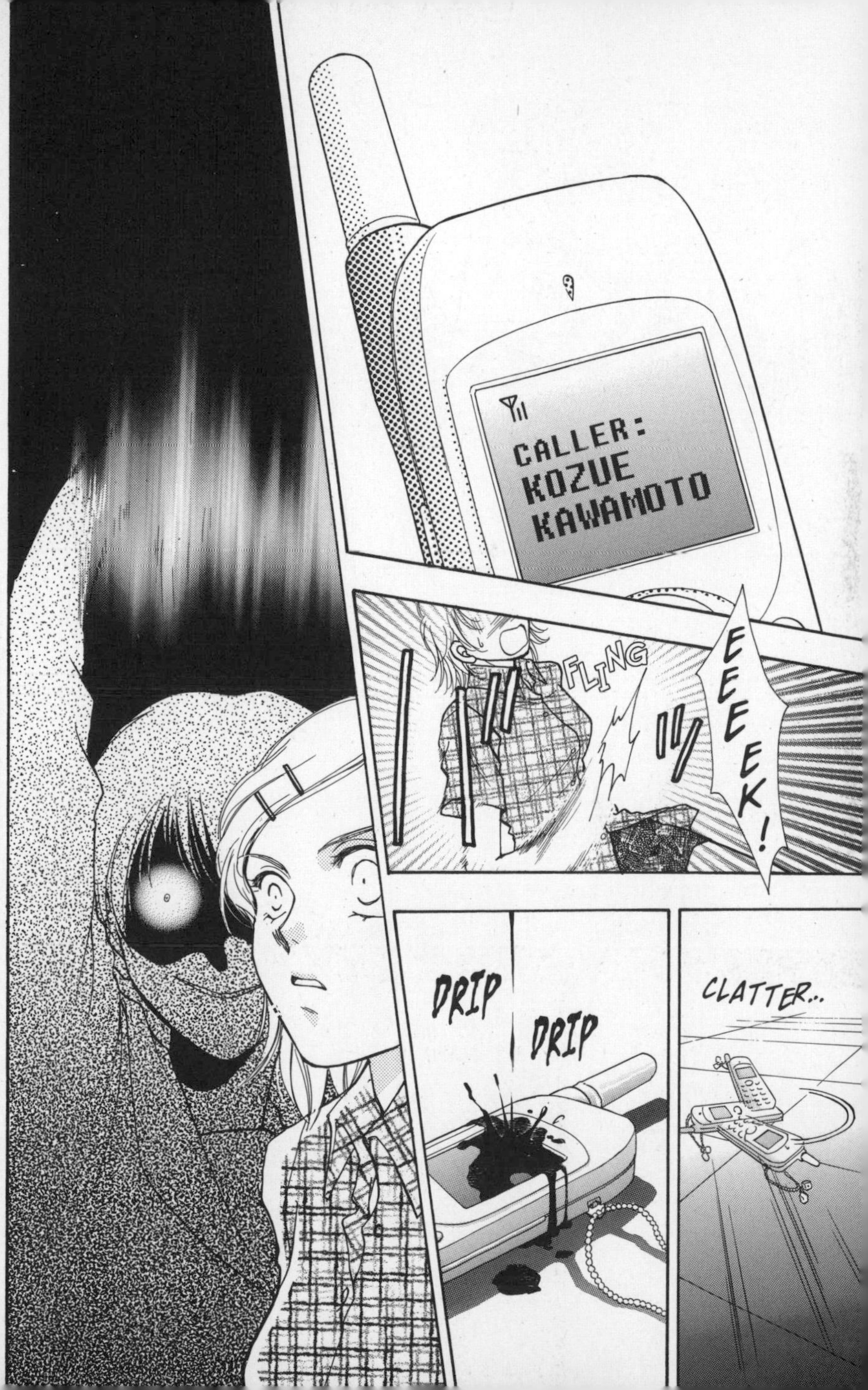
CALLER:
KOZUE
KAWAMOTO
EEEEEK!
FLING
CLATTER...
DRIP
DRIP

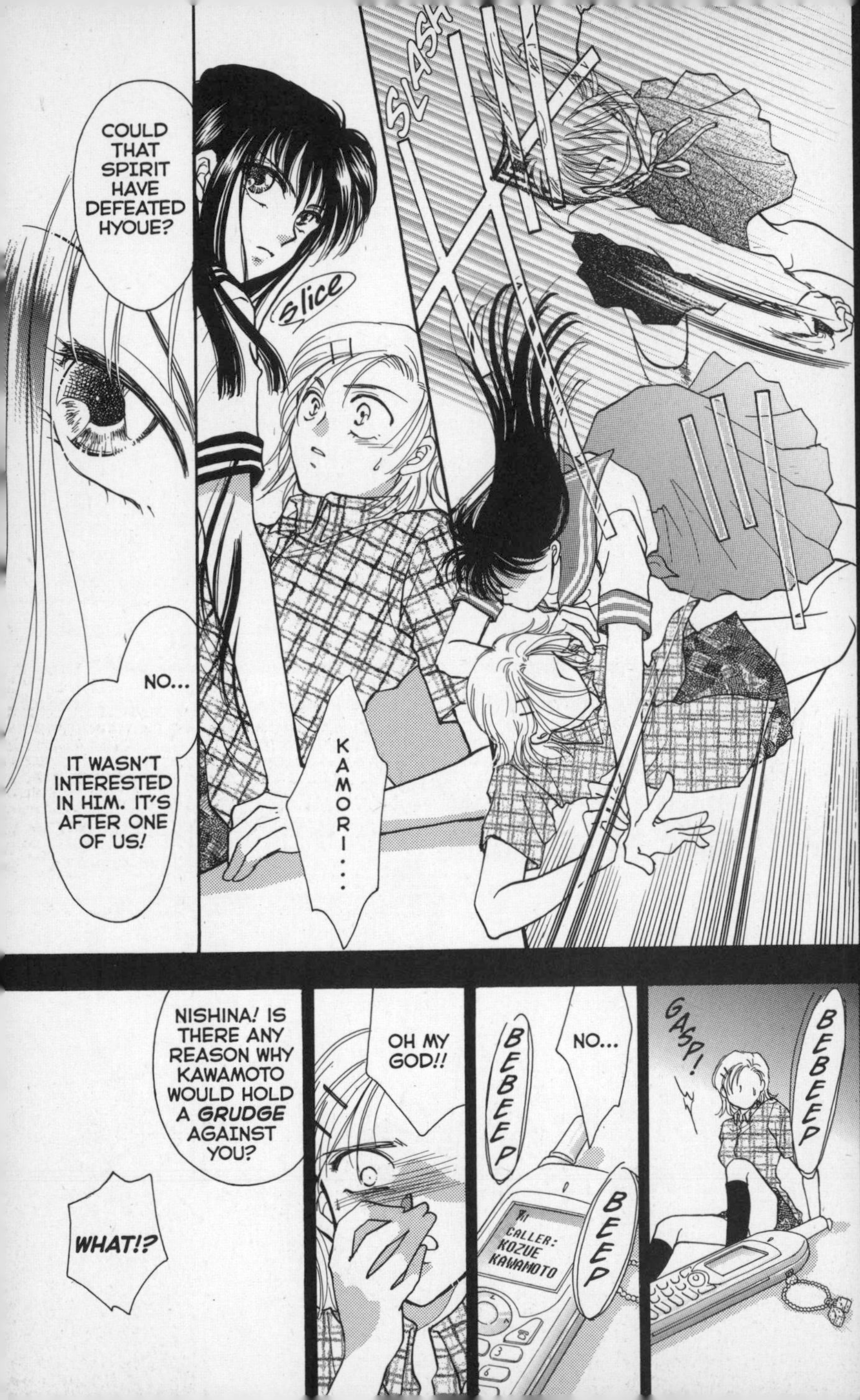
SLASH
Slice
KAMORI...
COULD THAT SPIRIT HAVE DEFEATED HYOUE?
NO...
IT WASN'T INTERESTED IN HIM. IT'S AFTER ONE OF US!
GASP!
BEBEEP
BEBEEP
BEEP
CALLER: KOZUE KAWAMOTO
NO...
OH MY GOD!!
NISHINA! IS THERE ANY REASON WHY KAWAMOTO WOULD HOLD A GRUDGE AGAINST YOU?
WHAT!?

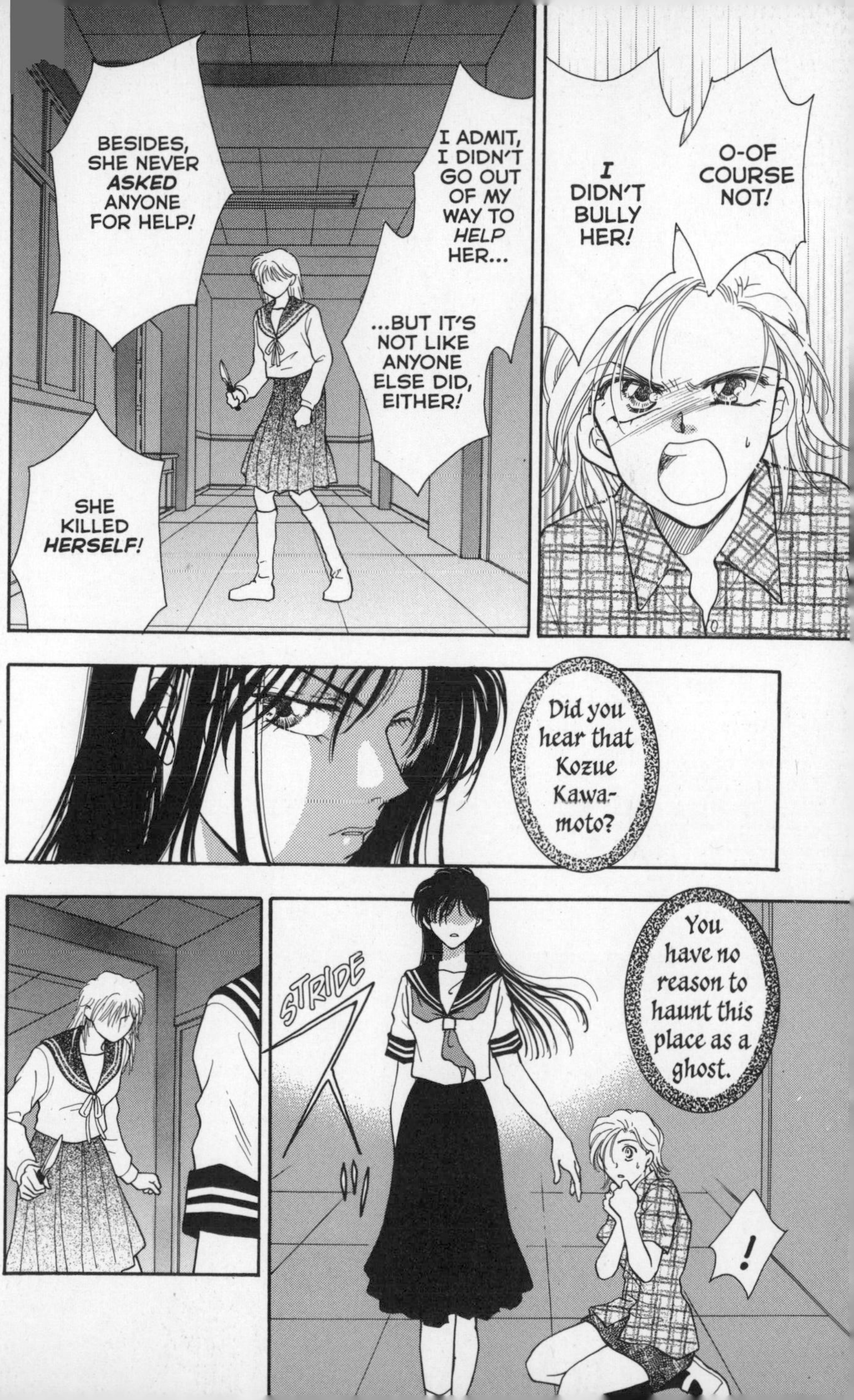
O-OF COURSE NOT!
I DIDN'T BULLY HER!
I ADMIT, I DIDN'T GO OUT OF MY WAY TO HELP HER...
...BUT IT'S NOT LIKE ANYONE ELSE DID, EITHER!
BESIDES, SHE NEVER ASKED ANYONE FOR HELP!
SHE KILLED HERSELF!
Did you hear that Kozue Kawamoto?
You have no reason to haunt this place as a ghost.
STRIDE
!

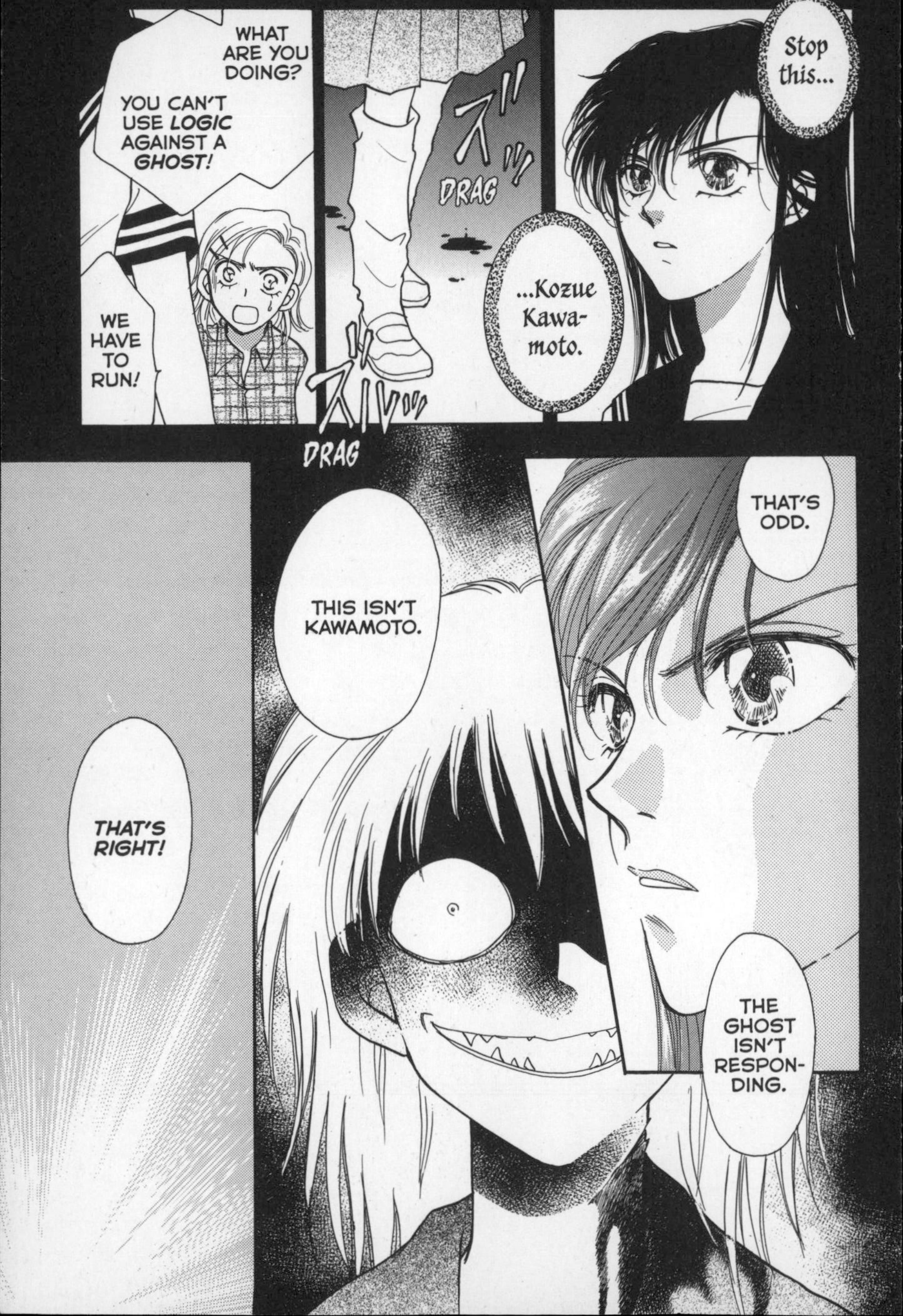

Stop this...
...Kozue Kawamoto.
DRAG
WHAT ARE YOU DOING?
YOU CAN'T USE *LOGIC* AGAINST A *GHOST!*
WE HAVE TO RUN!
DRAG
THAT'S ODD.
THE GHOST ISN'T RESPONDING.
THIS ISN'T KAWAMOTO.
THAT'S RIGHT!

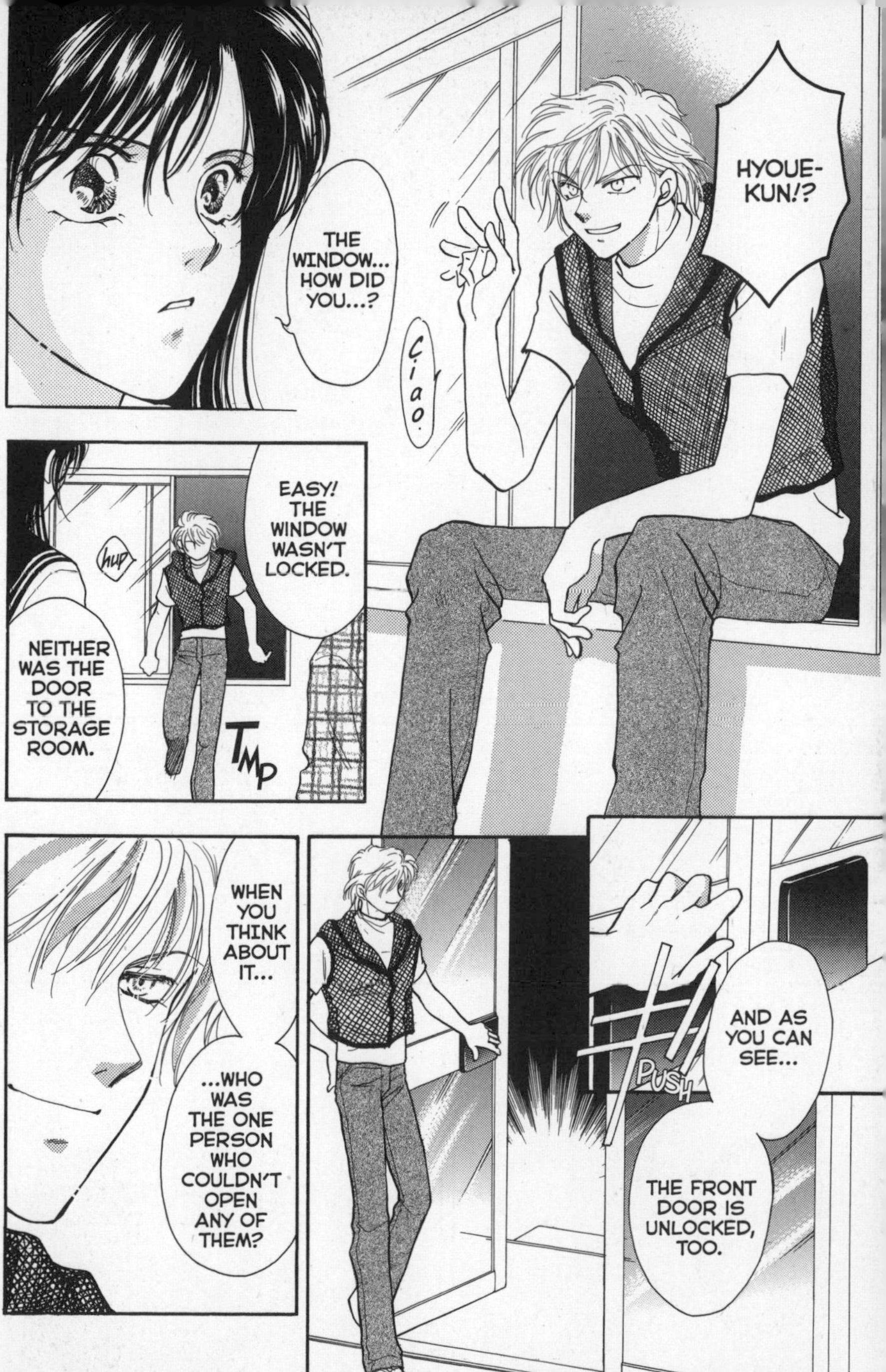
HYOUE-KUN!?
Ciao.
THE WINDOW... HOW DID YOU...?
EASY! THE WINDOW WASN'T LOCKED.
hup
NEITHER WAS THE DOOR TO THE STORAGE ROOM.
TMP
AND AS YOU CAN SEE...
PUSH
THE FRONT DOOR IS UNLOCKED, TOO.
WHEN YOU THINK ABOUT IT...
...WHO WAS THE ONE PERSON WHO COULDN'T OPEN ANY OF THEM?

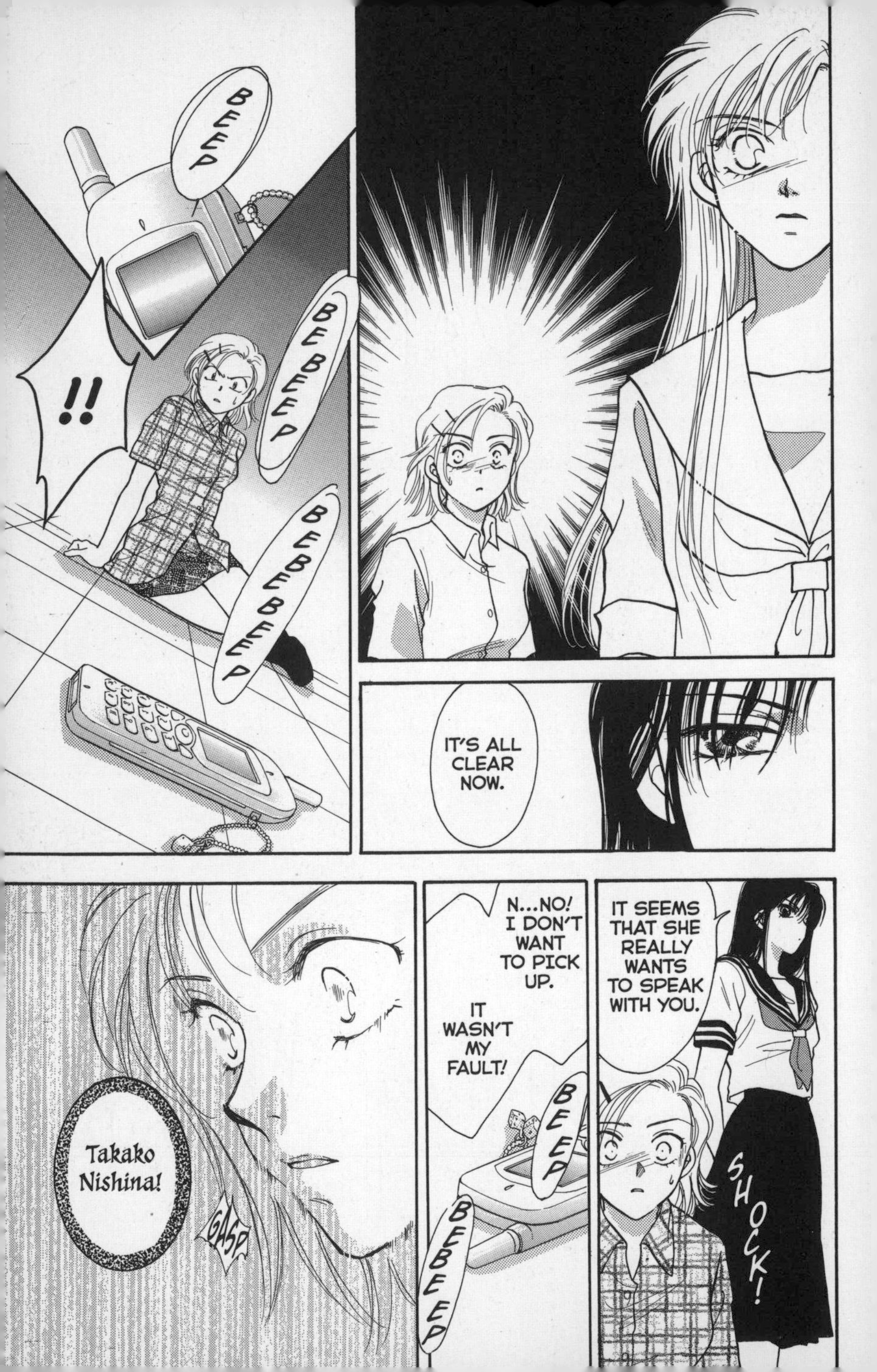
IT'S ALL CLEAR NOW.
BEEP
BEBEEP
!!
BEBEBEEP
IT SEEMS THAT SHE REALLY WANTS TO SPEAK WITH YOU.
SHOCK!
N...NO! I DON'T WANT TO PICK UP.
IT WASN'T MY FAULT!
BEEP
BEBEEP
Takako Nishina!
GASP

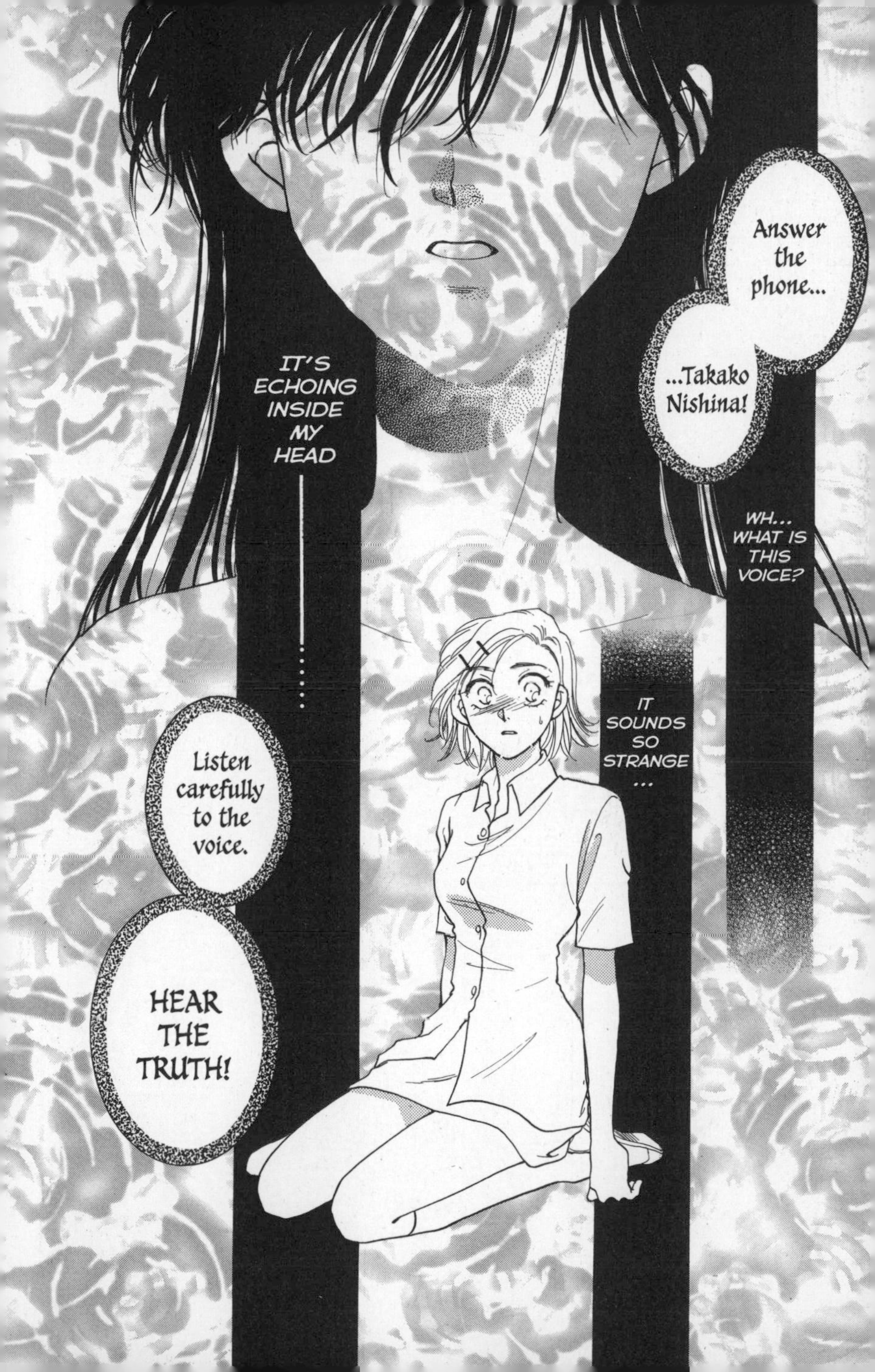
Answer the phone...
...Takako Nishina!
WH... WHAT IS THIS VOICE?
IT SOUNDS SO STRANGE ...
IT'S ECHOING INSIDE MY HEAD
......
Listen carefully to the voice.
HEAR THE TRUTH!

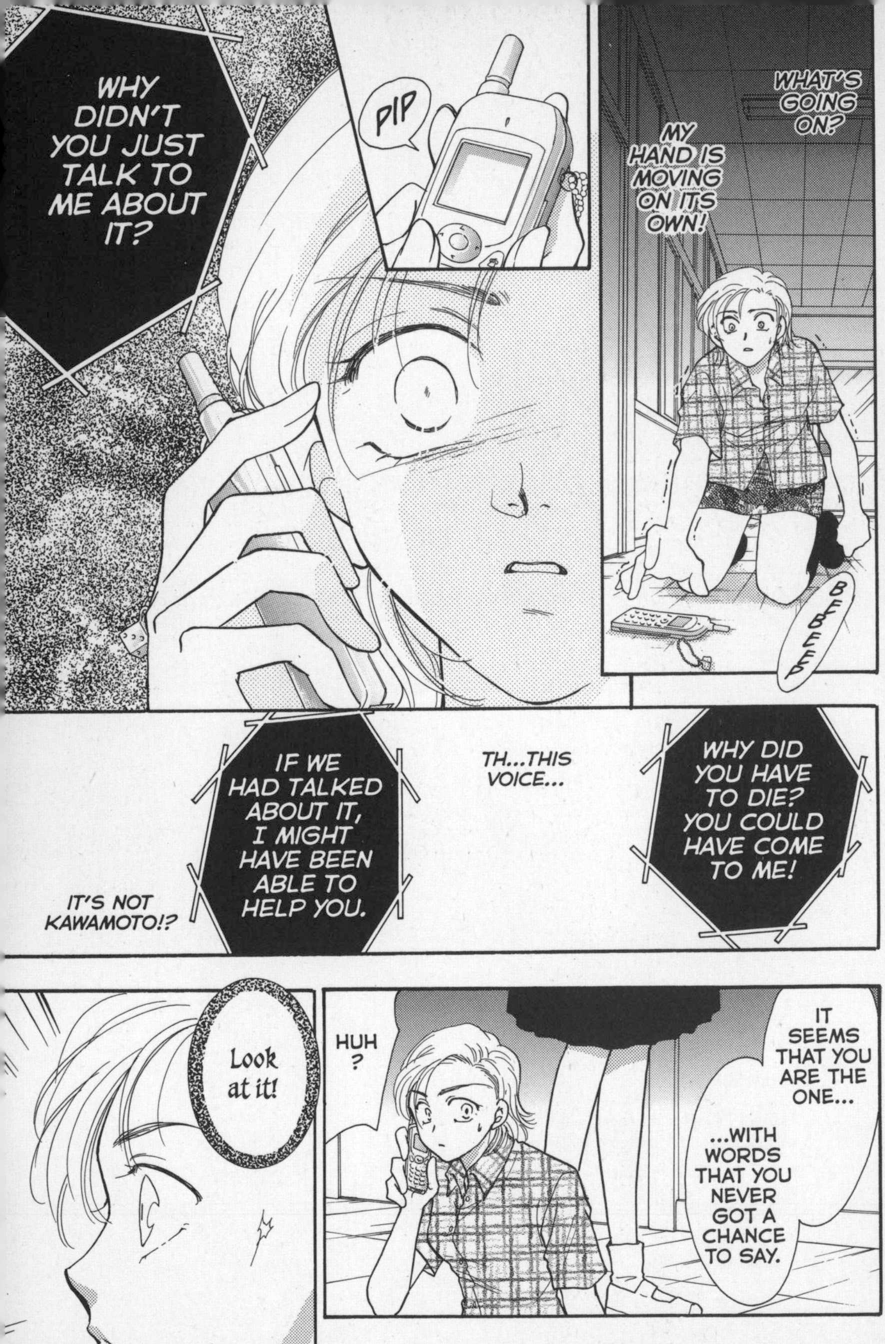

WHAT'S GOING ON?
MY HAND IS MOVING ON ITS OWN!
BEBEEP
PIP
WHY DIDN'T YOU JUST TALK TO ME ABOUT IT?
WHY DID YOU HAVE TO DIE? YOU COULD HAVE COME TO ME!
TH...THIS VOICE...
IF WE HAD TALKED ABOUT IT, I MIGHT HAVE BEEN ABLE TO HELP YOU.
IT'S NOT KAWAMOTO!?
IT SEEMS THAT YOU ARE THE ONE...
...WITH WORDS THAT YOU NEVER GOT A CHANCE TO SAY.
HUH?
Look at it!

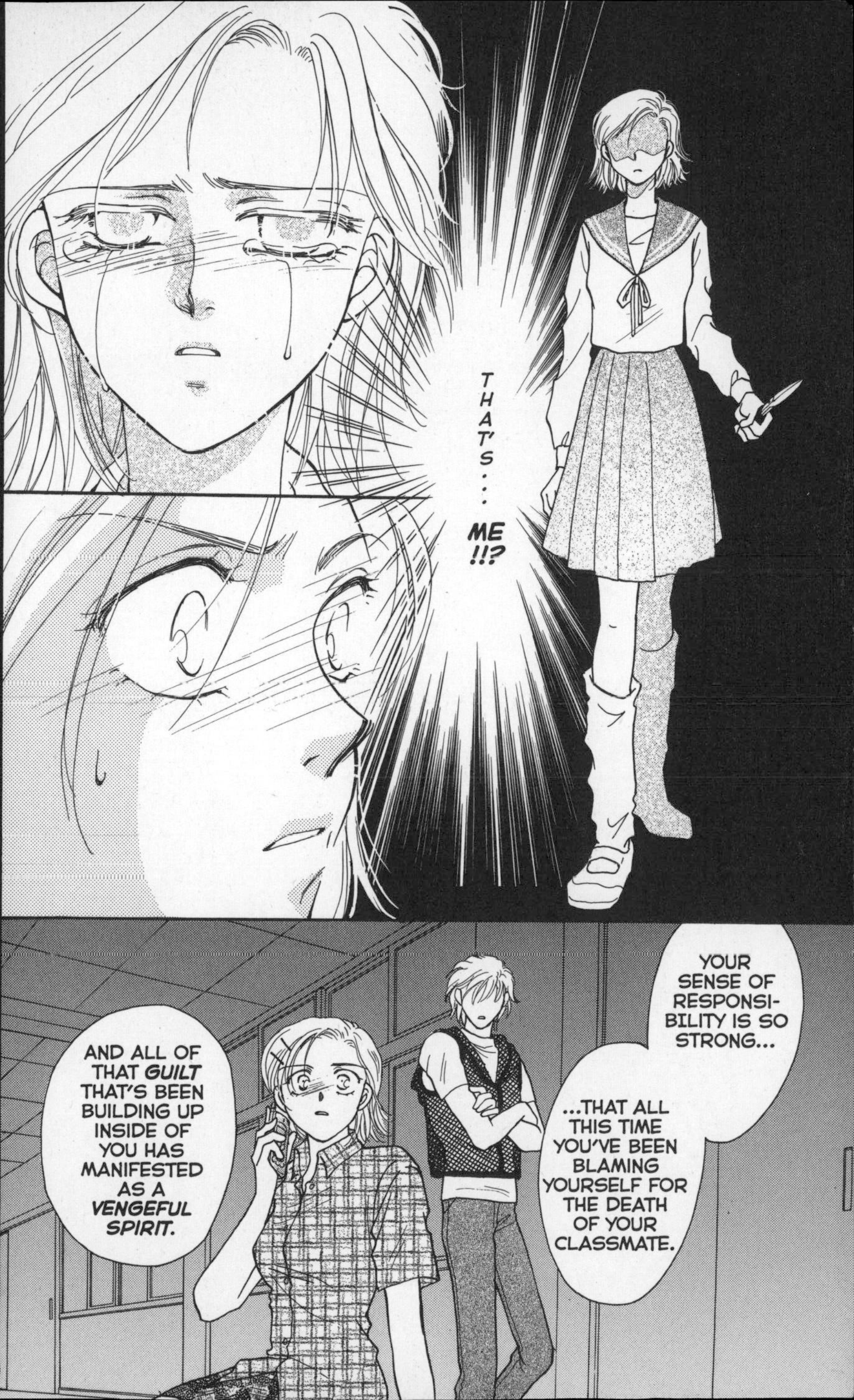
THAT'S... ME!!?
YOUR SENSE OF RESPONSI-BILITY IS SO STRONG...
...THAT ALL THIS TIME YOU'VE BEEN BLAMING YOURSELF FOR THE DEATH OF YOUR CLASSMATE.
AND ALL OF THAT *GUILT* THAT'S BEEN BUILDING UP INSIDE OF YOU HAS MANIFESTED AS A *VENGEFUL SPIRIT.*

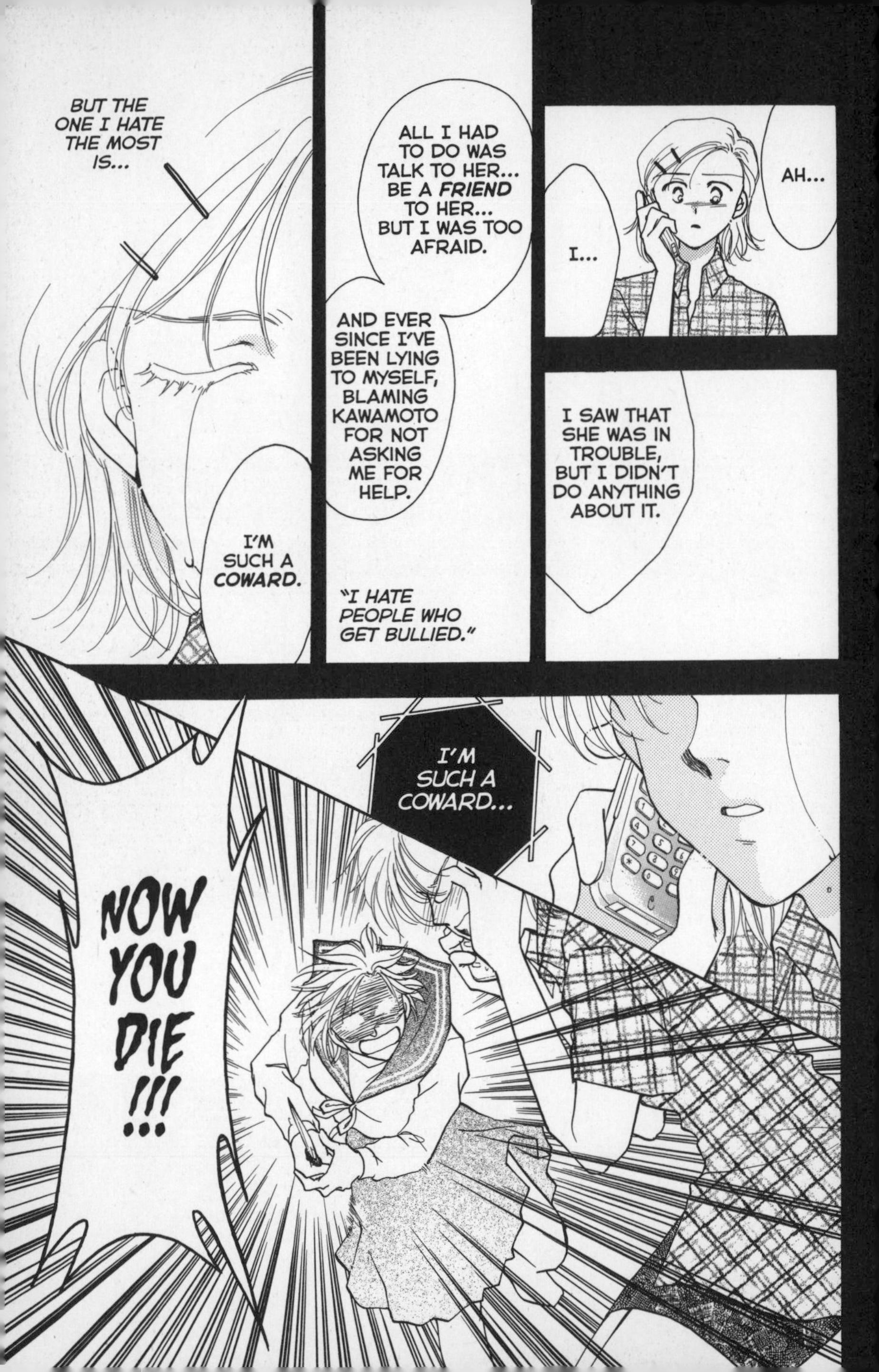
AH...
I...
I SAW THAT SHE WAS IN TROUBLE, BUT I DIDN'T DO ANYTHING ABOUT IT.
ALL I HAD TO DO WAS TALK TO HER... BE A *FRIEND* TO HER... BUT I WAS TOO AFRAID.
AND EVER SINCE I'VE BEEN LYING TO MYSELF, BLAMING KAWAMOTO FOR NOT ASKING ME FOR HELP.
"I HATE PEOPLE WHO GET BULLIED."
BUT THE ONE I HATE THE MOST IS...
I'M SUCH A *COWARD.*
I'M SUCH A COWARD...
NOW YOU DIE!!!

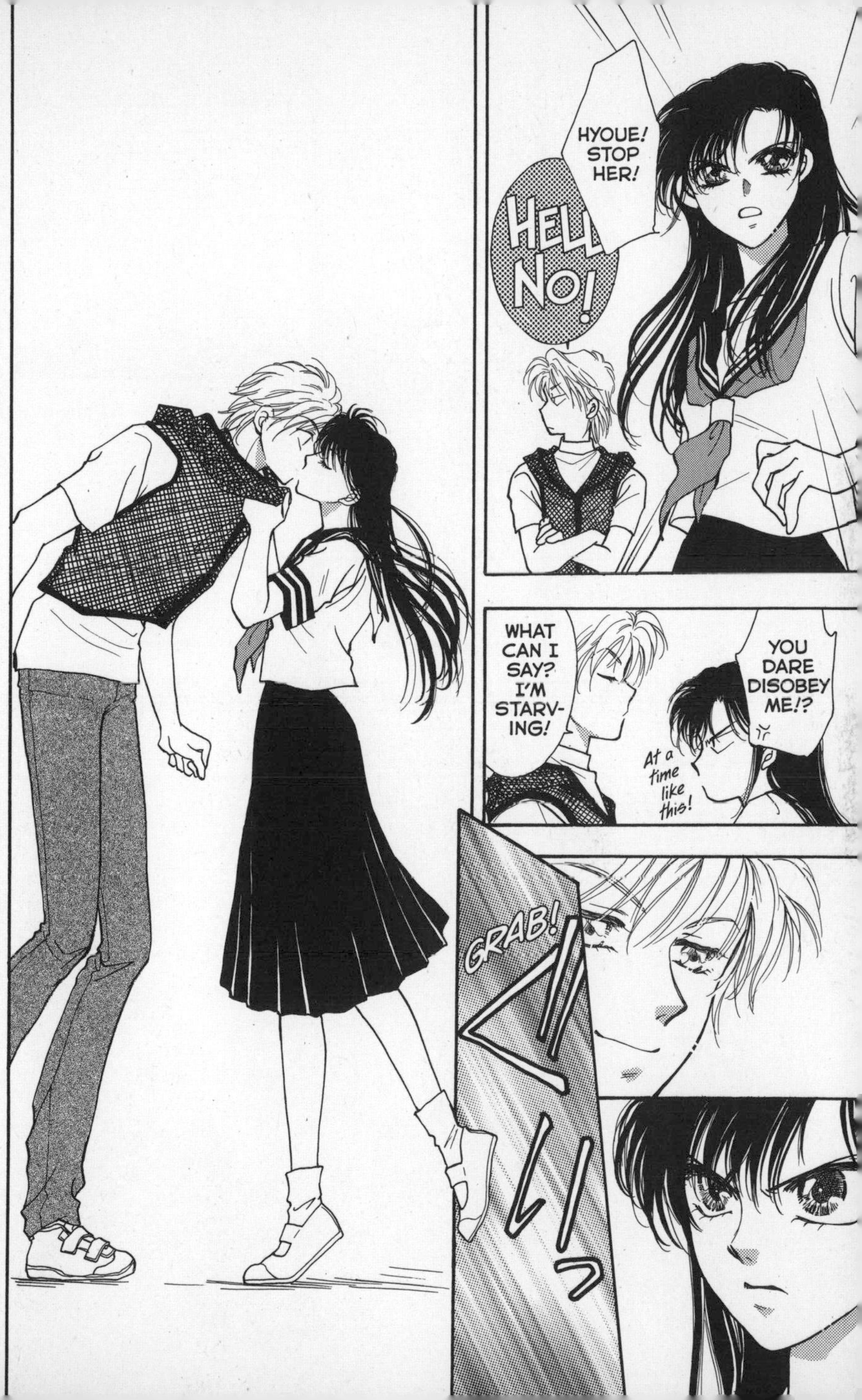
HYOUE! STOP HER!
HELL NO!
YOU DARE DISOBEY ME!?
At a time like this!
WHAT CAN I SAY? I'M STARVING!
GRAB!

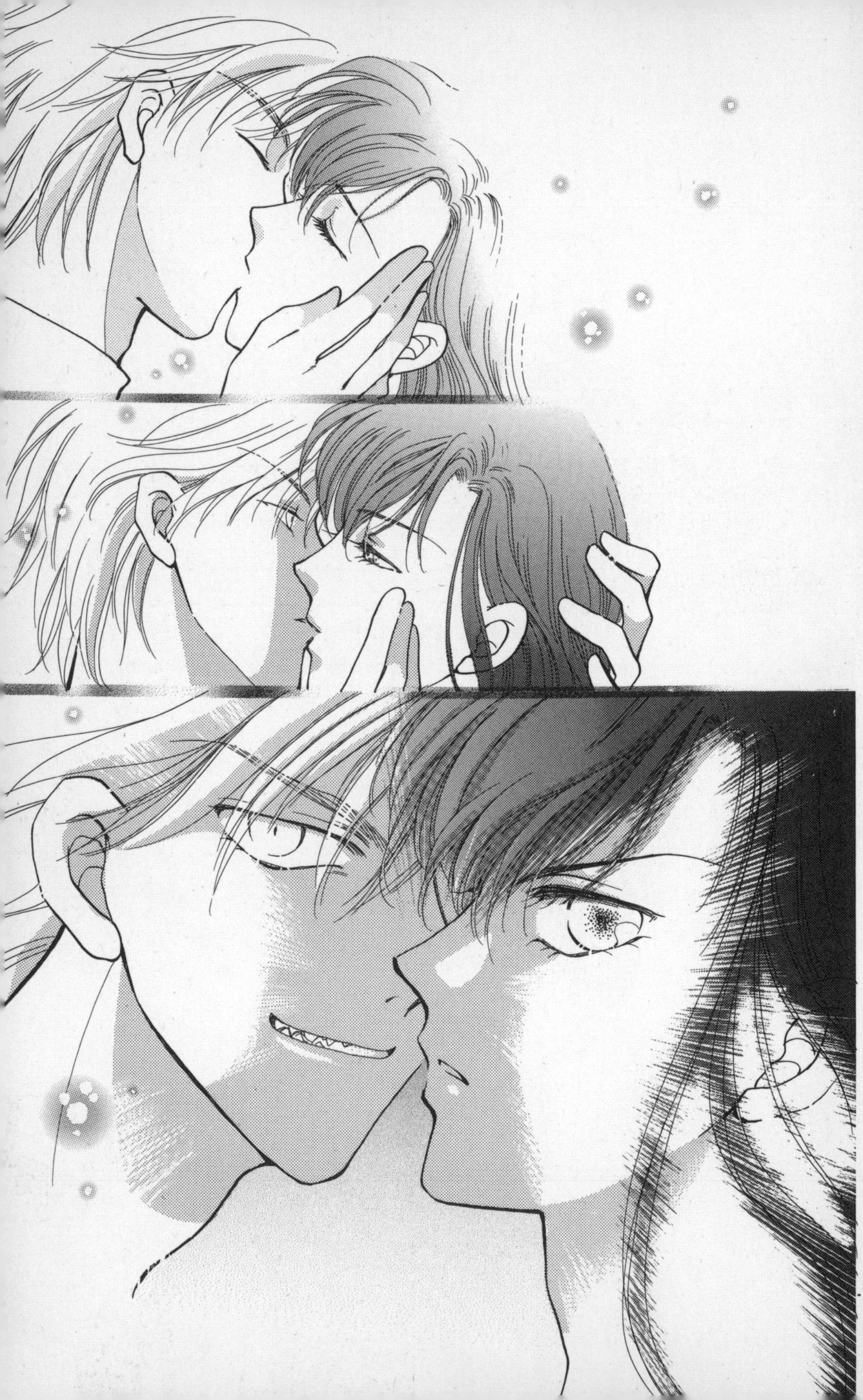

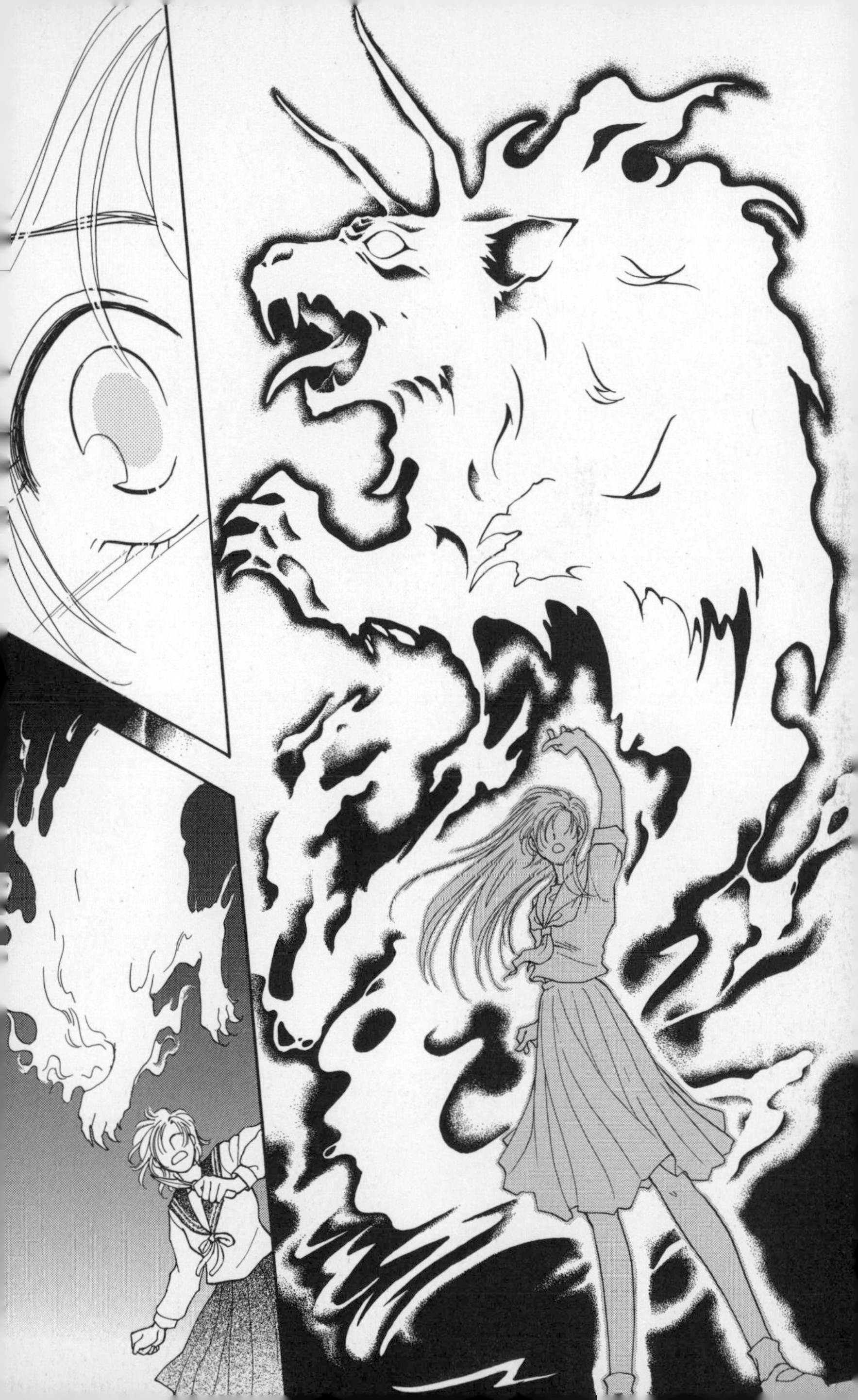

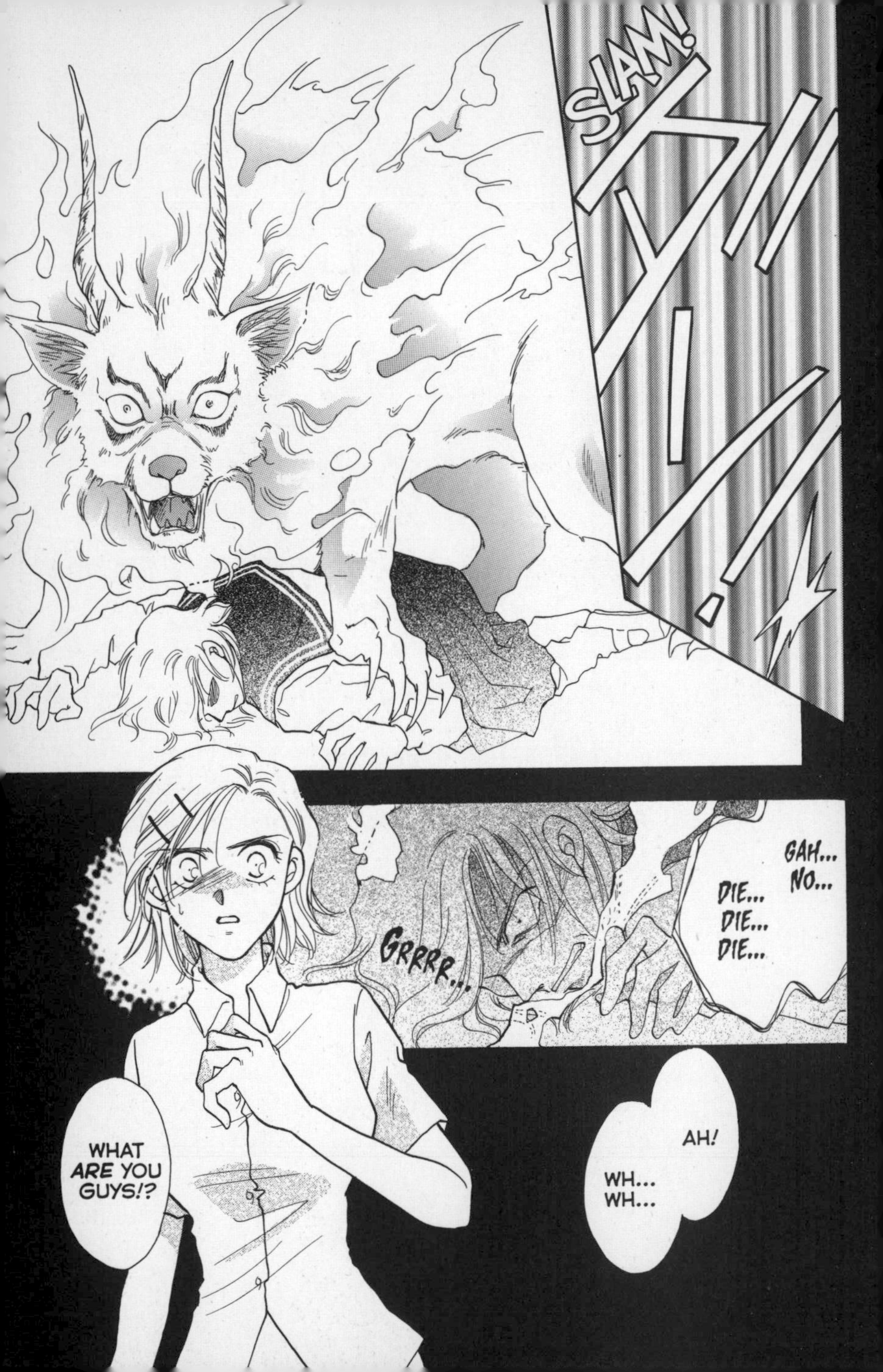
SLAM!
GAH... NO...
DIE... DIE... DIE...
GRRRR...
AH!
WH... WH...
WHAT ARE YOU GUYS!?

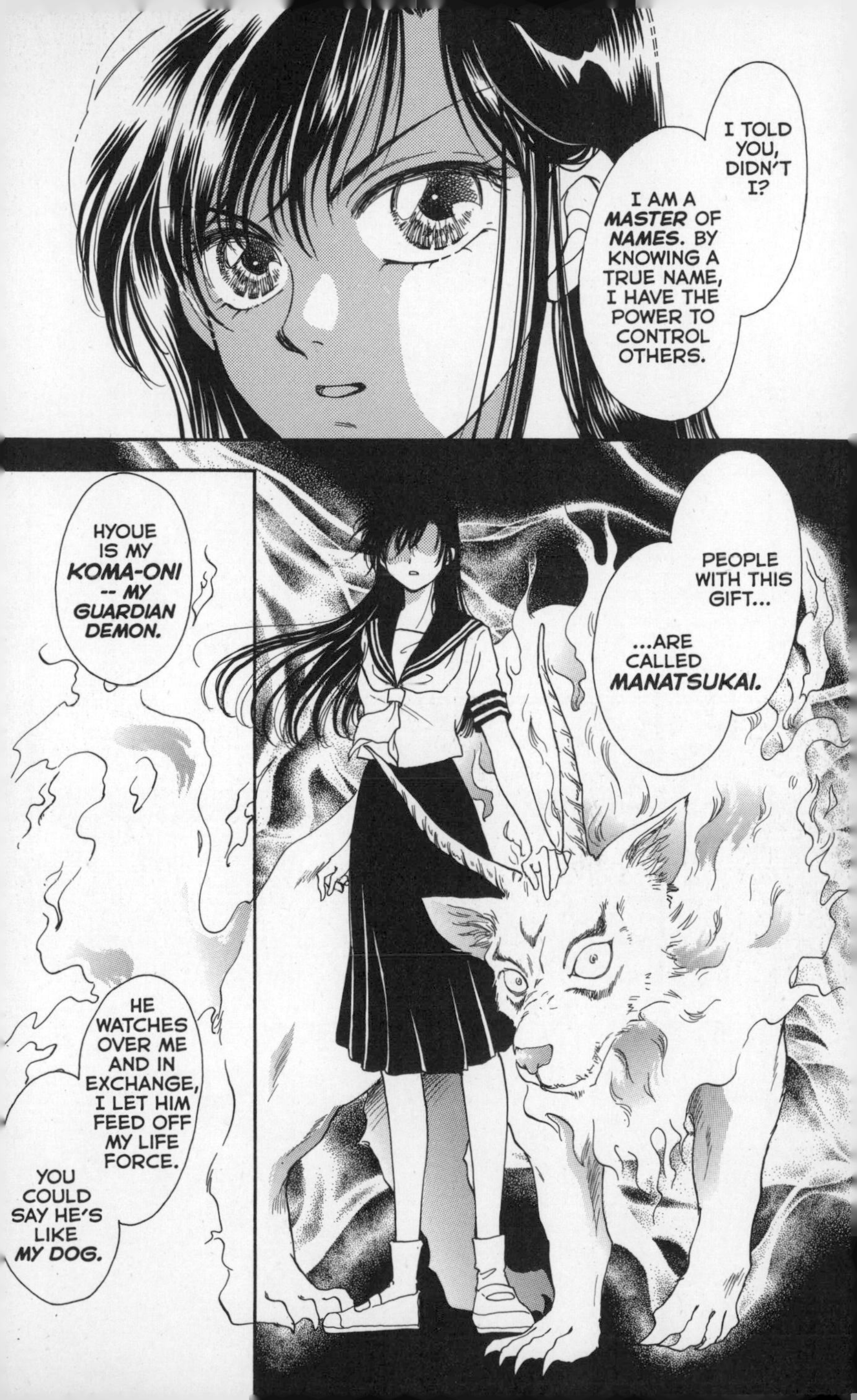
I TOLD YOU, DIDN'T I?
I AM A *MASTER* OF *NAMES*. BY KNOWING A TRUE NAME, I HAVE THE POWER TO CONTROL OTHERS.
PEOPLE WITH THIS GIFT...
...ARE CALLED *MANATSUKAI*.
HYOUE IS MY *KOMA-ONI* -- *MY GUARDIAN DEMON*.
HE WATCHES OVER ME AND IN EXCHANGE, I LET HIM FEED OFF MY LIFE FORCE.
YOU COULD SAY HE'S LIKE *MY DOG*.

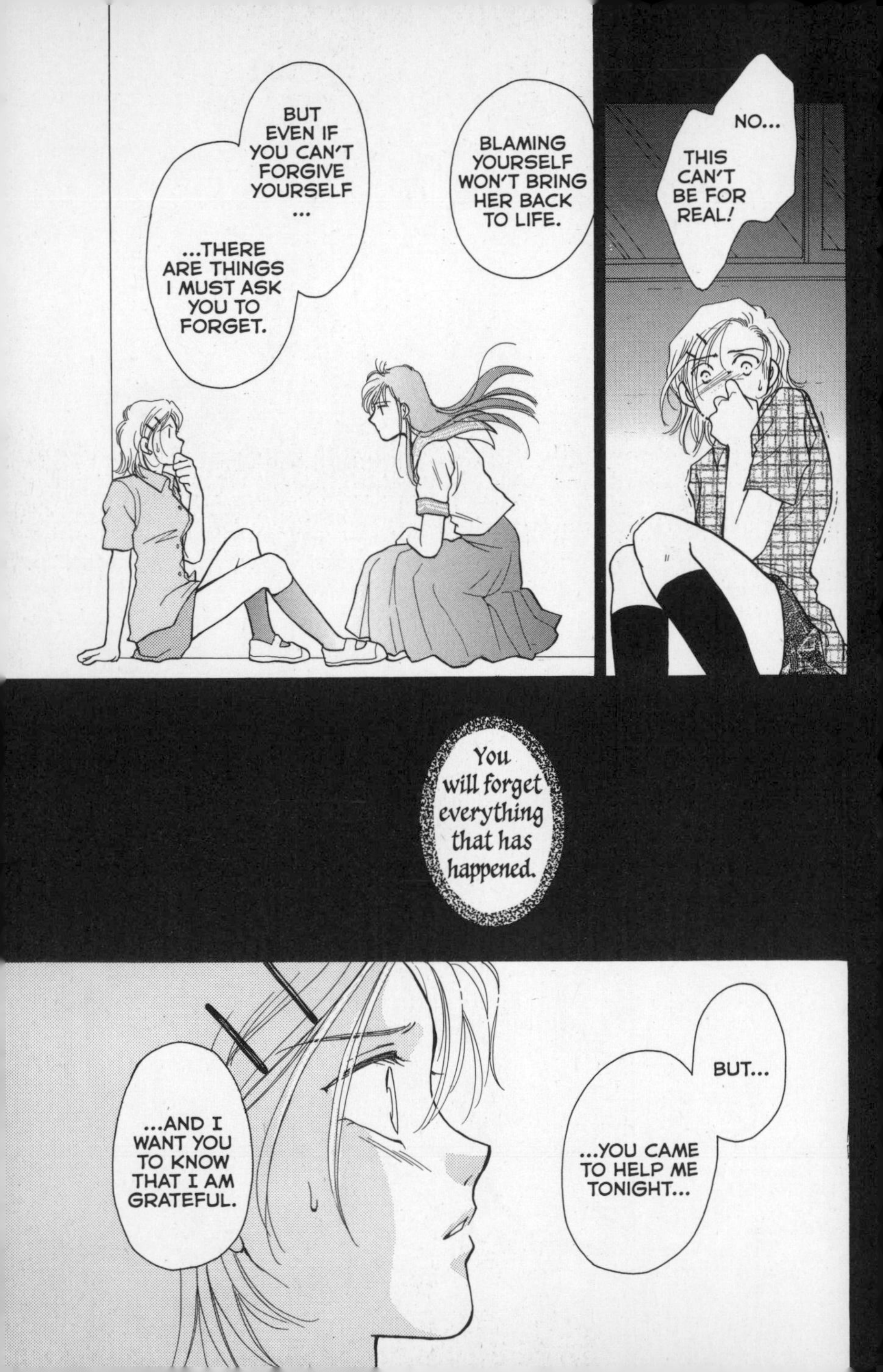
NO...
THIS CAN'T BE FOR REAL!
BLAMING YOURSELF WON'T BRING HER BACK TO LIFE.
BUT EVEN IF YOU CAN'T FORGIVE YOURSELF ...
...THERE ARE THINGS I MUST ASK YOU TO FORGET.
You will forget everything that has happened.
BUT...
...YOU CAME TO HELP ME TONIGHT...
...AND I WANT YOU TO KNOW THAT I AM GRATEFUL.

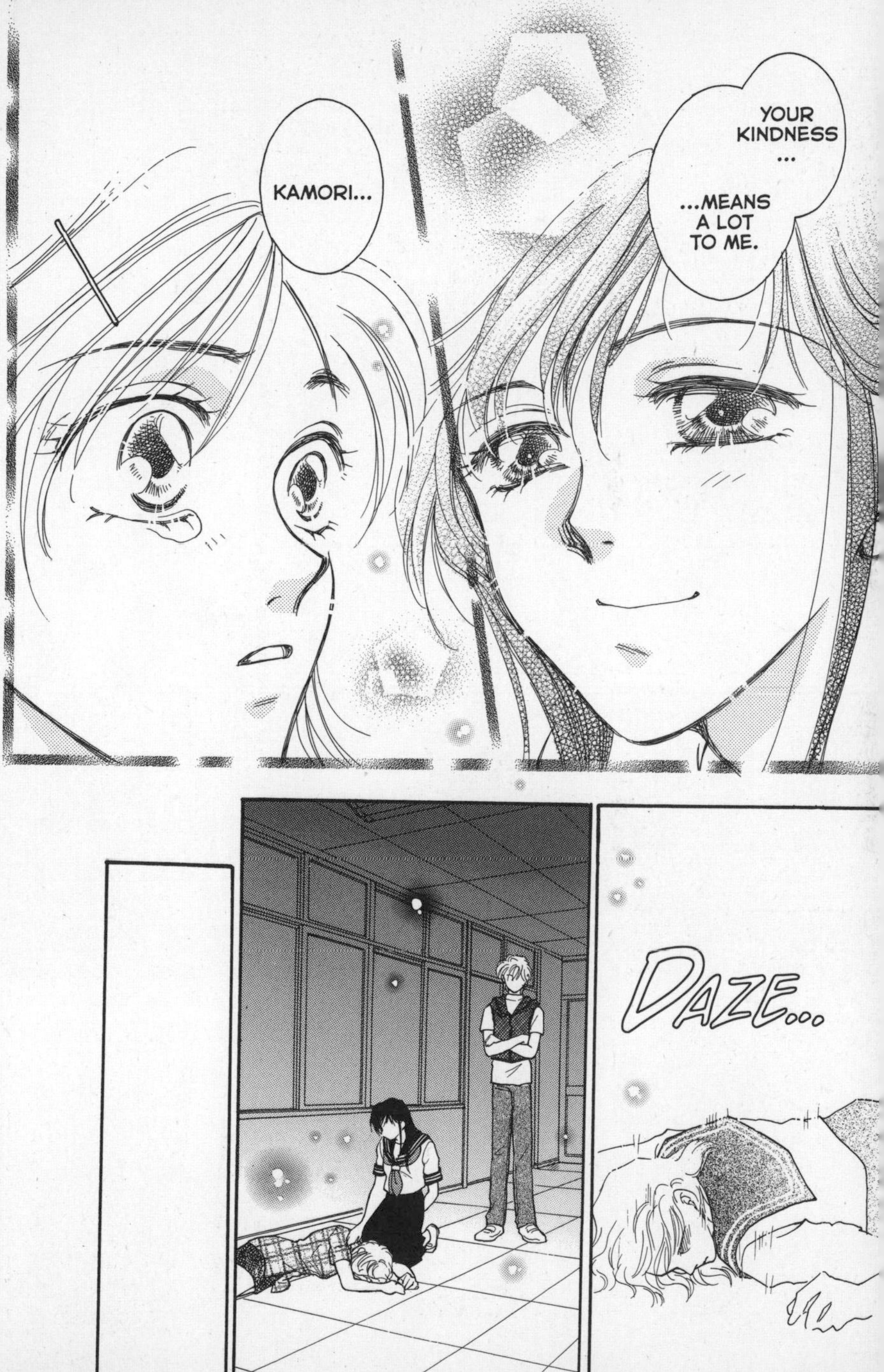
YOUR KINDNESS ... ...MEANS A LOT TO ME.
KAMORI...
DAZE...

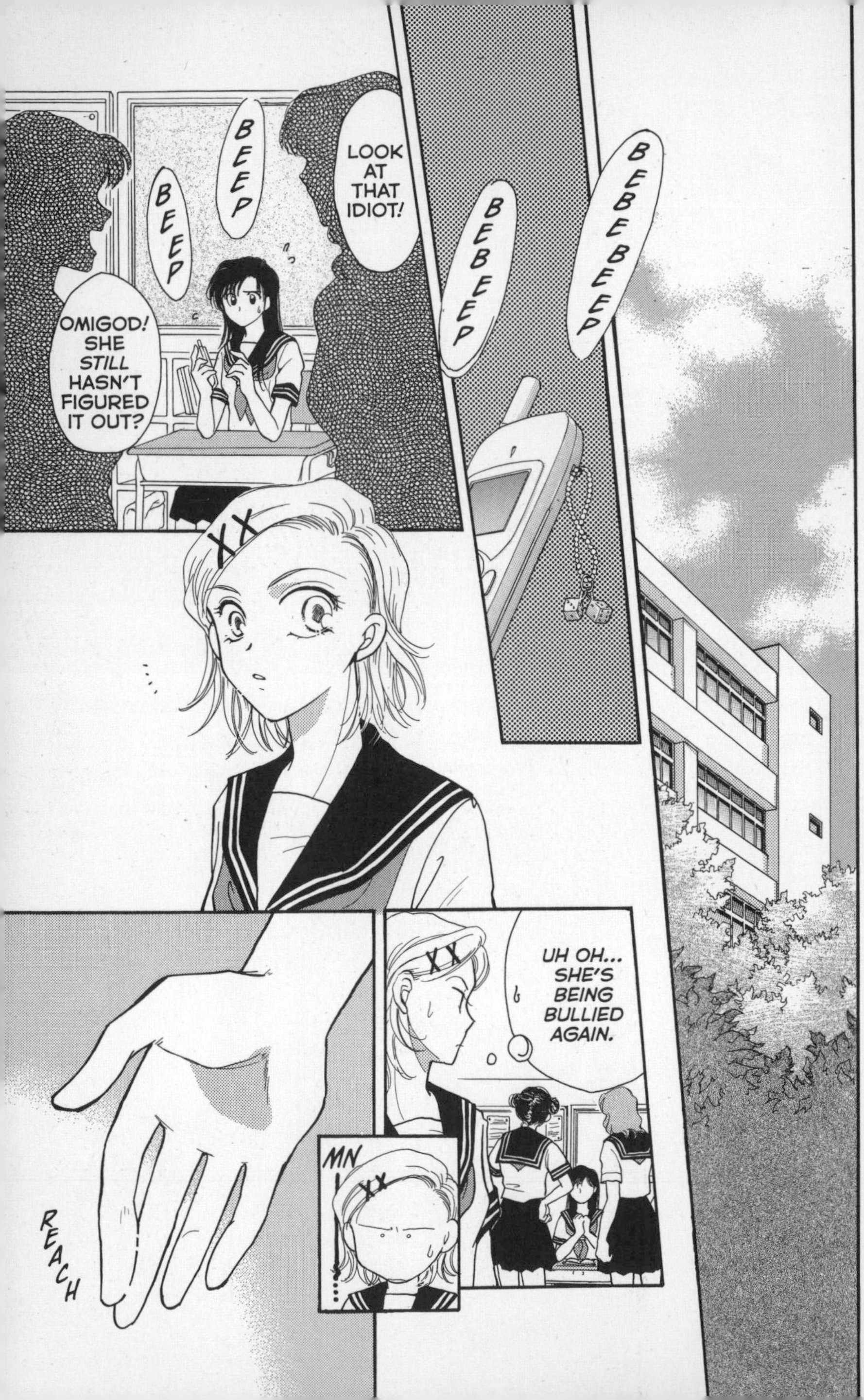
BEBEBEEP
BEBEEP
LOOK AT THAT IDIOT!
BEEP
BEEP
OMIGOD! SHE STILL HASN'T FIGURED IT OUT?
...
UH OH... SHE'S BEING BULLIED AGAIN.
MN
REACH

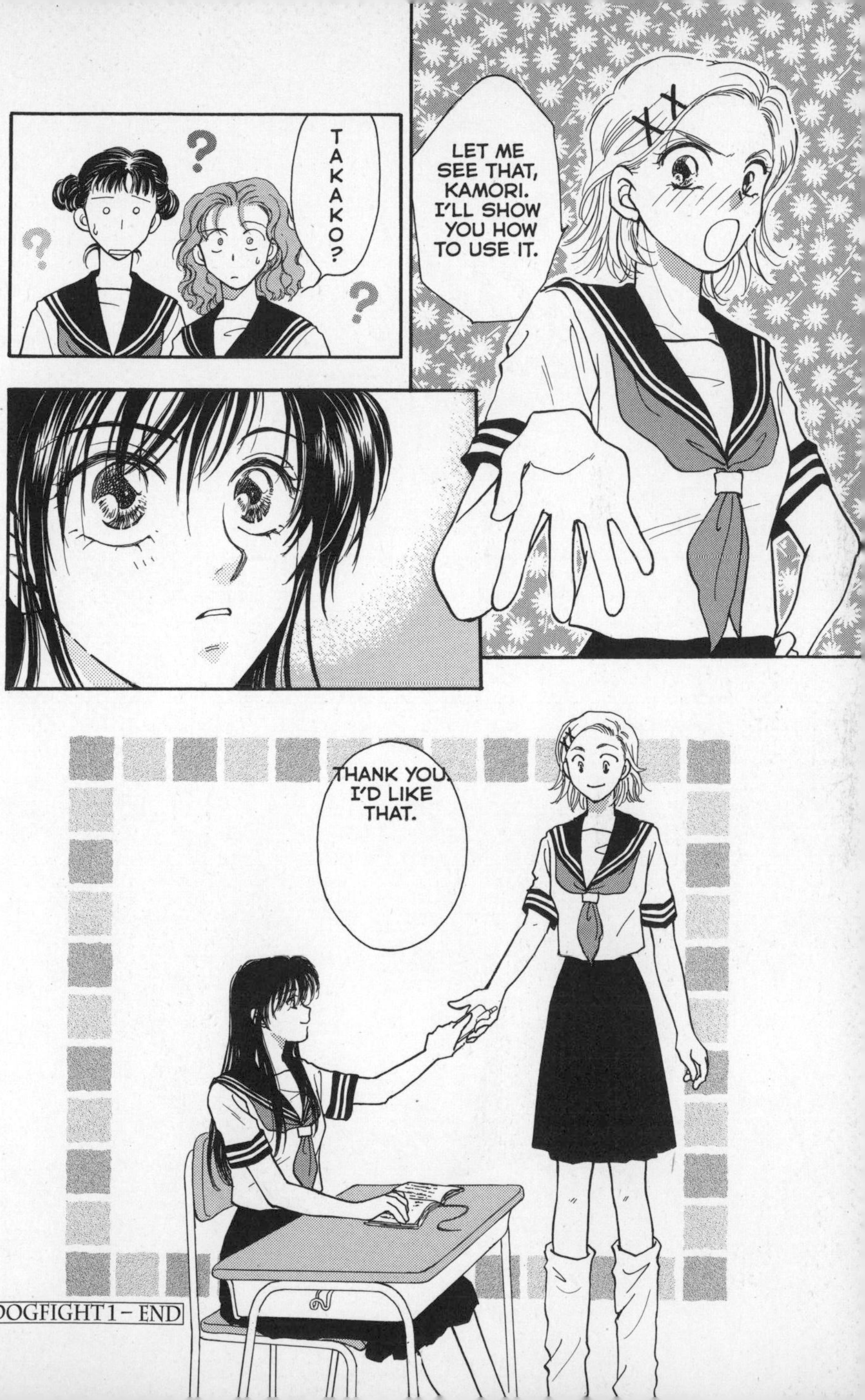
LET ME SEE THAT, KAMORI. I'LL SHOW YOU HOW TO USE IT.
TAKAKO?
THANK YOU. I'D LIKE THAT.
DOGFIGHT1 – END

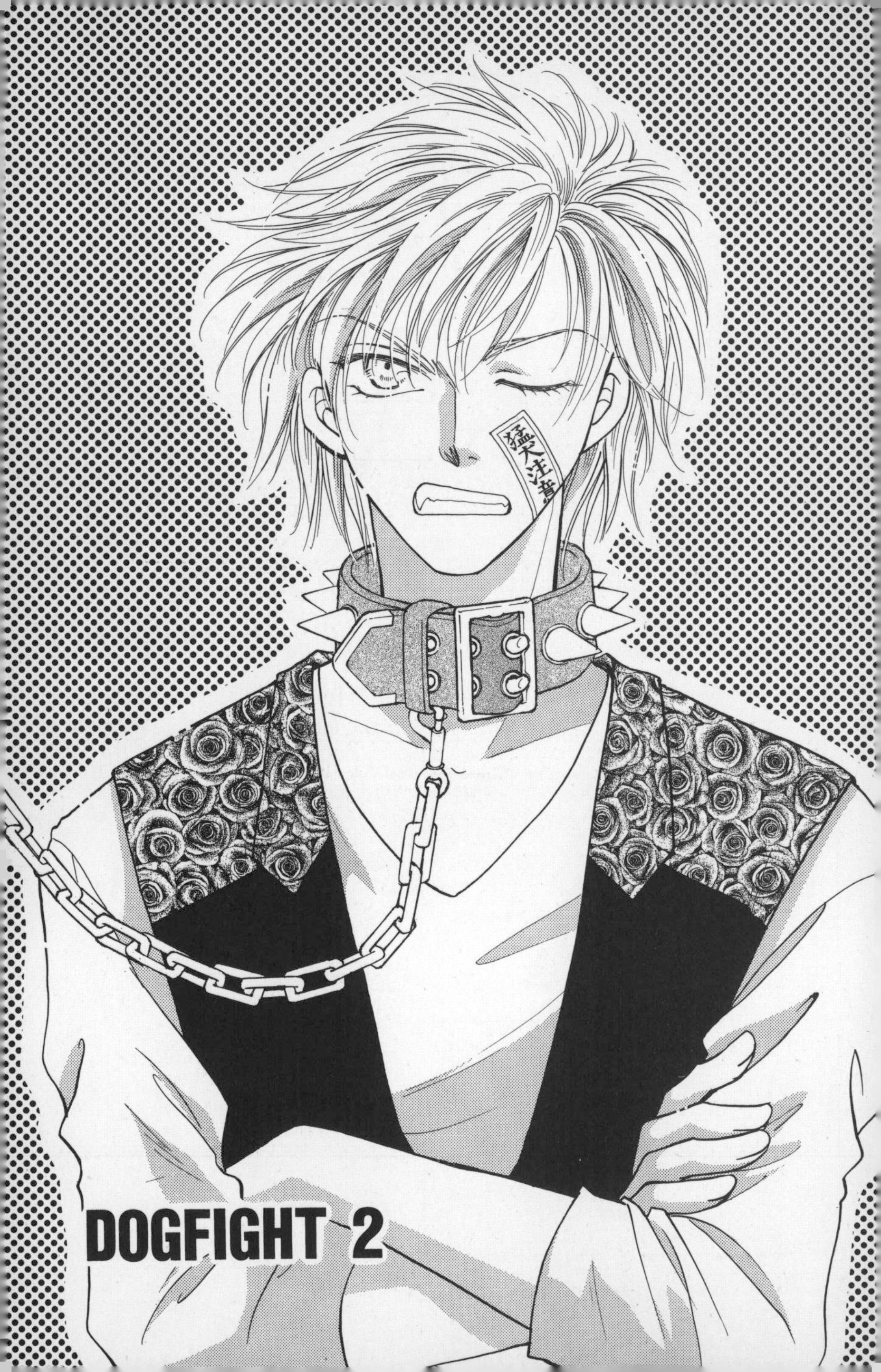
猛犬注意
DOGFIGHT 2

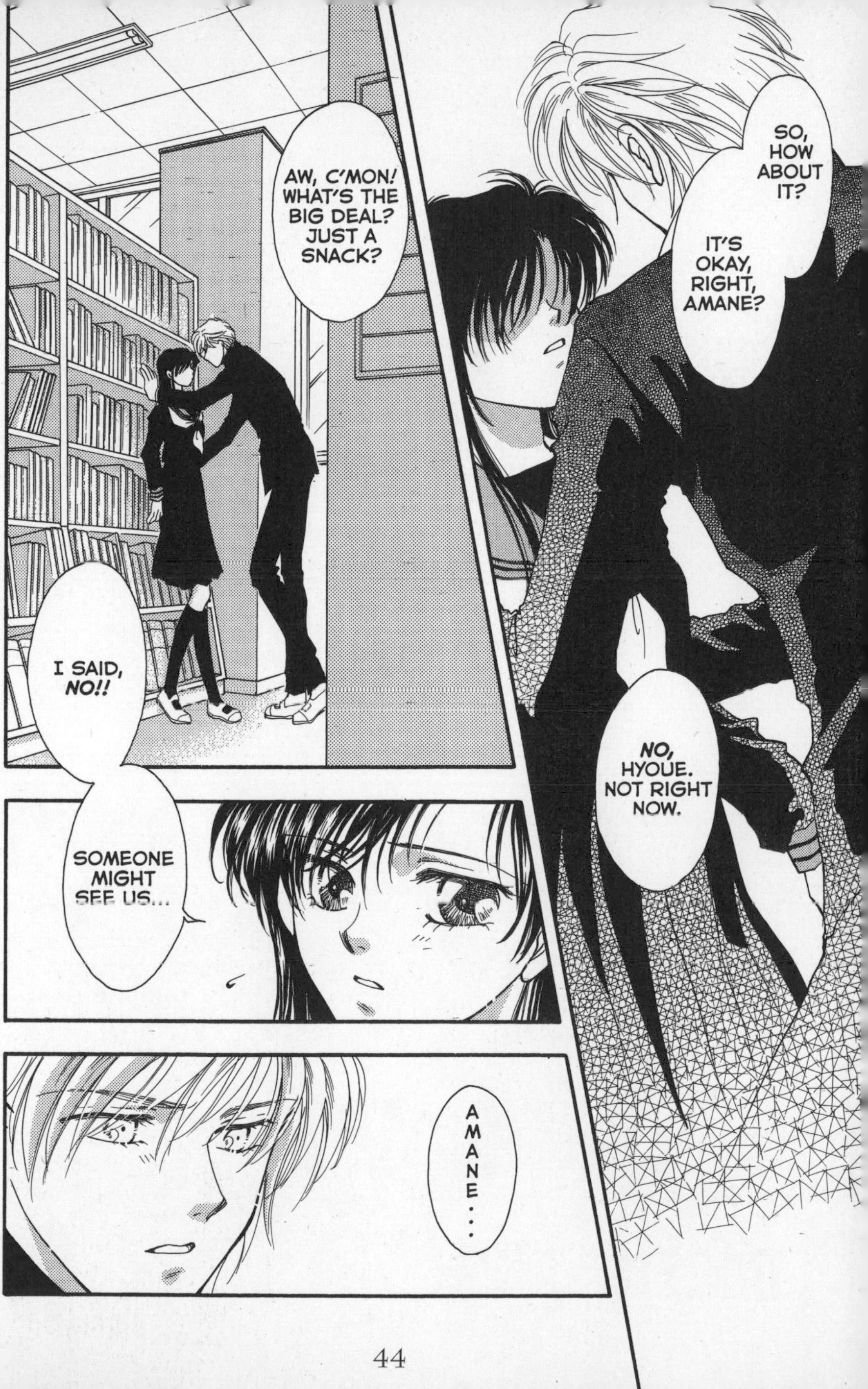
SO, HOW ABOUT IT?
IT'S OKAY, RIGHT, AMANE?
NO, HYOUE. NOT RIGHT NOW.
AW, C'MON! WHAT'S THE BIG DEAL? JUST A SNACK?
I SAID, *NO!!*
SOMEONE MIGHT SEE US...
AMANE...

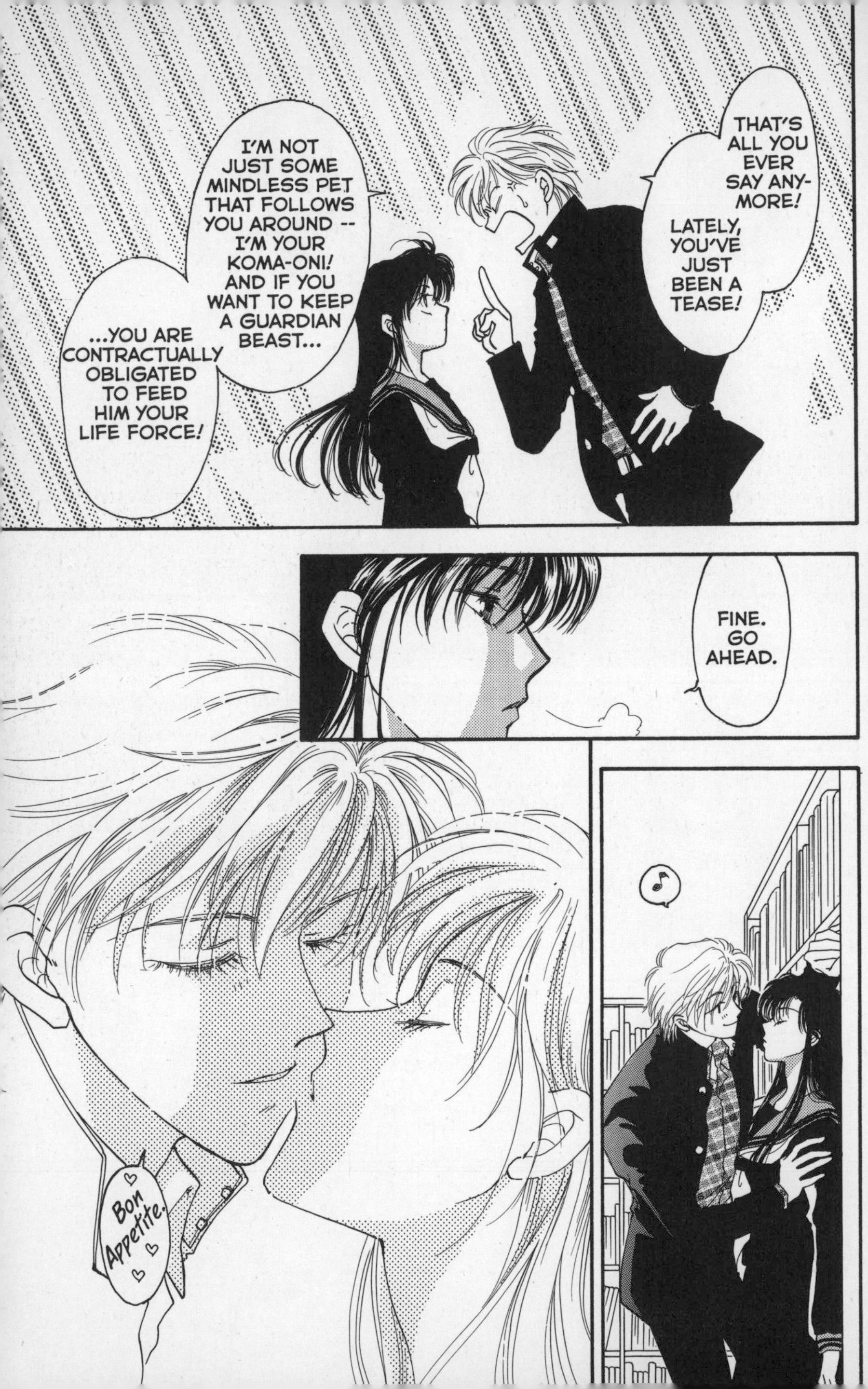
THAT'S ALL YOU EVER SAY ANY-MORE!
LATELY, YOU'VE JUST BEEN A TEASE!
I'M NOT JUST SOME MINDLESS PET THAT FOLLOWS YOU AROUND -- I'M YOUR KOMA-ONI! AND IF YOU WANT TO KEEP A GUARDIAN BEAST...
...YOU ARE CONTRACTUALLY OBLIGATED TO FEED HIM YOUR LIFE FORCE!
FINE. GO AHEAD.
Bon Appetite.

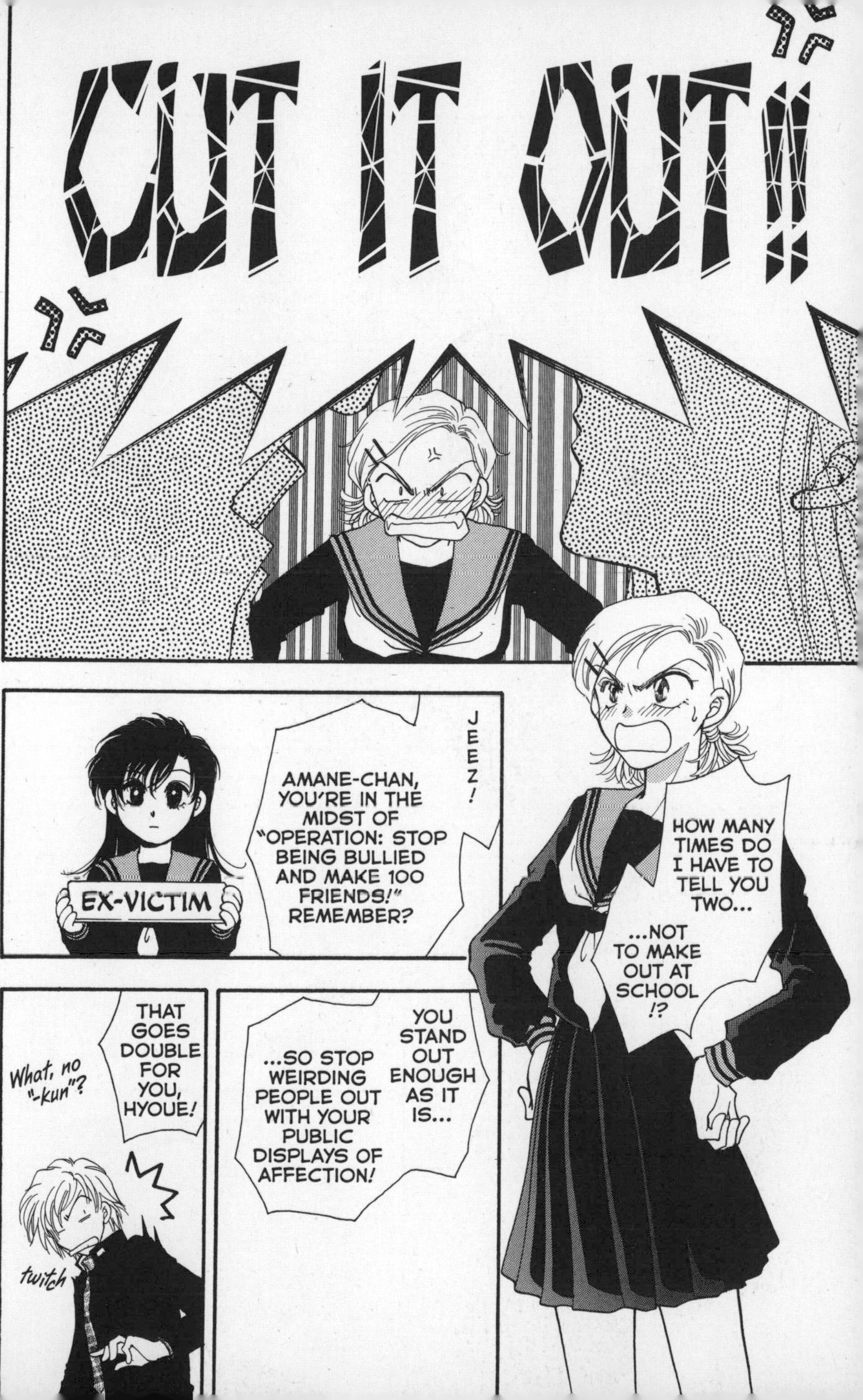
CUT IT OUT!!
HOW MANY TIMES DO I HAVE TO TELL YOU TWO...
...NOT TO MAKE OUT AT SCHOOL!?
JEEZ!
AMANE-CHAN, YOU'RE IN THE MIDST OF "OPERATION: STOP BEING BULLIED AND MAKE 100 FRIENDS!" REMEMBER?
EX-VICTIM
YOU STAND OUT ENOUGH AS IT IS...
...SO STOP WEIRDING PEOPLE OUT WITH YOUR PUBLIC DISPLAYS OF AFFECTION!
THAT GOES DOUBLE FOR YOU, HYOUE!
What, no "-kun"?
twitch

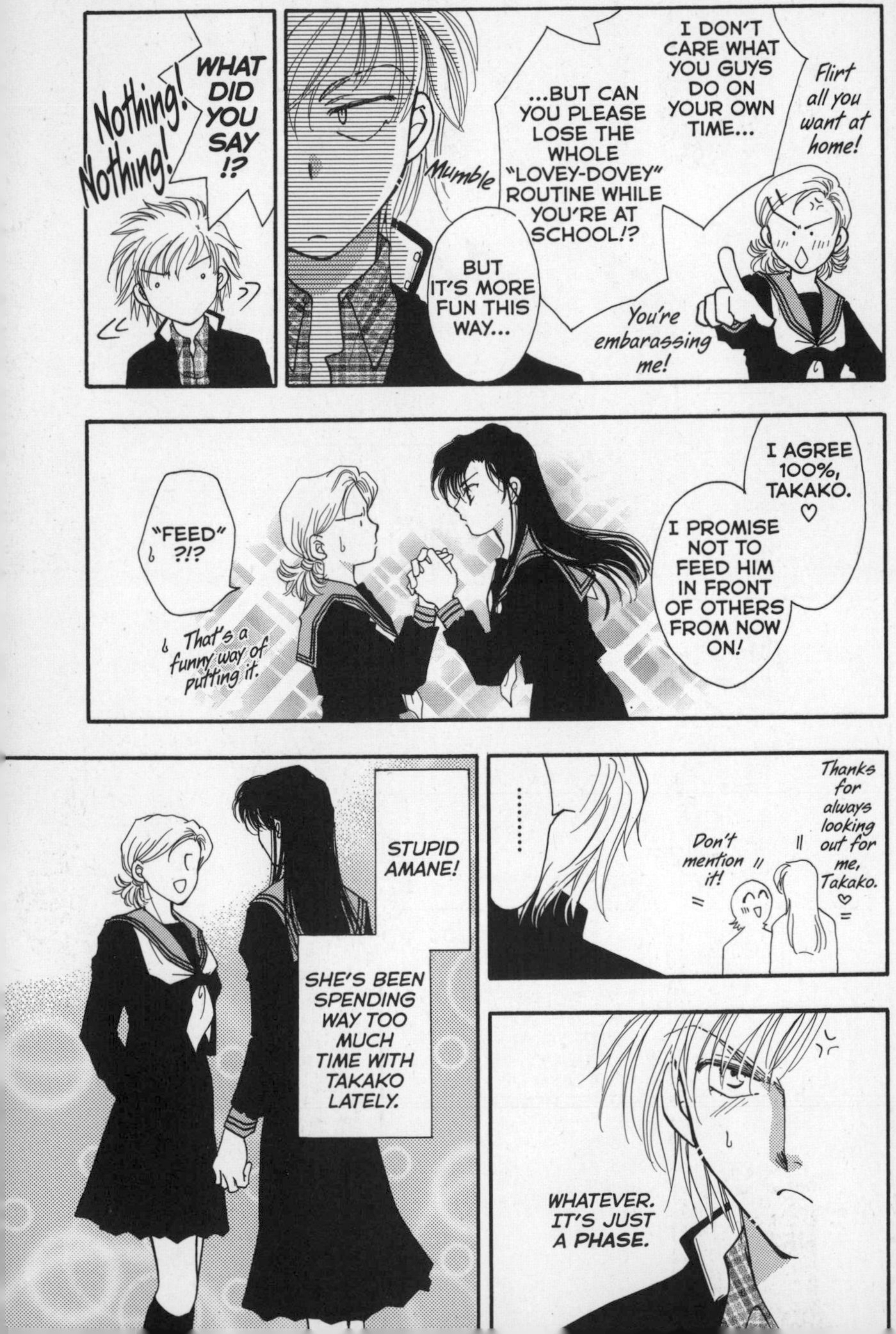
I DON'T CARE WHAT YOU GUYS DO ON YOUR OWN TIME...
Flirt all you want at home!
...BUT CAN YOU PLEASE LOSE THE WHOLE "LOVEY-DOVEY" ROUTINE WHILE YOU'RE AT SCHOOL!?
You're embarassing me!
Mumble
BUT IT'S MORE FUN THIS WAY...
WHAT DID YOU SAY !?
Nothing! Nothing!
I AGREE 100%, TAKAKO. ♡
I PROMISE NOT TO FEED HIM IN FRONT OF OTHERS FROM NOW ON!
"FEED" ?!?
That's a funny way of putting it.
......
Thanks for always looking out for me, Takako. ♡
Don't mention it!
WHATEVER. IT'S JUST A PHASE.
STUPID AMANE!
SHE'S BEEN SPENDING WAY TOO MUCH TIME WITH TAKAKO LATELY.

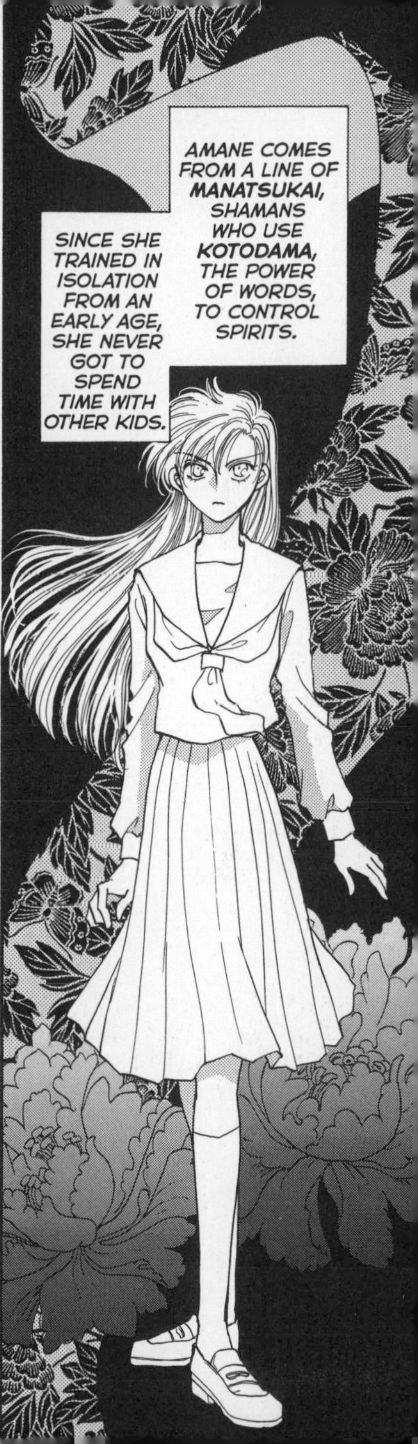
AMANE COMES FROM A LINE OF **MANATSUKAI,** SHAMANS WHO USE **KOTODAMA,** THE POWER OF WORDS, TO CONTROL SPIRITS.
SINCE SHE TRAINED IN ISOLATION FROM AN EARLY AGE, SHE NEVER GOT TO SPEND TIME WITH OTHER KIDS.

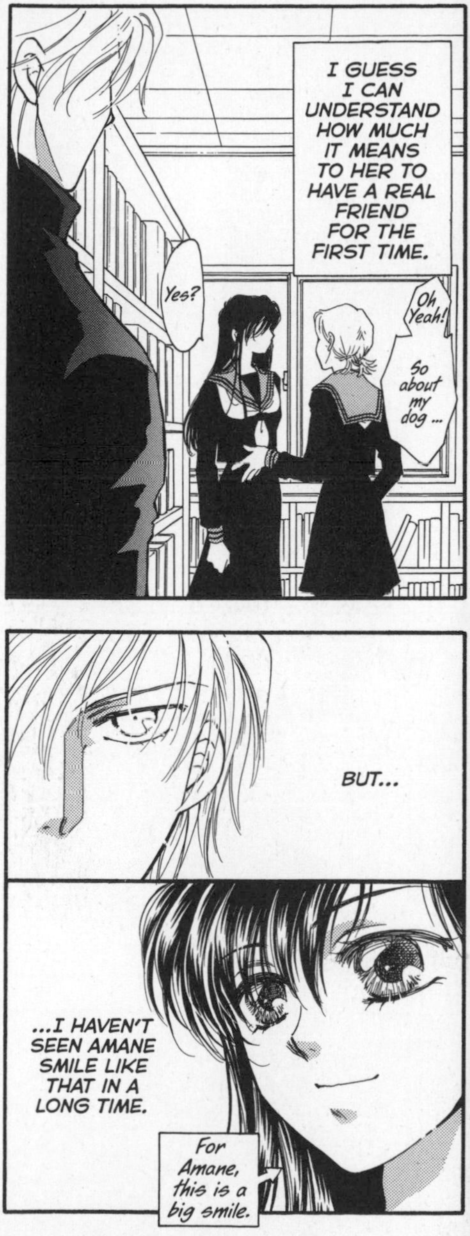
I GUESS I CAN UNDERSTAND HOW MUCH IT MEANS TO HER TO HAVE A REAL FRIEND FOR THE FIRST TIME.
Oh Yeah!
So about my dog ...
Yes?
BUT...
...I HAVEN'T SEEN AMANE SMILE LIKE THAT IN A LONG TIME.
For Amane, this is a big smile.

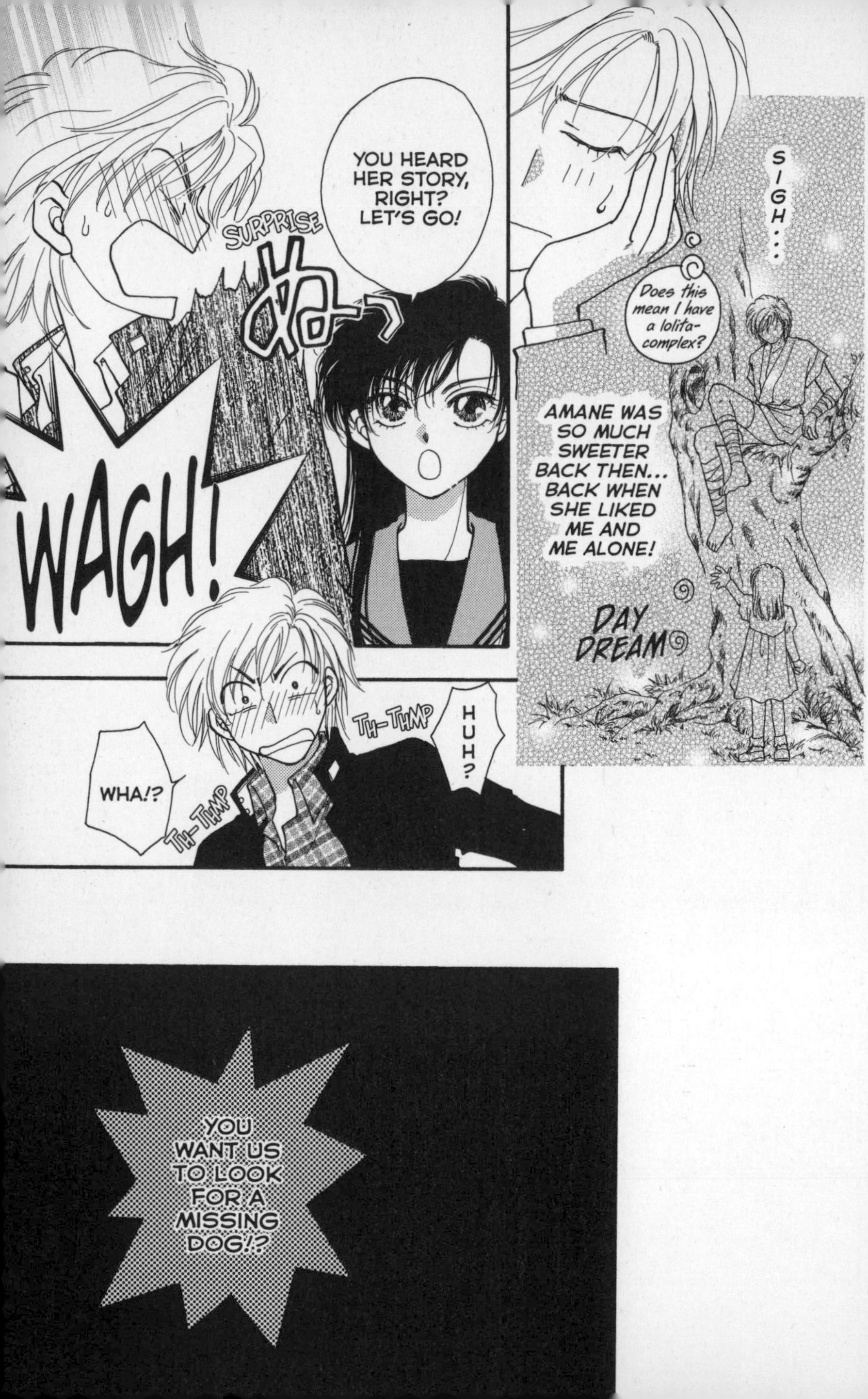
S I G H . . .
Does this mean I have a lolita-complex?
AMANE WAS SO MUCH SWEETER BACK THEN... BACK WHEN SHE LIKED ME AND ME ALONE!
DAY DREAM
YOU HEARD HER STORY, RIGHT? LET'S GO!
SURPRISE
ぬっ
WAGH!
HUH?
TH-THMP
WHA!?
TH-THMP
YOU WANT US TO LOOK FOR A MISSING DOG!?

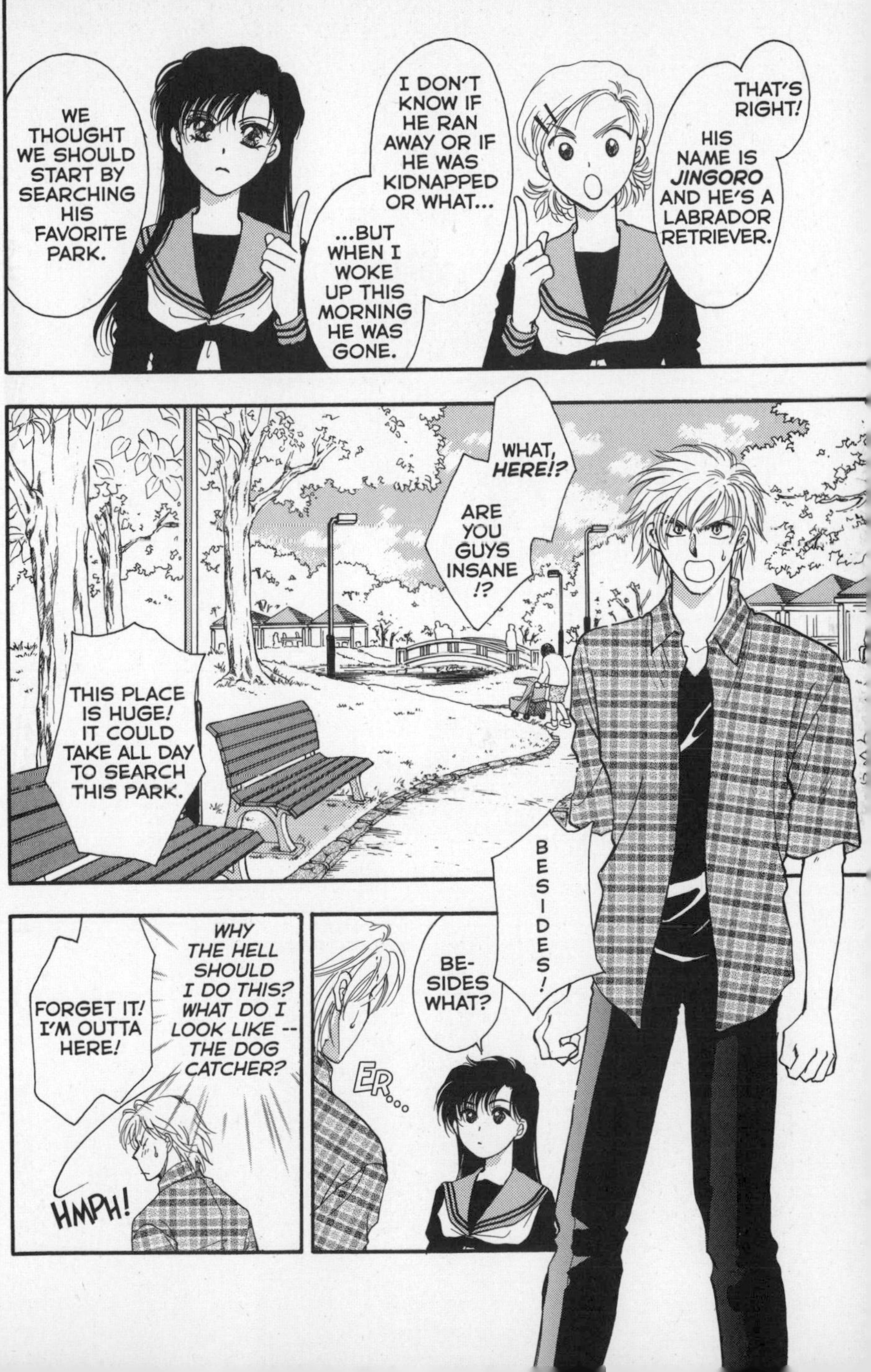
THAT'S RIGHT!
HIS NAME IS JINGORO AND HE'S A LABRADOR RETRIEVER.
I DON'T KNOW IF HE RAN AWAY OR IF HE WAS KIDNAPPED OR WHAT...
...BUT WHEN I WOKE UP THIS MORNING HE WAS GONE.
WE THOUGHT WE SHOULD START BY SEARCHING HIS FAVORITE PARK.
WHAT, HERE!?
ARE YOU GUYS INSANE!?
THIS PLACE IS HUGE! IT COULD TAKE ALL DAY TO SEARCH THIS PARK.
BESIDES!
BE-SIDES WHAT?
ER...
WHY THE HELL SHOULD I DO THIS? WHAT DO I LOOK LIKE -- THE DOG CATCHER?
FORGET IT! I'M OUTTA HERE!
HMPH!

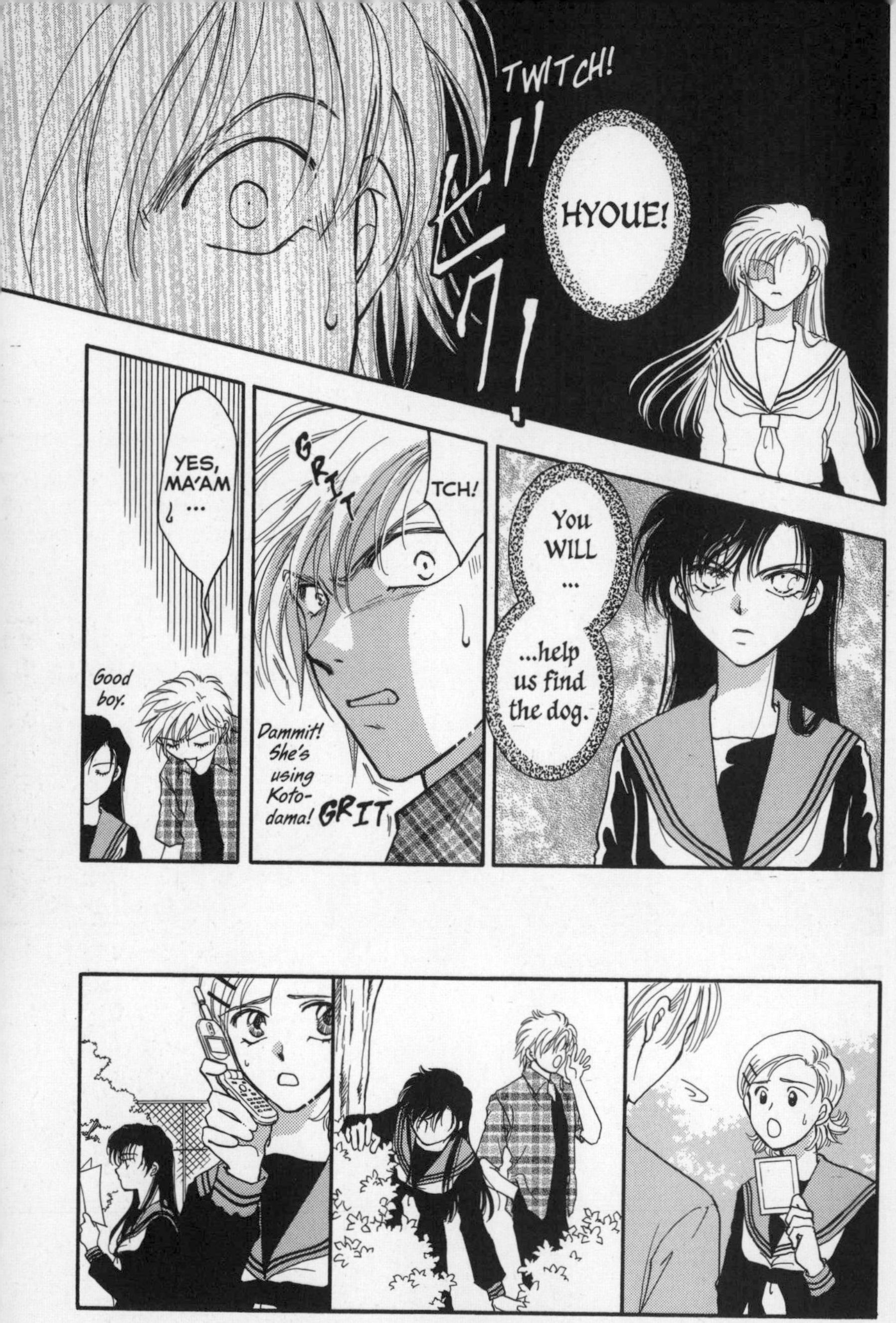
TWITCH!
HYOUE!
You WILL ...
...help us find the dog.
TCH!
GRIT
Dammit! She's using Koto-dama!
GRIT
YES, MA'AM ...
Good boy.

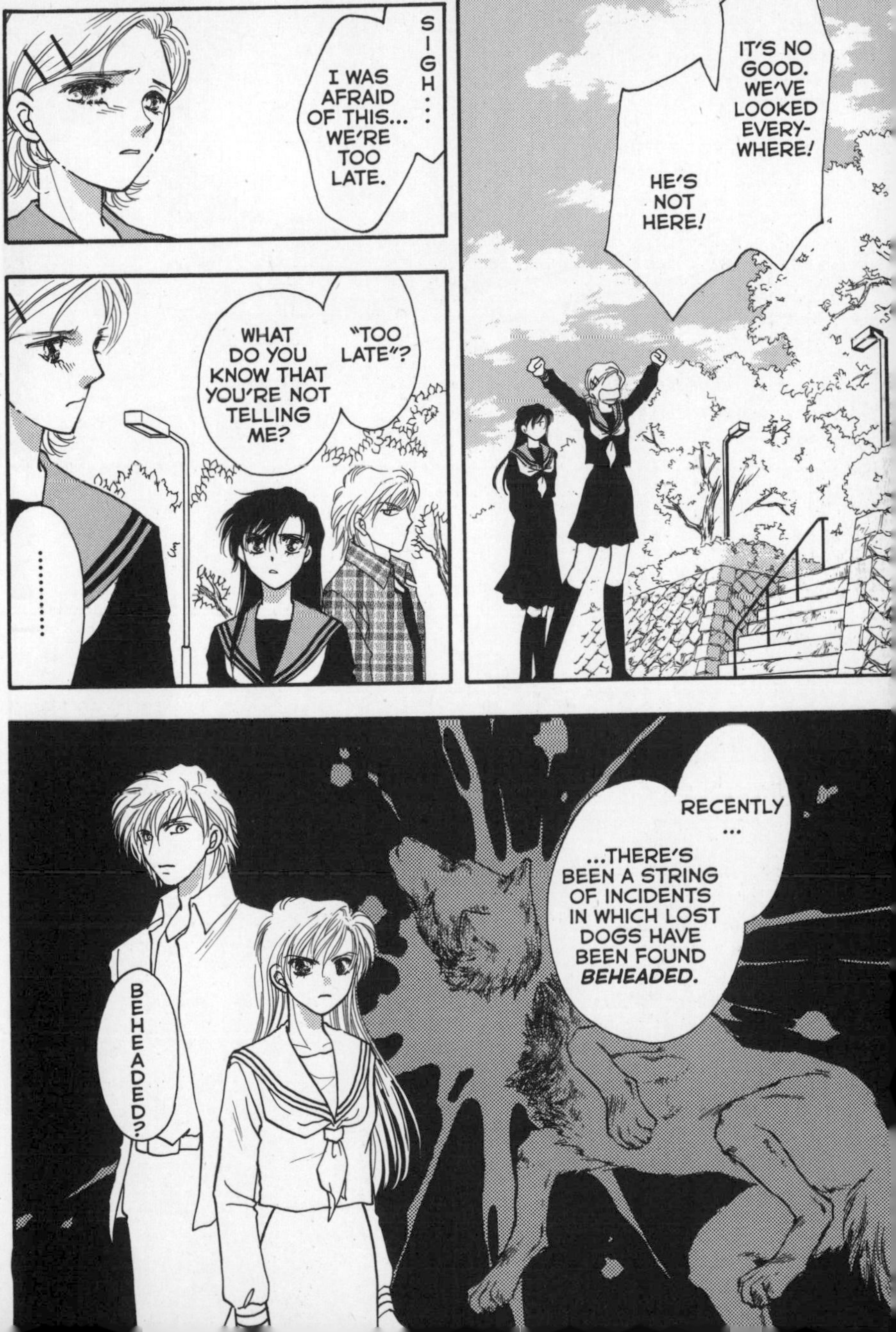
IT'S NO GOOD. WE'VE LOOKED EVERY-WHERE!
HE'S NOT HERE!
SIGH...
I WAS AFRAID OF THIS... WE'RE TOO LATE.
"TOO LATE"?
WHAT DO YOU KNOW THAT YOU'RE NOT TELLING ME?
....
RECENTLY...
...THERE'S BEEN A STRING OF INCIDENTS IN WHICH LOST DOGS HAVE BEEN FOUND *BEHEADED*.
BEHEADED?

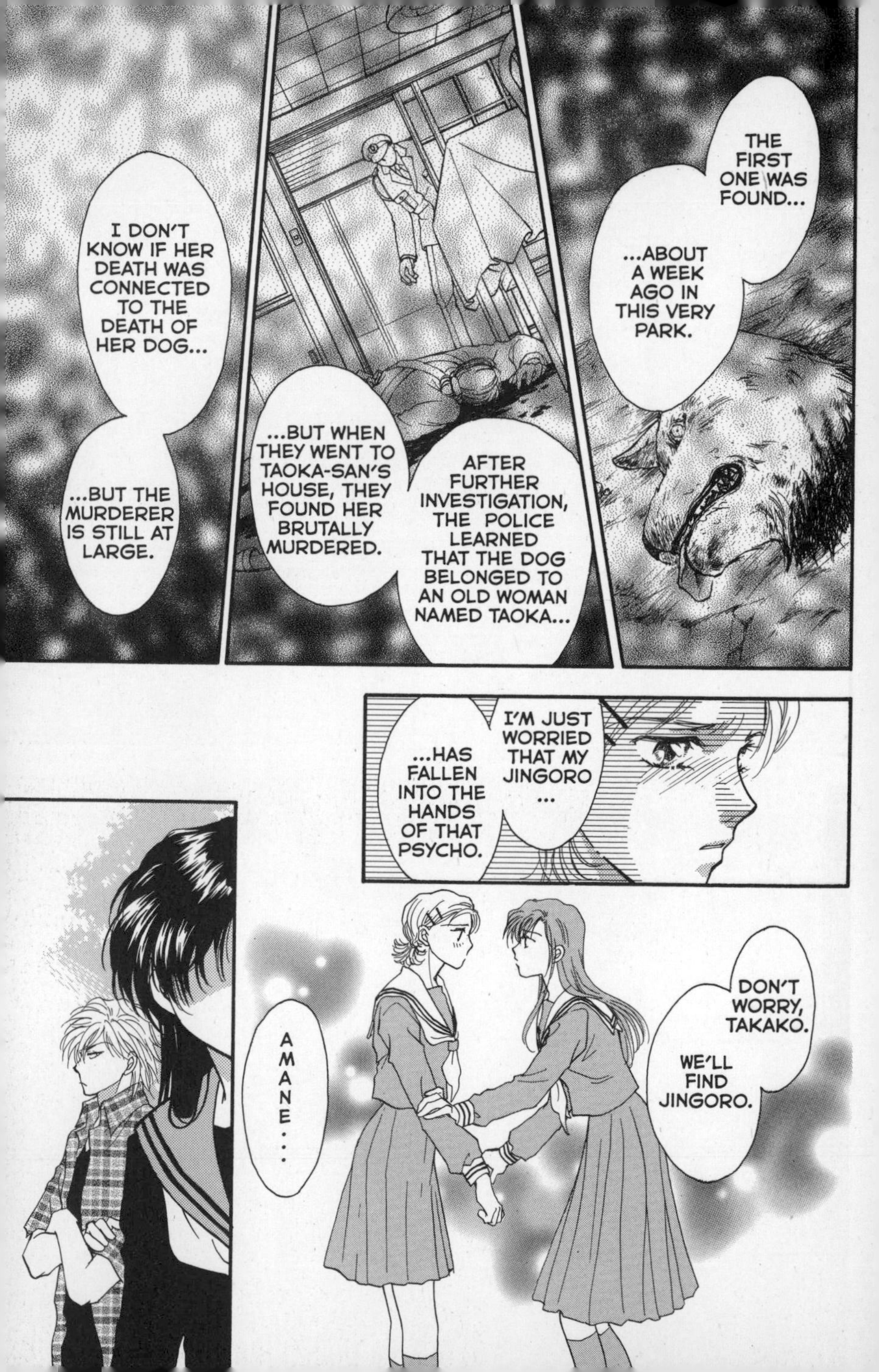
THE FIRST ONE WAS FOUND...
...ABOUT A WEEK AGO IN THIS VERY PARK.
AFTER FURTHER INVESTIGATION, THE POLICE LEARNED THAT THE DOG BELONGED TO AN OLD WOMAN NAMED TAOKA...
...BUT WHEN THEY WENT TO TAOKA-SAN'S HOUSE, THEY FOUND HER BRUTALLY MURDERED.
I DON'T KNOW IF HER DEATH WAS CONNECTED TO THE DEATH OF HER DOG...
...BUT THE MURDERER IS STILL AT LARGE.
I'M JUST WORRIED THAT MY JINGORO ...
...HAS FALLEN INTO THE HANDS OF THAT PSYCHO.
DON'T WORRY, TAKAKO.
WE'LL FIND JINGORO.
AMANE...

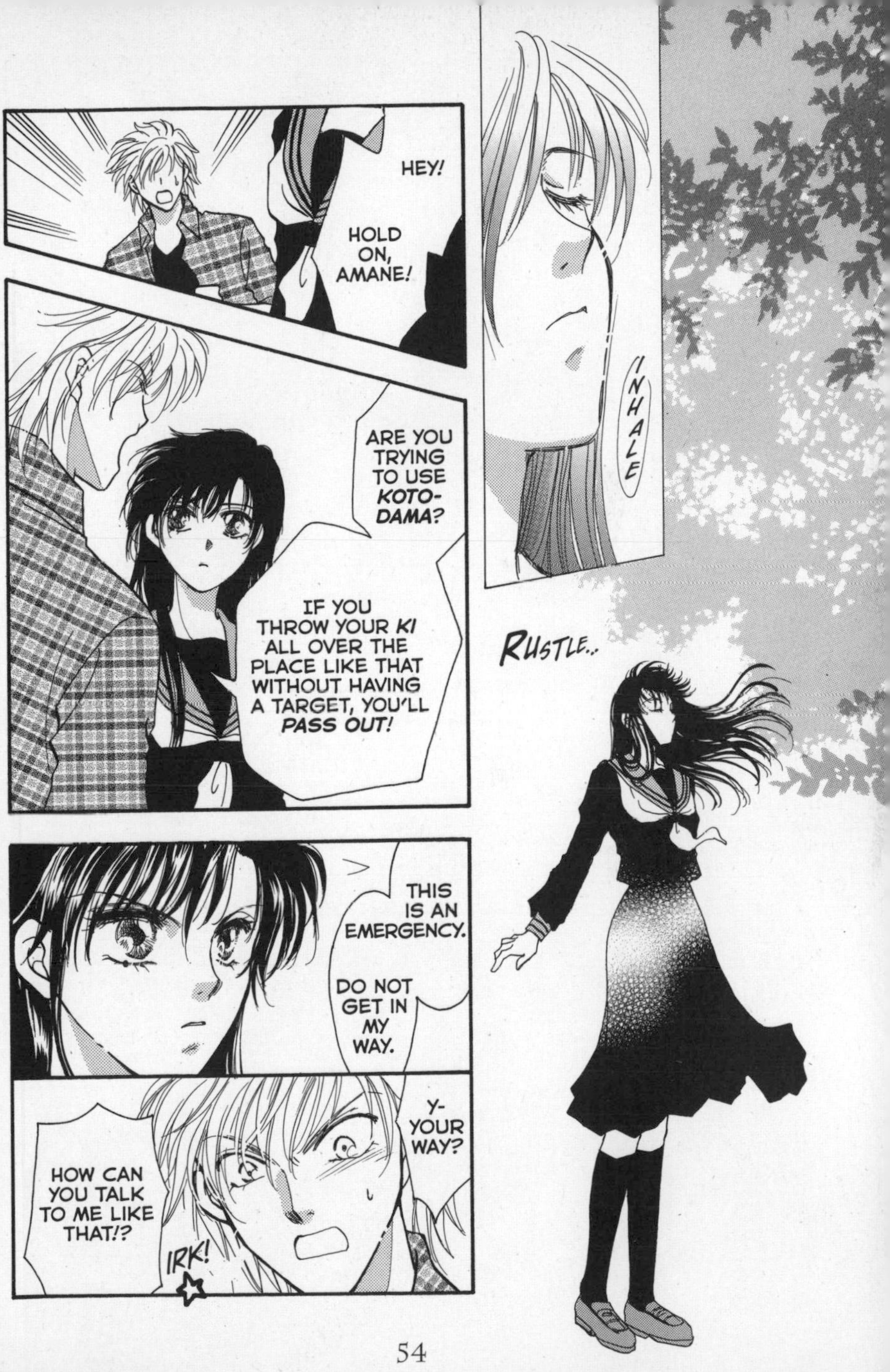
INHALE
RUSTLE..
HEY!
HOLD ON, AMANE!
ARE YOU TRYING TO USE KOTO-DAMA?
IF YOU THROW YOUR KI ALL OVER THE PLACE LIKE THAT WITHOUT HAVING A TARGET, YOU'LL PASS OUT!
THIS IS AN EMERGENCY.
DO NOT GET IN MY WAY.
Y-YOUR WAY?
HOW CAN YOU TALK TO ME LIKE THAT!?
IRK!

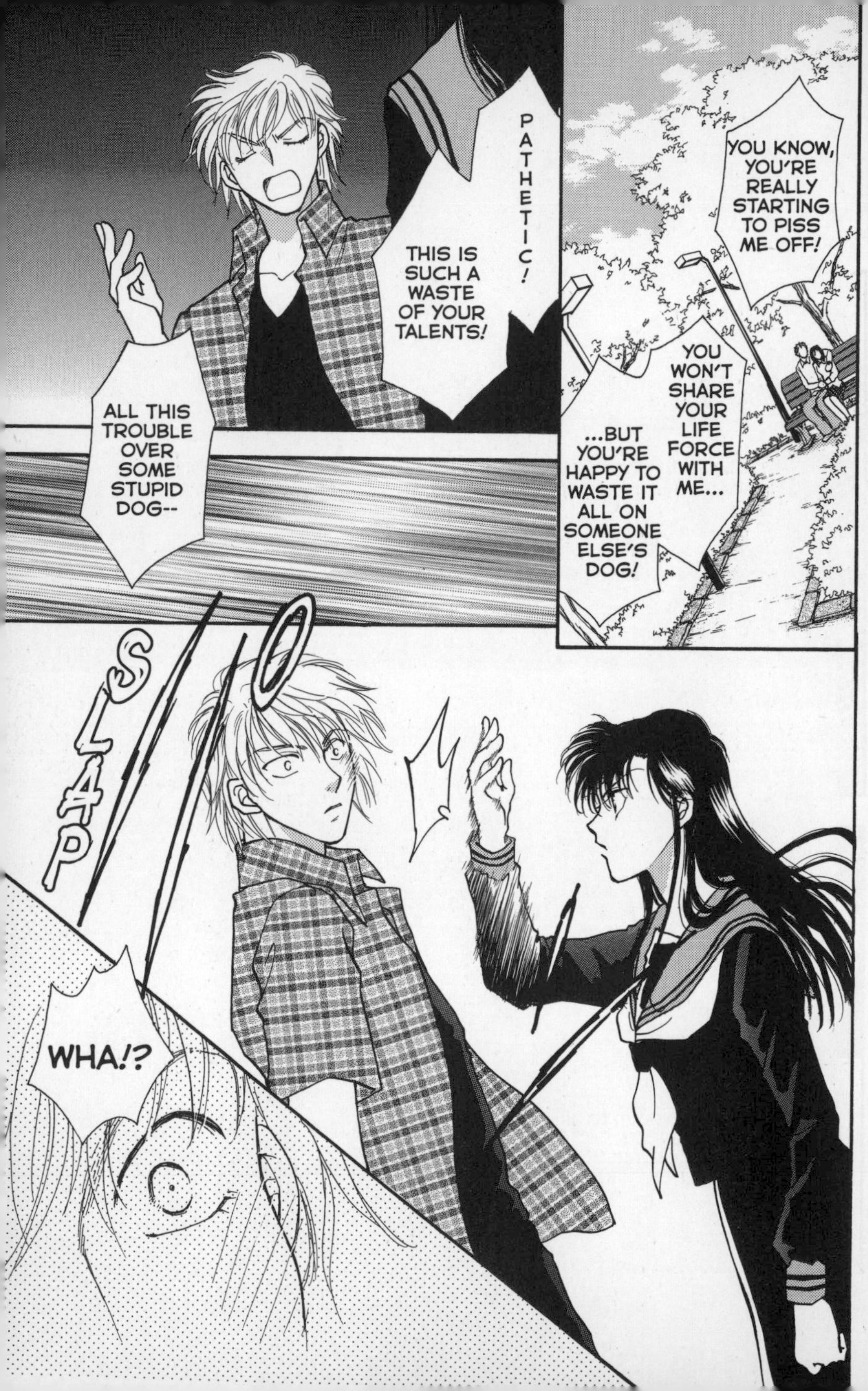
YOU KNOW, YOU'RE REALLY STARTING TO PISS ME OFF!
YOU WON'T SHARE YOUR LIFE FORCE WITH ME...
...BUT YOU'RE HAPPY TO WASTE IT ALL ON SOMEONE ELSE'S DOG!
PATHETIC!
THIS IS SUCH A WASTE OF YOUR TALENTS!
ALL THIS TROUBLE OVER SOME STUPID DOG--
SLAP
WHA!?

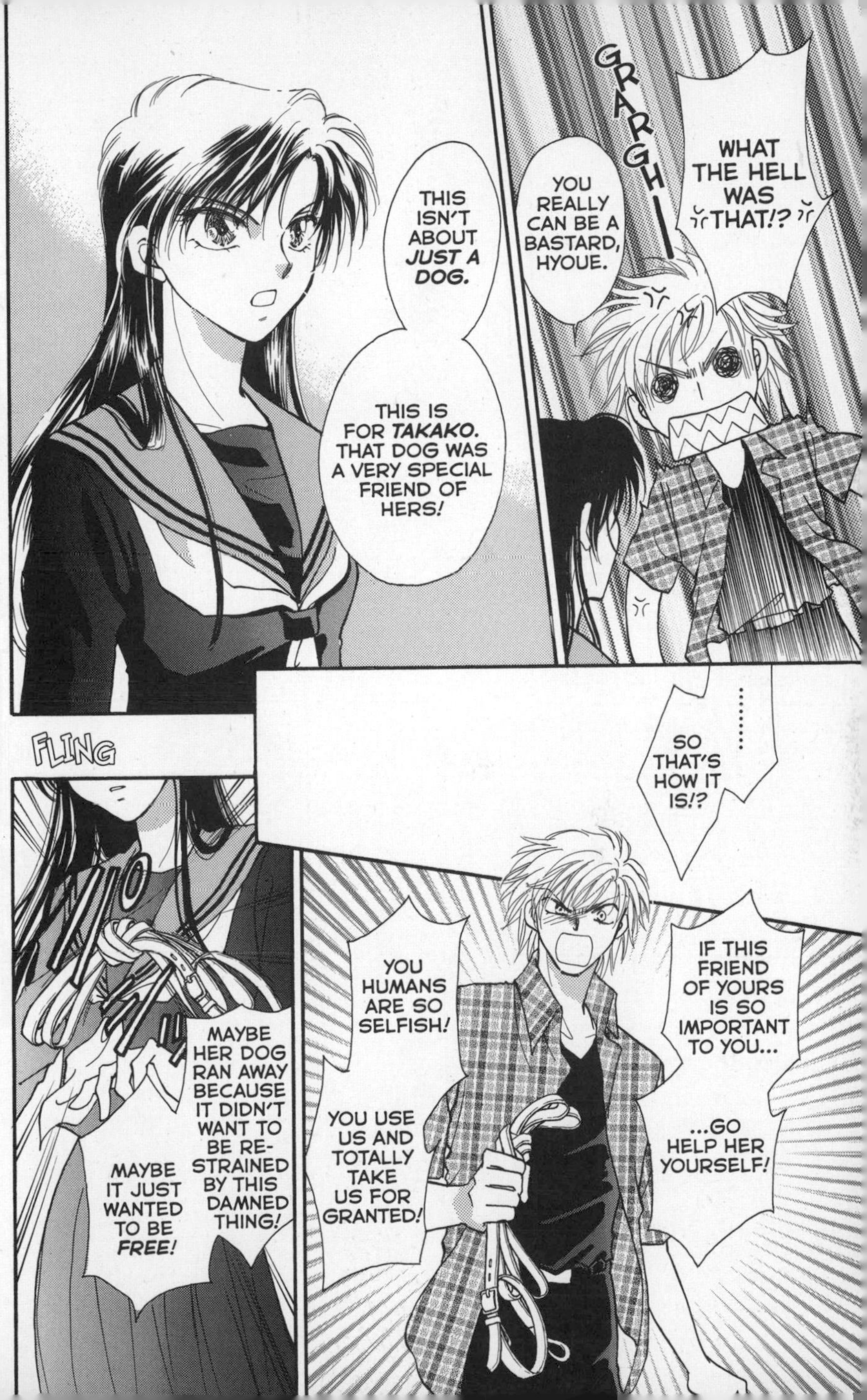
GRARGH
WHAT THE HELL WAS THAT!?
YOU REALLY CAN BE A BASTARD, HYOUE.
THIS ISN'T ABOUT *JUST A DOG.*
THIS IS FOR *TAKAKO.* THAT DOG WAS A VERY SPECIAL FRIEND OF HERS!
......
SO THAT'S HOW IT IS!?
IF THIS FRIEND OF YOURS IS SO IMPORTANT TO YOU...
...GO HELP HER YOURSELF!
YOU HUMANS ARE SO SELFISH!
YOU USE US AND TOTALLY TAKE US FOR GRANTED!
FLING
MAYBE HER DOG RAN AWAY BECAUSE IT DIDN'T WANT TO BE RE-STRAINED BY THIS DAMNED THING!
MAYBE IT JUST WANTED TO BE *FREE!*

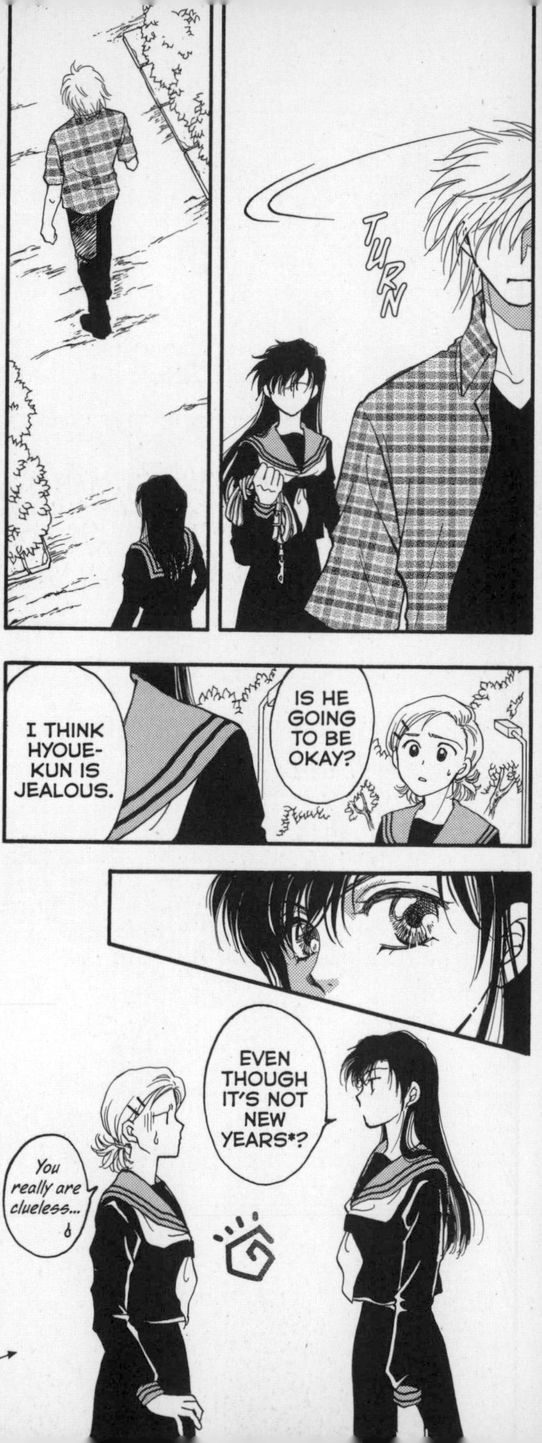
TURN
IS HE GOING TO BE OKAY?
I THINK HYOUE-KUN IS JEALOUS.
EVEN THOUGH IT'S NOT NEW YEARS*?
You really are clueless...

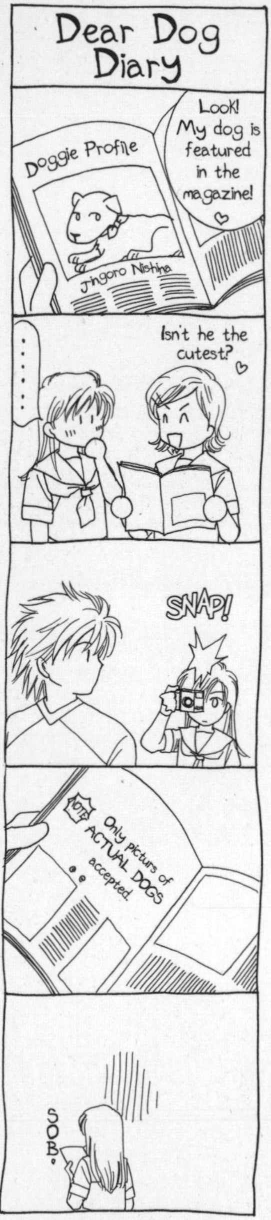
Dear Dog Diary
Look! My dog is featured in the magazine! ♡
Doggie Profile
Jingoro Nishina
......
Isn't he the cutest? ♡
SNAP!
NOTE
Only pictures of ACTUAL DOGS accepted.
SOB.

* Jealousy/New Years--
See Translator's Note
at the back of the book.

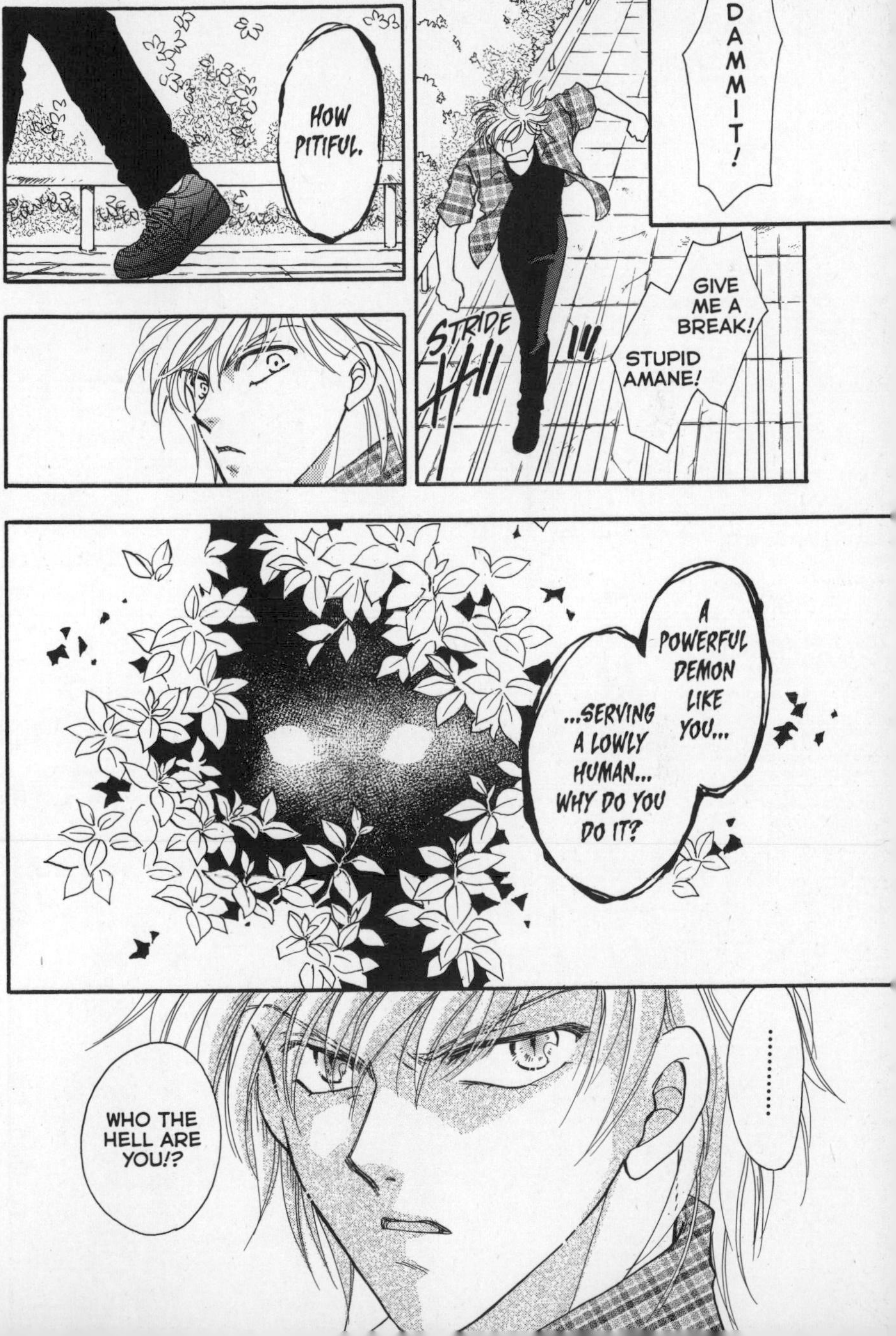
DAMMIT!
GIVE ME A BREAK!
STUPID AMANE!
STRIDE
HOW PITIFUL.
A POWERFUL DEMON LIKE YOU...
...SERVING A LOWLY HUMAN... WHY DO YOU DO IT?
......
WHO THE HELL ARE YOU!?

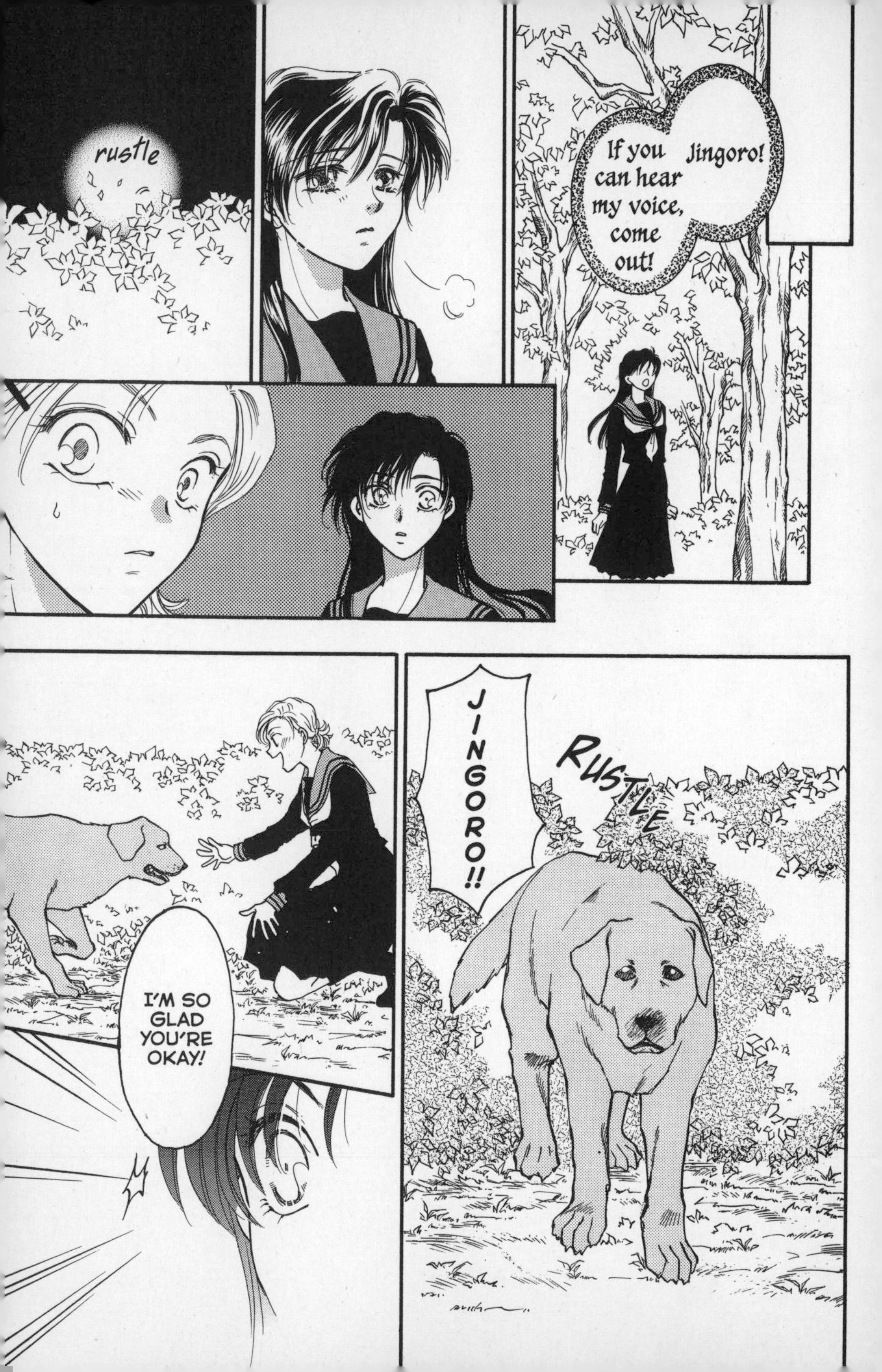
Jingoro! If you can hear my voice, come out!
rustle
JINGORO!!
RUSTLE
I'M SO GLAD YOU'RE OKAY!

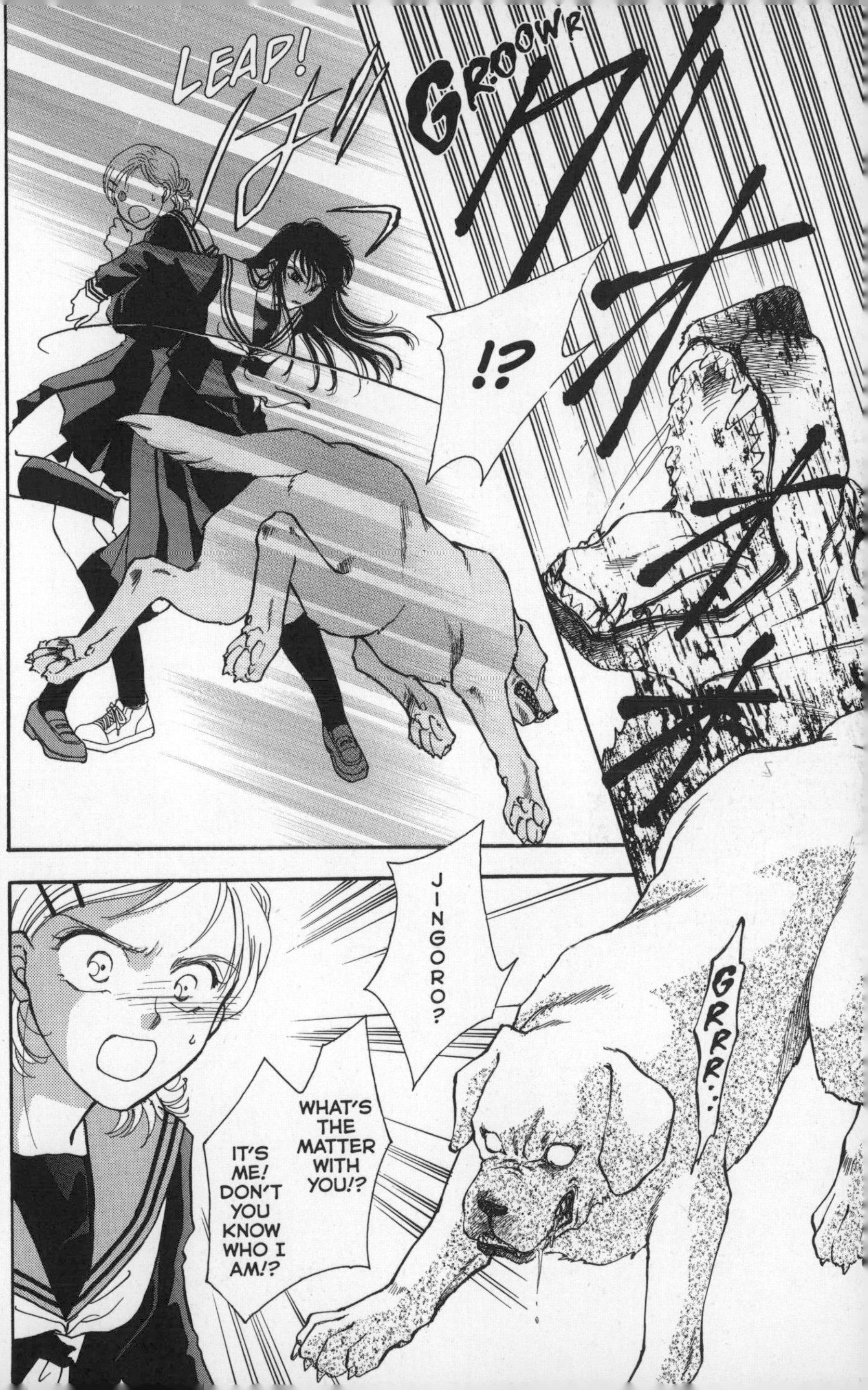
GROOW'R
LEAP!
!?
JINGORO?
GRRR...
WHAT'S THE MATTER WITH YOU!?
IT'S ME! DON'T YOU KNOW WHO I AM!?

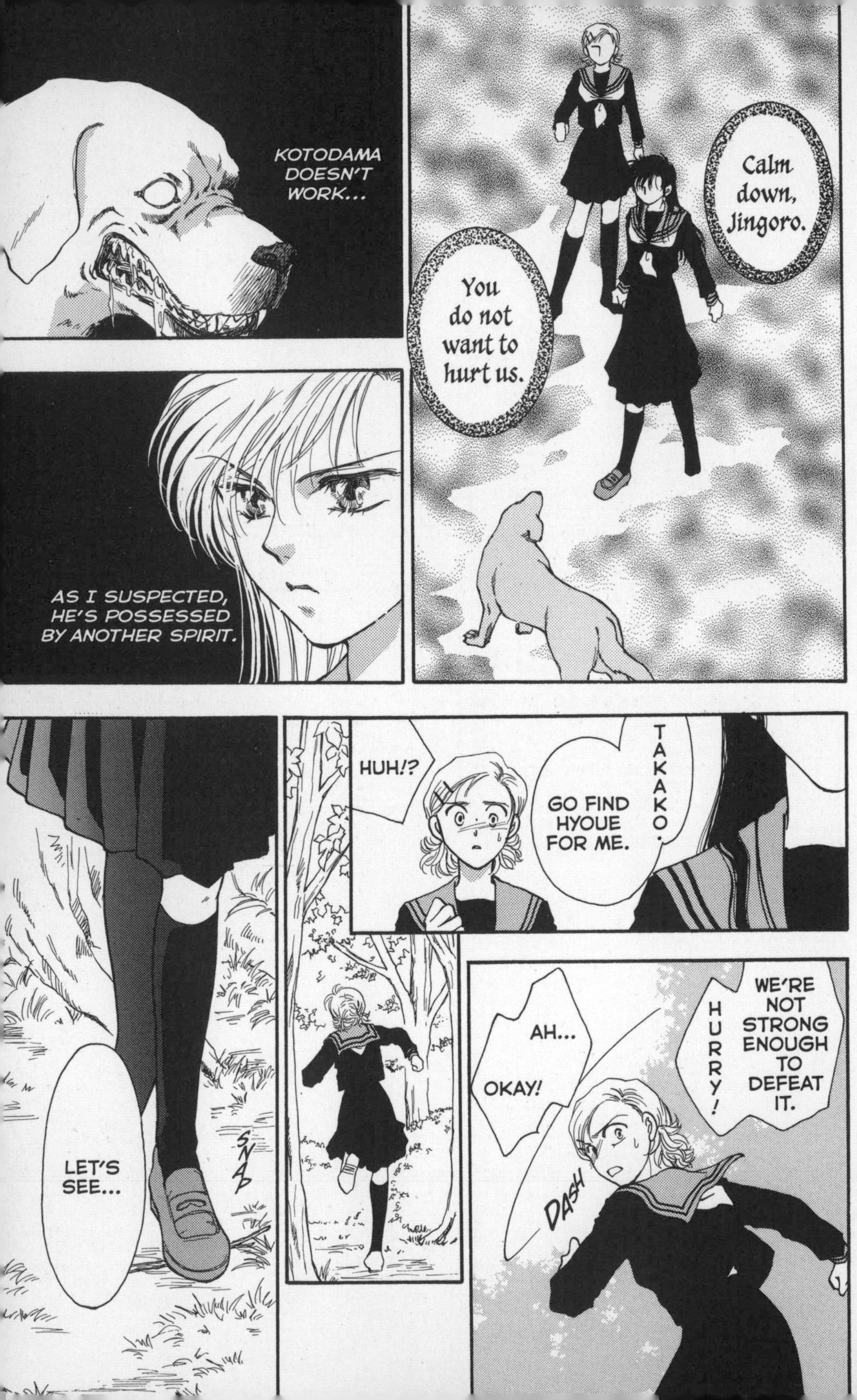
Calm down, Jingoro.
You do not want to hurt us.
KOTODAMA DOESN'T WORK...
AS I SUSPECTED, HE'S POSSESSED BY ANOTHER SPIRIT.
TAKAKO.
GO FIND HYOUE FOR ME.
HUH!?
WE'RE NOT STRONG ENOUGH TO DEFEAT IT.
HURRY!
AH...
OKAY!
DASH
SNAP
LET'S SEE...

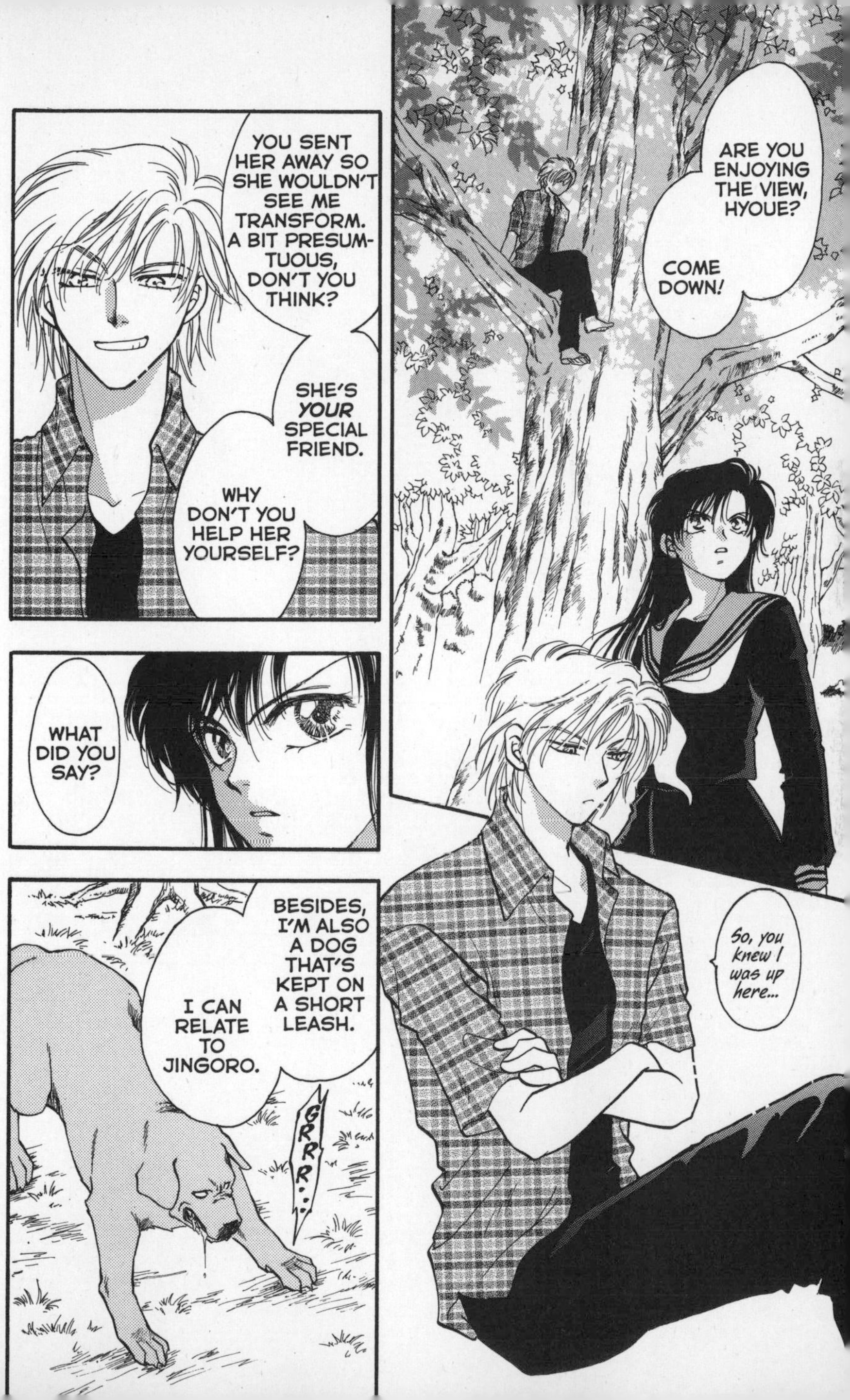
ARE YOU ENJOYING THE VIEW, HYOUE?
COME DOWN!
So, you knew I was up here...
YOU SENT HER AWAY SO SHE WOULDN'T SEE ME TRANSFORM. A BIT PRESUM-TUOUS, DON'T YOU THINK?
SHE'S *YOUR* SPECIAL FRIEND.
WHY DON'T YOU HELP HER YOURSELF?
WHAT DID YOU SAY?
BESIDES, I'M ALSO A DOG THAT'S KEPT ON A SHORT LEASH.
I CAN RELATE TO JINGORO.
GRRR...

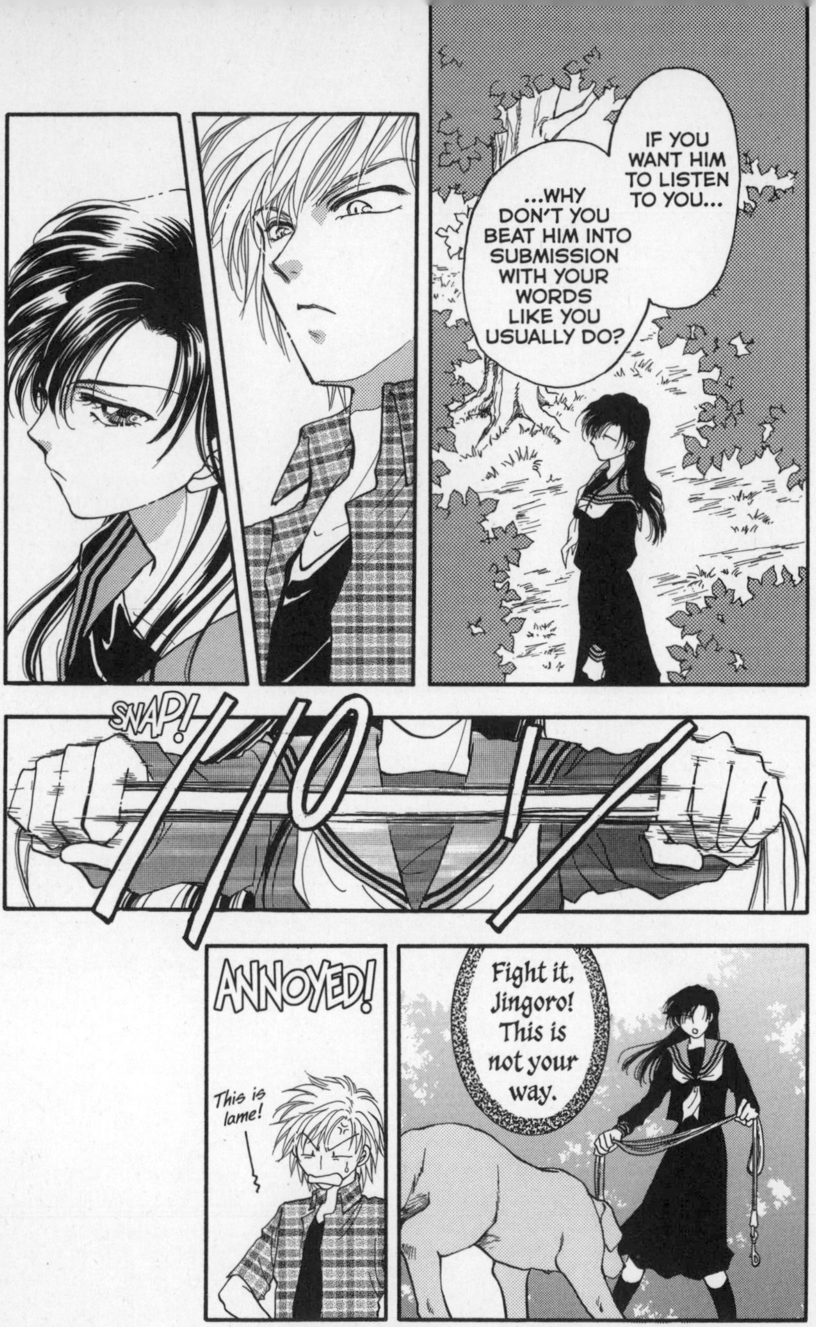
IF YOU WANT HIM TO LISTEN TO YOU...
...WHY DON'T YOU BEAT HIM INTO SUBMISSION WITH YOUR WORDS LIKE YOU USUALLY DO?
SNAP!
Fight it, Jingoro! This is not your way.
ANNOYED!
This is lame!

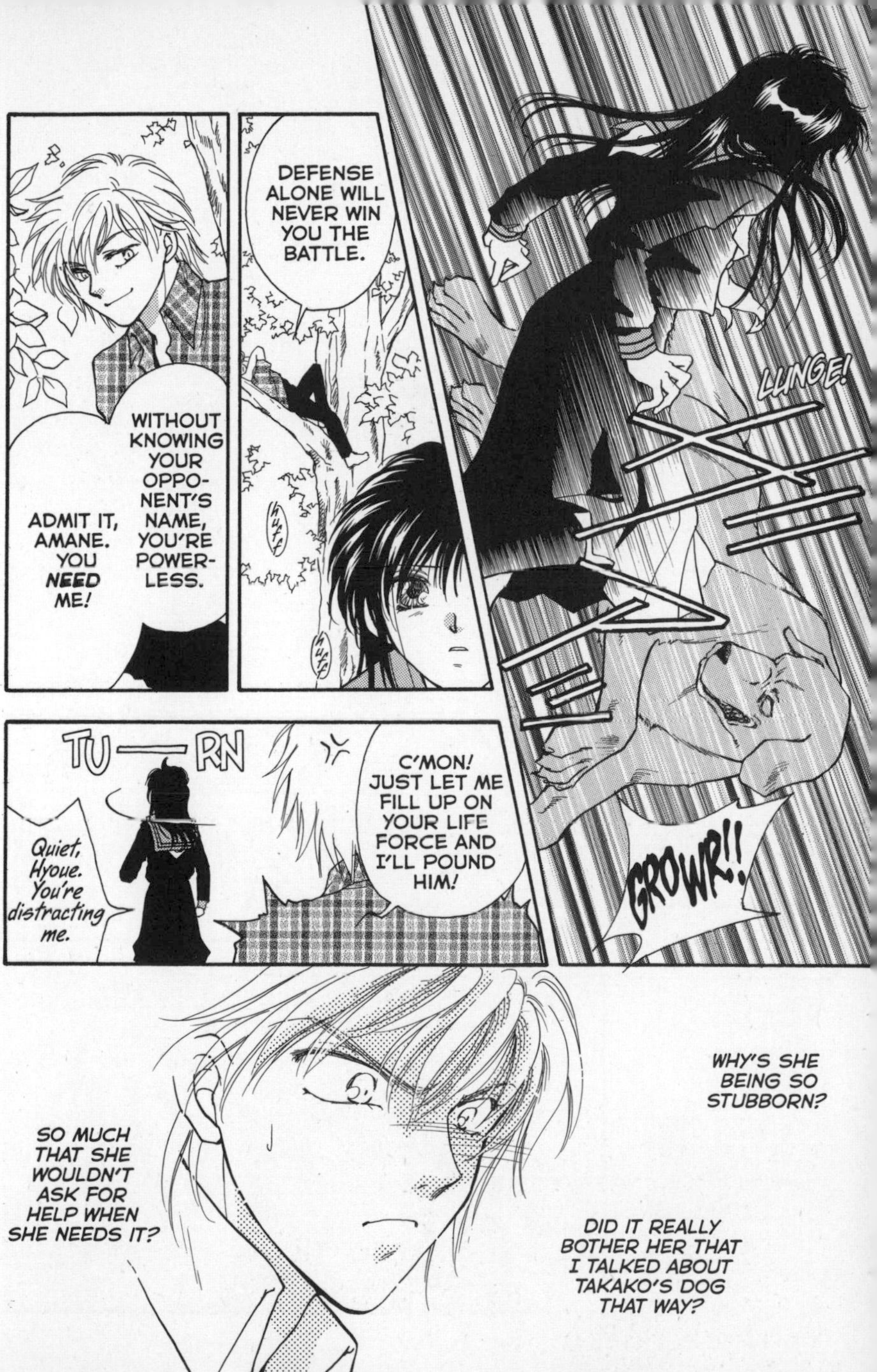
LUNGE!
GROWR!!
DEFENSE ALONE WILL NEVER WIN YOU THE BATTLE.
huff
huff
WITHOUT KNOWING YOUR OPPONENT'S NAME, YOU'RE POWERLESS.
ADMIT IT, AMANE. YOU **NEED** ME!
C'MON! JUST LET ME FILL UP ON YOUR LIFE FORCE AND I'LL POUND HIM!
TU——RN
Quiet, Hyoue. You're distracting me.
WHY'S SHE BEING SO STUBBORN?
SO MUCH THAT SHE WOULDN'T ASK FOR HELP WHEN SHE NEEDS IT?
DID IT REALLY BOTHER HER THAT I TALKED ABOUT TAKAKO'S DOG THAT WAY?

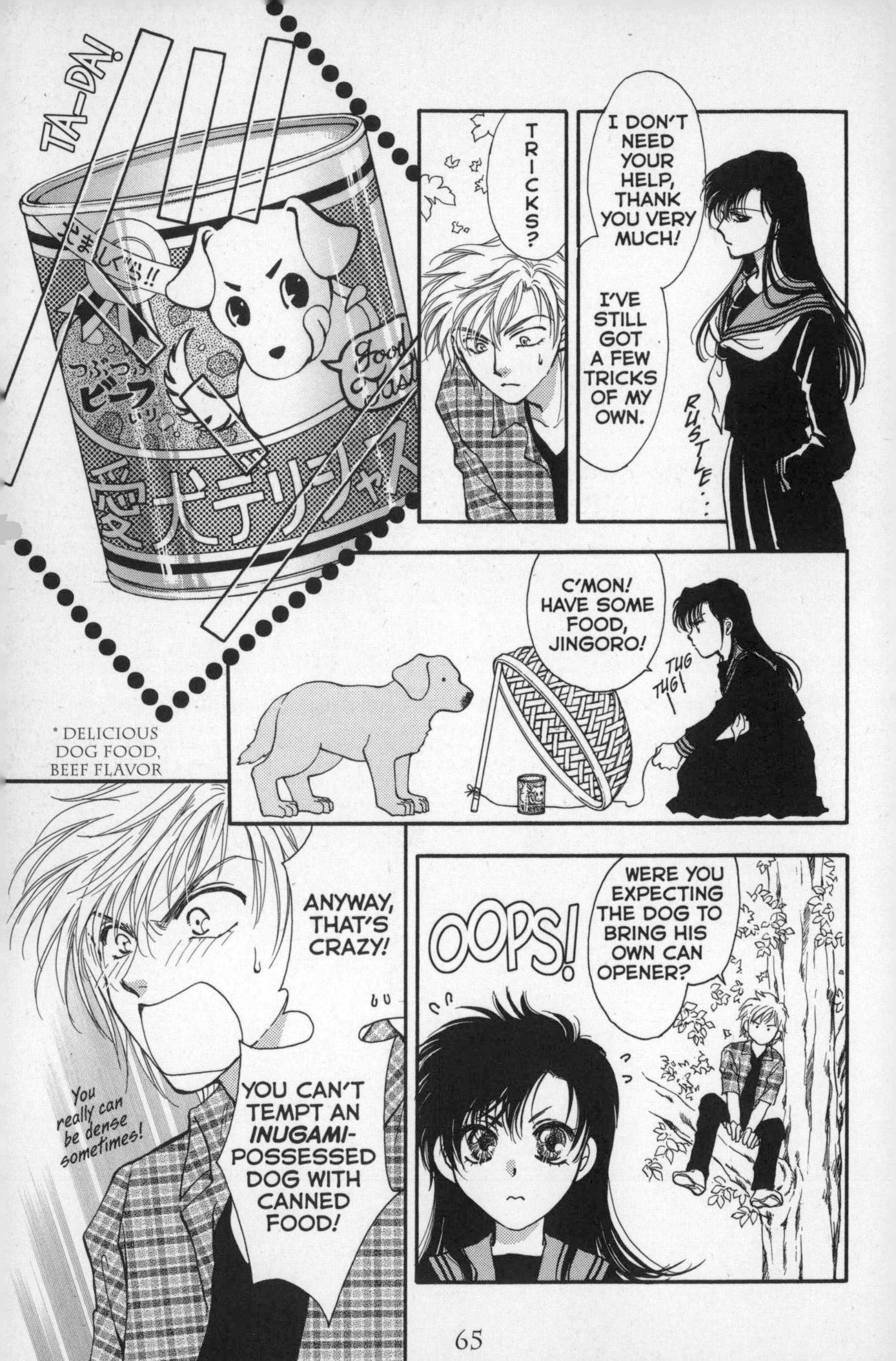
I DON'T NEED YOUR HELP, THANK YOU VERY MUCH!
I'VE STILL GOT A FEW TRICKS OF MY OWN.
RUSTLE...
TRICKS?
TA-DA!
愛犬デリシャス
C'MON! HAVE SOME FOOD, JINGORO!
TUG TUG
WERE YOU EXPECTING THE DOG TO BRING HIS OWN CAN OPENER?
OOPS!
ANYWAY, THAT'S CRAZY!
YOU CAN'T TEMPT AN *INUGAMI*-POSSESSED DOG WITH CANNED FOOD!
You really can be dense sometimes!

* DELICIOUS DOG FOOD, BEEF FLAVOR

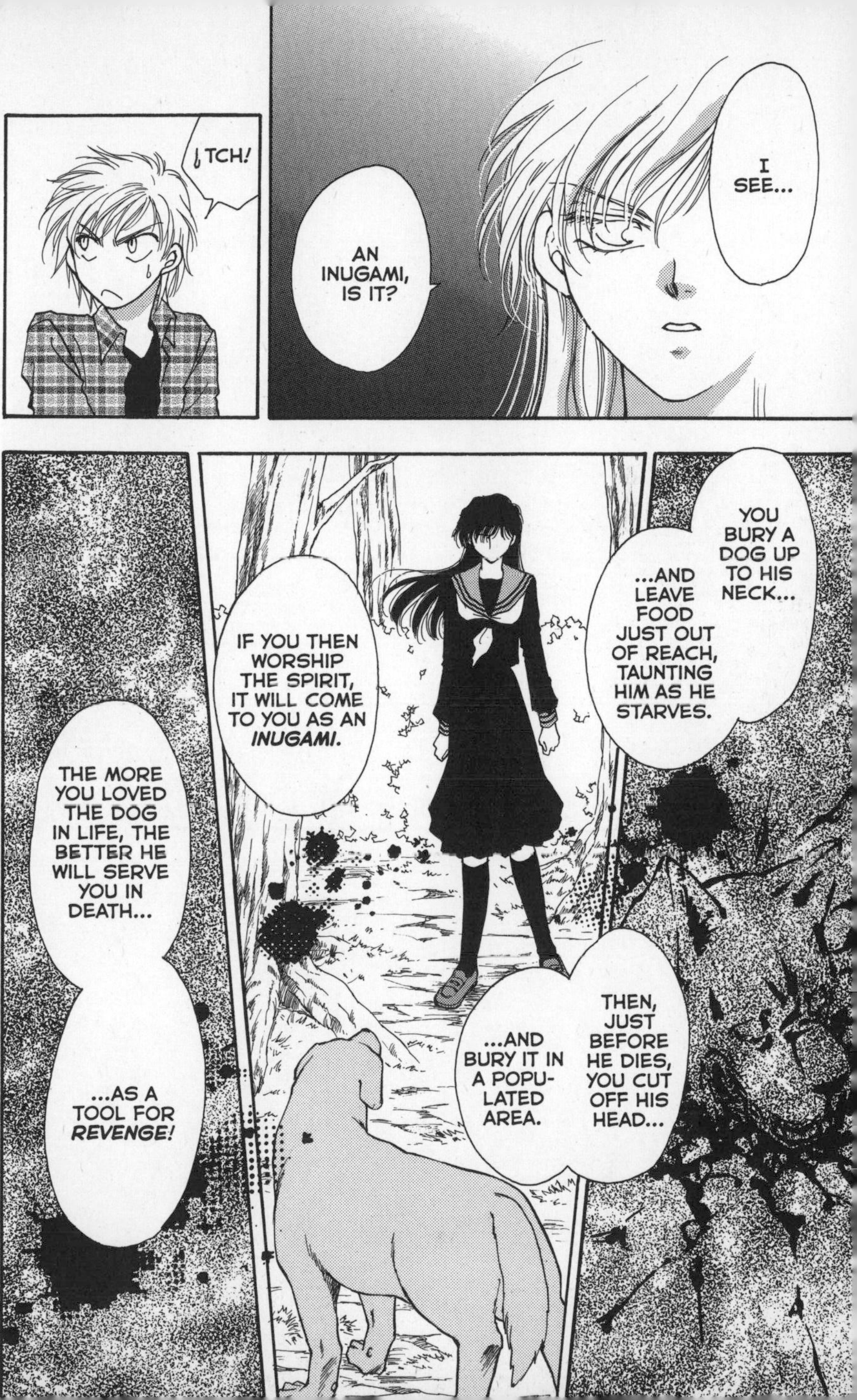
I SEE...
AN INUGAMI, IS IT?
TCH!
YOU BURY A DOG UP TO HIS NECK...
...AND LEAVE FOOD JUST OUT OF REACH, TAUNTING HIM AS HE STARVES.
THEN, JUST BEFORE HE DIES, YOU CUT OFF HIS HEAD...
...AND BURY IT IN A POPU-LATED AREA.
IF YOU THEN WORSHIP THE SPIRIT, IT WILL COME TO YOU AS AN *INUGAMI*.
THE MORE YOU LOVED THE DOG IN LIFE, THE BETTER HE WILL SERVE YOU IN DEATH...
...AS A TOOL FOR *REVENGE!*

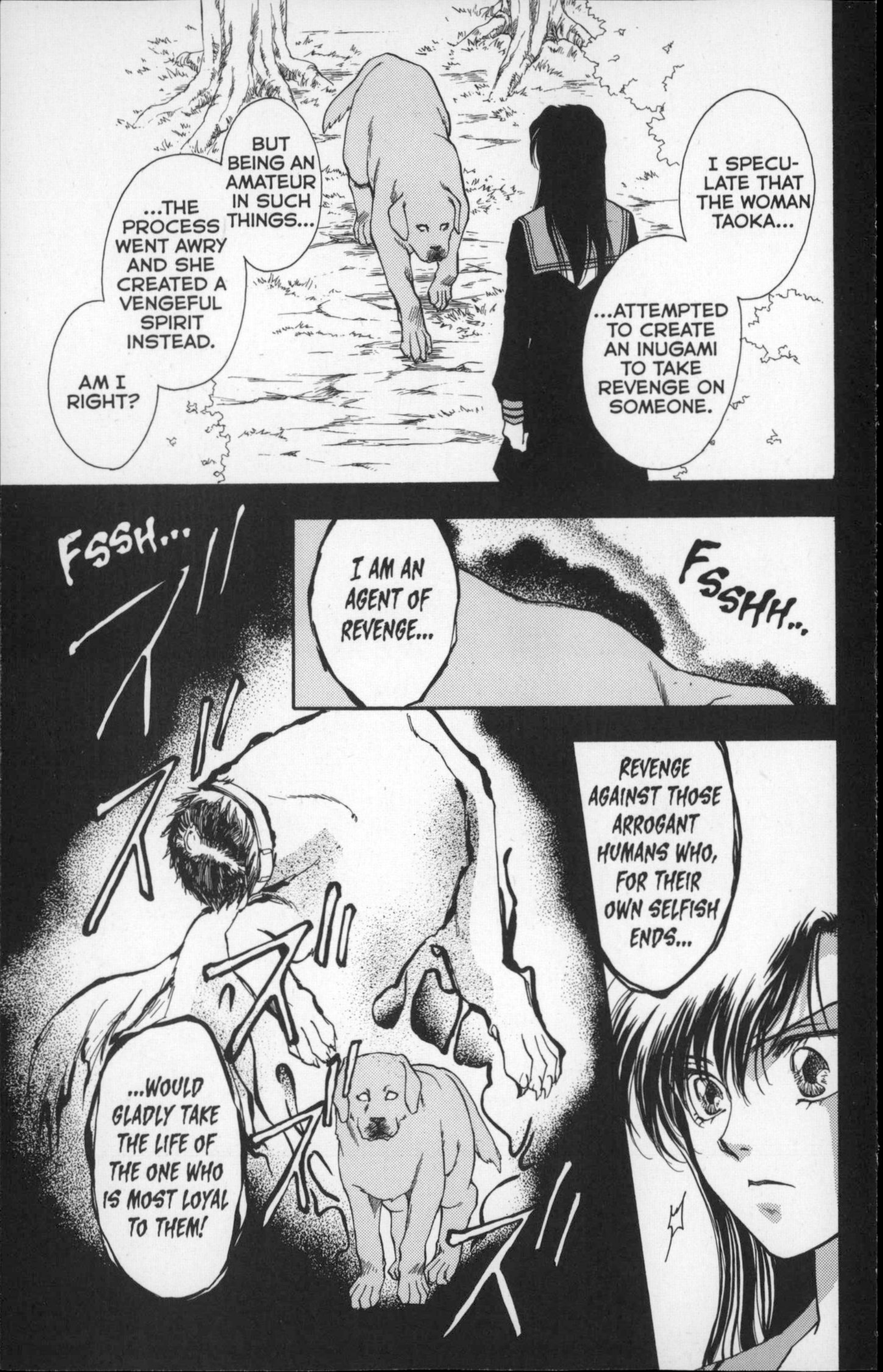
I SPECU- LATE THAT THE WOMAN TAOKA...
...ATTEMPTED TO CREATE AN INUGAMI TO TAKE REVENGE ON SOMEONE.
BUT BEING AN AMATEUR IN SUCH THINGS...
...THE PROCESS WENT AWRY AND SHE CREATED A VENGEFUL SPIRIT INSTEAD.
AM I RIGHT?
FSSHH...
I AM AN AGENT OF REVENGE...
FSSH...
REVENGE AGAINST THOSE ARROGANT HUMANS WHO, FOR THEIR OWN SELFISH ENDS...
...WOULD GLADLY TAKE THE LIFE OF THE ONE WHO IS MOST LOYAL TO THEM!

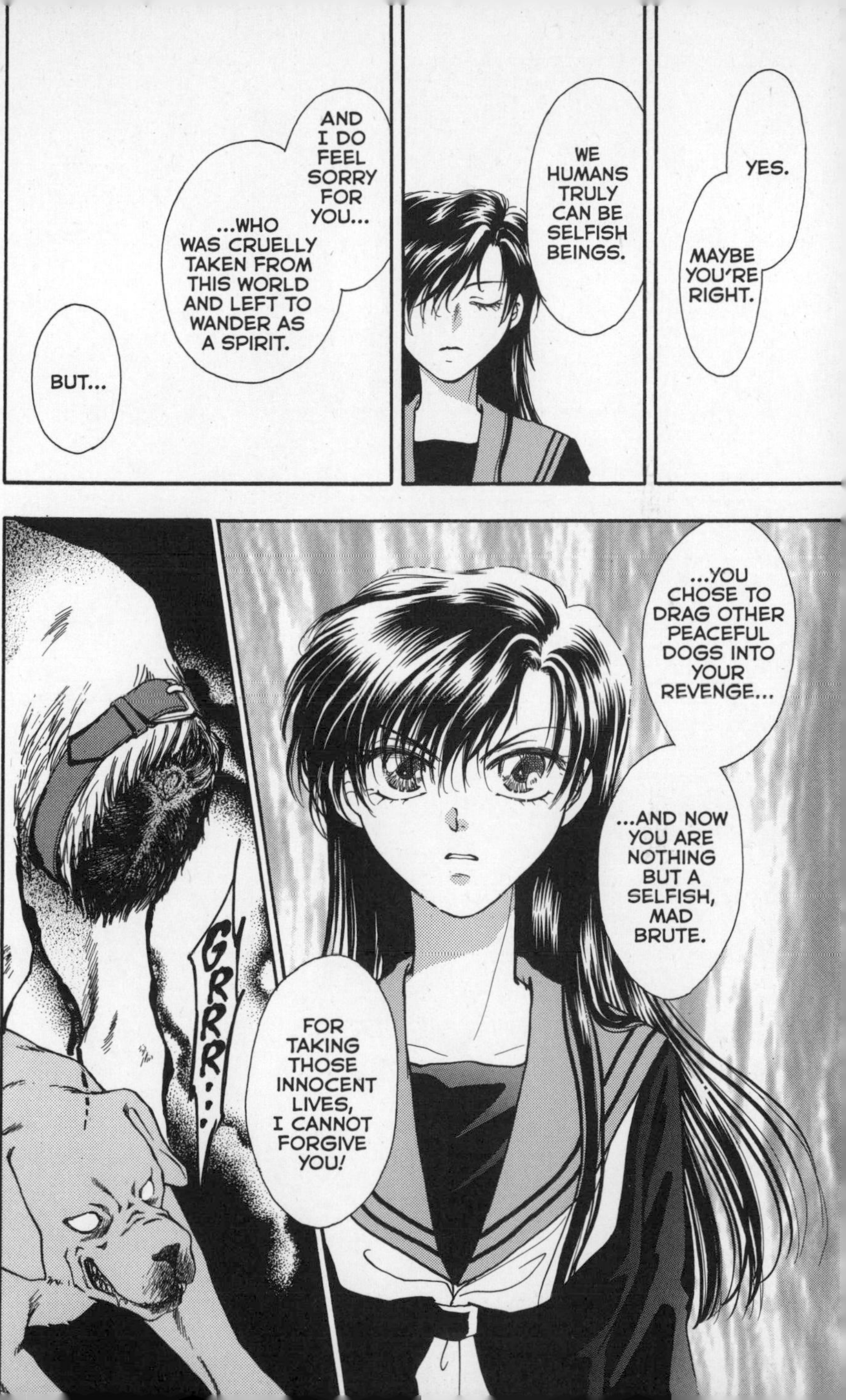
YES.
MAYBE YOU'RE RIGHT.
WE HUMANS TRULY CAN BE SELFISH BEINGS.
AND I DO FEEL SORRY FOR YOU...
...WHO WAS CRUELLY TAKEN FROM THIS WORLD AND LEFT TO WANDER AS A SPIRIT.
BUT...
...YOU CHOSE TO DRAG OTHER PEACEFUL DOGS INTO YOUR REVENGE...
...AND NOW YOU ARE NOTHING BUT A SELFISH, MAD BRUTE.
FOR TAKING THOSE INNOCENT LIVES, I CANNOT FORGIVE YOU!
GRRR...

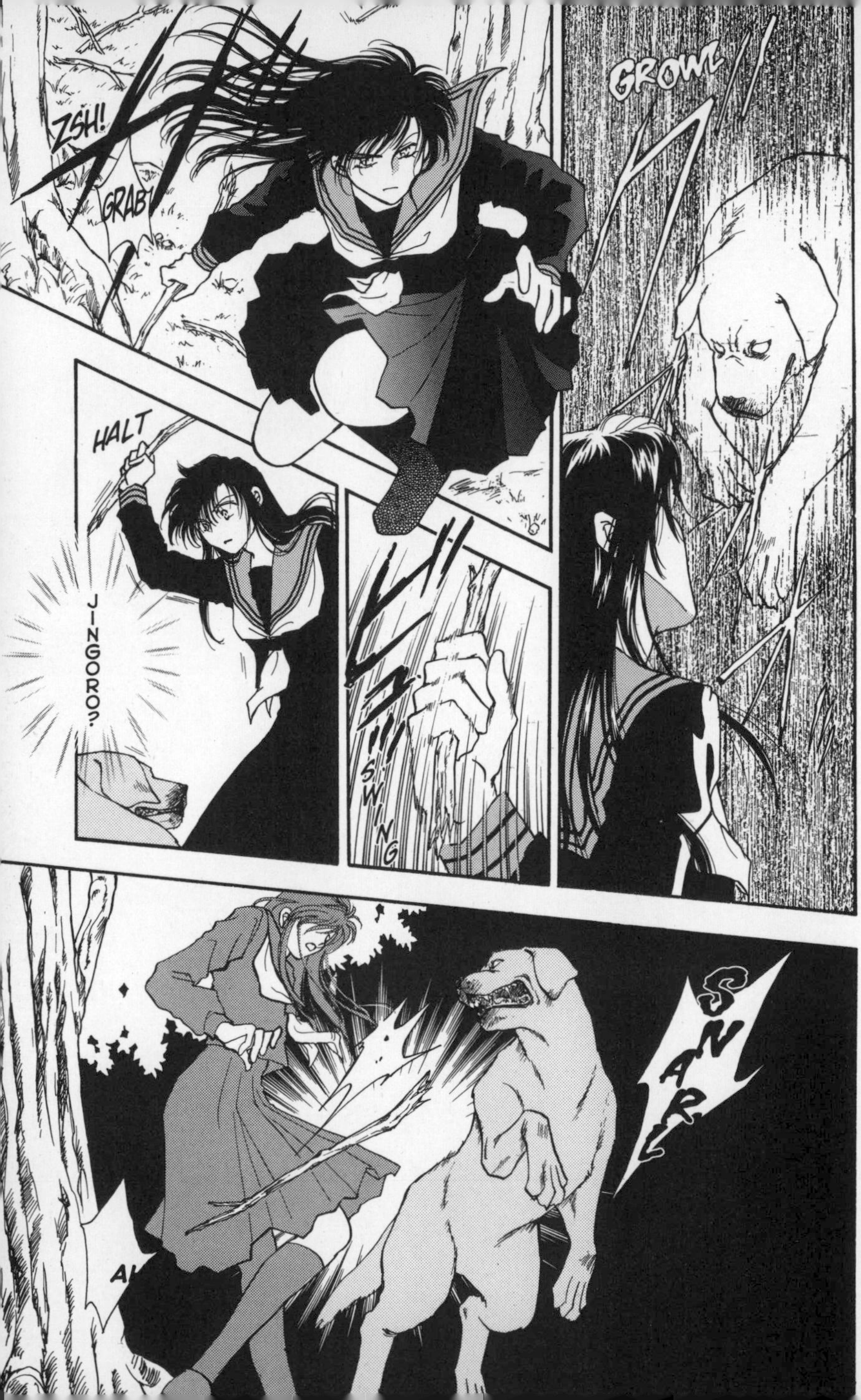
GROWL
ZSH!
GRAB
SWING
HALT
JINGORO?
SNARL

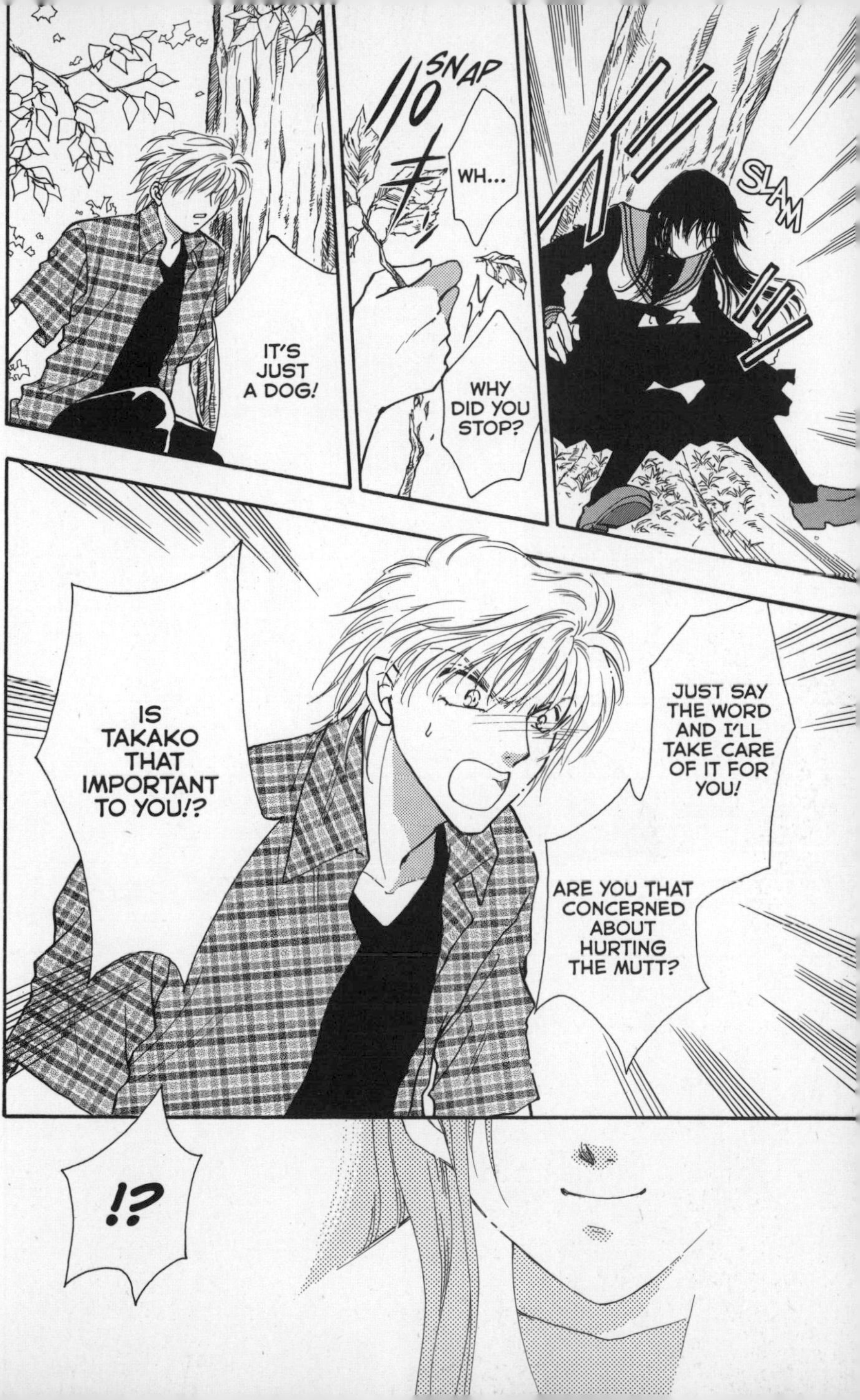
SLAM
SNAP
WH...
WHY DID YOU STOP?
IT'S JUST A DOG!
JUST SAY THE WORD AND I'LL TAKE CARE OF IT FOR YOU!
ARE YOU THAT CONCERNED ABOUT HURTING THE MUTT?
IS TAKAKO THAT IMPORTANT TO YOU!?
!?

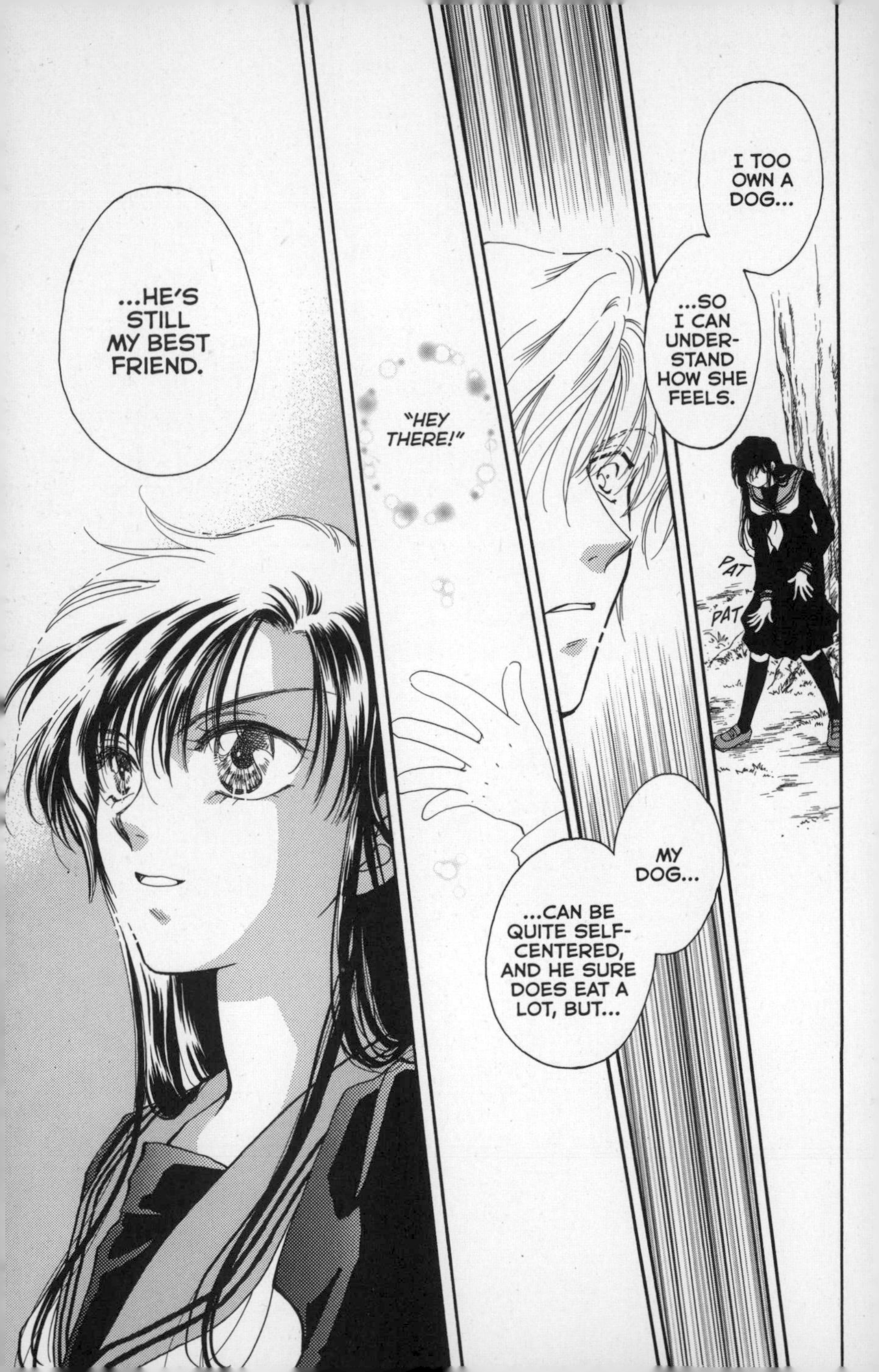
I TOO OWN A DOG...
...SO I CAN UNDER-STAND HOW SHE FEELS.
PAT PAT
MY DOG...
...CAN BE QUITE SELF-CENTERED, AND HE SURE DOES EAT A LOT, BUT...
"HEY THERE!"
...HE'S STILL MY BEST FRIEND.

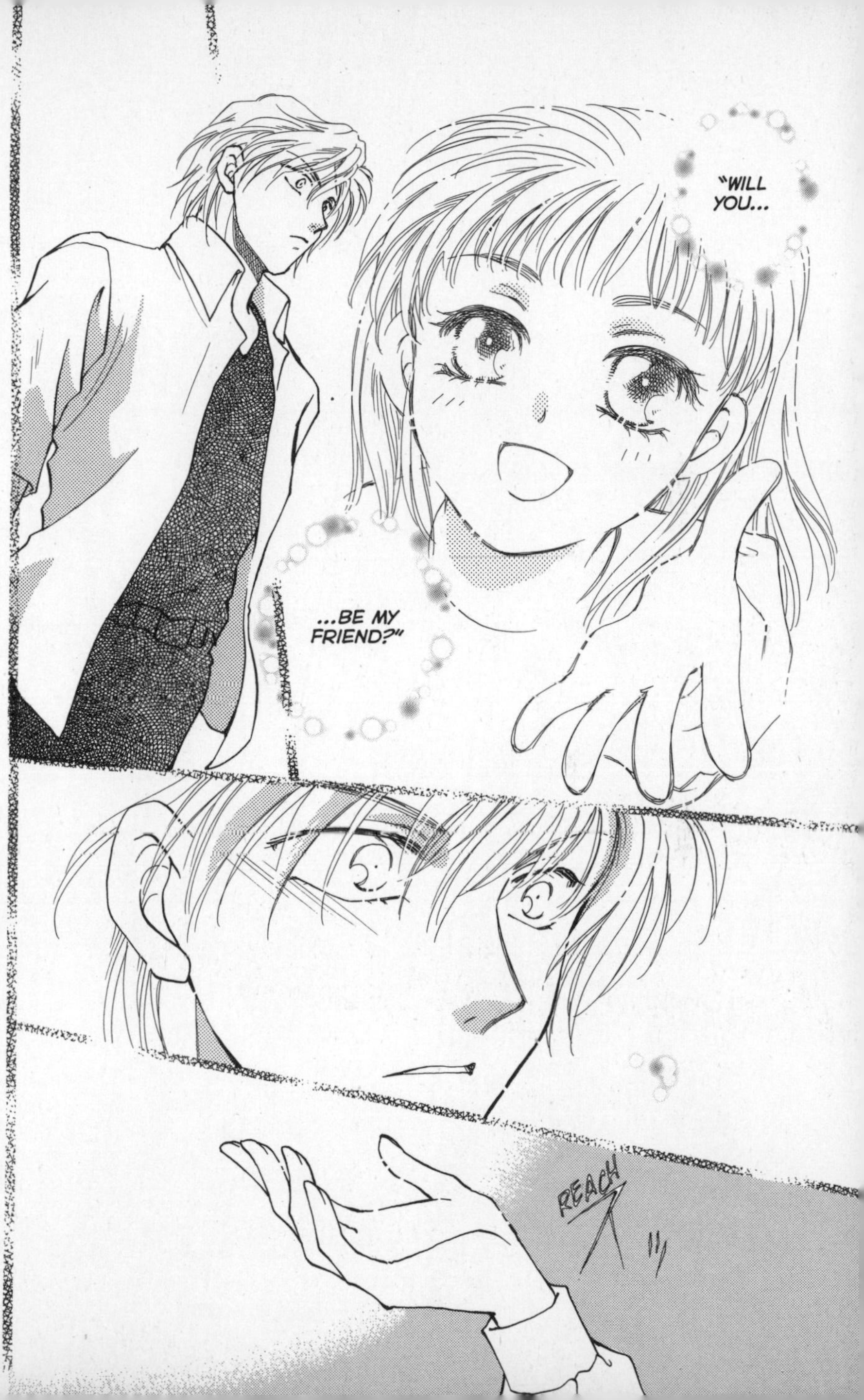
"WILL YOU...
...BE MY FRIEND?"
REACH

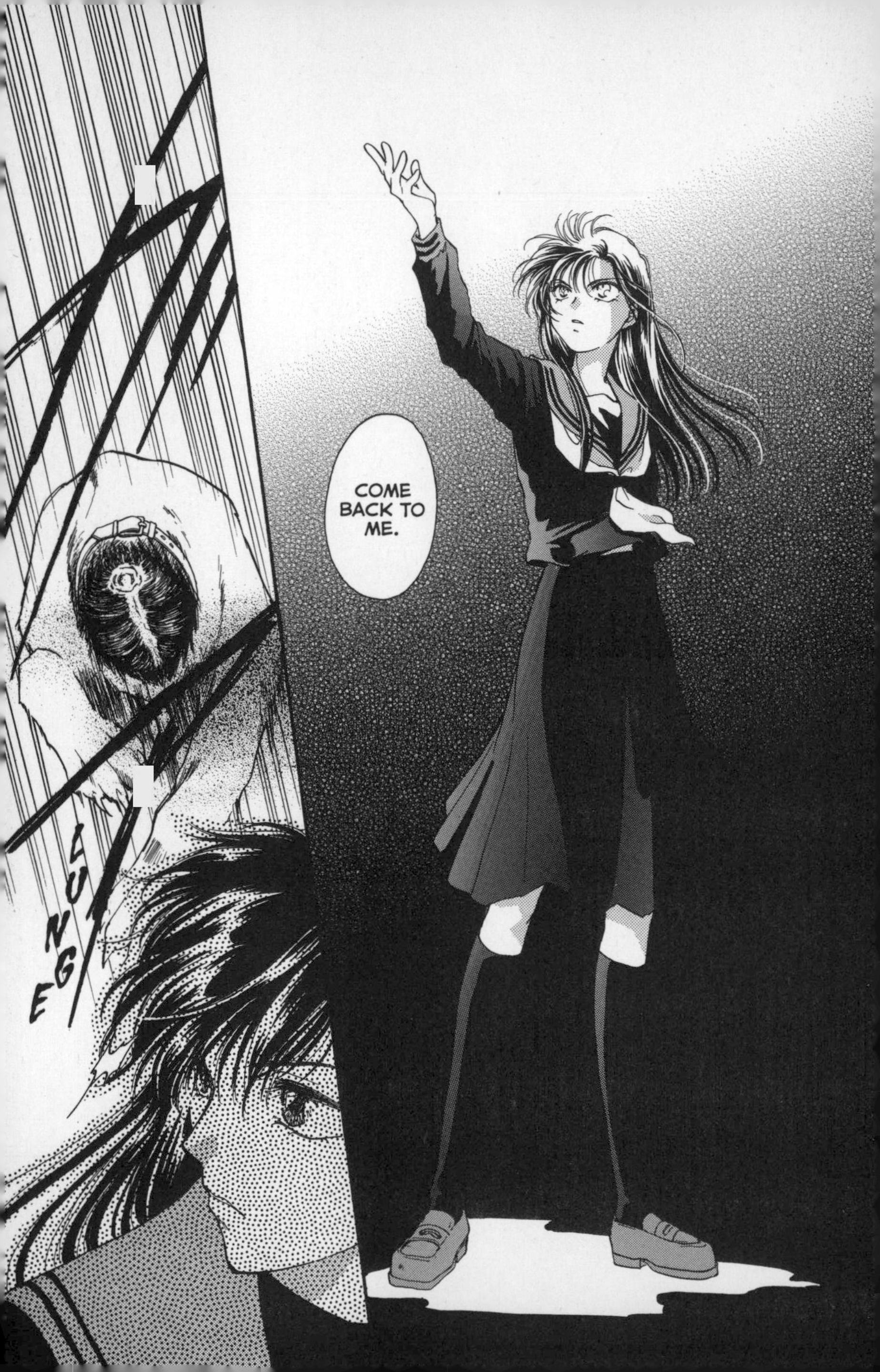
COME BACK TO ME.
LUNGE

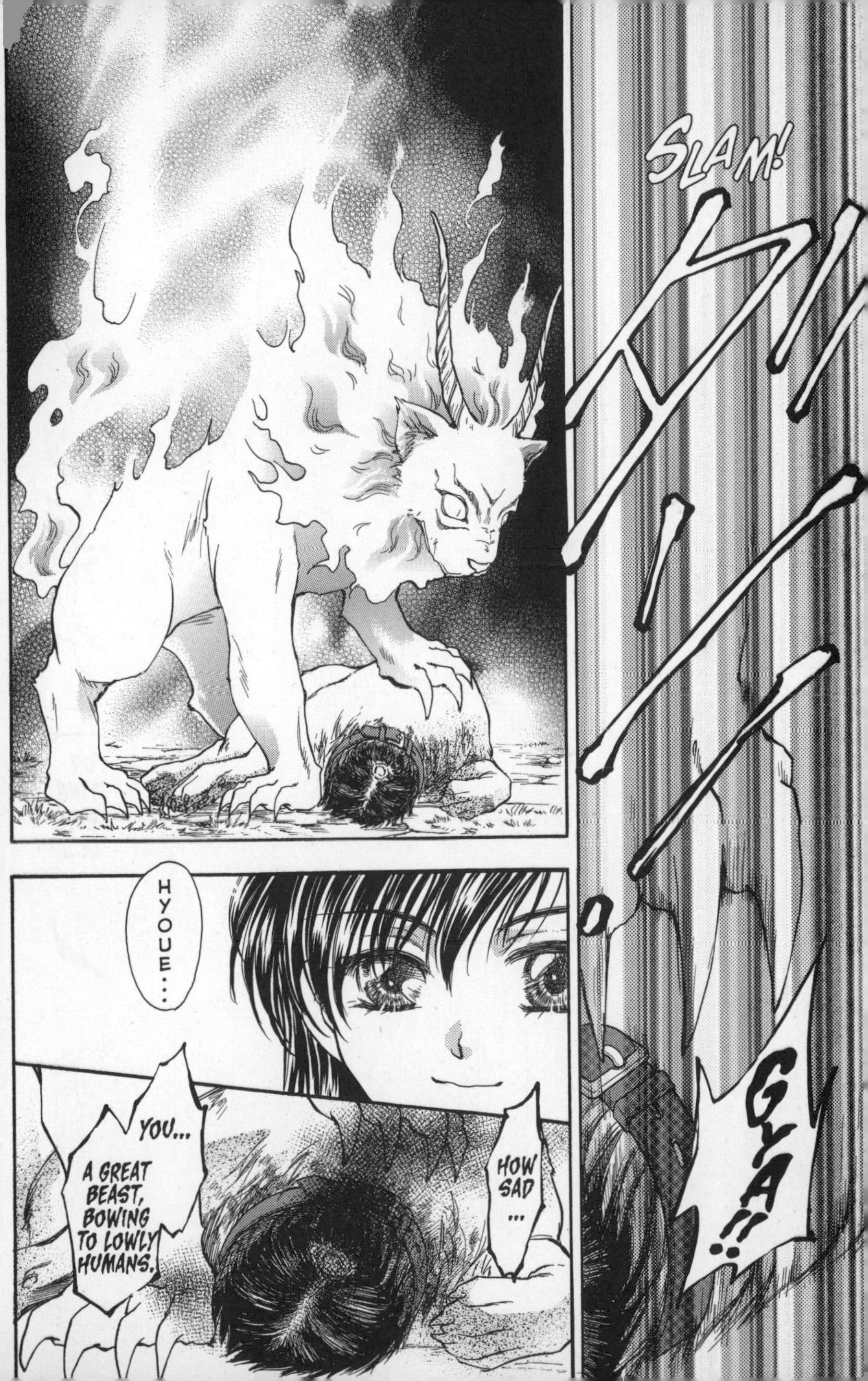

SLAM!
GYA!!
HYOUE...
HOW SAD...
YOU...
A GREAT BEAST, BOWING TO LOWLY HUMANS.

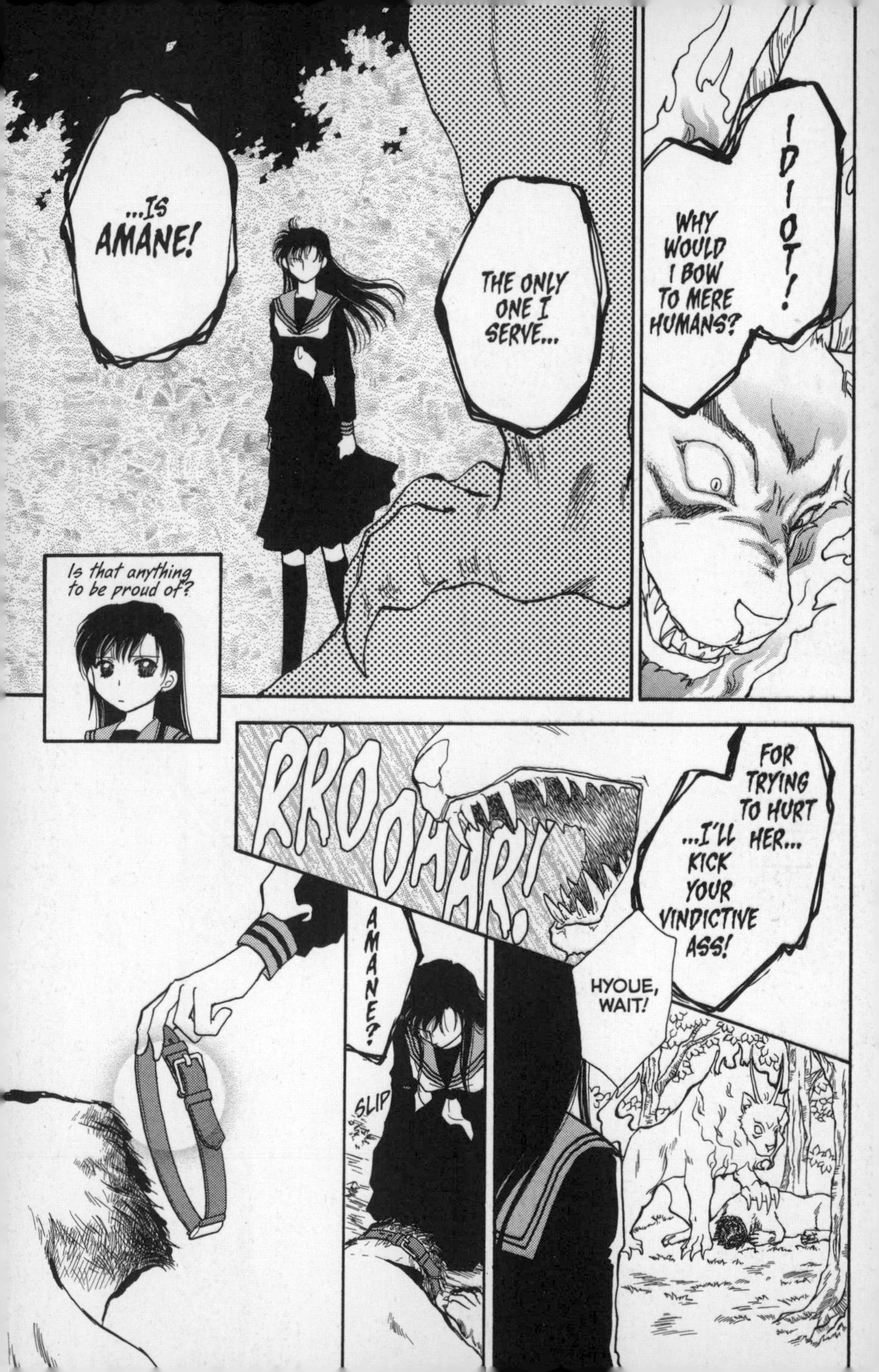
IDIOT!
WHY WOULD I BOW TO MERE HUMANS?
THE ONLY ONE I SERVE...
...IS AMANE!
Is that anything to be proud of?
FOR TRYING TO HURT HER...
...I'LL KICK YOUR VINDICTIVE ASS!
RROOOWAR!
HYOUE, WAIT!
AMANE?
SLIP

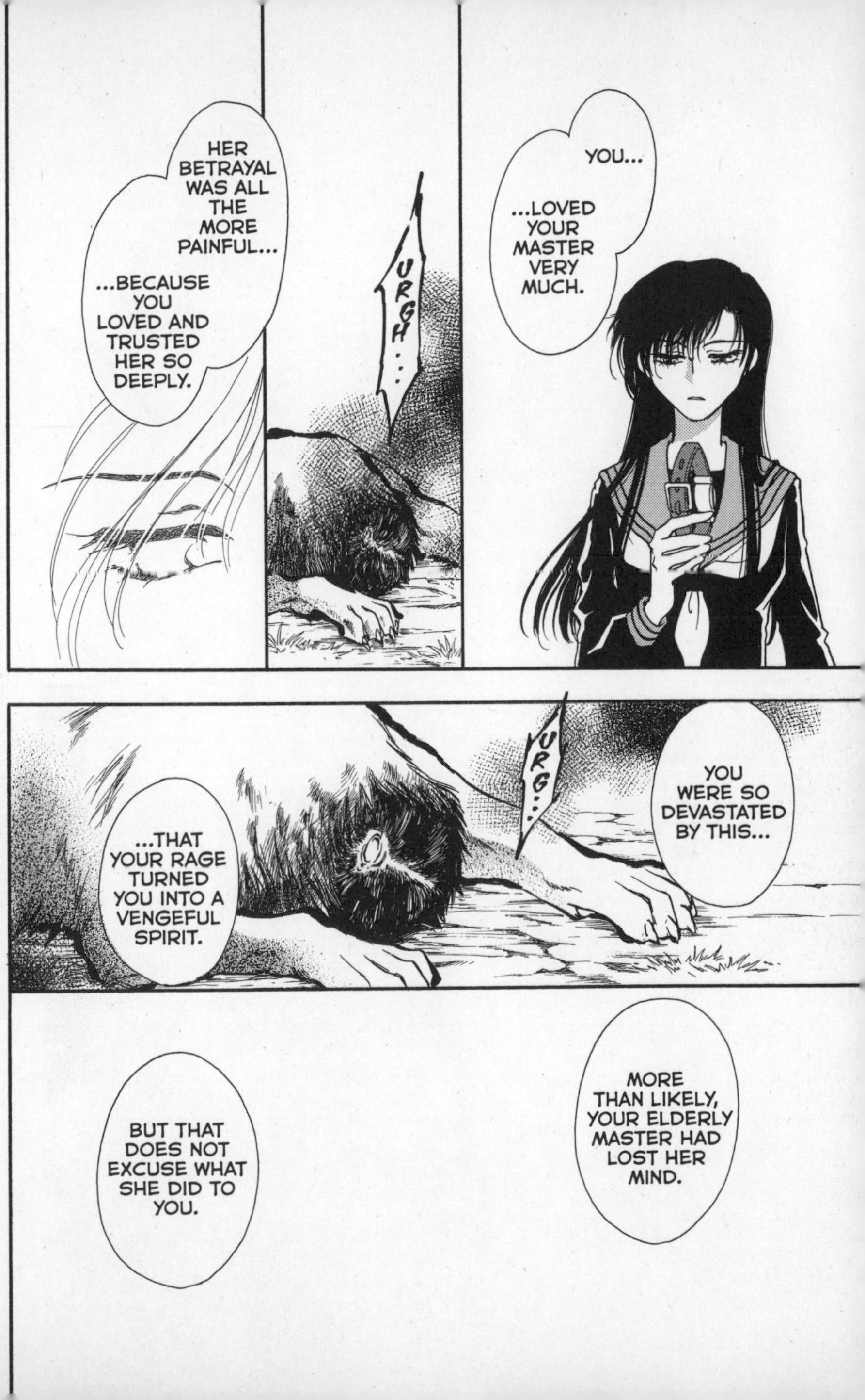
YOU...
...LOVED YOUR MASTER VERY MUCH.
URGH...
HER BETRAYAL WAS ALL THE MORE PAINFUL...
...BECAUSE YOU LOVED AND TRUSTED HER SO DEEPLY.
YOU WERE SO DEVASTATED BY THIS...
URG...
...THAT YOUR RAGE TURNED YOU INTO A VENGEFUL SPIRIT.
MORE THAN LIKELY, YOUR ELDERLY MASTER HAD LOST HER MIND.
BUT THAT DOES NOT EXCUSE WHAT SHE DID TO YOU.

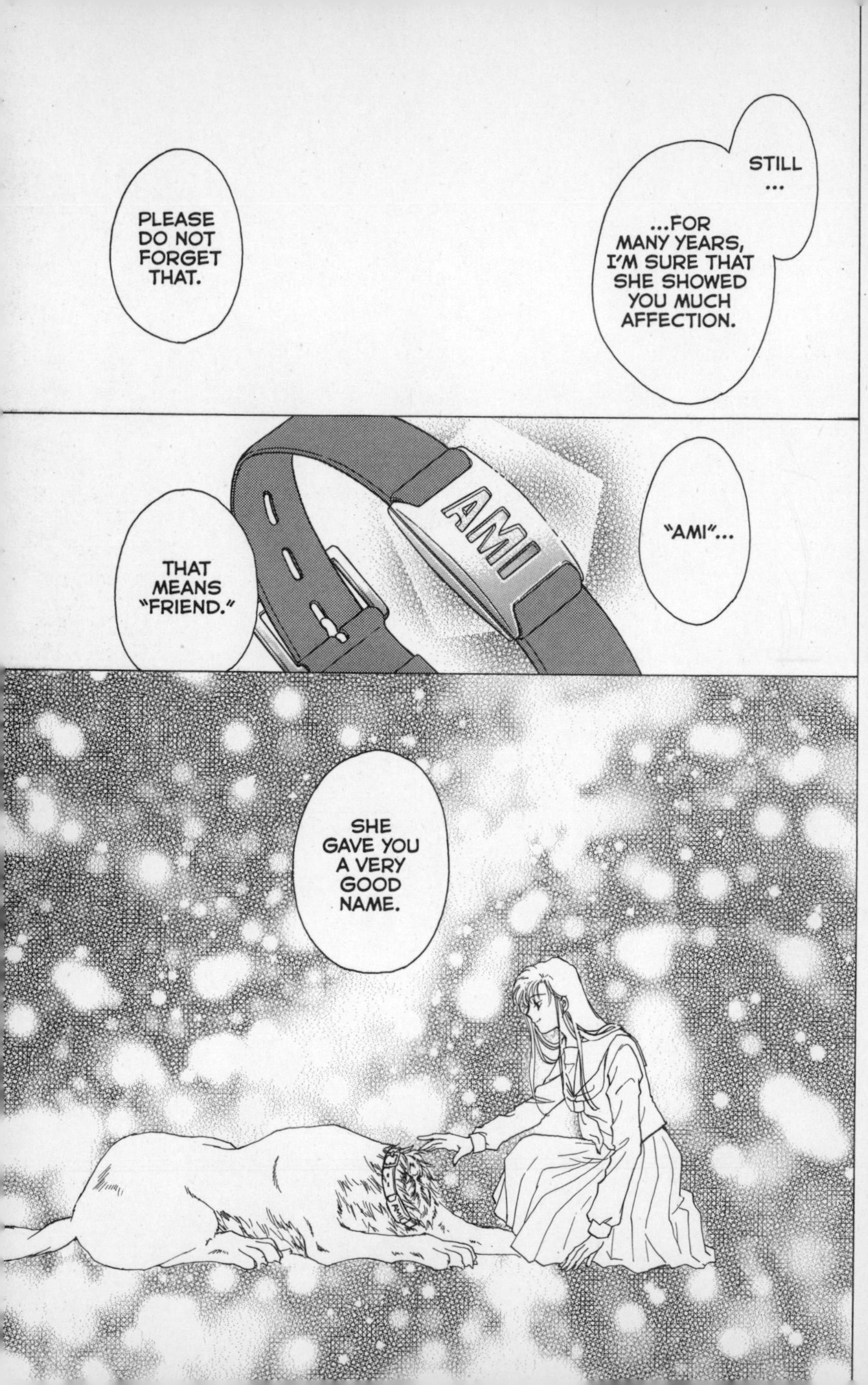
STILL ...
...FOR MANY YEARS, I'M SURE THAT SHE SHOWED YOU MUCH AFFECTION.
PLEASE DO NOT FORGET THAT.
"AMI"...
AMI
THAT MEANS "FRIEND."
SHE GAVE YOU A VERY GOOD NAME.

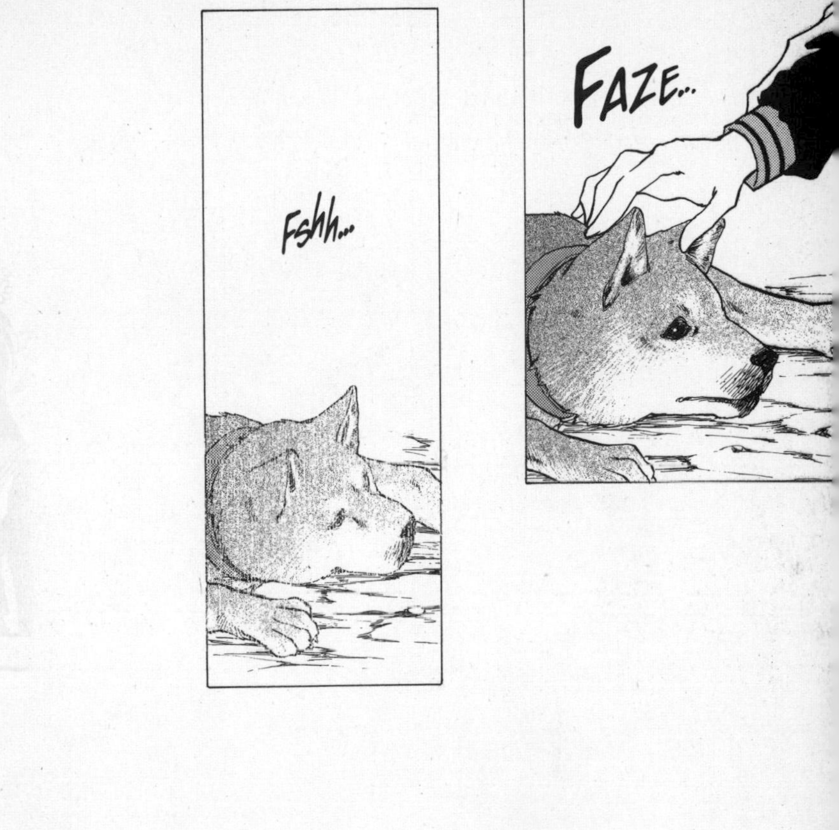
FAZE...
Fshh...

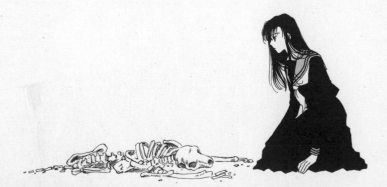

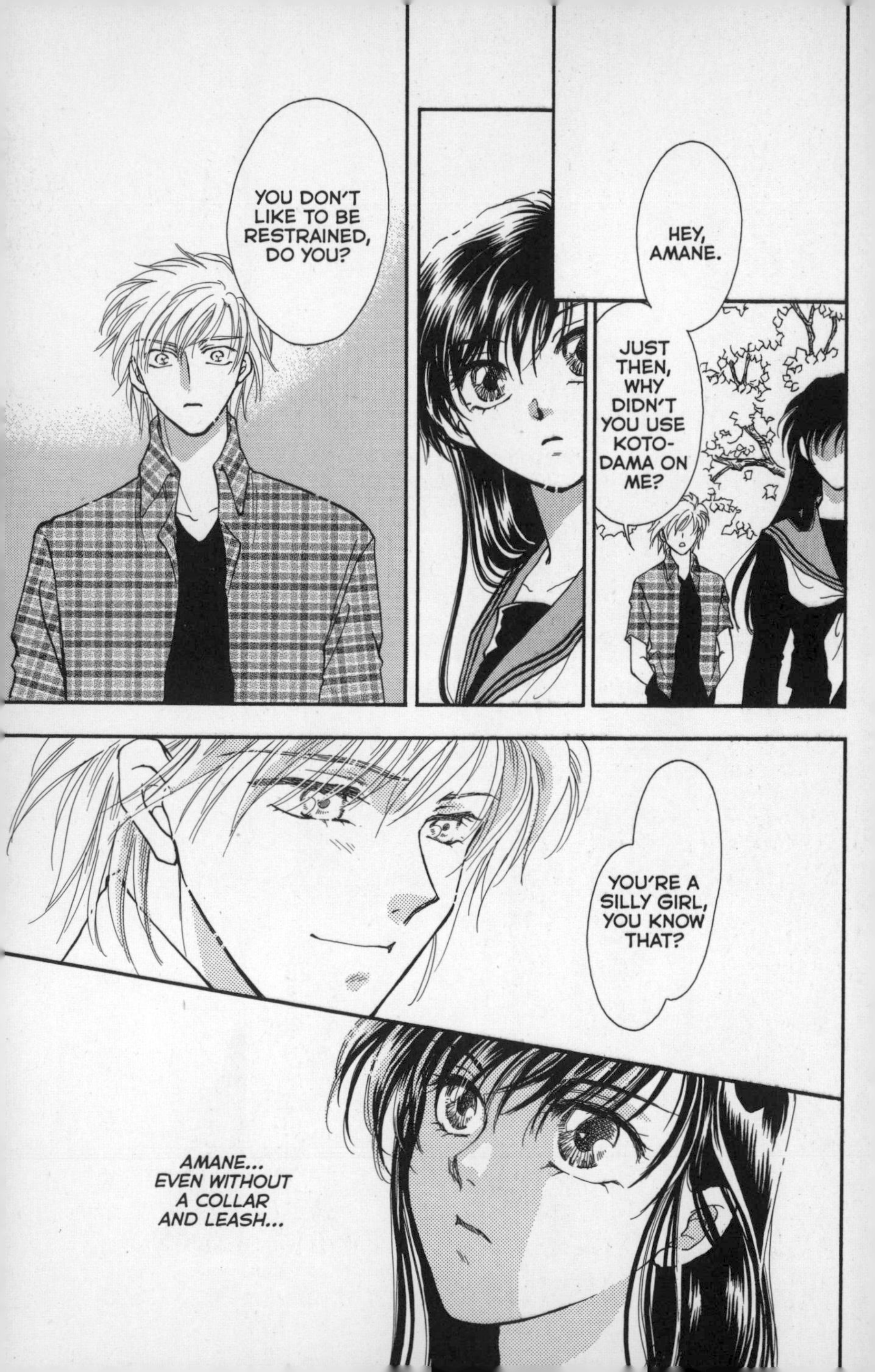
HEY, AMANE.
JUST THEN, WHY DIDN'T YOU USE KOTO-DAMA ON ME?
YOU DON'T LIKE TO BE RESTRAINED, DO YOU?
YOU'RE A SILLY GIRL, YOU KNOW THAT?
AMANE... EVEN WITHOUT A COLLAR AND LEASH...

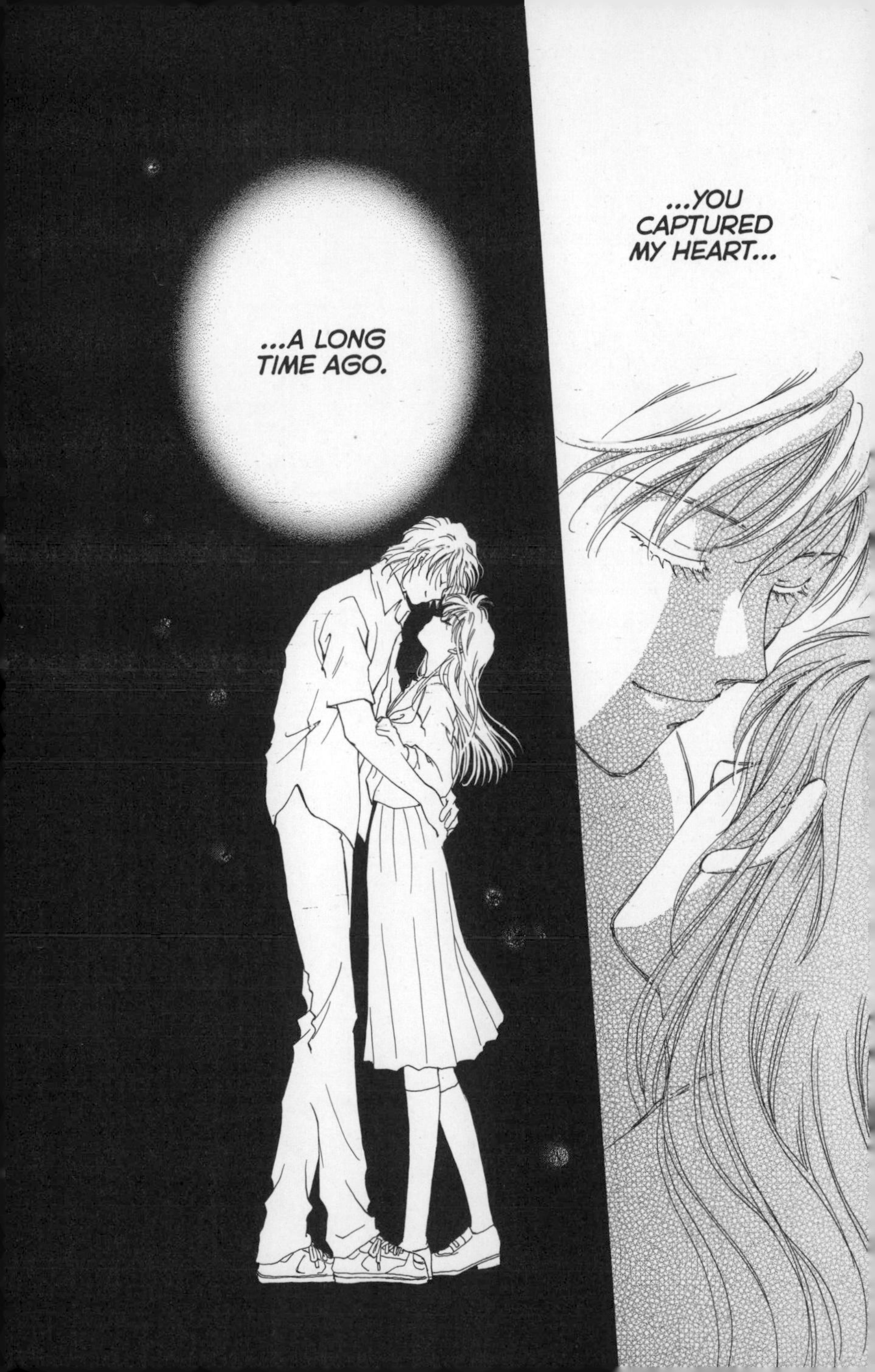
...YOU CAPTURED MY HEART...
...A LONG TIME AGO.

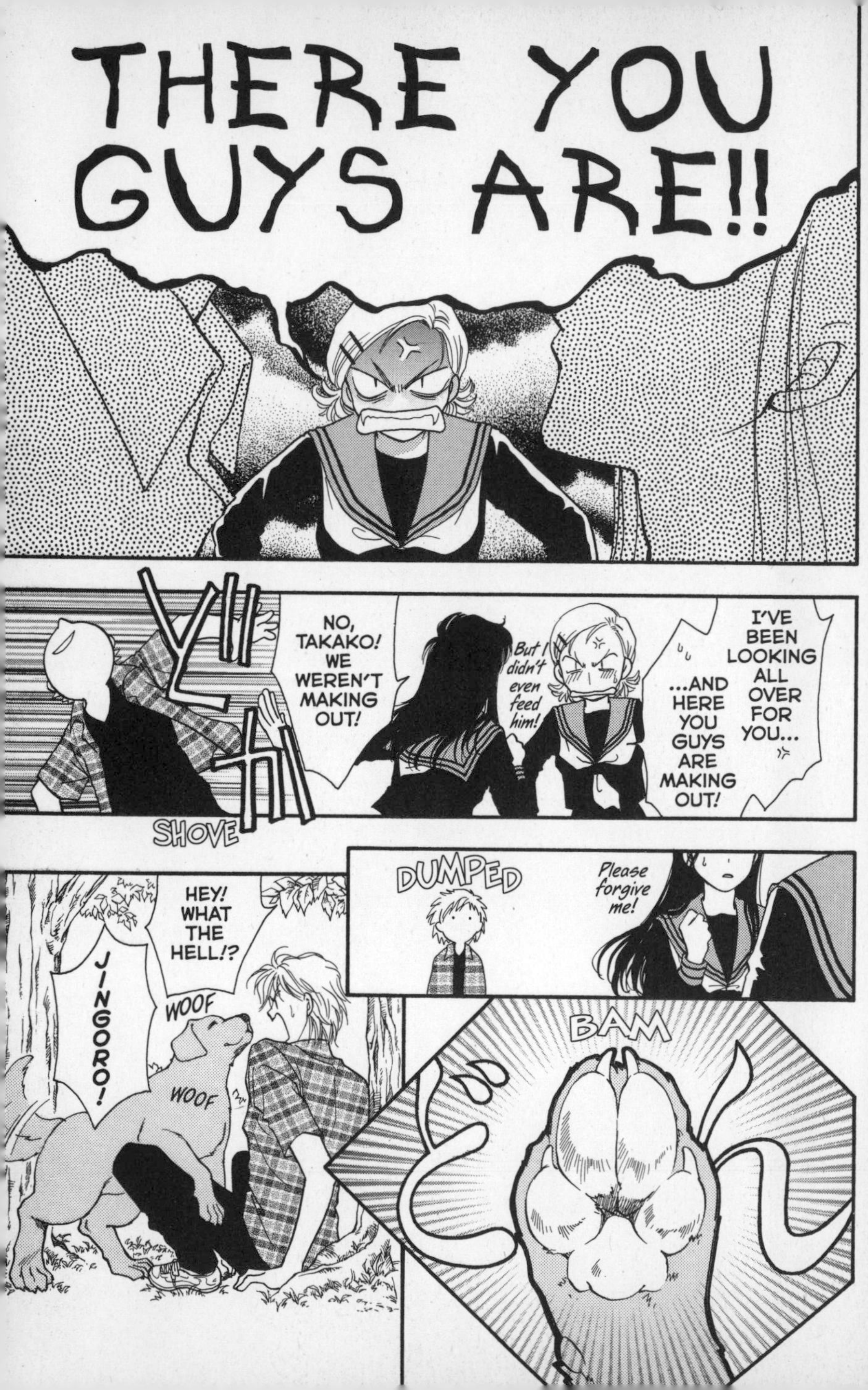
THERE YOU GUYS ARE!!
I'VE BEEN LOOKING ALL OVER FOR YOU...
...AND HERE YOU GUYS ARE MAKING OUT!
But I didn't even feed him!
NO, TAKAKO! WE WEREN'T MAKING OUT!
SHOVE
Please forgive me!
DUMPED
BAM
HEY! WHAT THE HELL!?
JINGORO!
WOOF
WOOF

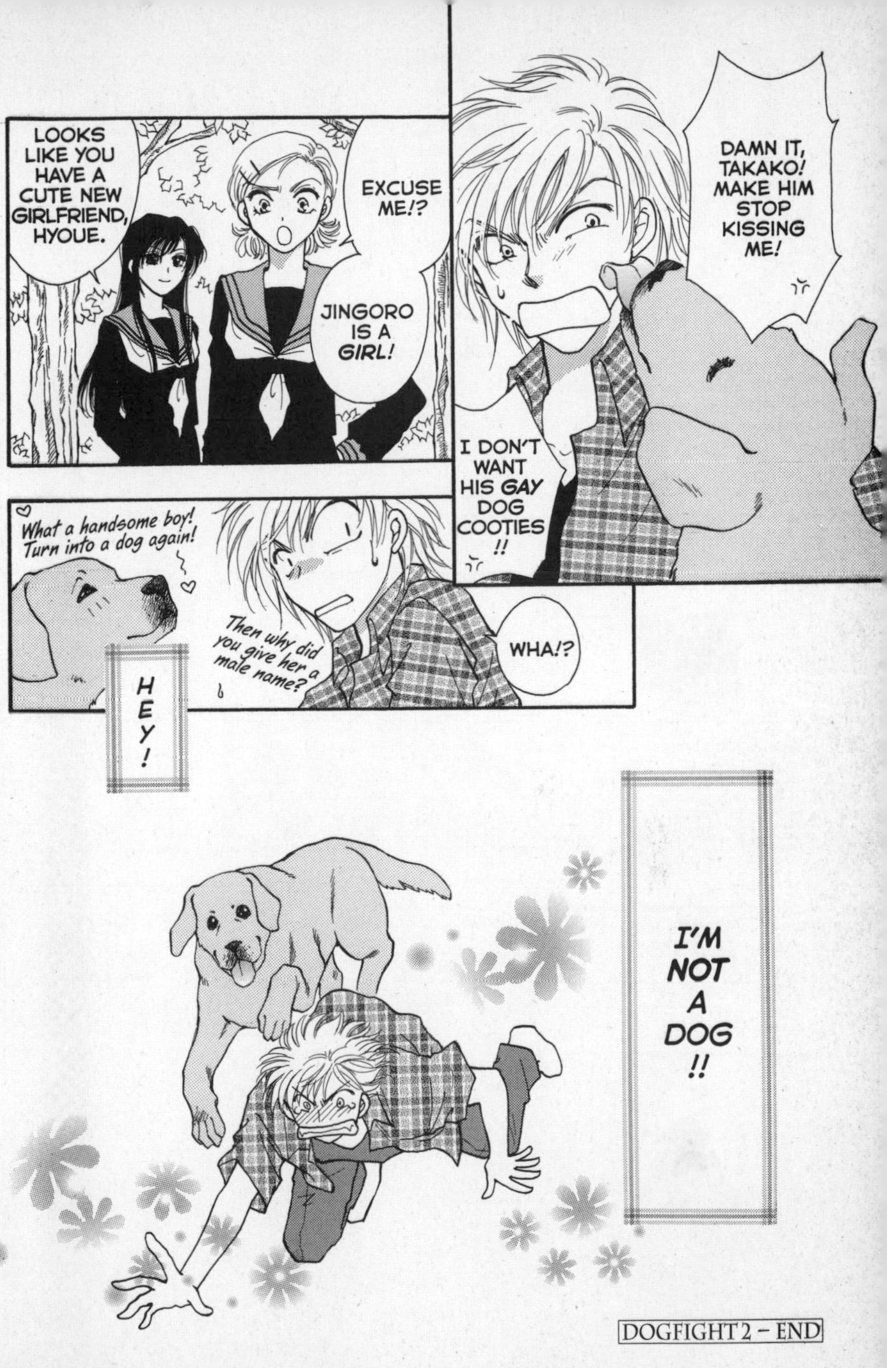
DAMN IT, TAKAKO! MAKE HIM STOP KISSING ME!
I DON'T WANT HIS GAY DOG COOTIES!!
LOOKS LIKE YOU HAVE A CUTE NEW GIRLFRIEND, HYOUE.
EXCUSE ME!?
JINGORO IS A GIRL!
WHA!?
Then why did you give her a male name?
HEY!
What a handsome boy! Turn into a dog again!
I'M NOT A DOG!!

DOGFIGHT 2 – END

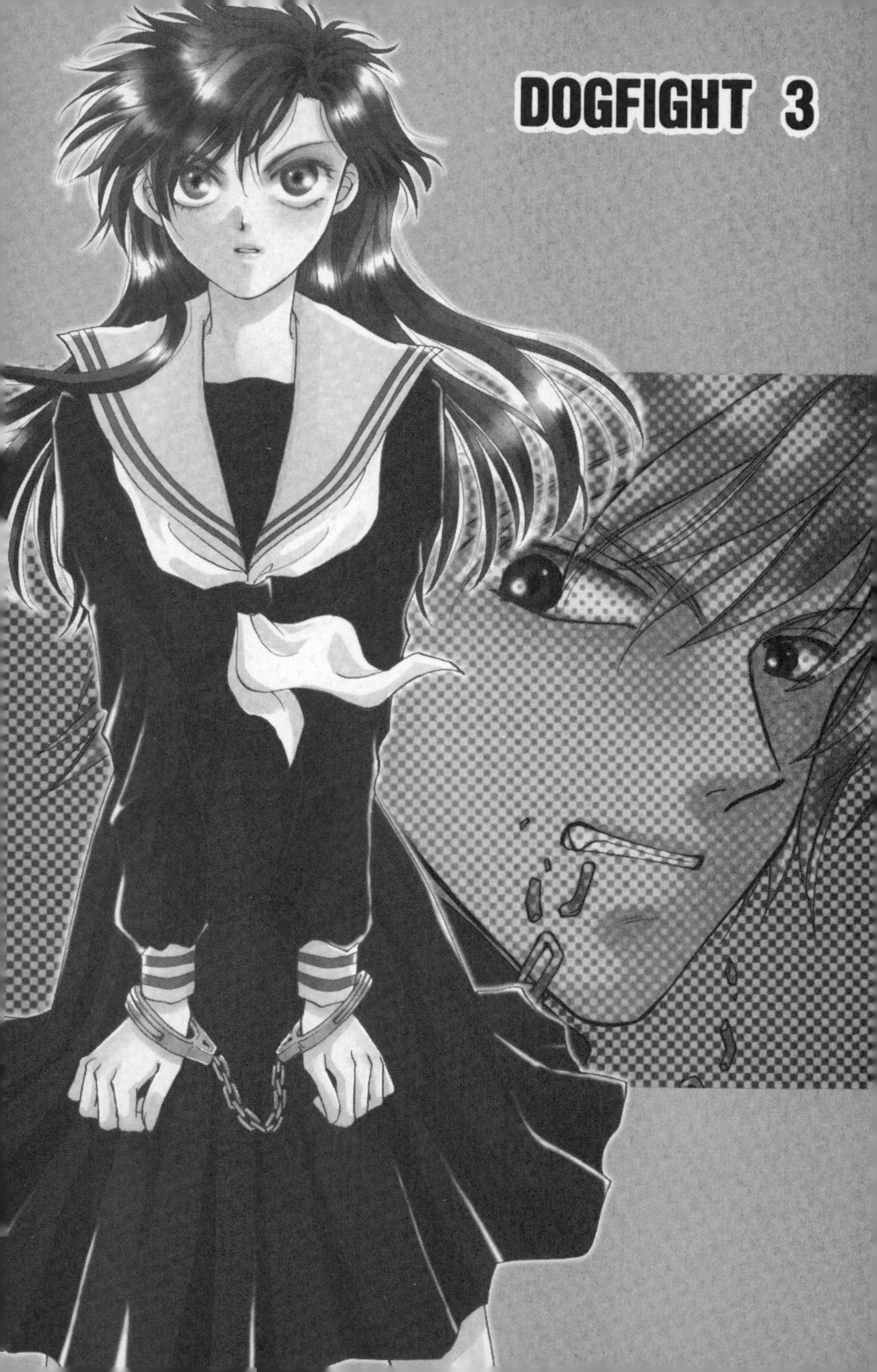
DOGFIGHT 3

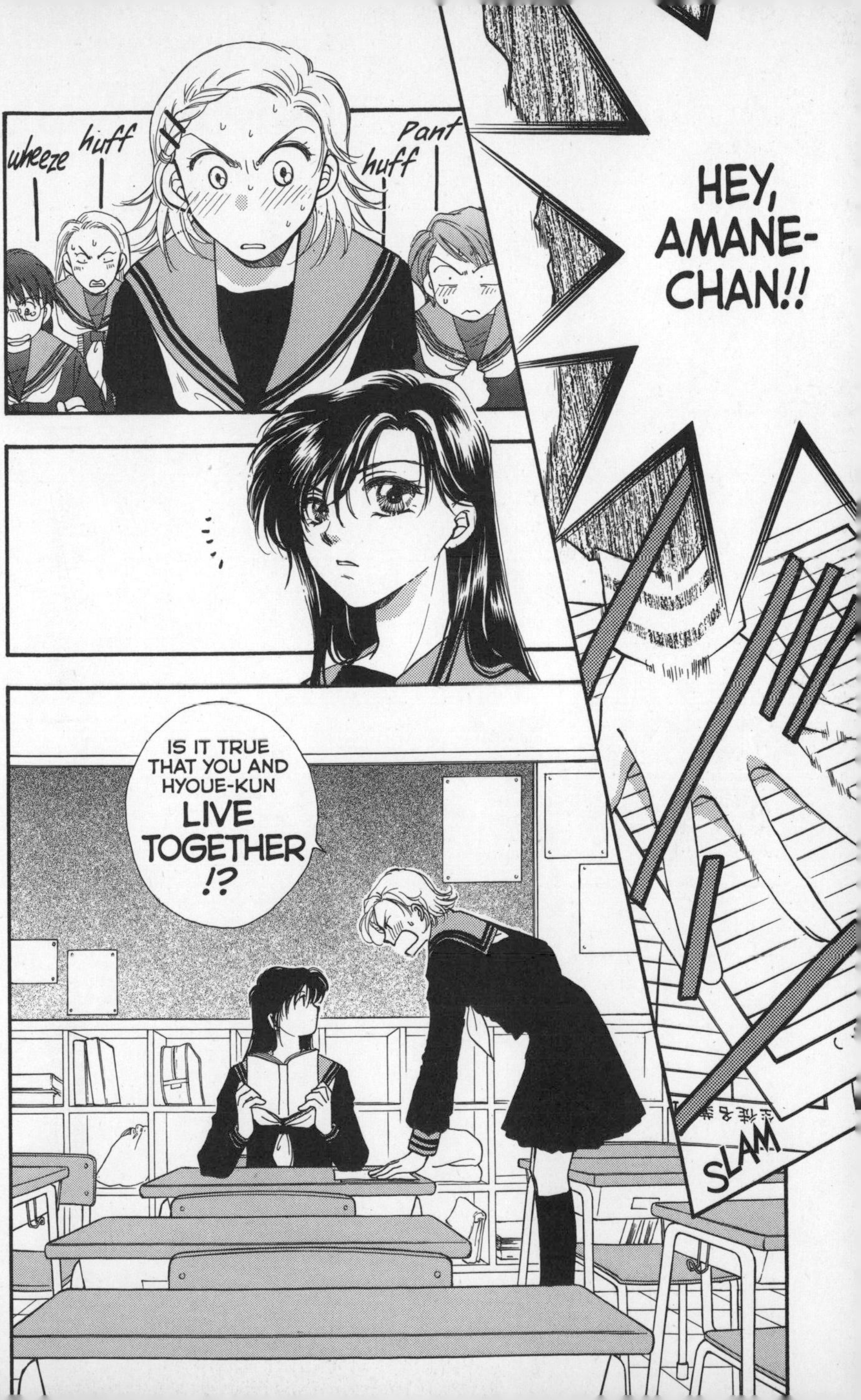
HEY, AMANE-CHAN!!
SLAM
Pant
huff
huff
wheeze
IS IT TRUE THAT YOU AND HYOUE-KUN LIVE TOGETHER !?

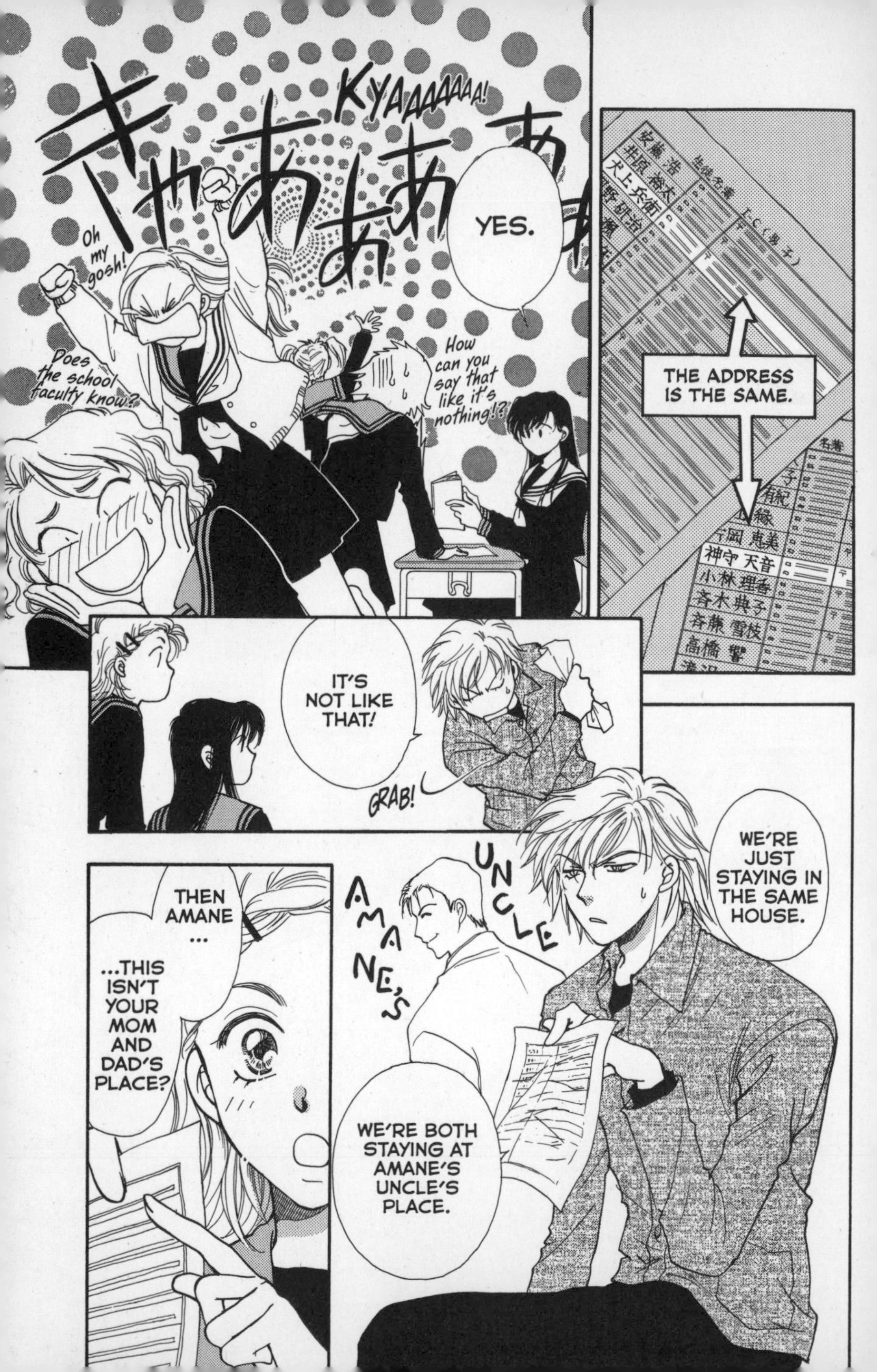

安藤 浩
井原 裕太
犬上 兵衛
生徒名簿
THE ADDRESS IS THE SAME.
神守 天音
小林 理香
斉木 典子
斉藤 雪枝
高橋 響
YES.
KYAAAAAAA!
きゃあああ
Oh my gosh!
Does the school faculty know!?
How can you say that like it's nothing!?
IT'S NOT LIKE THAT!
GRAB!
WE'RE JUST STAYING IN THE SAME HOUSE.
UNCLE
AMANE'S
THEN AMANE ...
...THIS ISN'T YOUR MOM AND DAD'S PLACE?
WE'RE BOTH STAYING AT AMANE'S UNCLE'S PLACE.

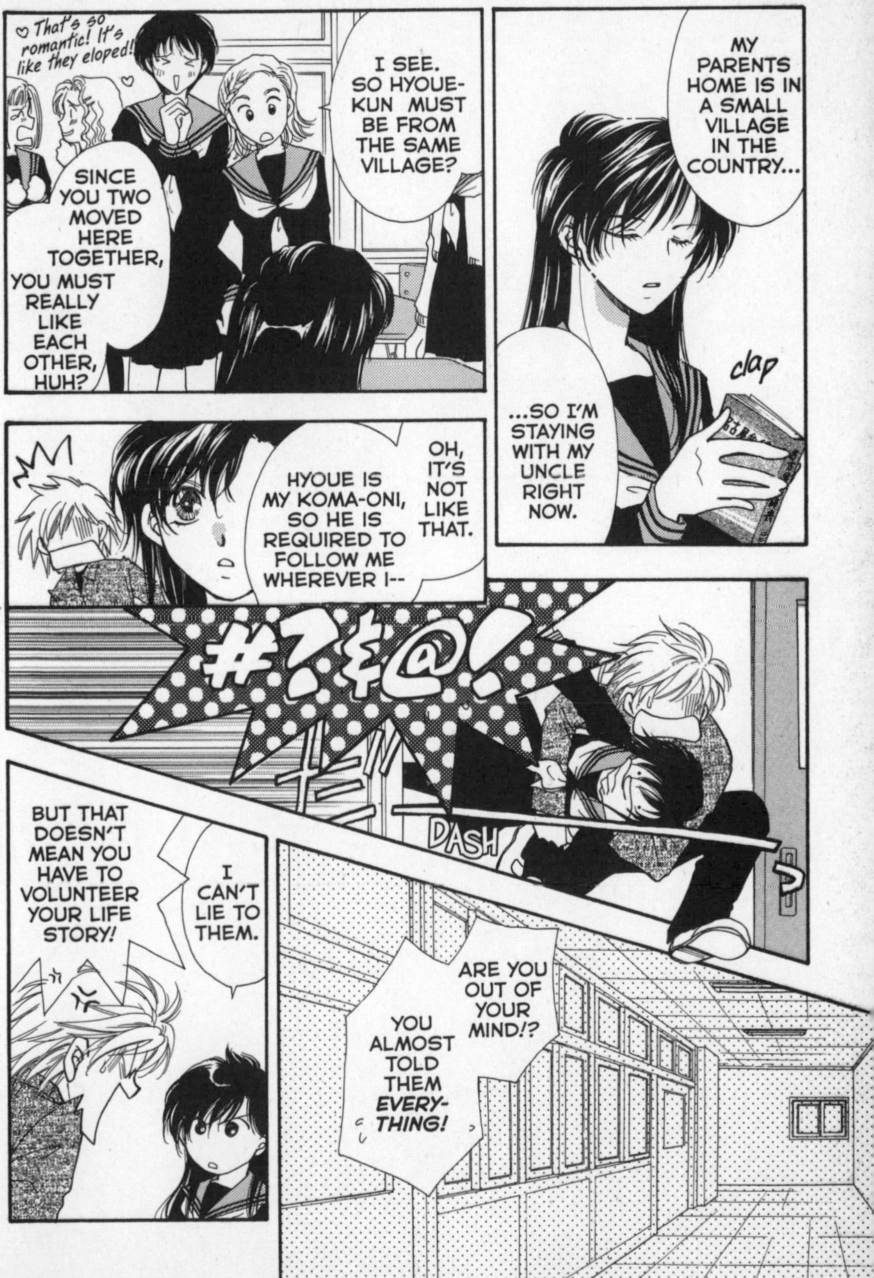
MY PARENTS HOME IS IN A SMALL VILLAGE IN THE COUNTRY...
...SO I'M STAYING WITH MY UNCLE RIGHT NOW.
clap
I SEE. SO HYOUE-KUN MUST BE FROM THE SAME VILLAGE?
♡ That's so romantic! It's like they eloped!
SINCE YOU TWO MOVED HERE TOGETHER, YOU MUST REALLY LIKE EACH OTHER, HUH?
OH, IT'S NOT LIKE THAT.
HYOUE IS MY KOMA-ONI, SO HE IS REQUIRED TO FOLLOW ME WHEREVER I--
#?&@!
DASH
ARE YOU OUT OF YOUR MIND!?
YOU ALMOST TOLD THEM *EVERY-THING!*
I CAN'T LIE TO THEM.
BUT THAT DOESN'T MEAN YOU HAVE TO VOLUNTEER YOUR LIFE STORY!

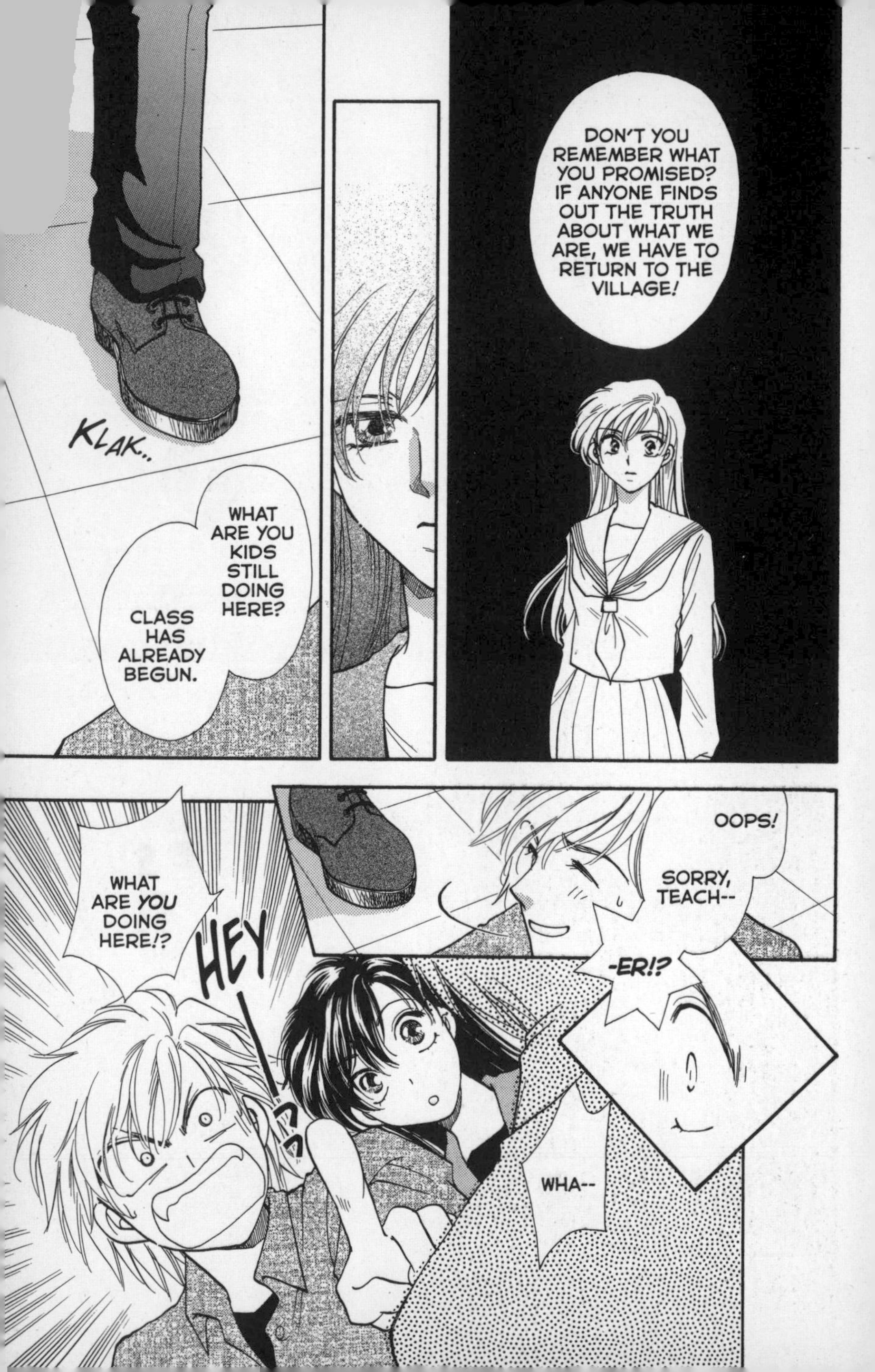
DON'T YOU REMEMBER WHAT YOU PROMISED? IF ANYONE FINDS OUT THE TRUTH ABOUT WHAT WE ARE, WE HAVE TO RETURN TO THE VILLAGE!
KLAK..
WHAT ARE YOU KIDS STILL DOING HERE?
CLASS HAS ALREADY BEGUN.
OOPS!
SORRY, TEACH--
-ER!?
WHAT ARE *YOU* DOING HERE!?
HEY
WHA--

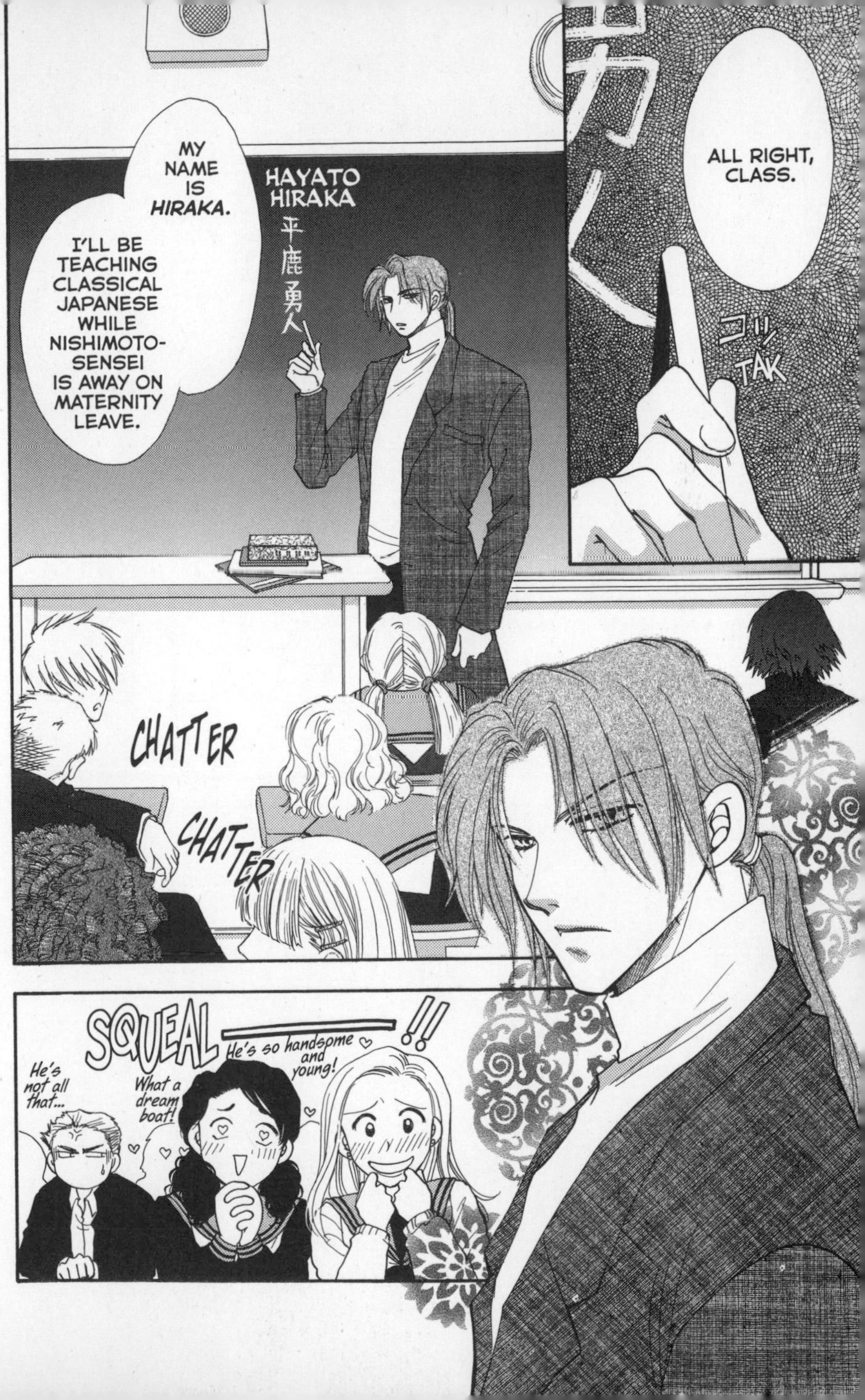
ALL RIGHT, CLASS.
コツ
TAK
HAYATO HIRAKA
平鹿勇人
MY NAME IS HIRAKA.
I'LL BE TEACHING CLASSICAL JAPANESE WHILE NISHIMOTO-SENSEI IS AWAY ON MATERNITY LEAVE.
CHATTER
CHATTER
SQUEAL——!!
He's so handsome and young!
What a dream boat!
He's not all that...

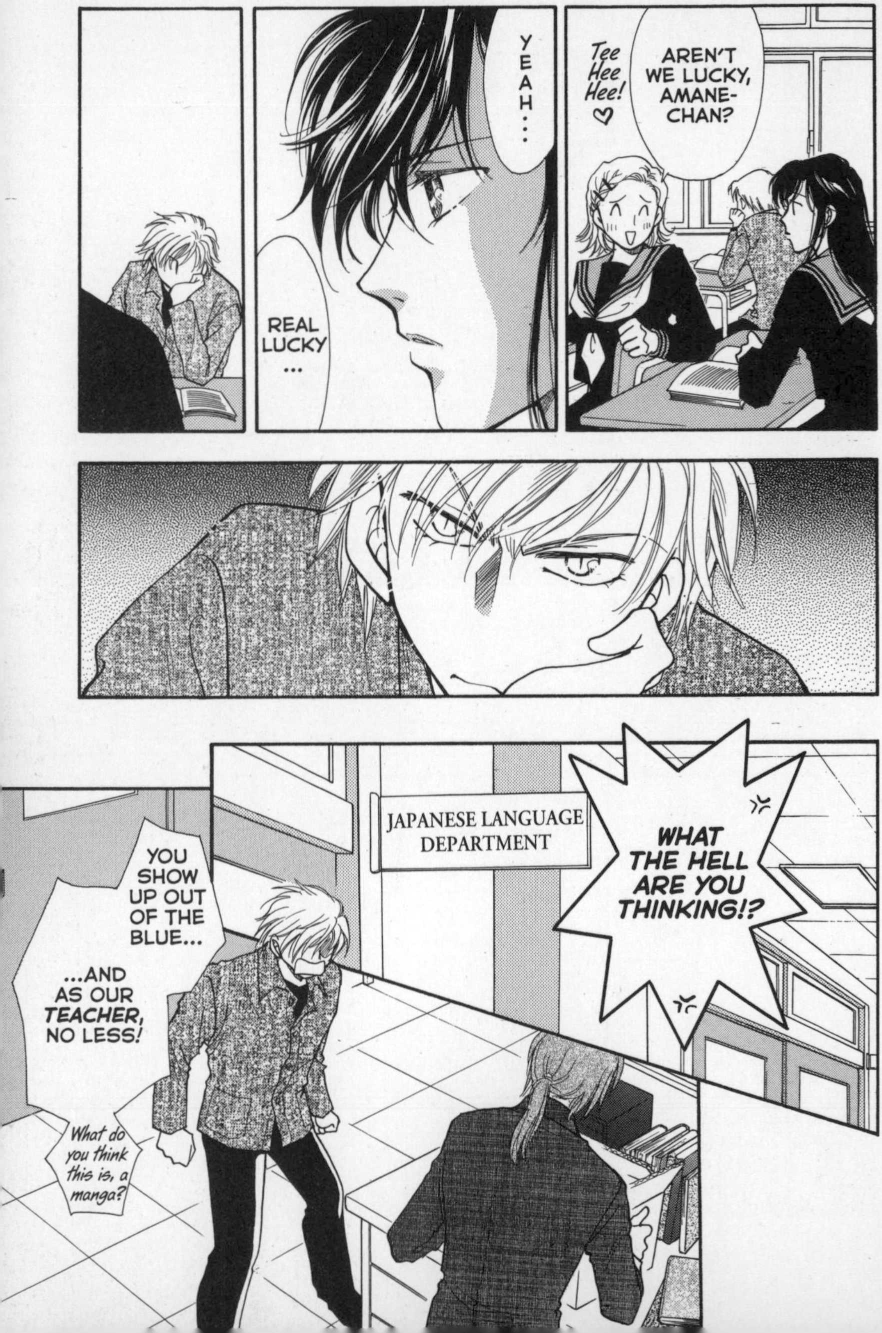
AREN'T WE LUCKY, AMANE-CHAN?
Tee Hee Hee! ♡
YEAH...
REAL LUCKY ...
JAPANESE LANGUAGE DEPARTMENT
WHAT THE HELL ARE YOU THINKING!?
YOU SHOW UP OUT OF THE BLUE...
...AND AS OUR TEACHER, NO LESS!
What do you think this is, a manga?

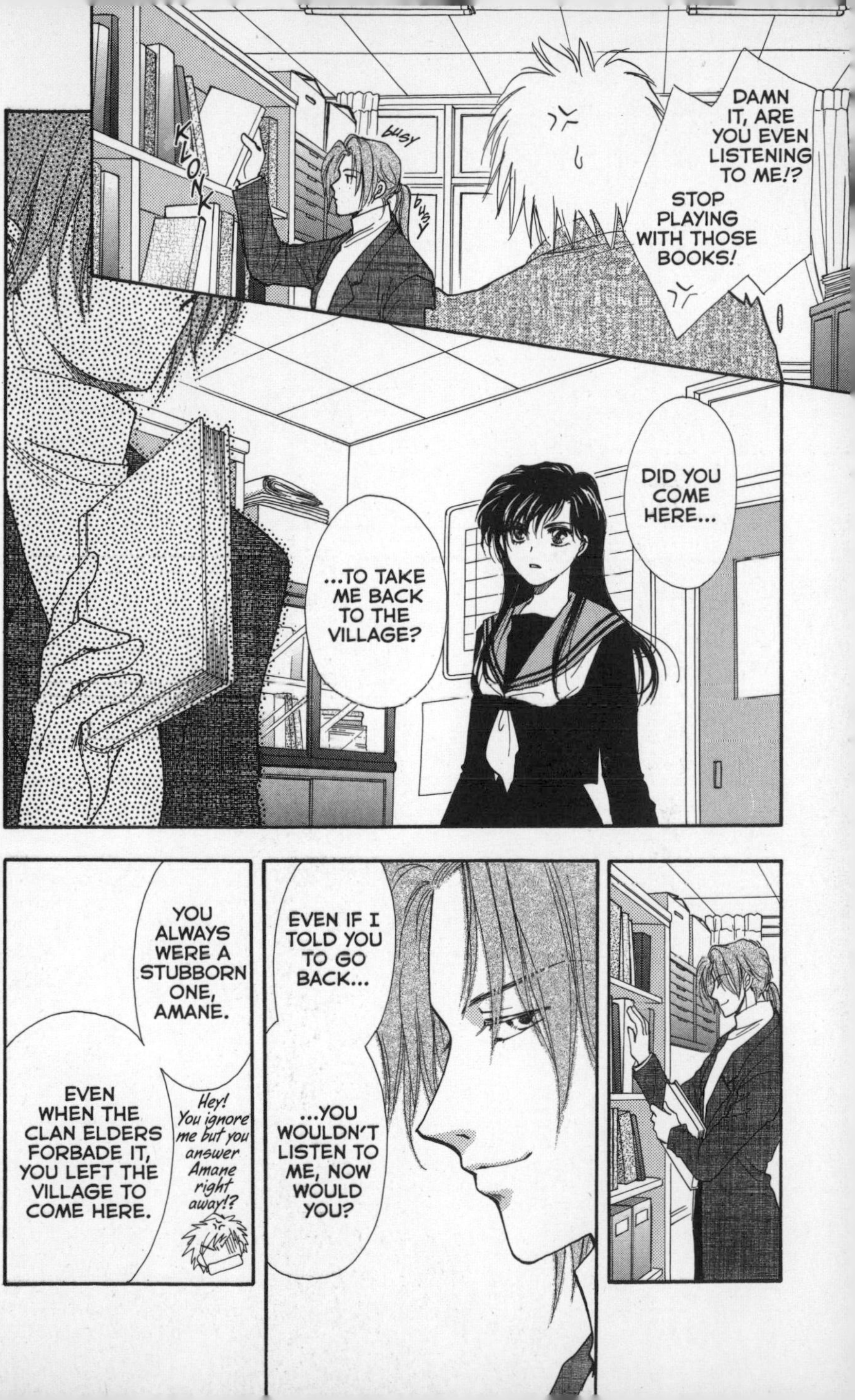
DAMN IT, ARE YOU EVEN LISTENING TO ME!?
STOP PLAYING WITH THOSE BOOKS!
busy
busy
KVONK
DID YOU COME HERE...
...TO TAKE ME BACK TO THE VILLAGE?
EVEN IF I TOLD YOU TO GO BACK...
...YOU WOULDN'T LISTEN TO ME, NOW WOULD YOU?
YOU ALWAYS WERE A STUBBORN ONE, AMANE.
Hey! You ignore me but you answer Amane right away!?
EVEN WHEN THE CLAN ELDERS FORBADE IT, YOU LEFT THE VILLAGE TO COME HERE.

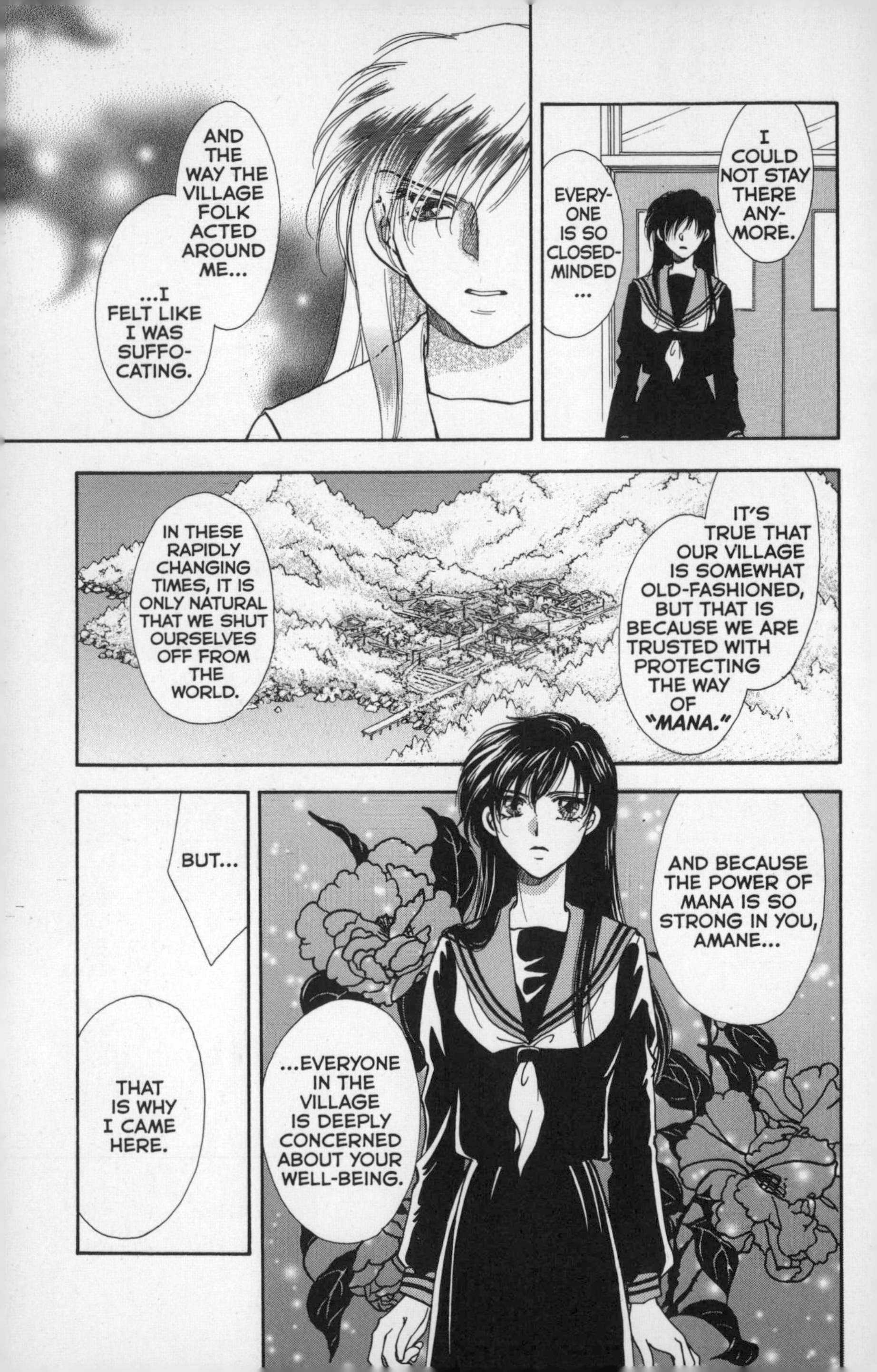
I COULD NOT STAY THERE ANYMORE.
EVERYONE IS SO CLOSED-MINDED...
AND THE WAY THE VILLAGE FOLK ACTED AROUND ME...
...I FELT LIKE I WAS SUFFOCATING.
IT'S TRUE THAT OUR VILLAGE IS SOMEWHAT OLD-FASHIONED, BUT THAT IS BECAUSE WE ARE TRUSTED WITH PROTECTING THE WAY OF *"MANA."*
IN THESE RAPIDLY CHANGING TIMES, IT IS ONLY NATURAL THAT WE SHUT OURSELVES OFF FROM THE WORLD.
AND BECAUSE THE POWER OF MANA IS SO STRONG IN YOU, AMANE...
...EVERYONE IN THE VILLAGE IS DEEPLY CONCERNED ABOUT YOUR WELL-BEING.
BUT...
THAT IS WHY I CAME HERE.

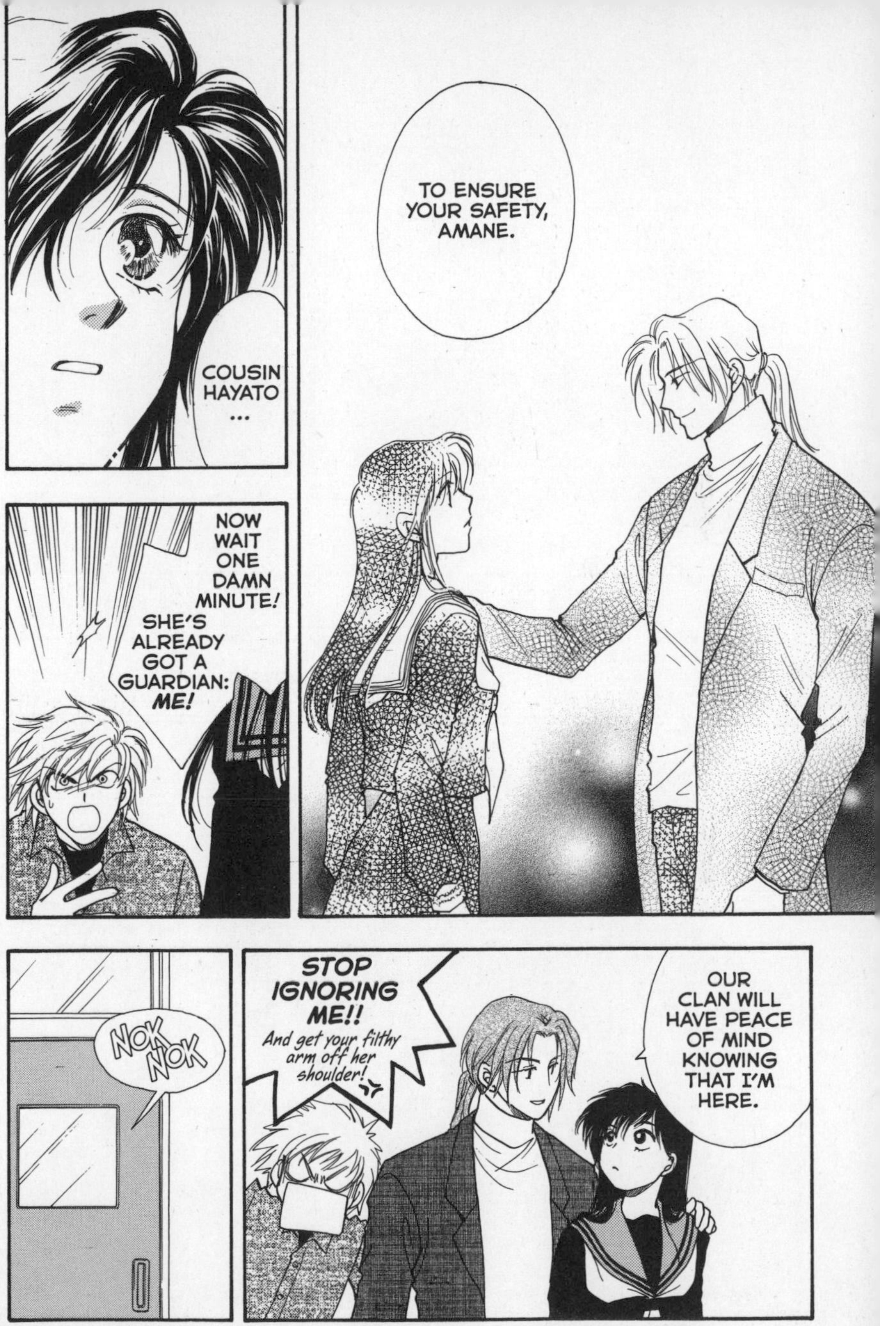
TO ENSURE YOUR SAFETY, AMANE.
COUSIN HAYATO ...
NOW WAIT ONE DAMN MINUTE!
SHE'S ALREADY GOT A GUARDIAN: *ME!*
OUR CLAN WILL HAVE PEACE OF MIND KNOWING THAT I'M HERE.
STOP IGNORING ME!!
And get your filthy arm off her shoulder!
NOK NOK

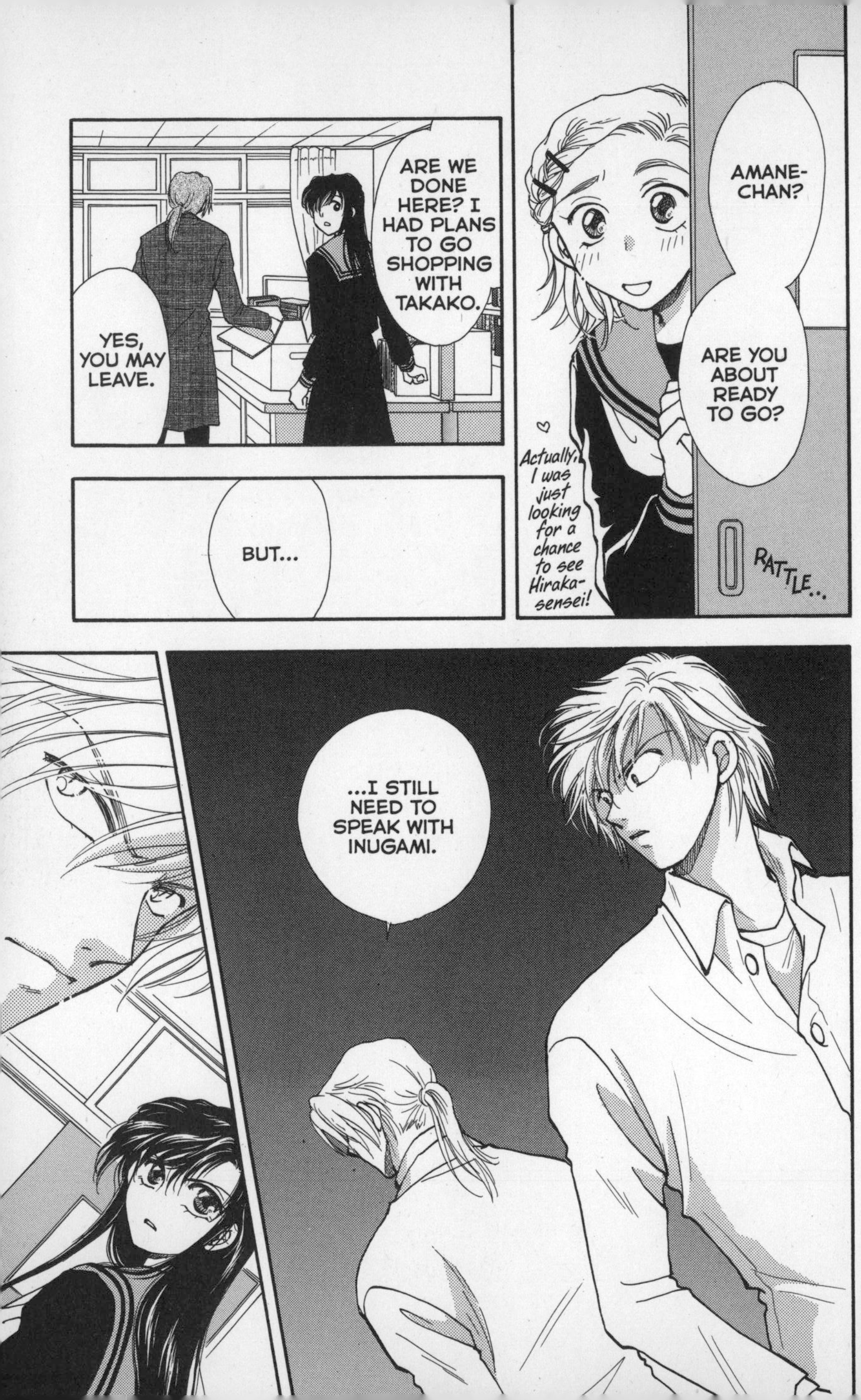
AMANE-CHAN?
ARE YOU ABOUT READY TO GO?
Actually, I was just looking for a chance to see Hiraka-sensei!
RATTLE...
ARE WE DONE HERE? I HAD PLANS TO GO SHOPPING WITH TAKAKO.
YES, YOU MAY LEAVE.
BUT...
...I STILL NEED TO SPEAK WITH INUGAMI.

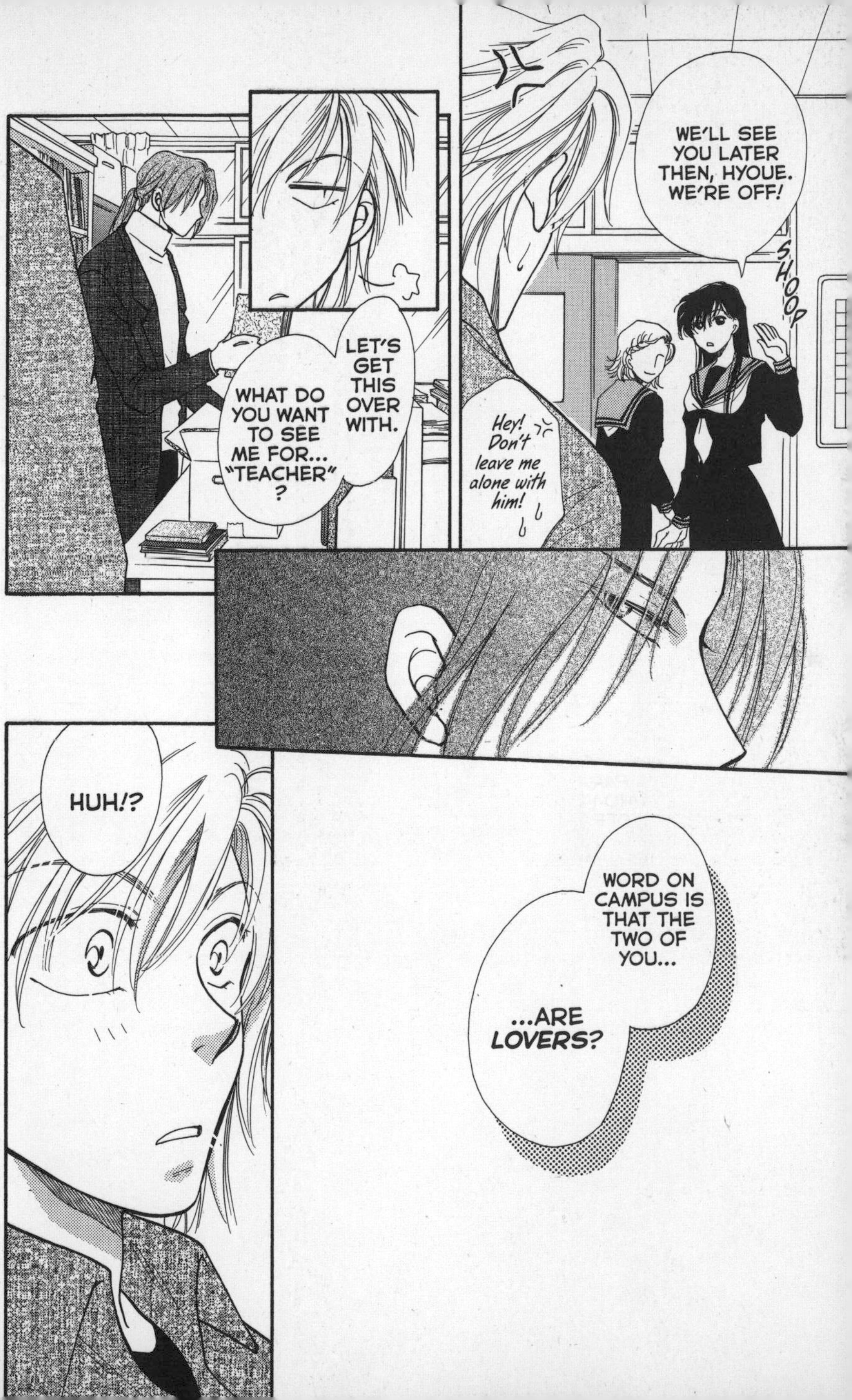
WE'LL SEE YOU LATER THEN, HYOUE. WE'RE OFF!
SHOOP
Hey! Don't leave me alone with him!
LET'S GET THIS OVER WITH.
WHAT DO YOU WANT TO SEE ME FOR... "TEACHER"?
WORD ON CAMPUS IS THAT THE TWO OF YOU...
...ARE LOVERS?
HUH!?

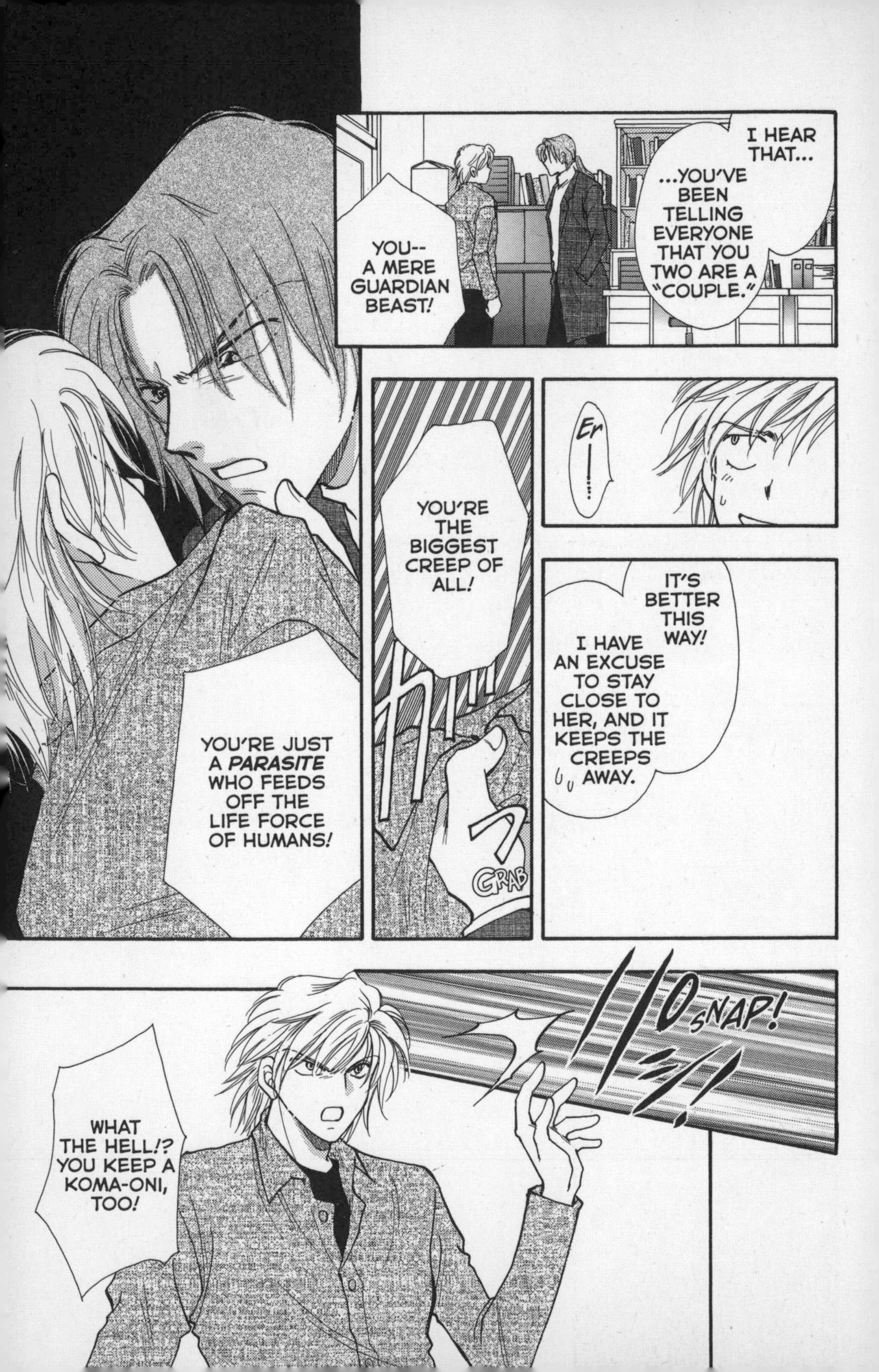
I HEAR THAT...
...YOU'VE BEEN TELLING EVERYONE THAT YOU TWO ARE A "COUPLE."
YOU-- A MERE GUARDIAN BEAST!
Er......
IT'S BETTER THIS WAY!
I HAVE AN EXCUSE TO STAY CLOSE TO HER, AND IT KEEPS THE CREEPS AWAY.
YOU'RE THE BIGGEST CREEP OF ALL!
GRAB
YOU'RE JUST A *PARASITE* WHO FEEDS OFF THE LIFE FORCE OF HUMANS!
SNAP!
WHAT THE HELL!? YOU KEEP A KOMA-ONI, TOO!

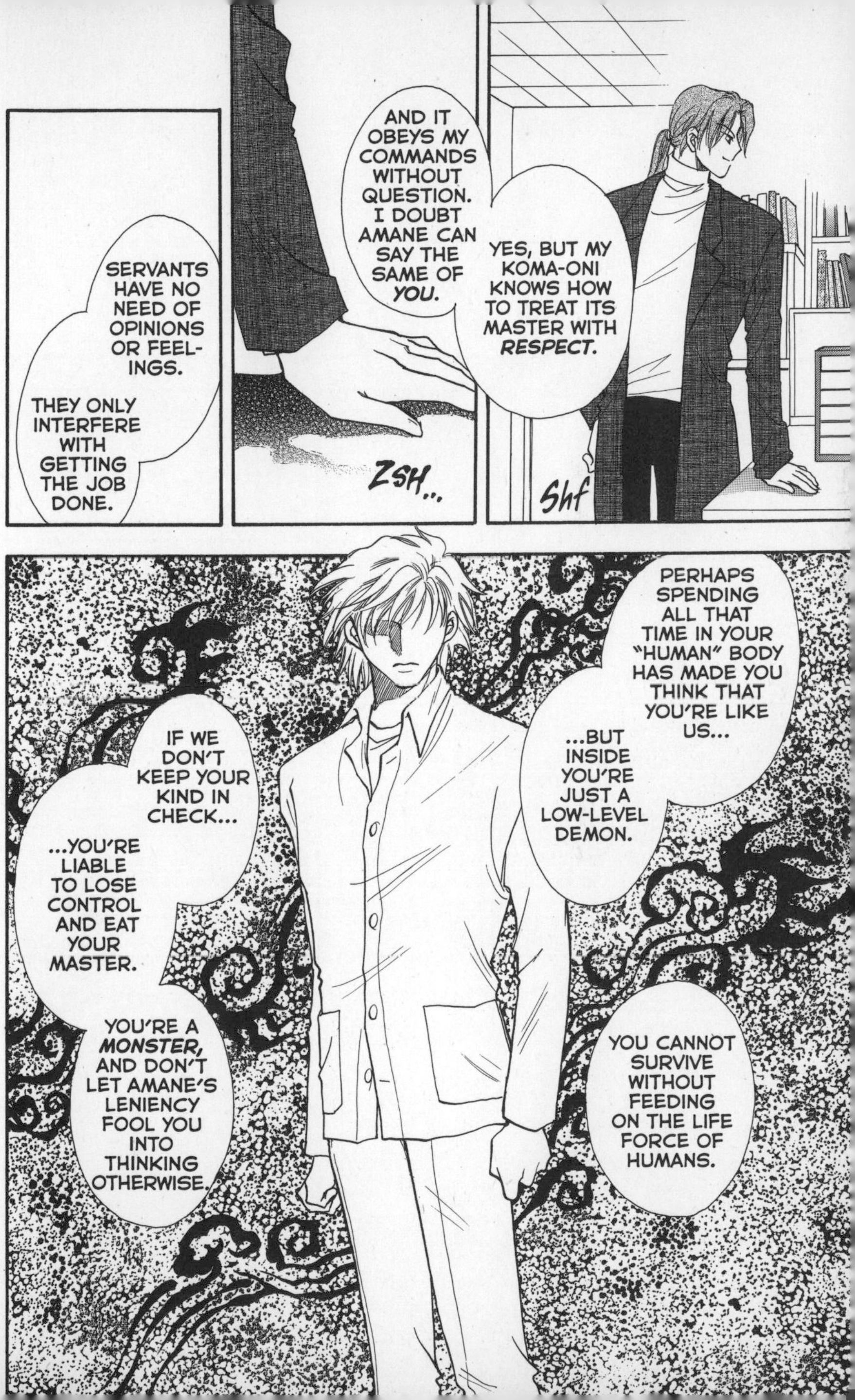
YES, BUT MY KOMA-ONI KNOWS HOW TO TREAT ITS MASTER WITH *RESPECT*.
Shf
AND IT OBEYS MY COMMANDS WITHOUT QUESTION. I DOUBT AMANE CAN SAY THE SAME OF *YOU*.
ZSH...
SERVANTS HAVE NO NEED OF OPINIONS OR FEEL-INGS.
THEY ONLY INTERFERE WITH GETTING THE JOB DONE.
PERHAPS SPENDING ALL THAT TIME IN YOUR "HUMAN" BODY HAS MADE YOU THINK THAT YOU'RE LIKE US...
...BUT INSIDE YOU'RE JUST A LOW-LEVEL DEMON.
YOU CANNOT SURVIVE WITHOUT FEEDING ON THE LIFE FORCE OF HUMANS.
IF WE DON'T KEEP YOUR KIND IN CHECK...
...YOU'RE LIABLE TO LOSE CONTROL AND EAT YOUR MASTER.
YOU'RE A ***MONSTER,*** AND DON'T LET AMANE'S LENIENCY FOOL YOU INTO THINKING OTHERWISE.

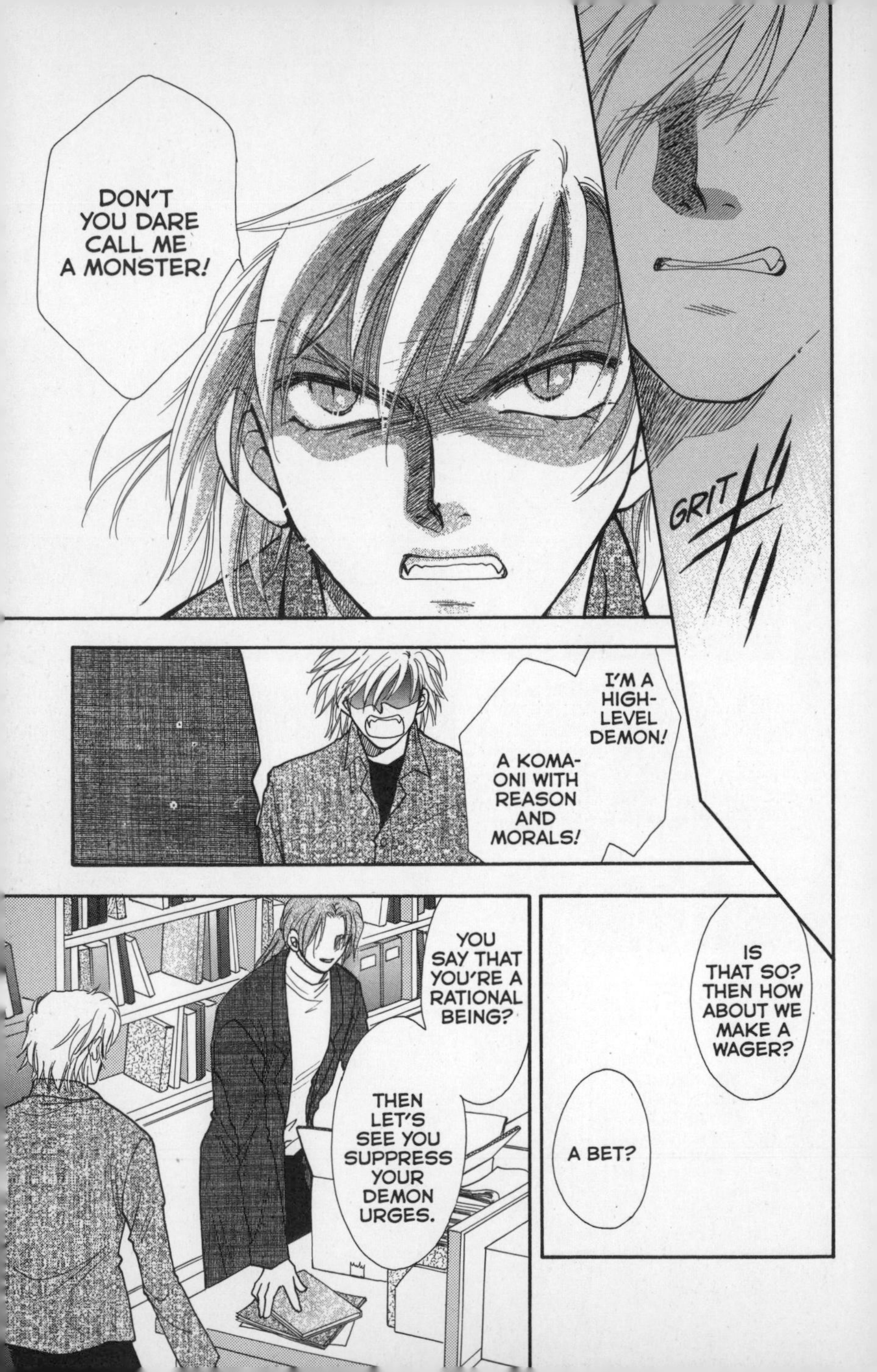
GRIT
DON'T YOU DARE CALL ME A MONSTER!
I'M A HIGH-LEVEL DEMON!
A KOMA-ONI WITH REASON AND MORALS!
IS THAT SO? THEN HOW ABOUT WE MAKE A WAGER?
A BET?
YOU SAY THAT YOU'RE A RATIONAL BEING?
THEN LET'S SEE YOU SUPPRESS YOUR DEMON URGES.

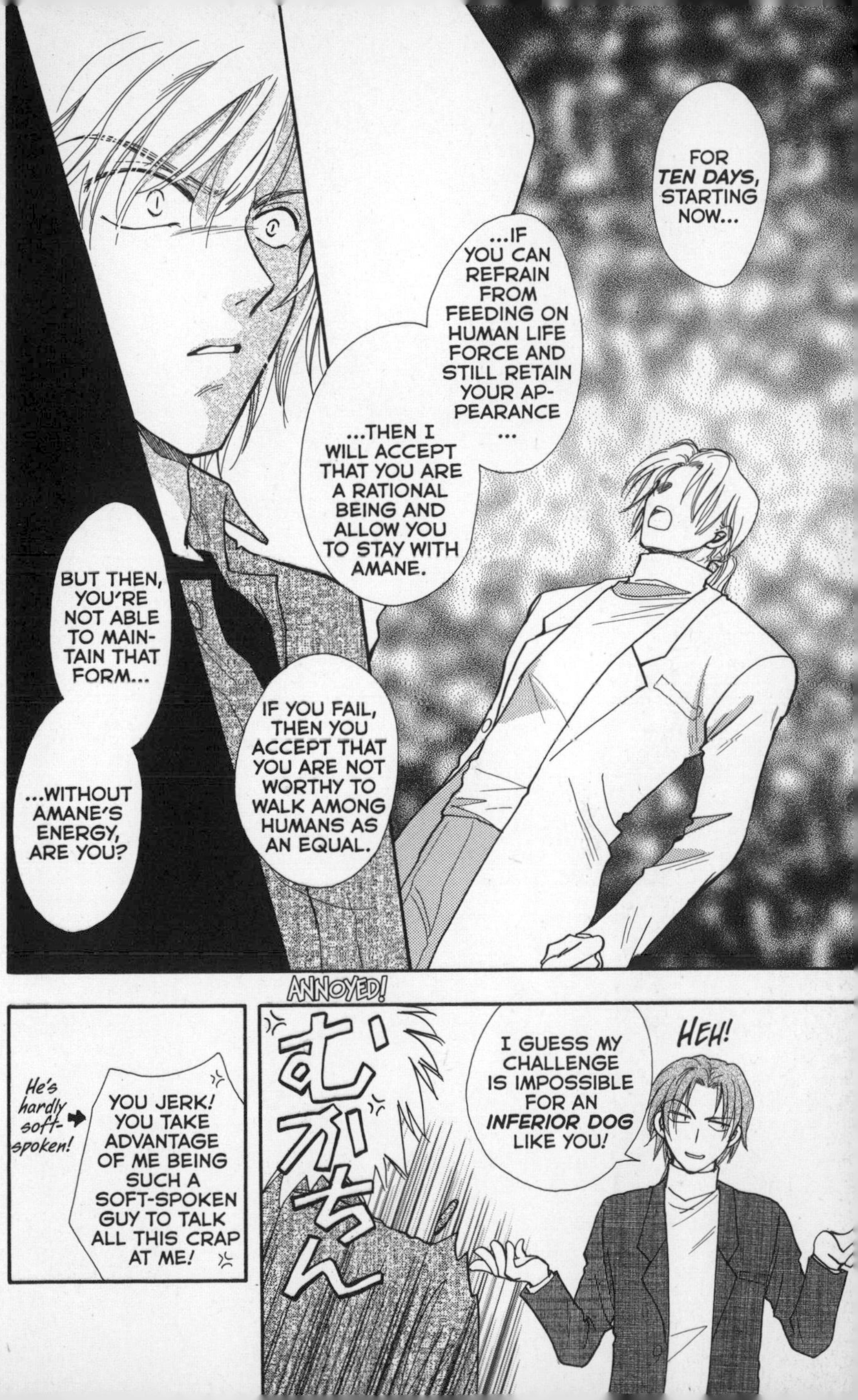
FOR TEN DAYS, STARTING NOW...
...IF YOU CAN REFRAIN FROM FEEDING ON HUMAN LIFE FORCE AND STILL RETAIN YOUR AP-PEARANCE...
...THEN I WILL ACCEPT THAT YOU ARE A RATIONAL BEING AND ALLOW YOU TO STAY WITH AMANE.
IF YOU FAIL, THEN YOU ACCEPT THAT YOU ARE NOT WORTHY TO WALK AMONG HUMANS AS AN EQUAL.
BUT THEN, YOU'RE NOT ABLE TO MAIN-TAIN THAT FORM...
...WITHOUT AMANE'S ENERGY, ARE YOU?
HEH!
I GUESS MY CHALLENGE IS IMPOSSIBLE FOR AN INFERIOR DOG LIKE YOU!
ANNOYED!
むかちん
YOU JERK! YOU TAKE ADVANTAGE OF ME BEING SUCH A SOFT-SPOKEN GUY TO TALK ALL THIS CRAP AT ME!
He's hardly soft-spoken!

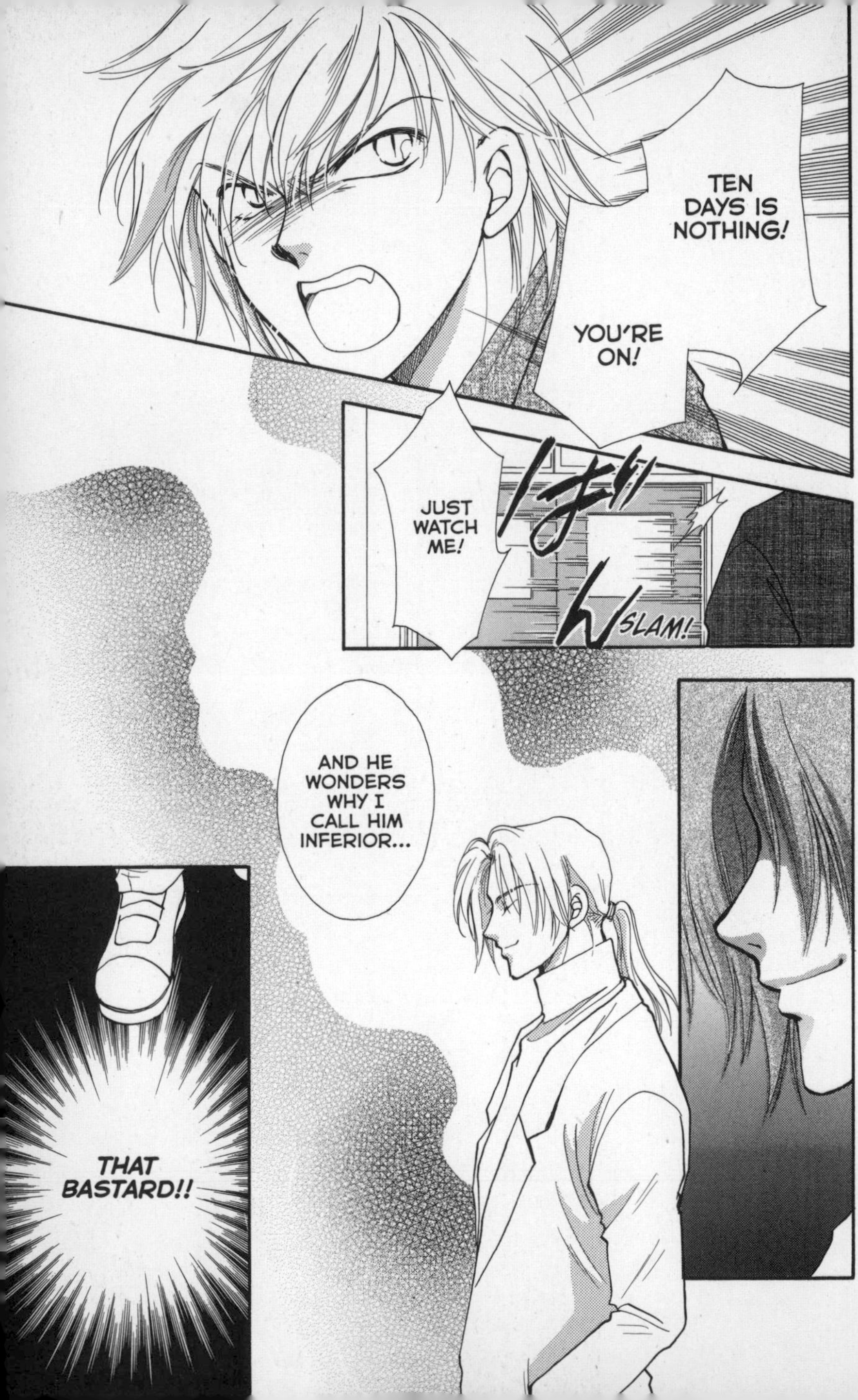
TEN DAYS IS NOTHING!
YOU'RE ON!
JUST WATCH ME!
ばん
SLAM!
AND HE WONDERS WHY I CALL HIM INFERIOR...
THAT BASTARD!!

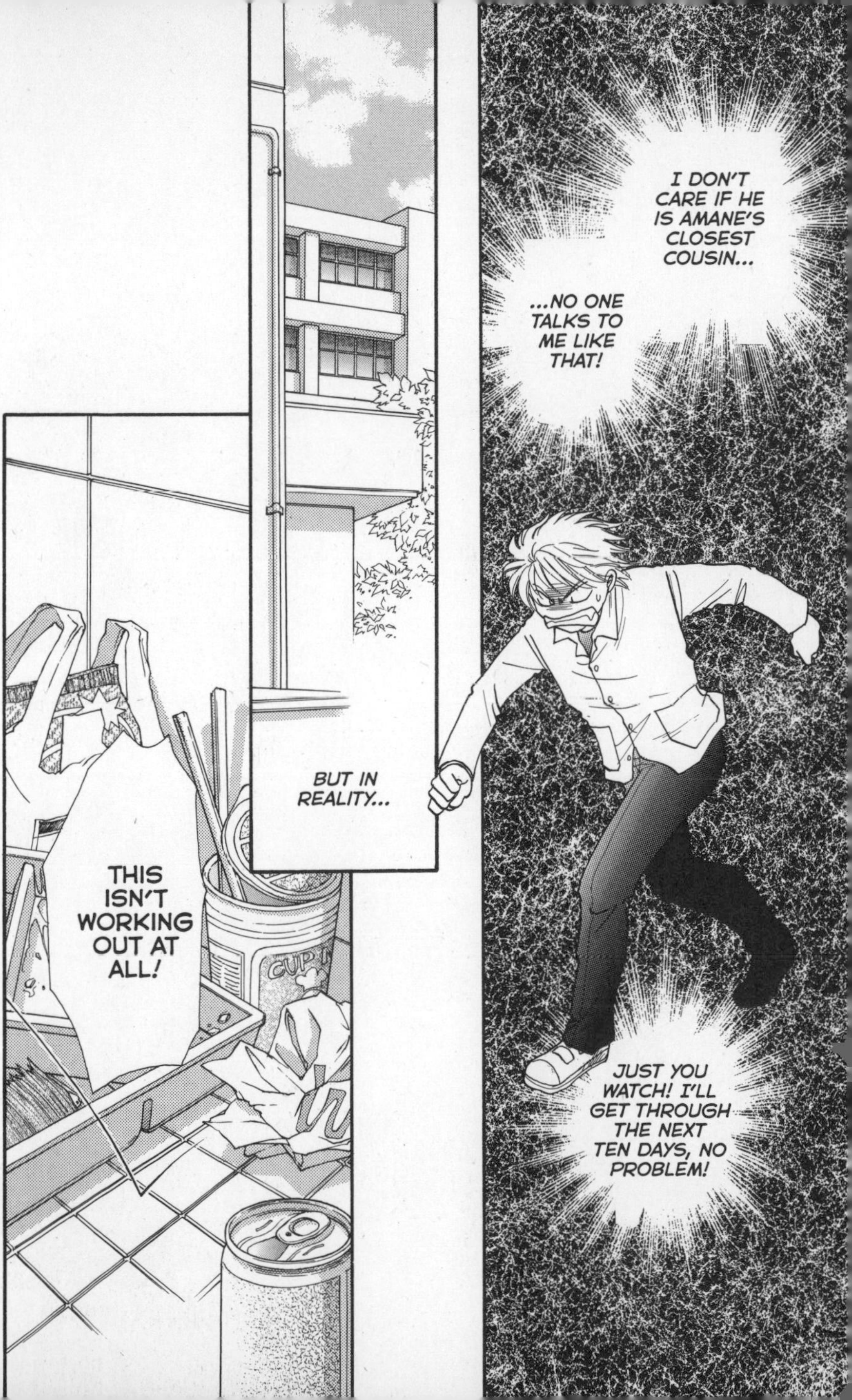
I DON'T CARE IF HE IS AMANE'S CLOSEST COUSIN...
...NO ONE TALKS TO ME LIKE THAT!
JUST YOU WATCH! I'LL GET THROUGH THE NEXT TEN DAYS, NO PROBLEM!
BUT IN REALITY...
THIS ISN'T WORKING OUT AT ALL!

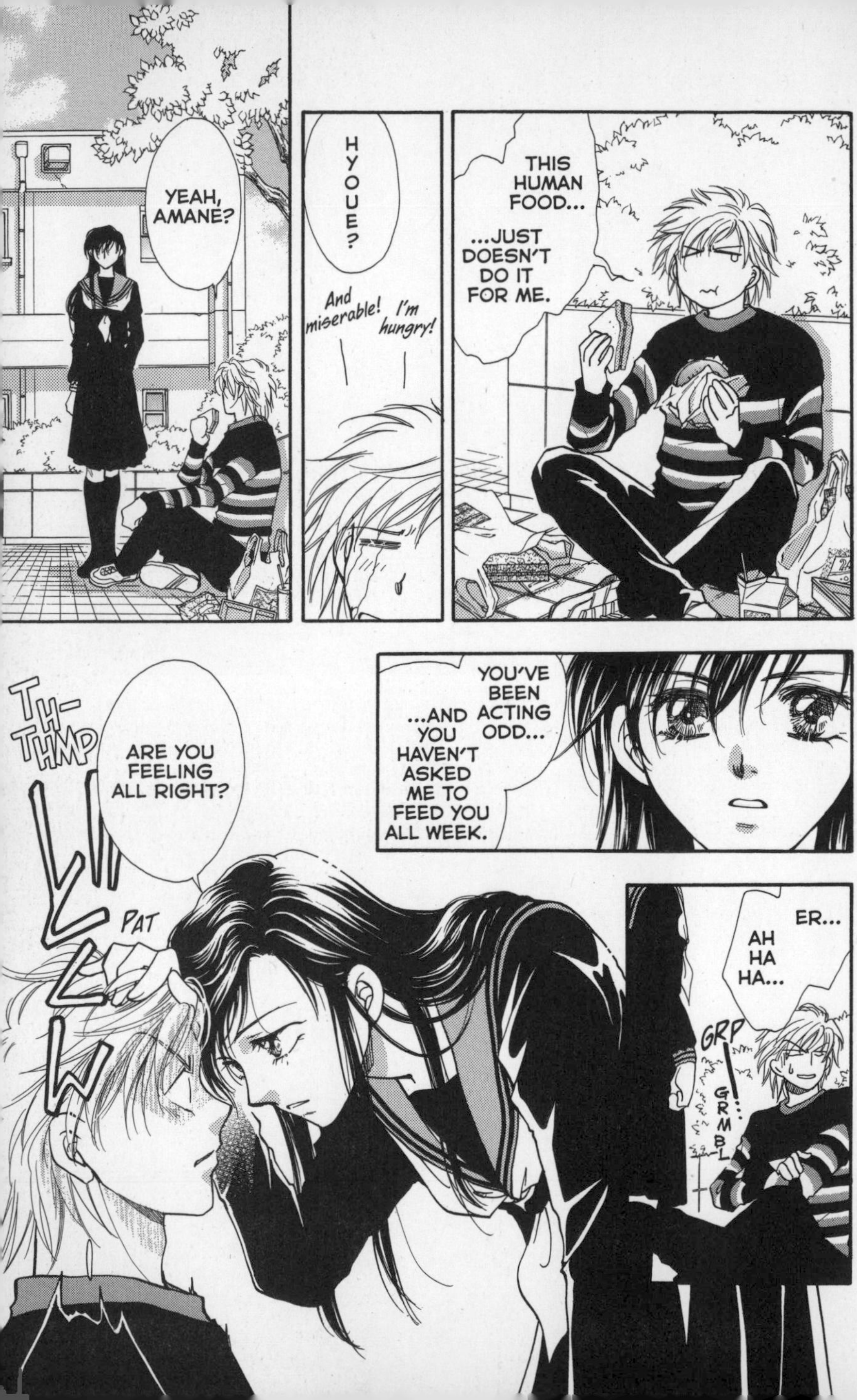
THIS HUMAN FOOD...
...JUST DOESN'T DO IT FOR ME.
HYOUE?
I'm hungry!
And miserable!
YEAH, AMANE?
YOU'VE BEEN ACTING ODD...
...AND YOU HAVEN'T ASKED ME TO FEED YOU ALL WEEK.
ER...
AH HA HA...
GRP
GRMBL
ARE YOU FEELING ALL RIGHT?
TH-THMP
PAT

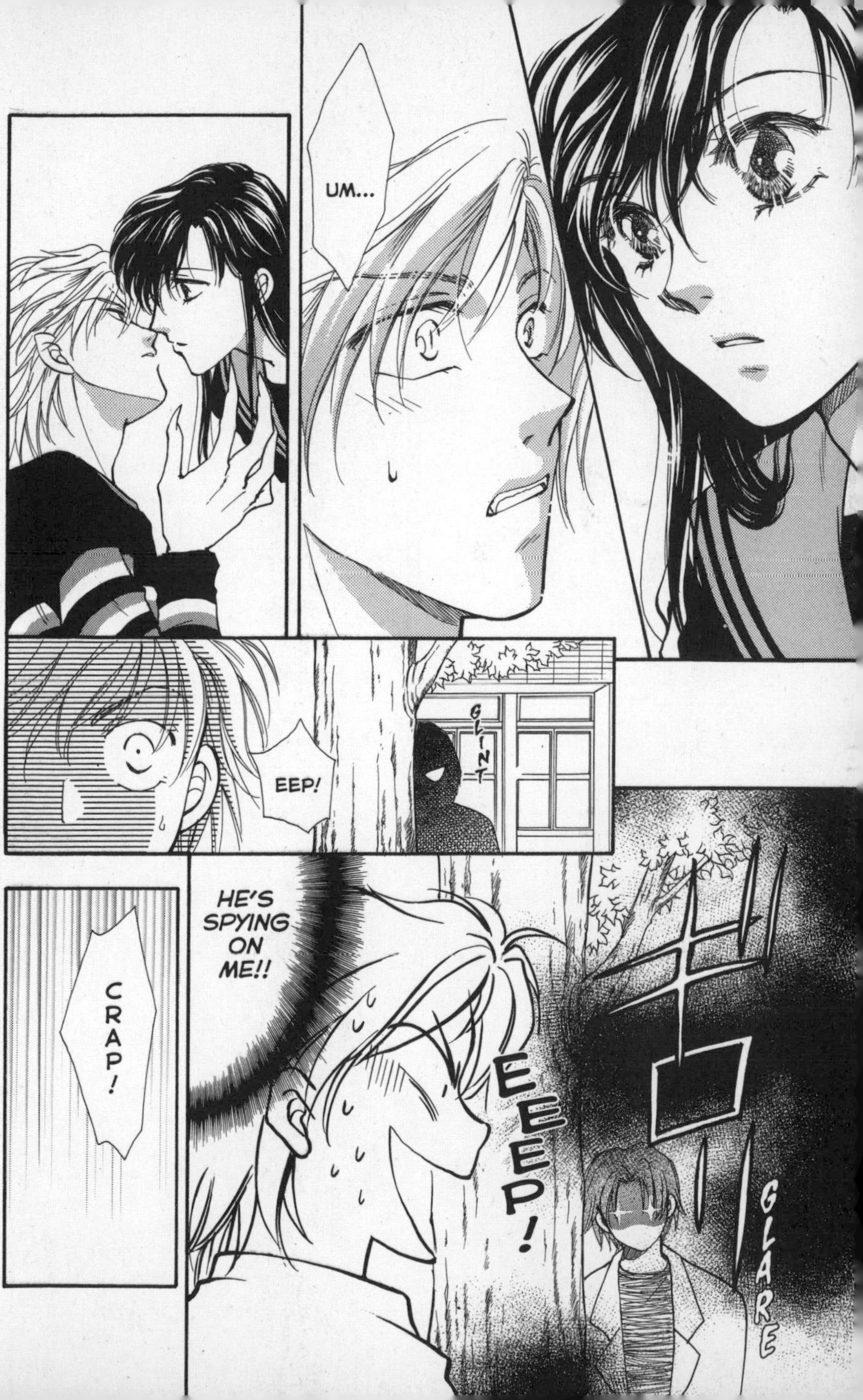
UM...
GLINT
EEP!
HE'S SPYING ON ME!!
EEEP!
GLARE
CRAP!

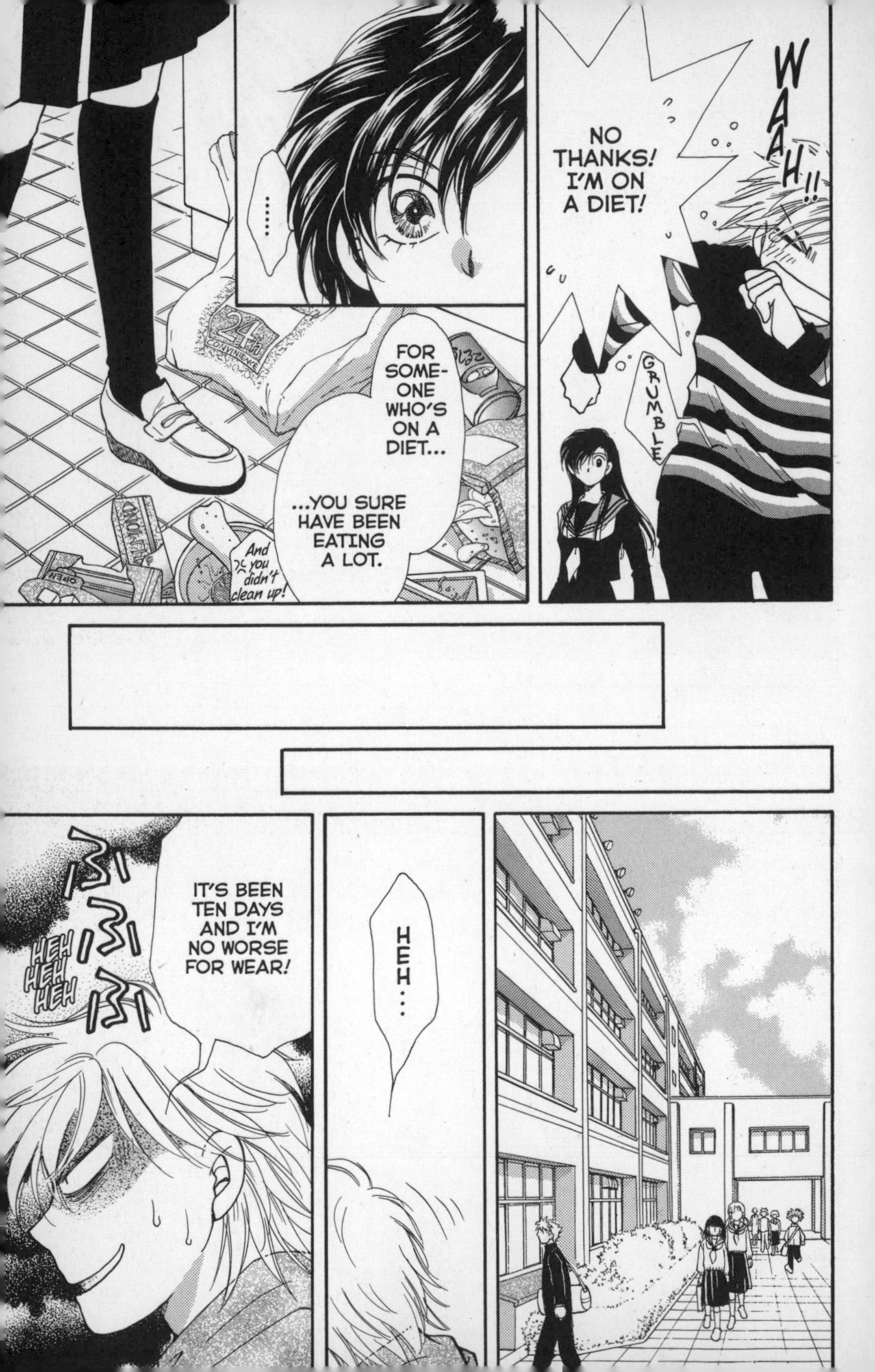
WAAH!!
NO THANKS! I'M ON A DIET!
GRUMBLE
......
FOR SOME-ONE WHO'S ON A DIET...
...YOU SURE HAVE BEEN EATING A LOT.
And you didn't clean up!
HEH...
IT'S BEEN TEN DAYS AND I'M NO WORSE FOR WEAR!
HEH HEH HEH

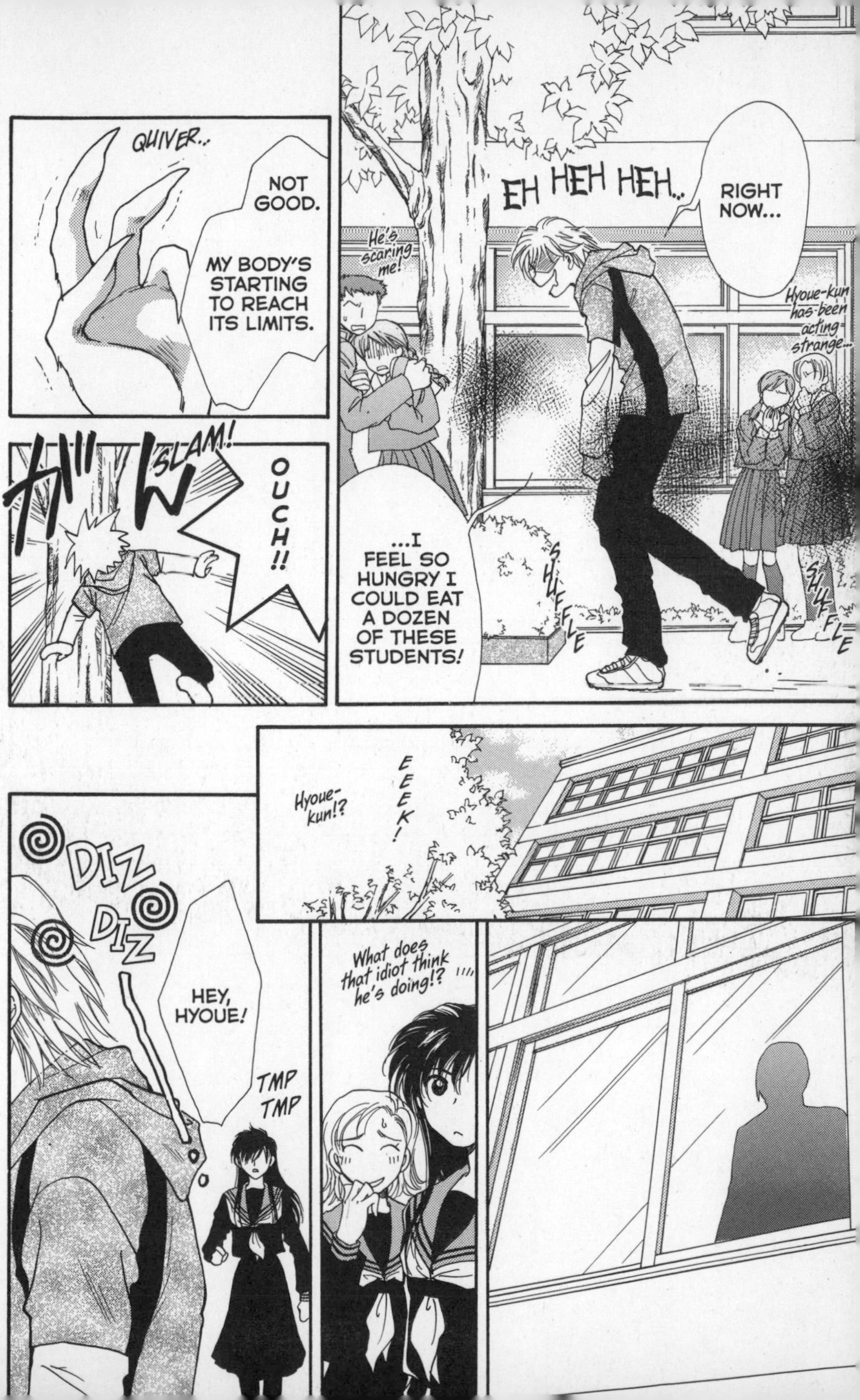
EH HEH HEH..
RIGHT NOW...
...I FEEL SO HUNGRY I COULD EAT A DOZEN OF THESE STUDENTS!
Hyoue-kun has been acting strange..
He's scaring me!
SHUFFLE
SHUFFLE
QUIVER..
NOT GOOD.
MY BODY'S STARTING TO REACH ITS LIMITS.
SLAM!
OUCH!!
EEEK!
Hyoue-kun!?
What does that idiot think he's doing!?
DIZ DIZ
HEY, HYOUE!
TMP TMP

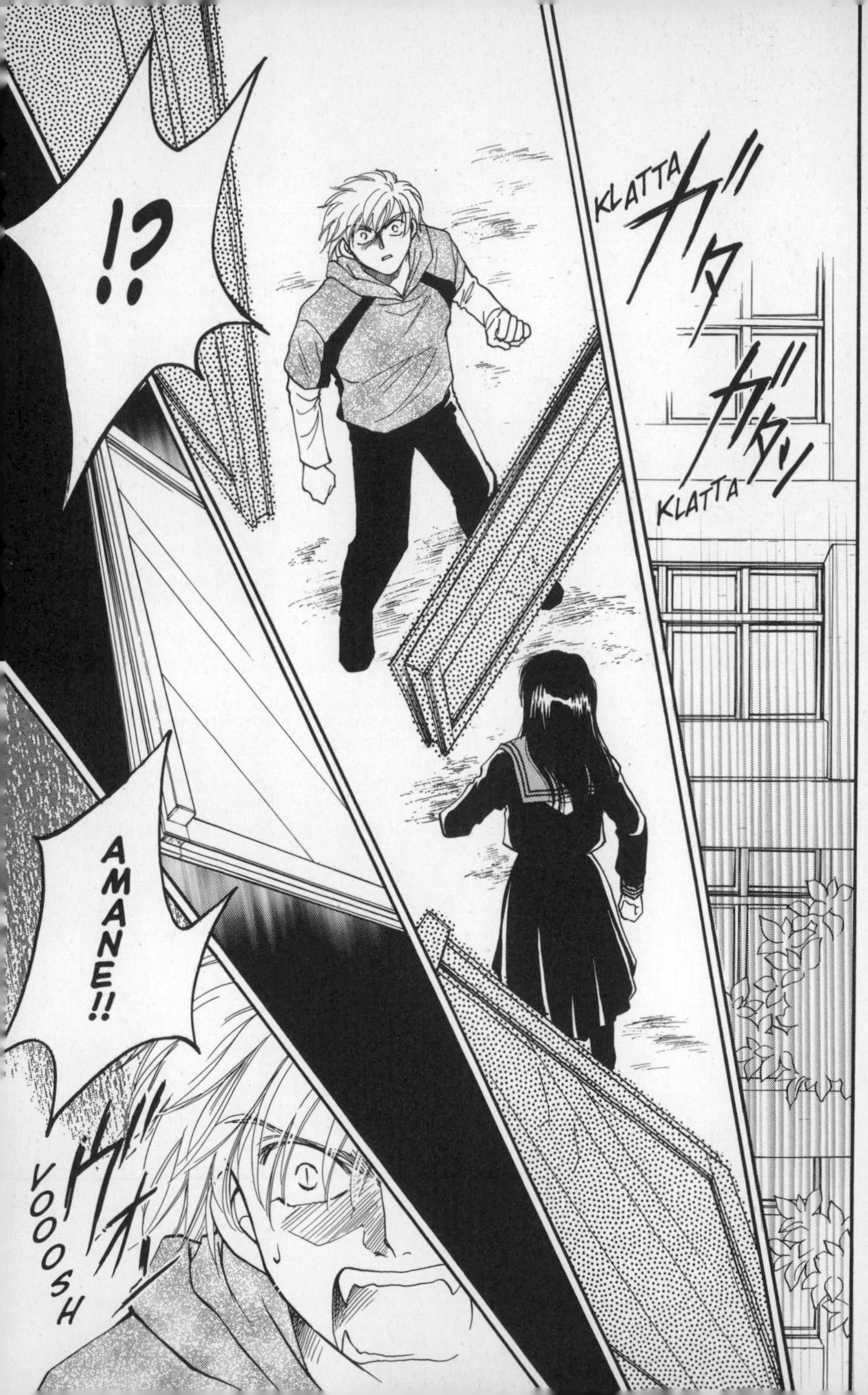
KLATTA
KLATTA
!?
AMANE!!
VOOOSH

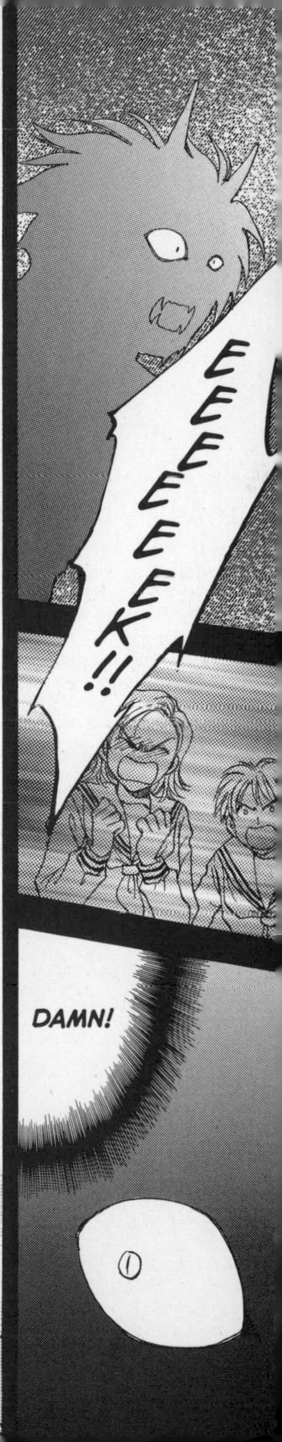
EEEEEEEK!!
DAMN!
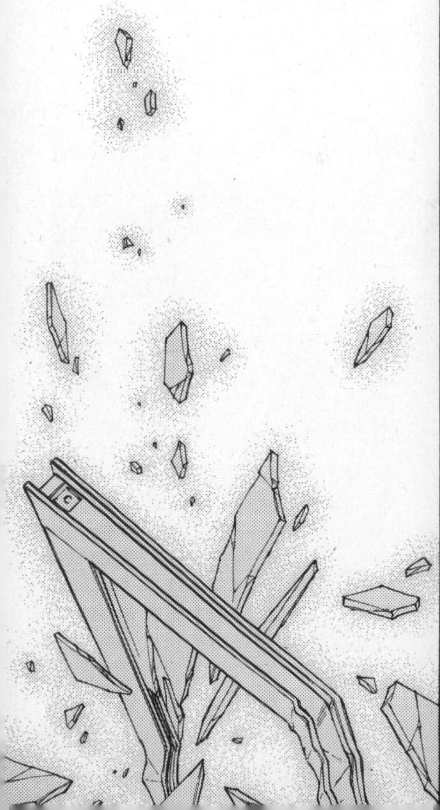

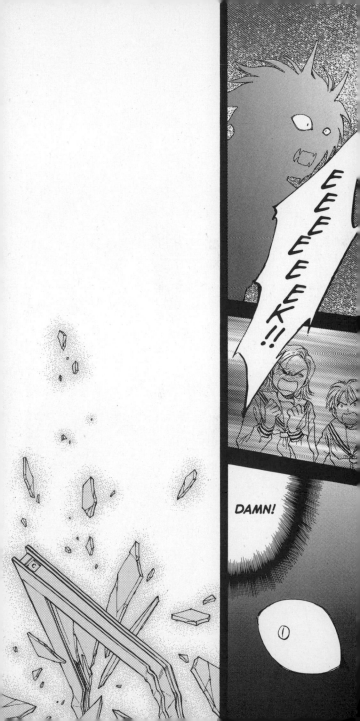

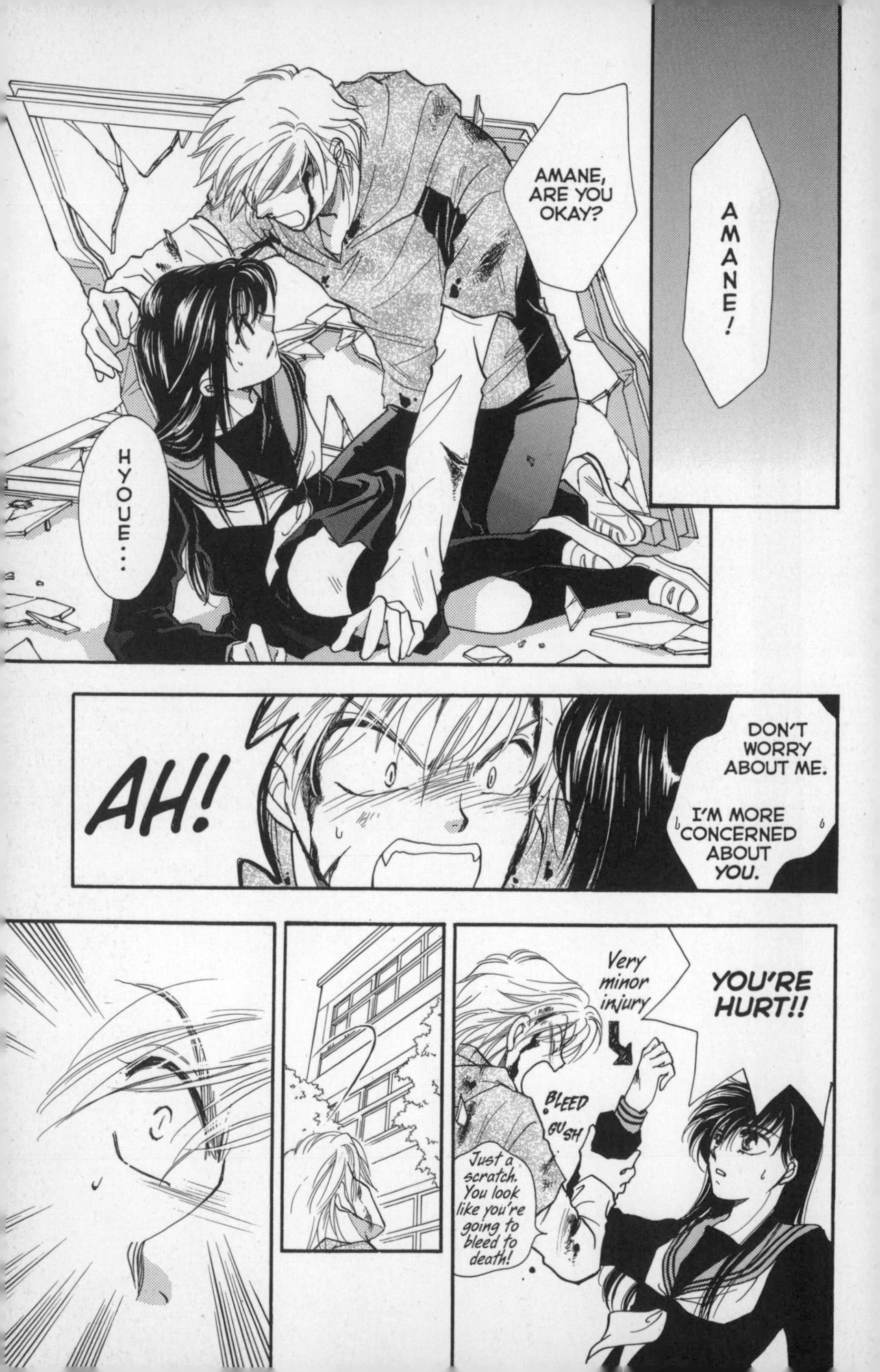
AMANE!
AMANE, ARE YOU OKAY?
HYOUE...
DON'T WORRY ABOUT ME.
I'M MORE CONCERNED ABOUT YOU.
AH!
YOU'RE HURT!!
Very minor injury
BLEED
GUSH
Just a scratch. You look like you're going to bleed to death!

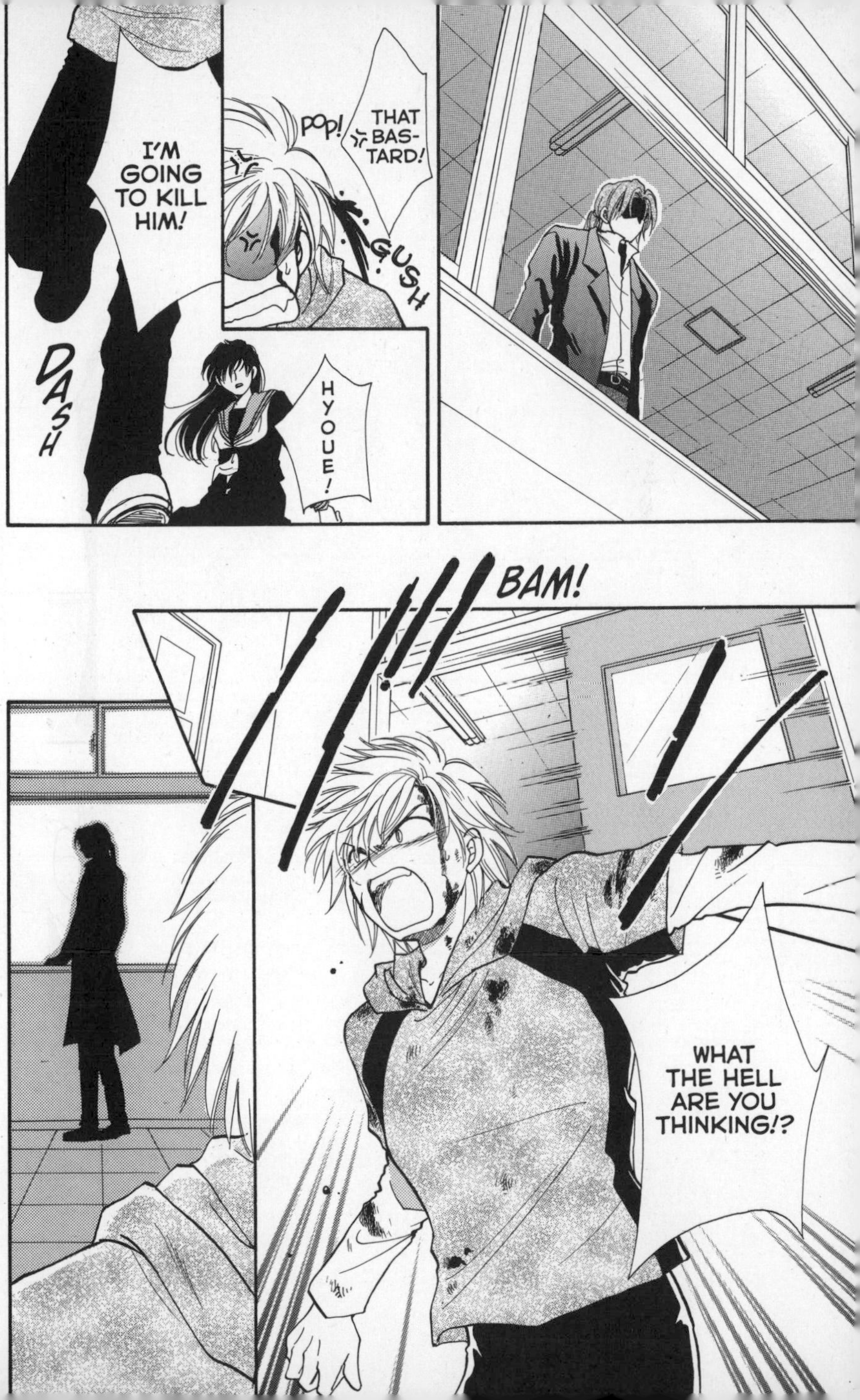
THAT BASTARD!
POP!
GUSH
HYOUE!
I'M GOING TO KILL HIM!
DASH
BAM!
WHAT THE HELL ARE YOU THINKING!?

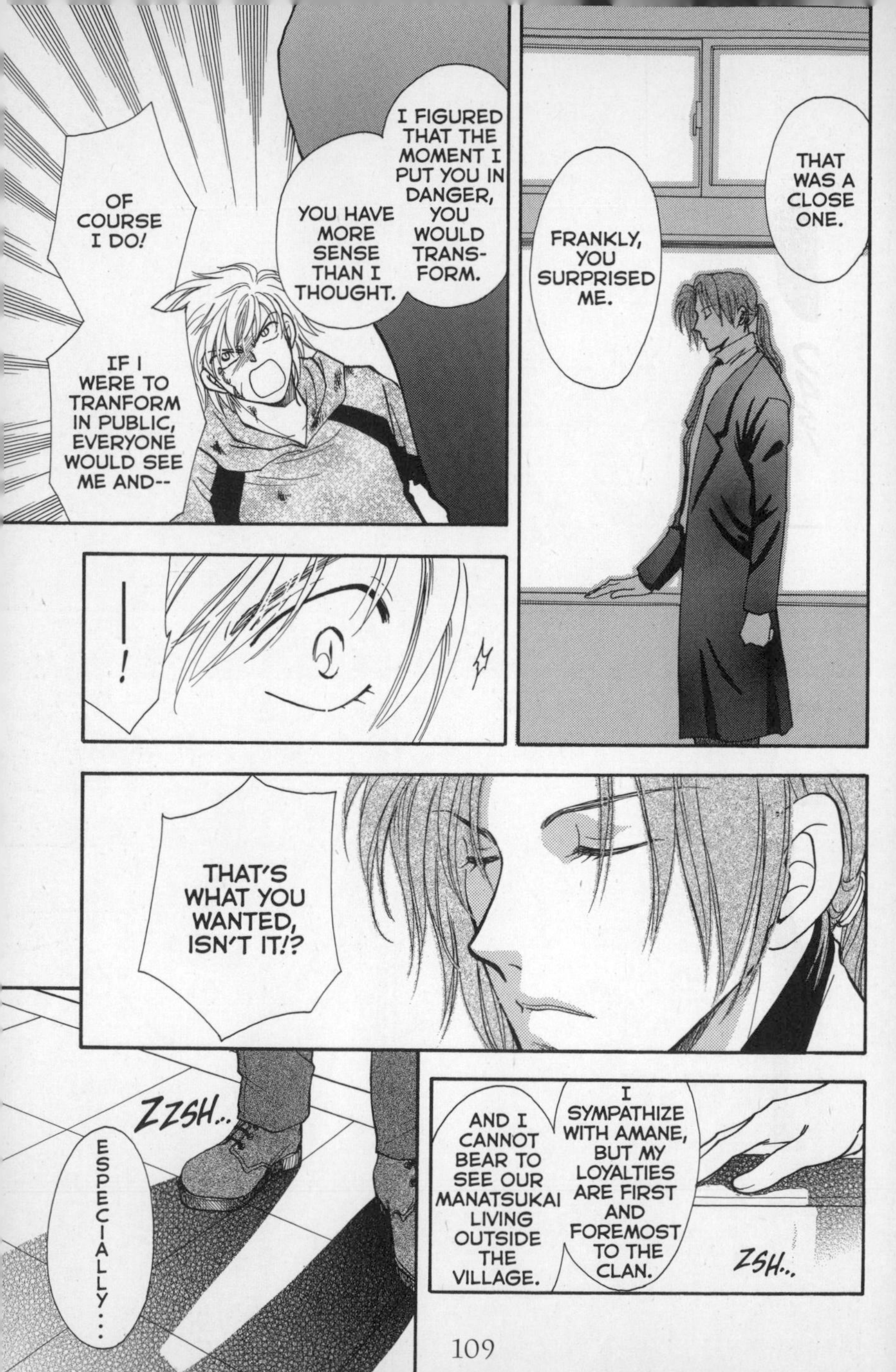
THAT WAS A CLOSE ONE.
FRANKLY, YOU SURPRISED ME.
I FIGURED THAT THE MOMENT I PUT YOU IN DANGER, YOU WOULD TRANS-FORM.
YOU HAVE MORE SENSE THAN I THOUGHT.
OF COURSE I DO!
IF I WERE TO TRANFORM IN PUBLIC, EVERYONE WOULD SEE ME AND--
--!
THAT'S WHAT YOU WANTED, ISN'T IT!?
I SYMPATHIZE WITH AMANE, BUT MY LOYALTIES ARE FIRST AND FOREMOST TO THE CLAN.
AND I CANNOT BEAR TO SEE OUR MANATSUKAI LIVING OUTSIDE THE VILLAGE.
ZSH...
ZZSH...
ESPECIALLY...

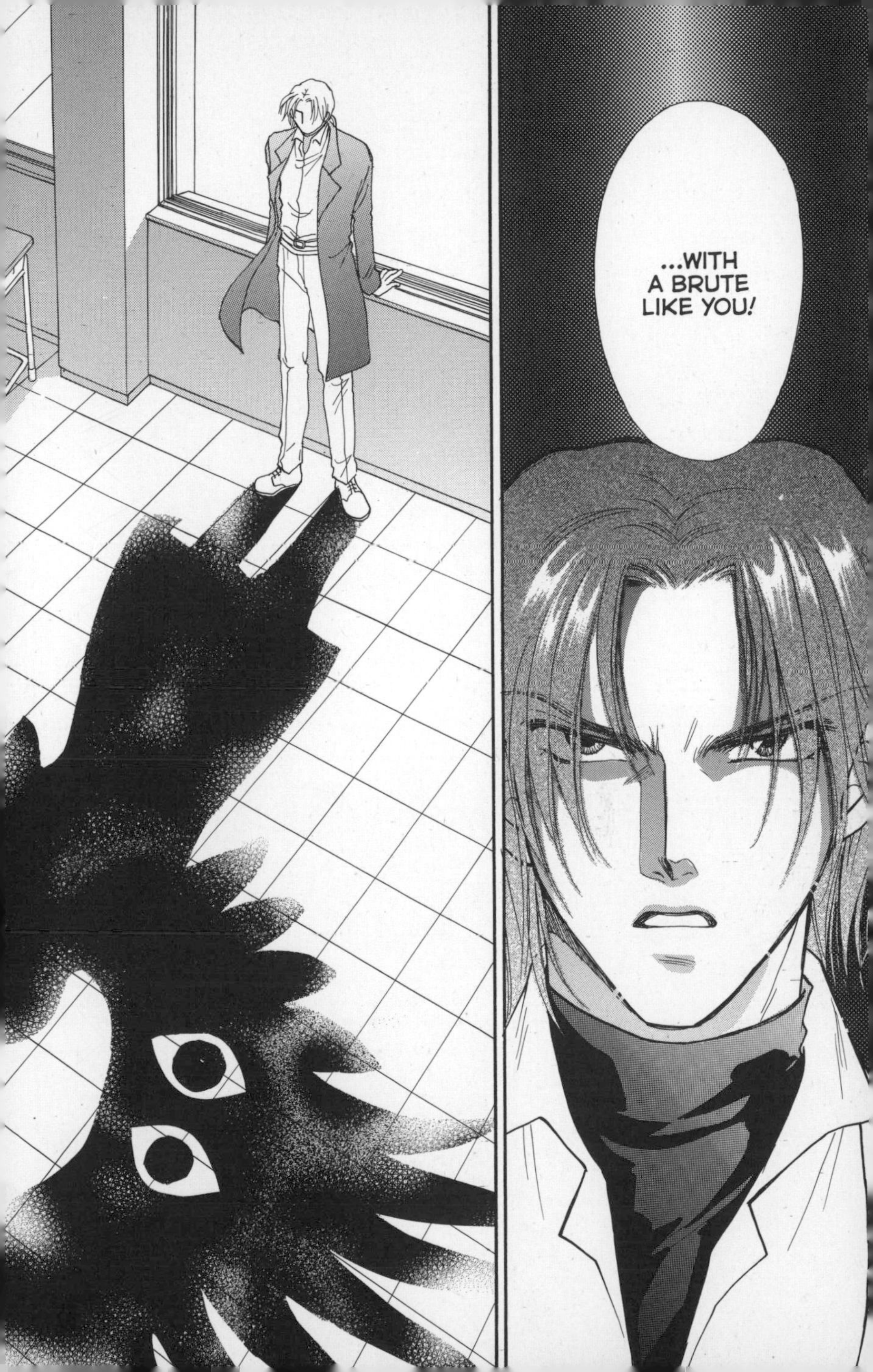
...WITH A BRUTE LIKE YOU!

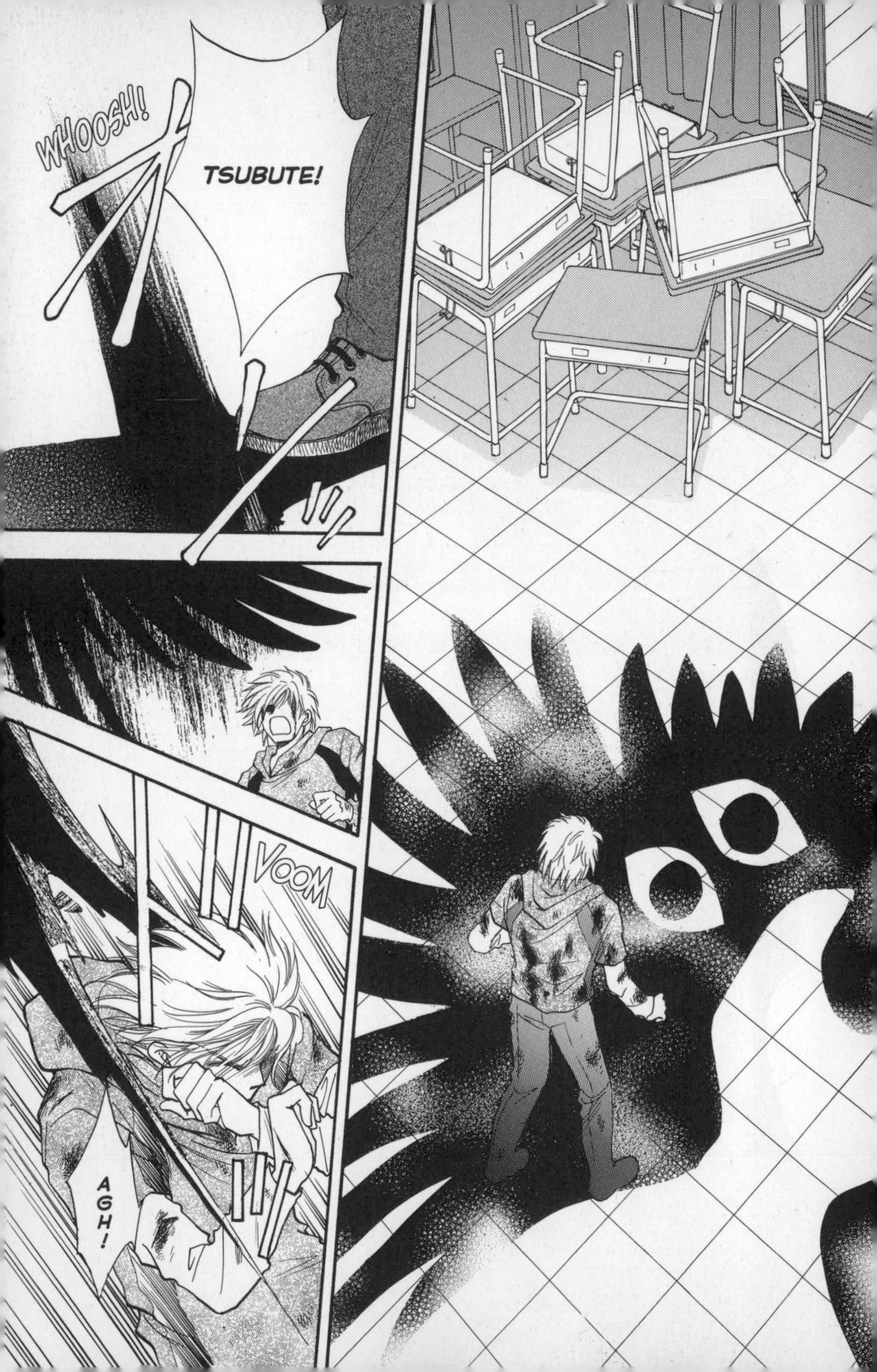
TSUBUTE!
WHOOSH!
VOOM
AGH!

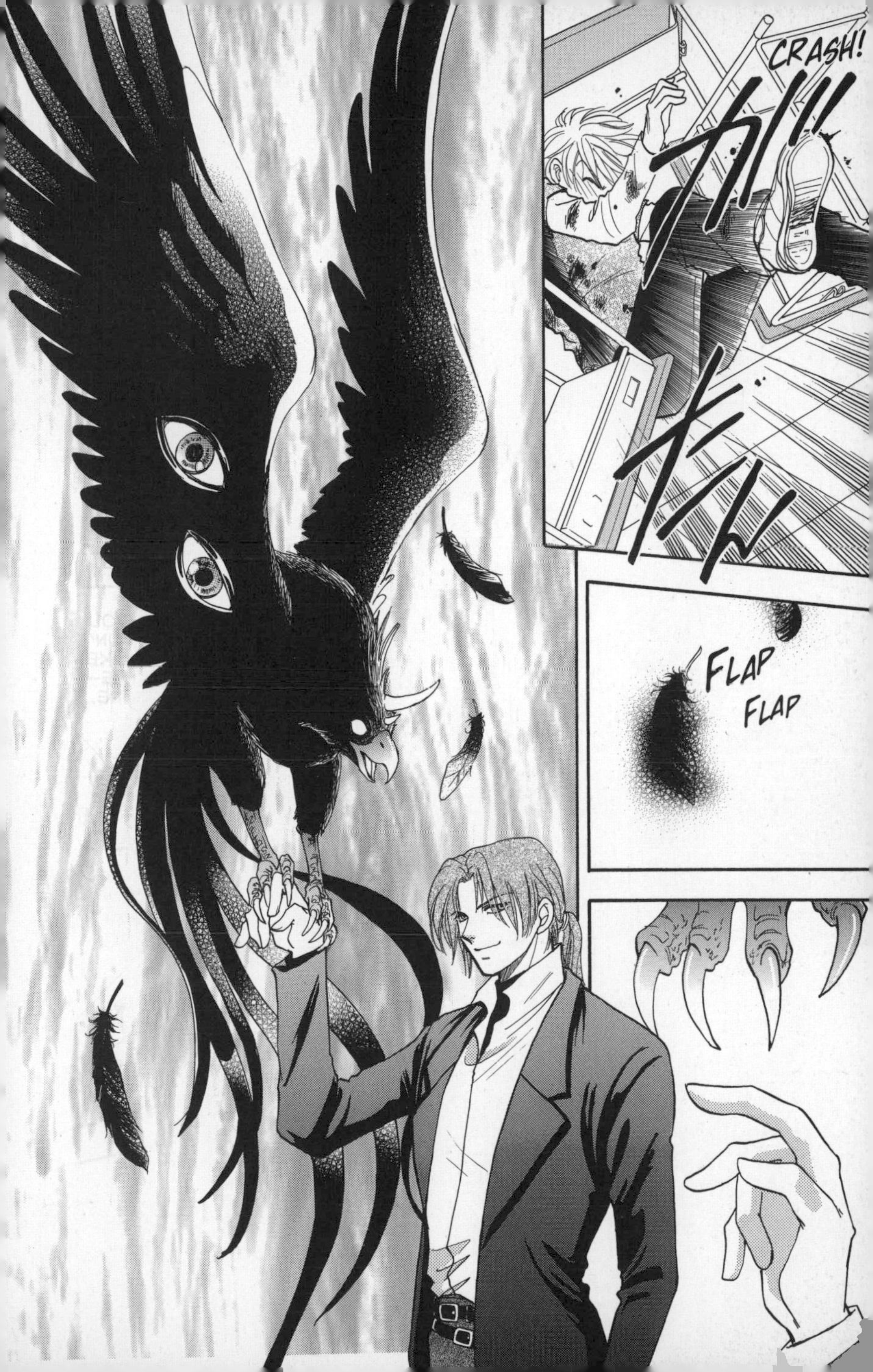
CRASH!
FLAP
FLAP

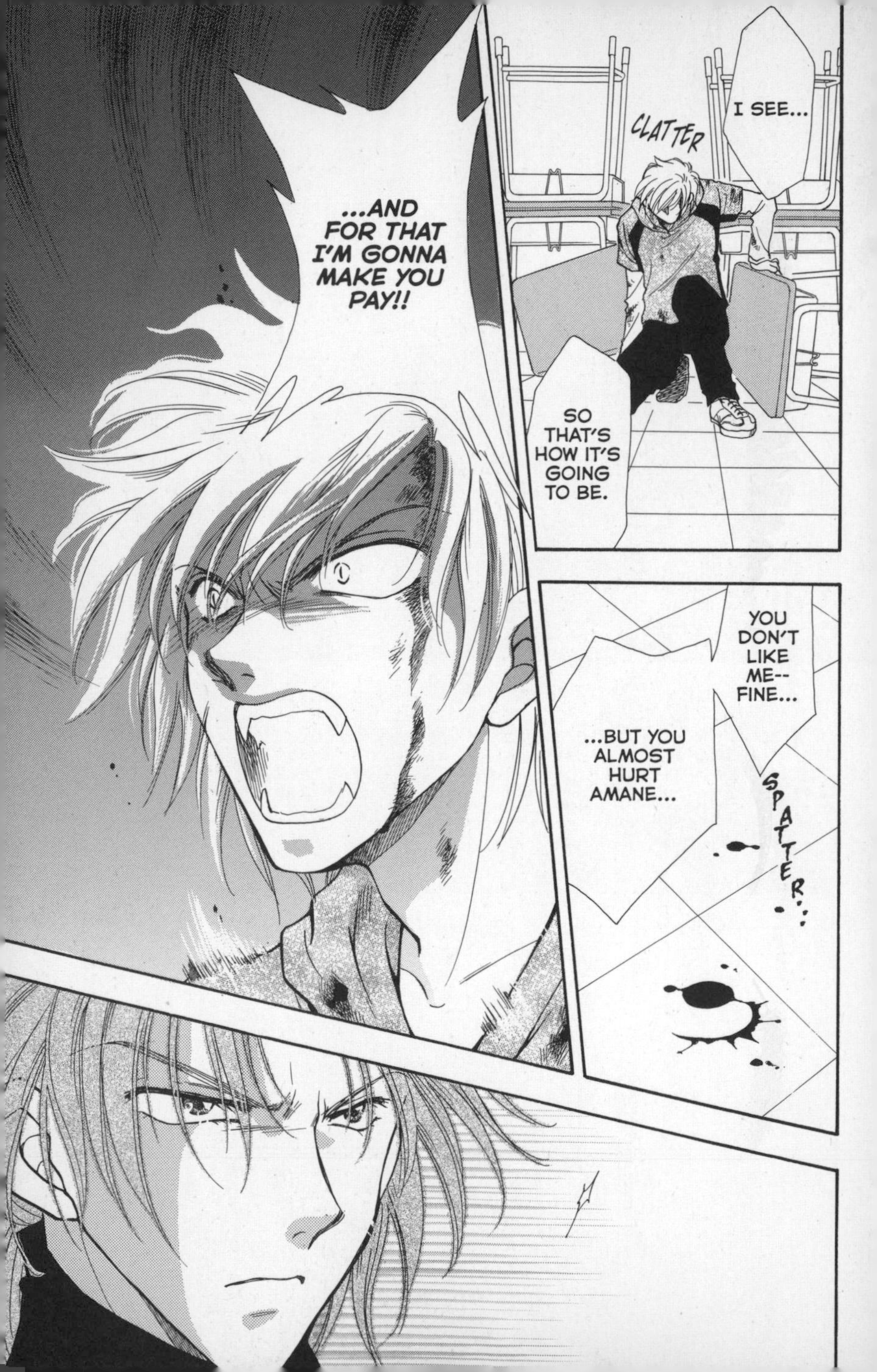
I SEE...
CLATTER
SO THAT'S HOW IT'S GOING TO BE.
YOU DON'T LIKE ME--FINE...
...BUT YOU ALMOST HURT AMANE...
SPATTER...
...AND FOR THAT I'M GONNA MAKE YOU PAY!!

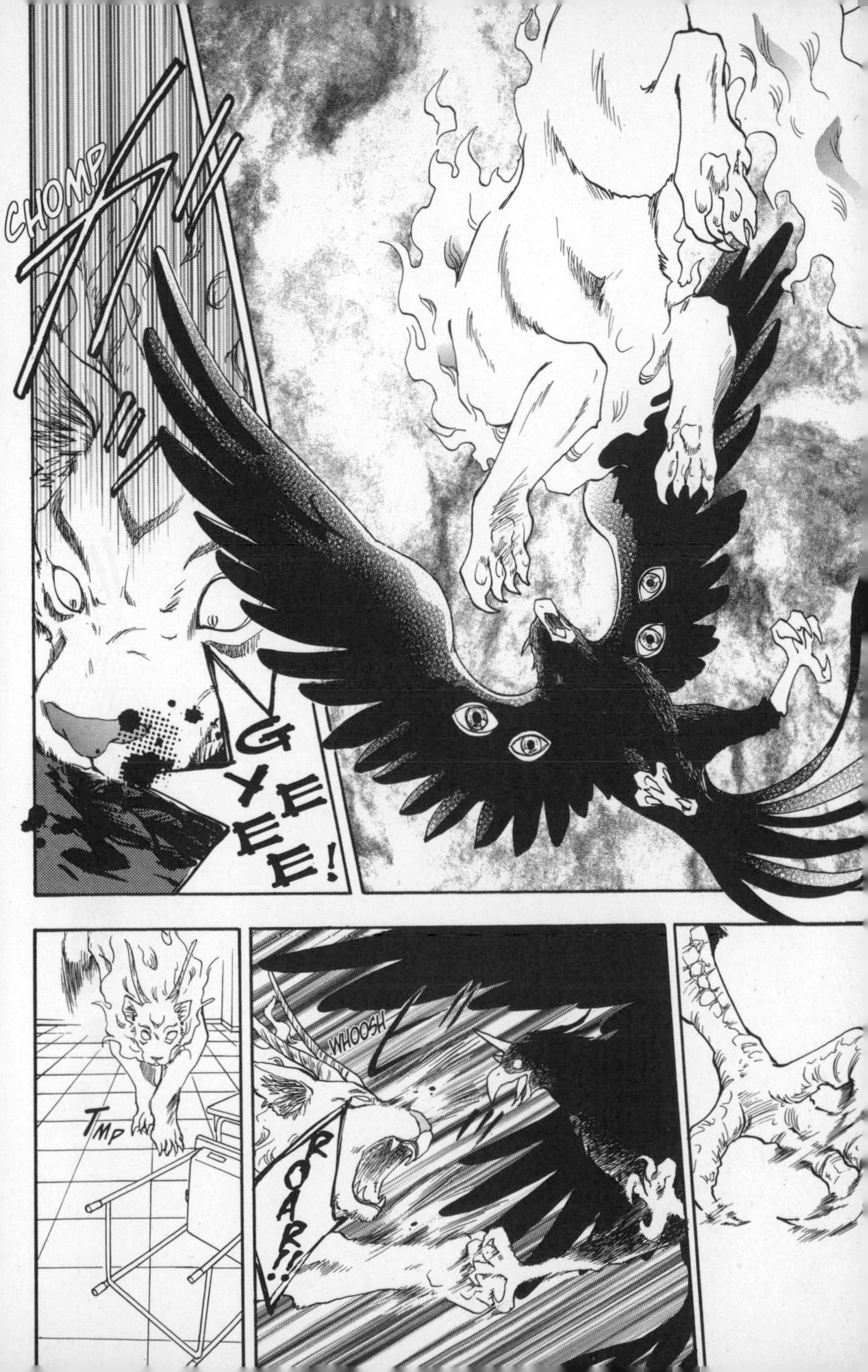
CHOMP
GYEEE!
WHOOSH
ROAR!!
TMP

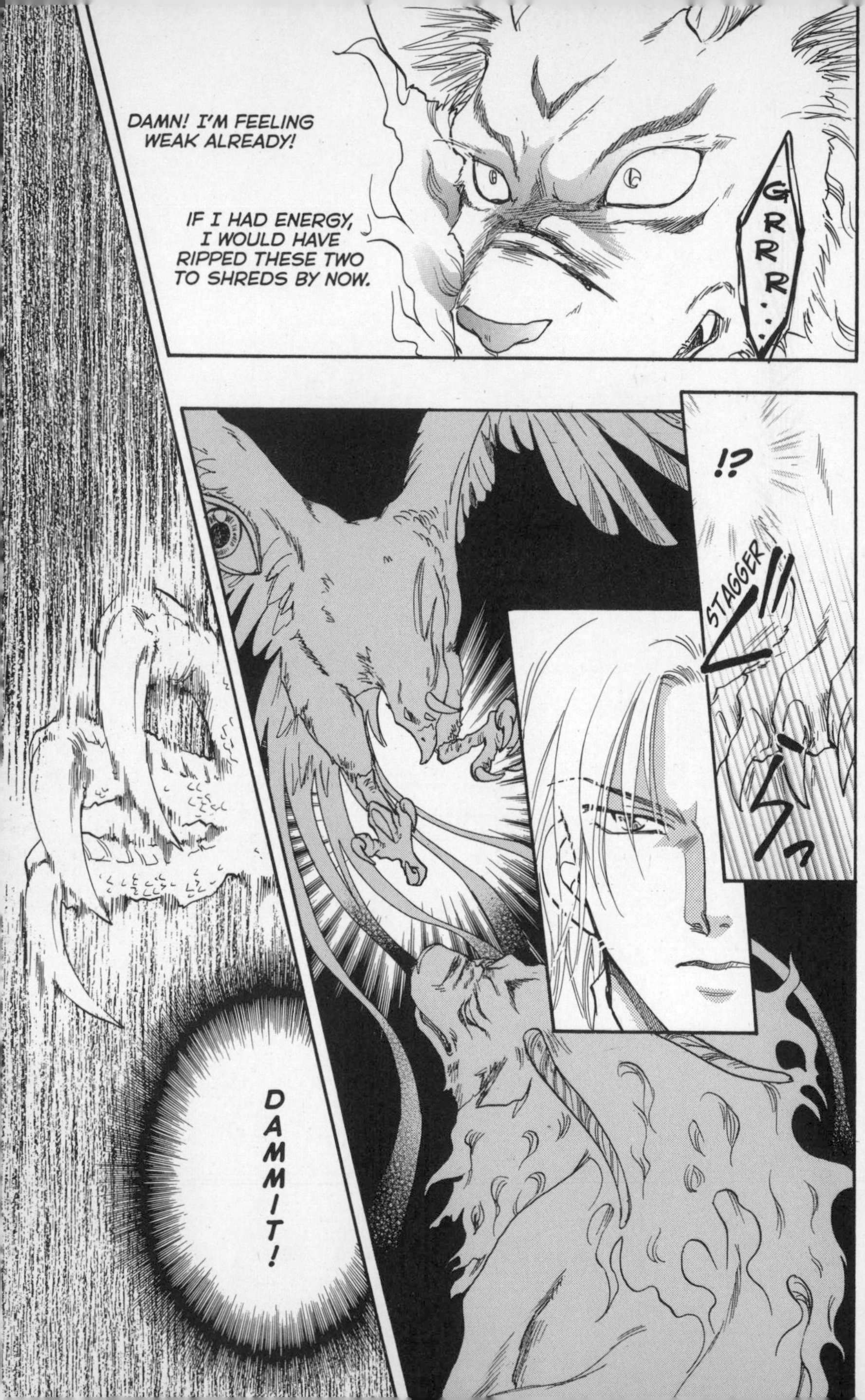
GRRR...
DAMN! I'M FEELING WEAK ALREADY!
IF I HAD ENERGY, I WOULD HAVE RIPPED THESE TWO TO SHREDS BY NOW.
!?
STAGGER
DAMMIT!

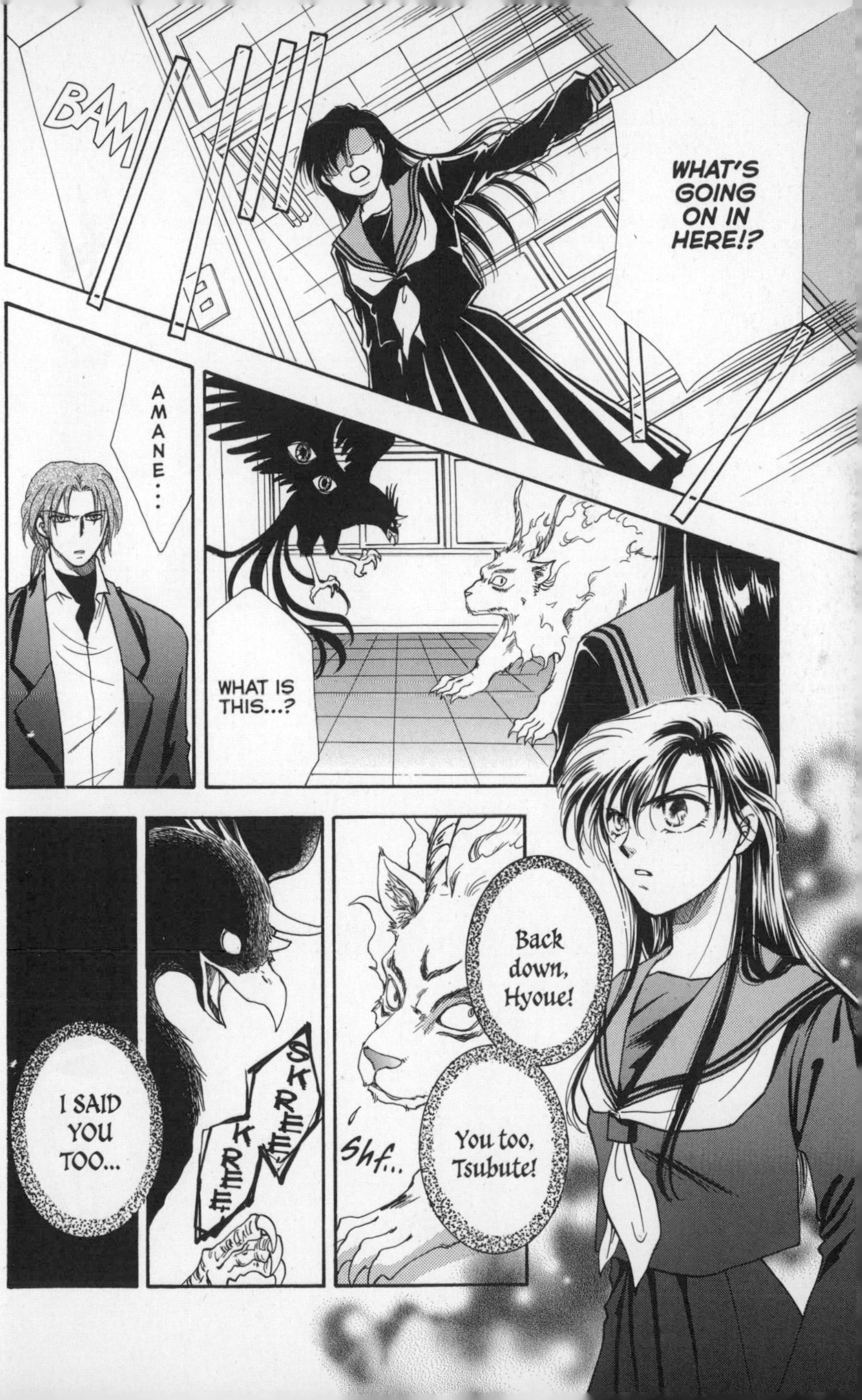
WHAT'S GOING ON IN HERE!?
BAM
WHAT IS THIS...?
AMANE...
Back down, Hyoue!
You too, Tsubute!
Shf...
SKREE
KREEE
I SAID YOU TOO...

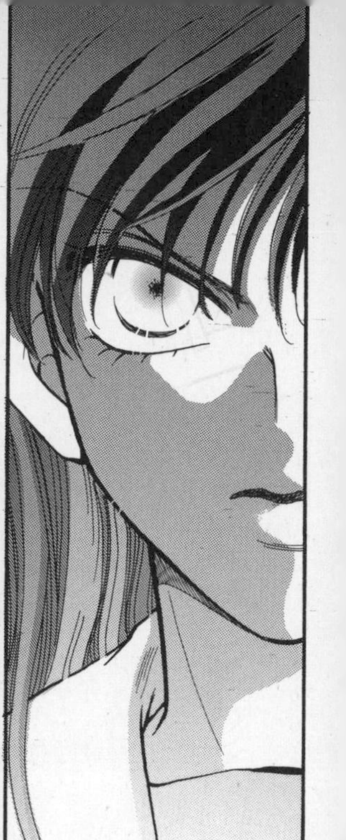

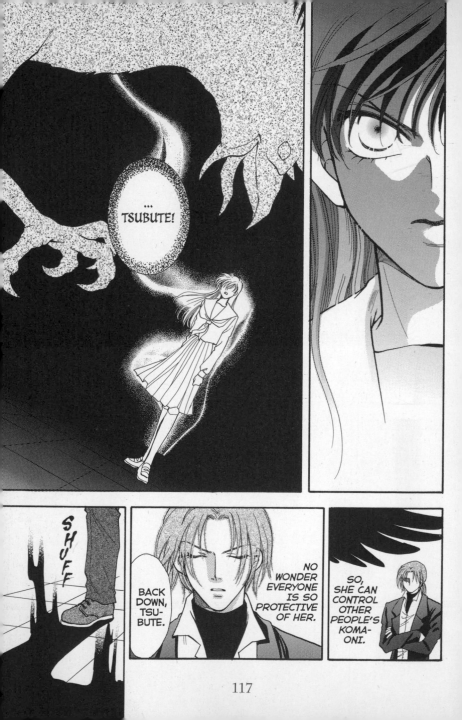

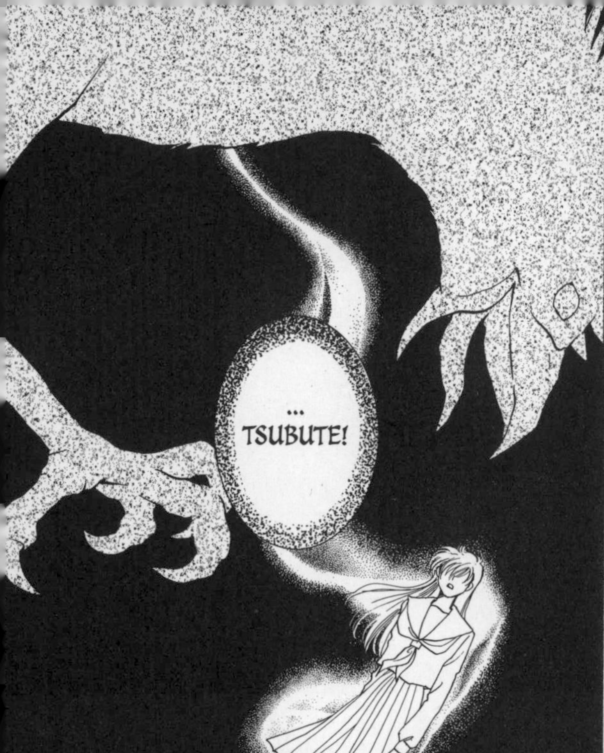
... TSUBUTE!

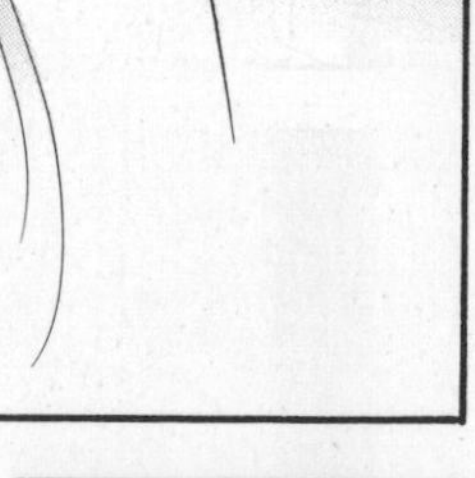
SO, SHE CAN CONTROL OTHER PEOPLE'S KOMA-ONI.

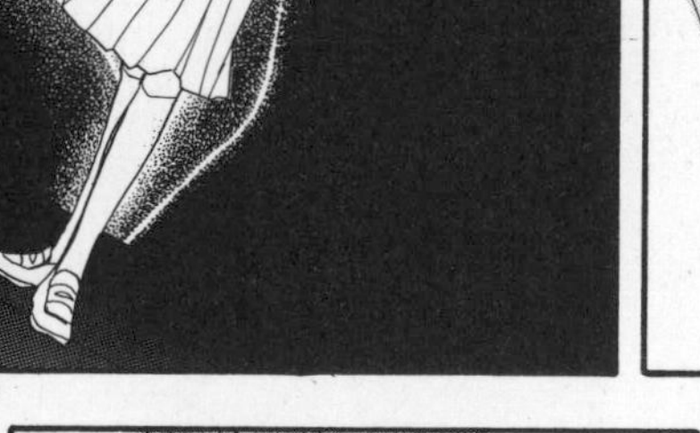
NO WONDER EVERYONE IS SO PROTECTIVE OF HER.
BACK DOWN, TSU-BUTE.

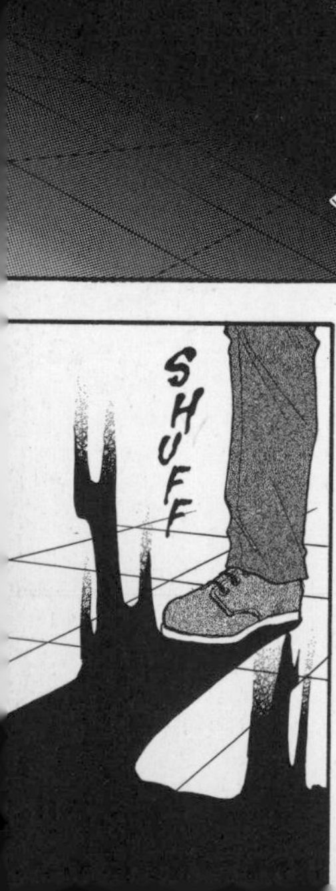
SHUFF

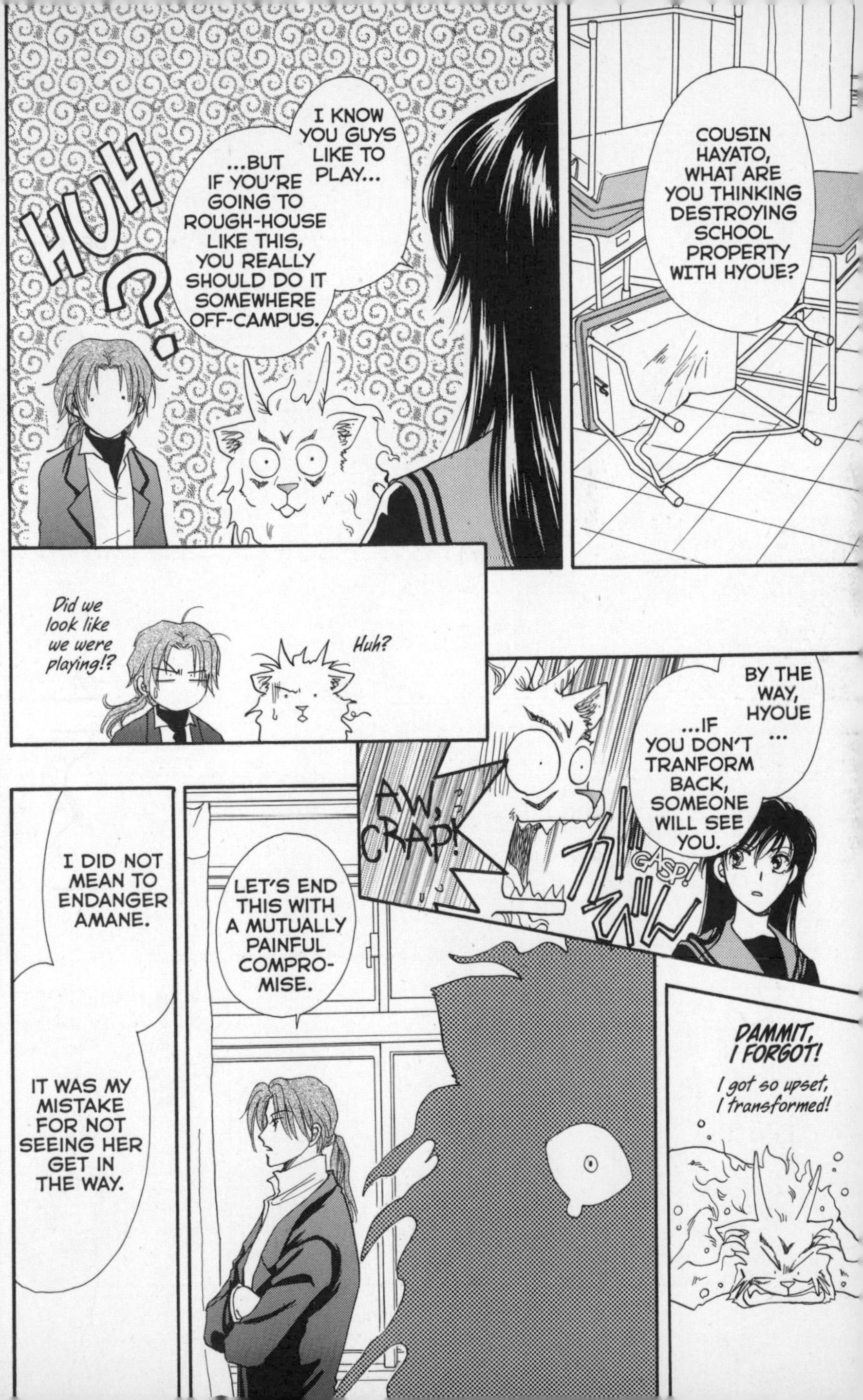
COUSIN HAYATO, WHAT ARE YOU THINKING DESTROYING SCHOOL PROPERTY WITH HYOUE?
I KNOW YOU GUYS LIKE TO PLAY...
...BUT IF YOU'RE GOING TO ROUGH-HOUSE LIKE THIS, YOU REALLY SHOULD DO IT SOMEWHERE OFF-CAMPUS.
HUH ?
Did we look like we were playing!?
Huh?
BY THE WAY, HYOUE ...
...IF YOU DON'T TRANFORM BACK, SOMEONE WILL SEE YOU.
GASP!
AW, CRAP!
DAMMIT, I FORGOT!
I got so upset, I transformed!
LET'S END THIS WITH A MUTUALLY PAINFUL COMPRO-MISE.
I DID NOT MEAN TO ENDANGER AMANE.
IT WAS MY MISTAKE FOR NOT SEEING HER GET IN THE WAY.

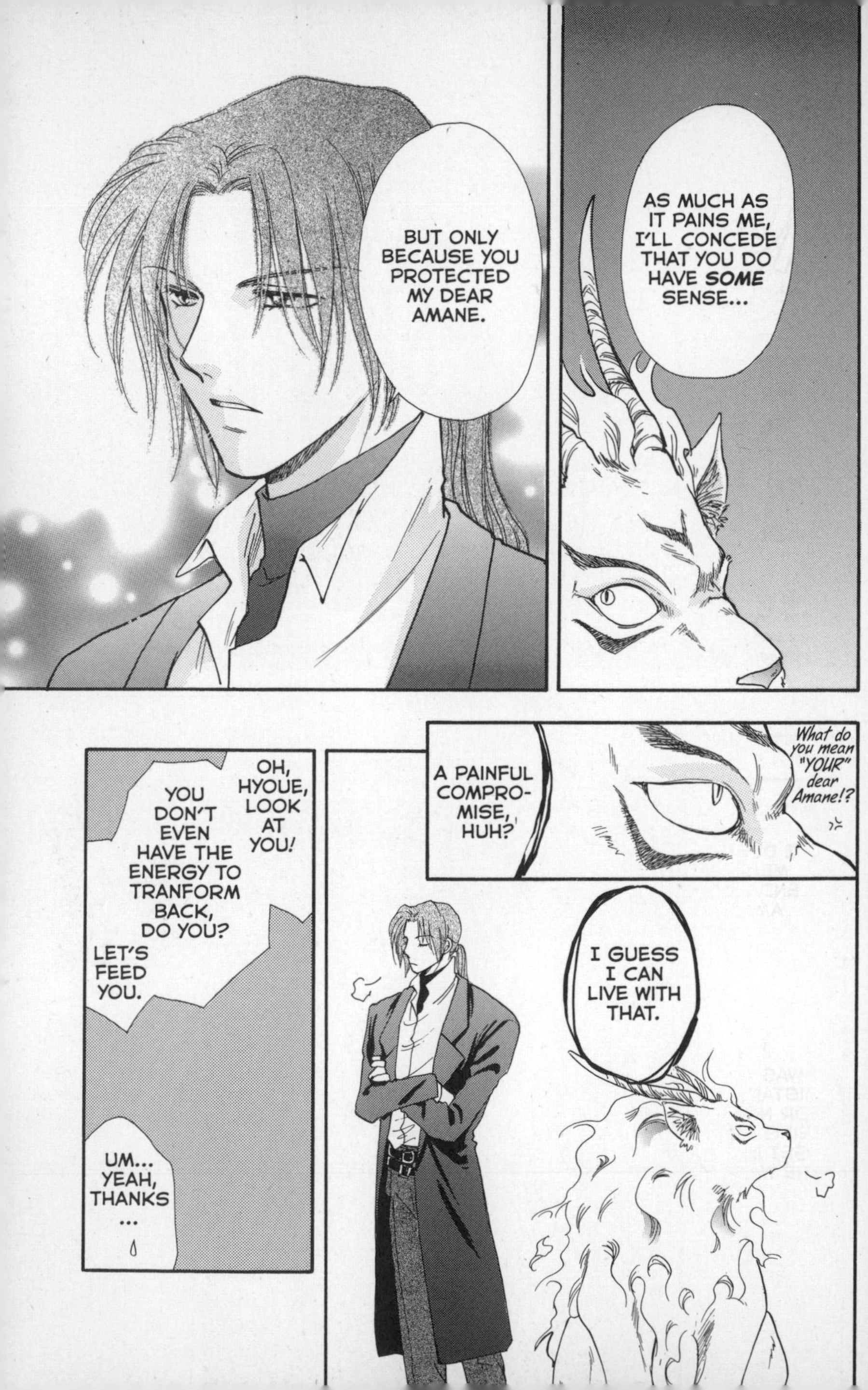
AS MUCH AS IT PAINS ME, I'LL CONCEDE THAT YOU DO HAVE **SOME** SENSE...
BUT ONLY BECAUSE YOU PROTECTED MY DEAR AMANE.
What do you mean "YOUR" dear Amane!?
A PAINFUL COMPROMISE, HUH?
I GUESS I CAN LIVE WITH THAT.
OH, HYOUE, LOOK AT YOU!
YOU DON'T EVEN HAVE THE ENERGY TO TRANFORM BACK, DO YOU?
LET'S FEED YOU.
UM... YEAH, THANKS ...

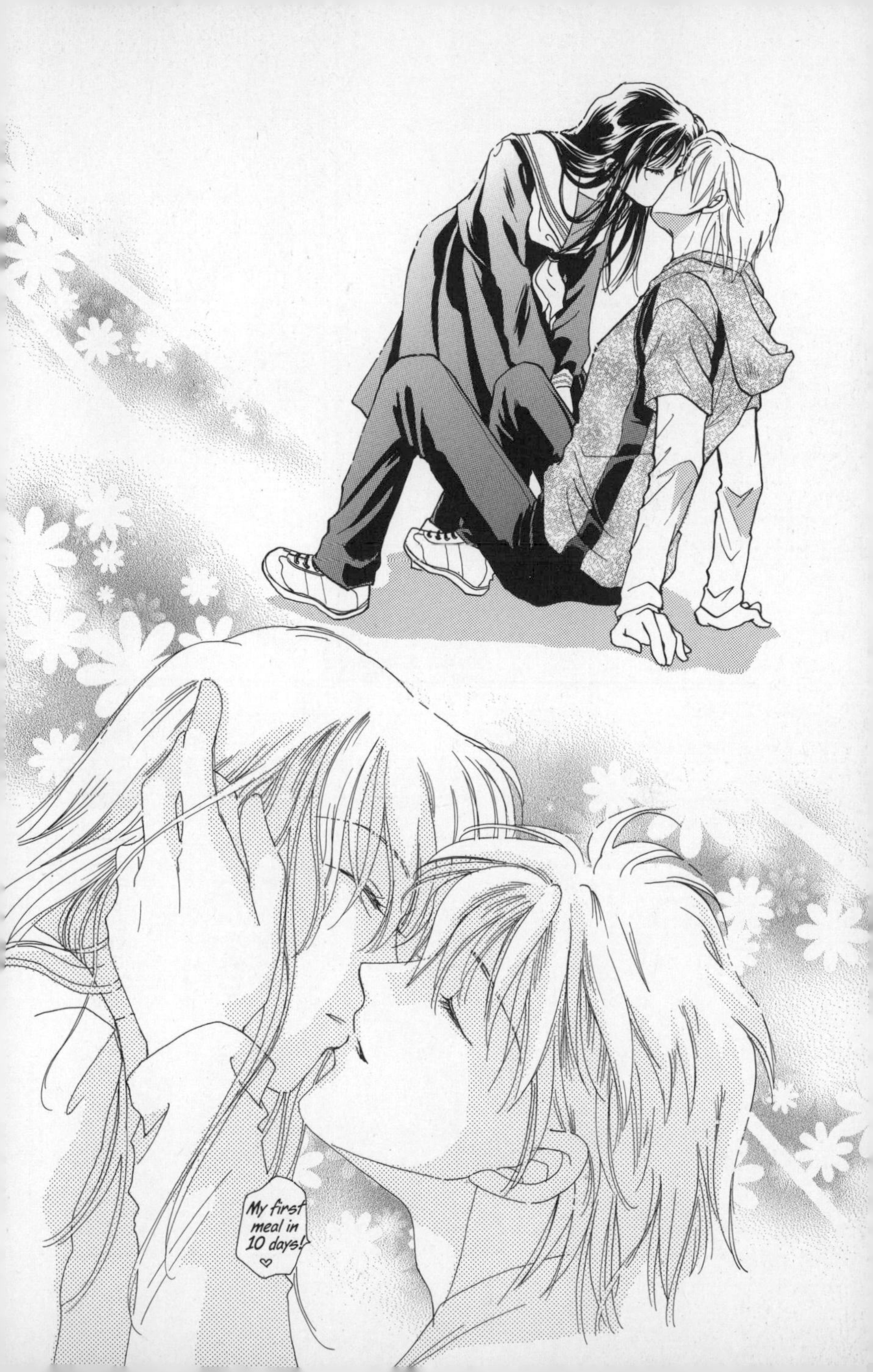
My first meal in 10 days! ♡

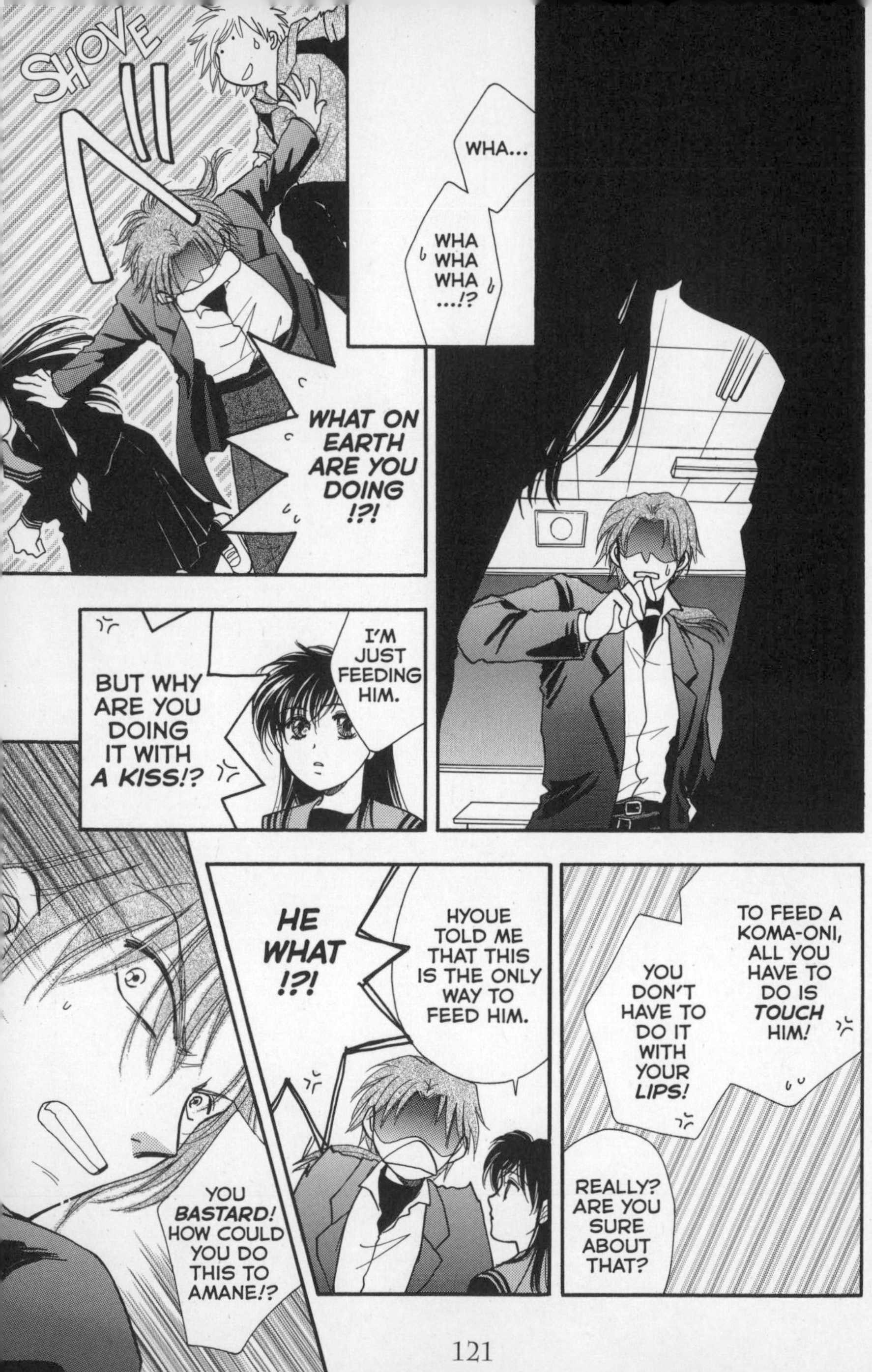
WHA...
WHA WHA WHA ...!?
SHOVE
WHAT ON EARTH ARE YOU DOING !?!
I'M JUST FEEDING HIM.
BUT WHY ARE YOU DOING IT WITH A KISS!?
TO FEED A KOMA-ONI, ALL YOU HAVE TO DO IS TOUCH HIM!
YOU DON'T HAVE TO DO IT WITH YOUR LIPS!
REALLY? ARE YOU SURE ABOUT THAT?
HYOUE TOLD ME THAT THIS IS THE ONLY WAY TO FEED HIM.
HE WHAT !?!
YOU BASTARD! HOW COULD YOU DO THIS TO AMANE!?

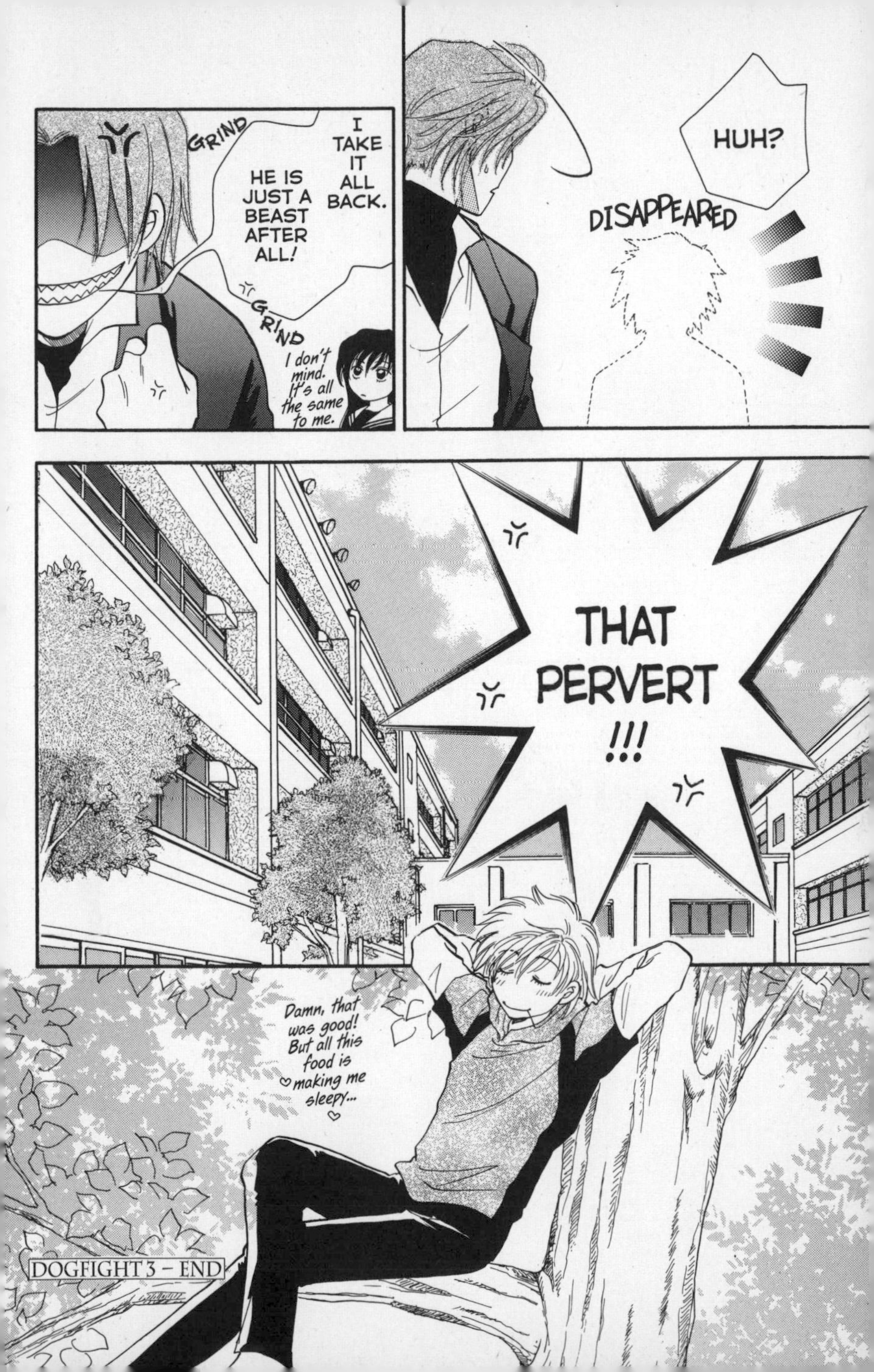
HUH?
DISAPPEARED
I TAKE IT ALL BACK.
HE IS JUST A BEAST AFTER ALL!
GRIND
GRIND
I don't mind. It's all the same to me.
THAT PERVERT !!!
Damn, that was good! But all this food is making me sleepy...
DOGFIGHT 3 – END

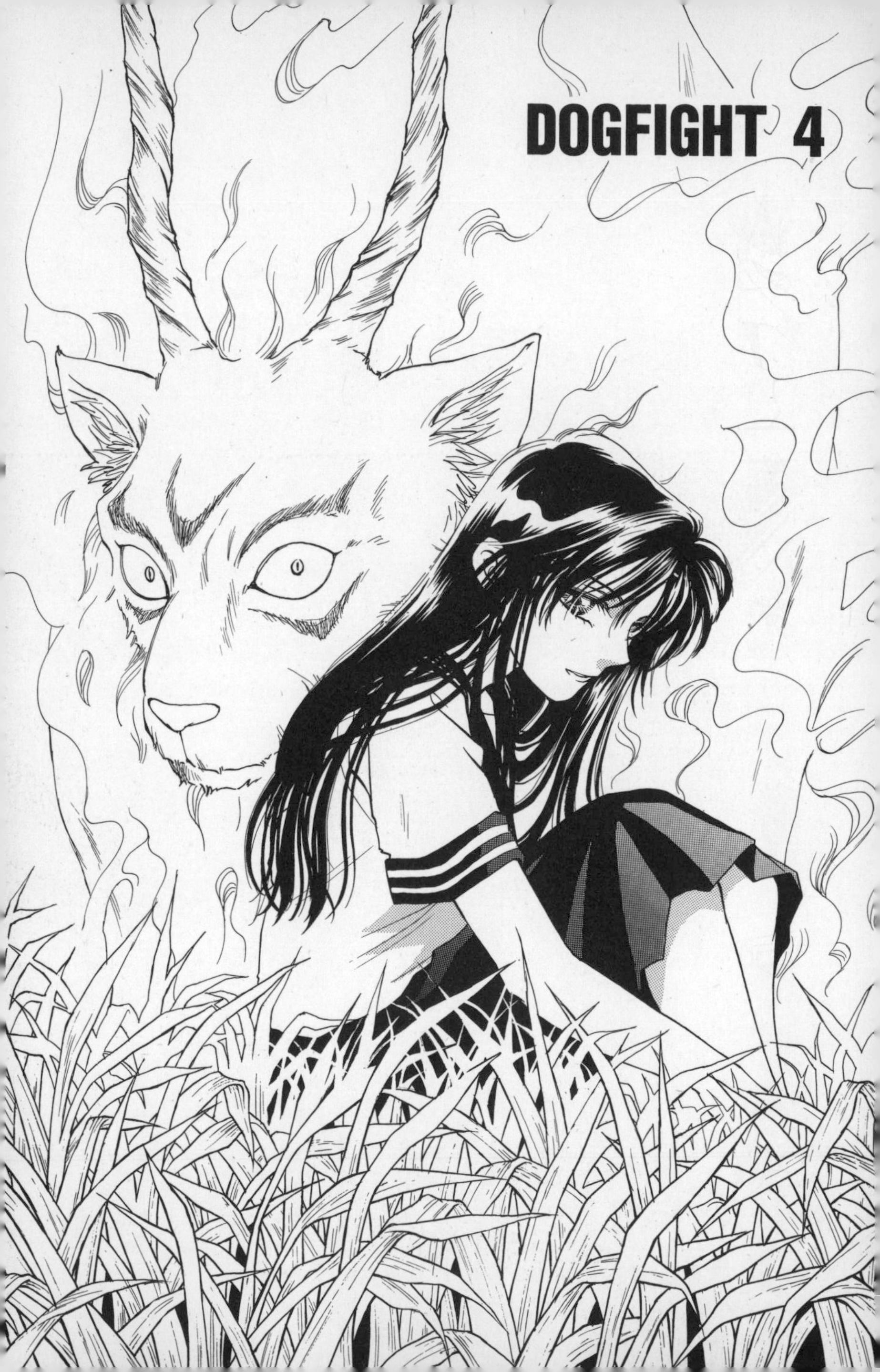
DOGFIGHT 4

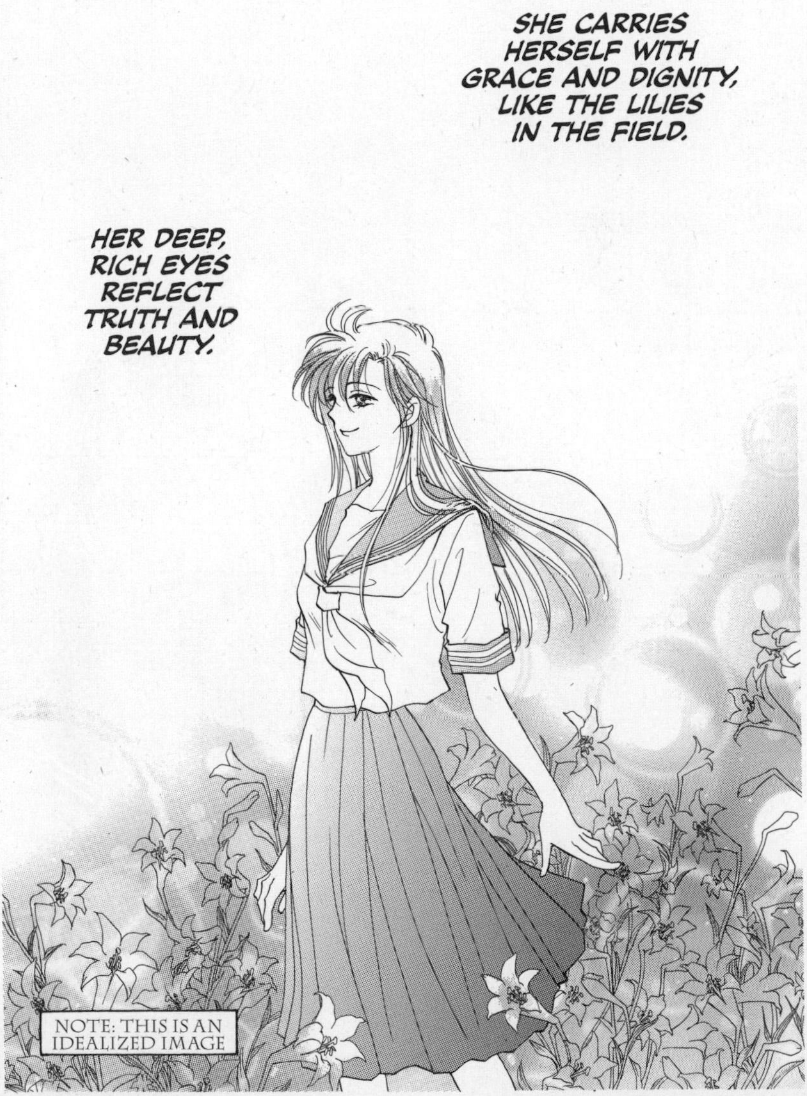
SHE CARRIES HERSELF WITH GRACE AND DIGNITY, LIKE THE LILIES IN THE FIELD.
HER DEEP, RICH EYES REFLECT TRUTH AND BEAUTY.
NOTE: THIS IS AN IDEALIZED IMAGE

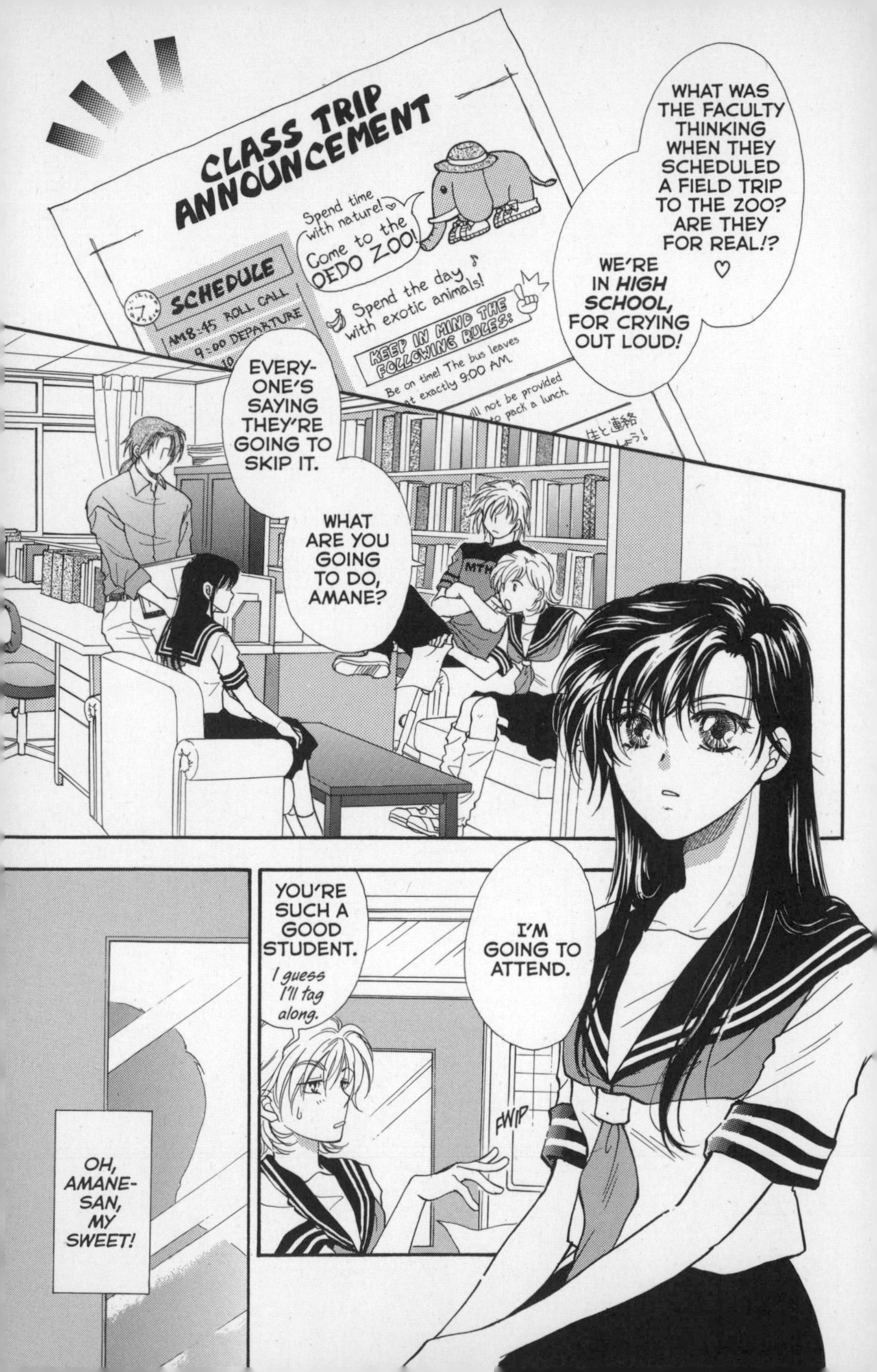
CLASS TRIP ANNOUNCEMENT
Spend time with nature! ♡
Come to the OEDO ZOO!
SCHEDULE
AM8:45 ROLL CALL
9:00 DEPARTURE
Spend the day with exotic animals! ♪
KEEP IN MIND THE FOLLOWING RULES:
Be on time! The bus leaves
WHAT WAS THE FACULTY THINKING WHEN THEY SCHEDULED A FIELD TRIP TO THE ZOO? ARE THEY FOR REAL!? ♡
WE'RE IN *HIGH SCHOOL,* FOR CRYING OUT LOUD!
EVERYONE'S SAYING THEY'RE GOING TO SKIP IT.
WHAT ARE YOU GOING TO DO, AMANE?
I'M GOING TO ATTEND.
FWIP
YOU'RE SUCH A GOOD STUDENT.
I guess I'll tag along.
OH, AMANE-SAN, MY SWEET!

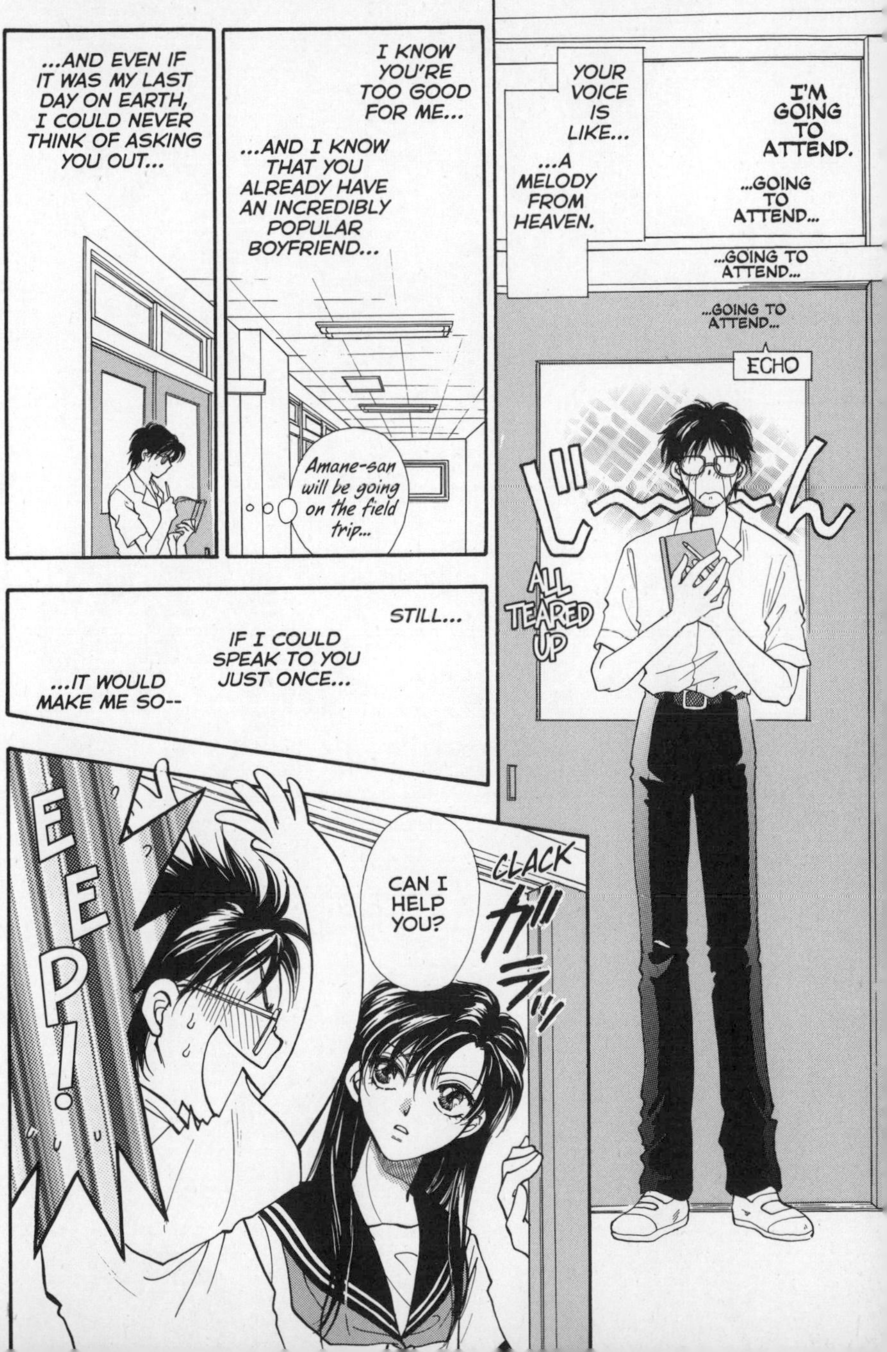
I'M GOING TO ATTEND.
...GOING TO ATTEND...
...GOING TO ATTEND...
...GOING TO ATTEND...
ECHO
YOUR VOICE IS LIKE...
...A MELODY FROM HEAVEN.
じ〜〜ん
ALL TEARED UP
I KNOW YOU'RE TOO GOOD FOR ME...
...AND I KNOW THAT YOU ALREADY HAVE AN INCREDIBLY POPULAR BOYFRIEND...
Amane-san will be going on the field trip...
...AND EVEN IF IT WAS MY LAST DAY ON EARTH, I COULD NEVER THINK OF ASKING YOU OUT...
STILL...
IF I COULD SPEAK TO YOU JUST ONCE...
...IT WOULD MAKE ME SO--
CLACK
ガラッ
CAN I HELP YOU?
EEP!

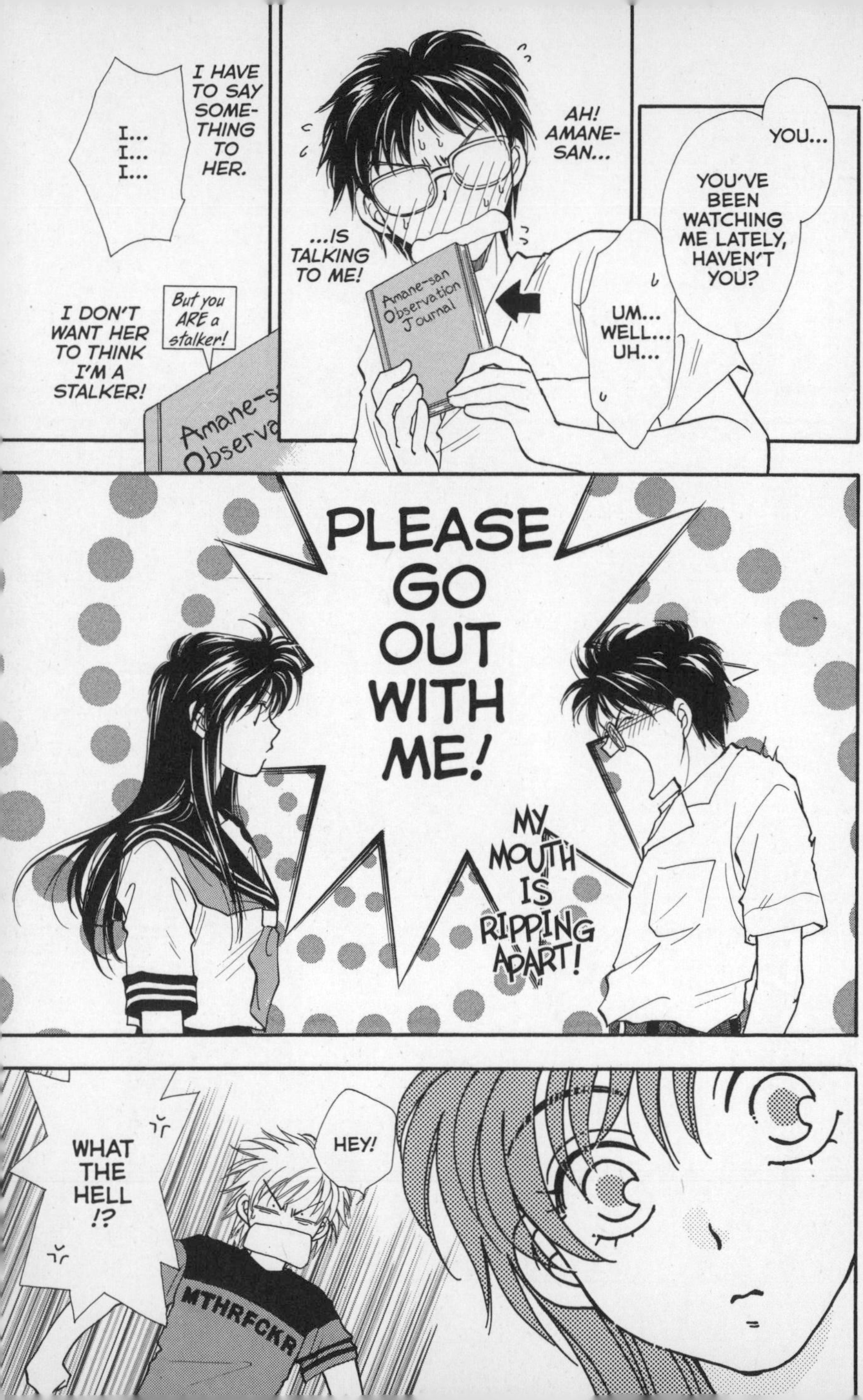
YOU...
YOU'VE BEEN WATCHING ME LATELY, HAVEN'T YOU?
UM... WELL... UH...
AH! AMANE-SAN...
...IS TALKING TO ME!
Amane-san Observation Journal
I HAVE TO SAY SOME-THING TO HER.
I... I... I...
I DON'T WANT HER TO THINK I'M A STALKER!
But you ARE a stalker!
PLEASE GO OUT WITH ME!
MY MOUTH IS RIPPING APART!
HEY!
WHAT THE HELL !?
MTHRFCKR

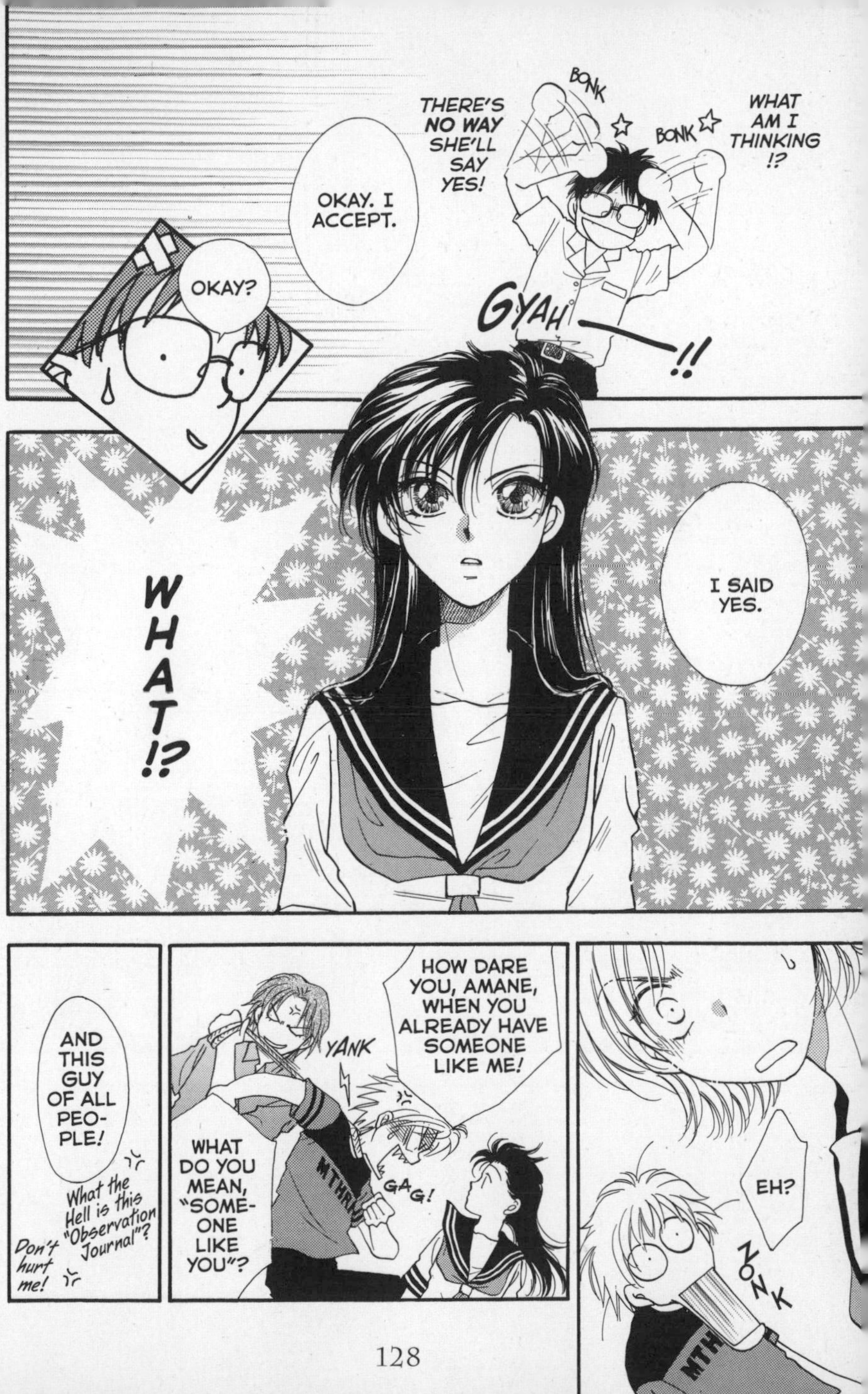
WHAT AM I THINKING !?
BONK
BONK
THERE'S NO WAY SHE'LL SAY YES!
OKAY. I ACCEPT.
GYAH—!!
OKAY?
I SAID YES.
WHAT!?
EH?
ZONK
HOW DARE YOU, AMANE, WHEN YOU ALREADY HAVE SOMEONE LIKE ME!
YANK
GAG!
WHAT DO YOU MEAN, "SOME-ONE LIKE YOU"?
AND THIS GUY OF ALL PEO-PLE!
What the Hell is this "Observation Journal"?
Don't hurt me!

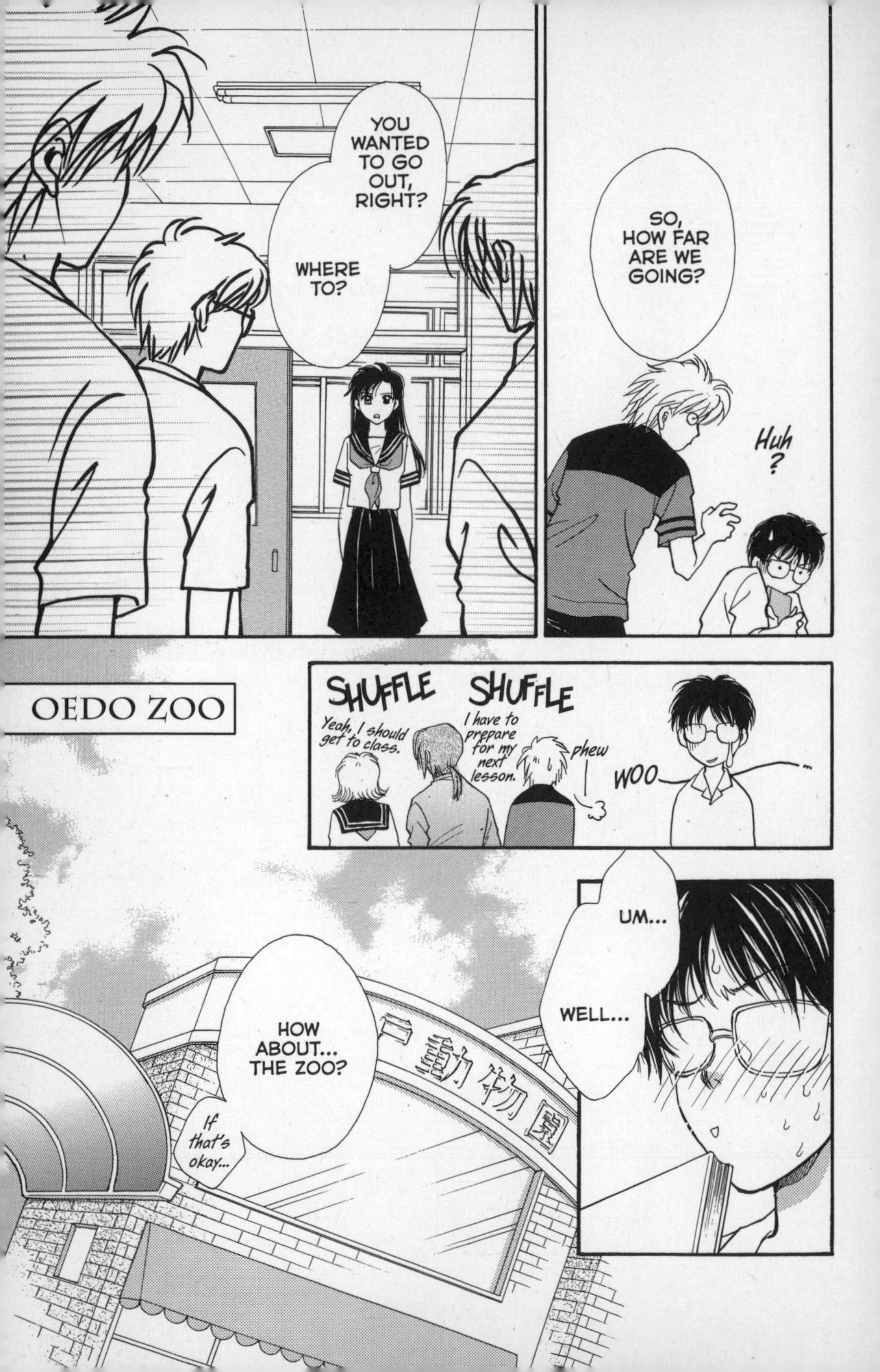
SO, HOW FAR ARE WE GOING?
Huh?
YOU WANTED TO GO OUT, RIGHT?
WHERE TO?
WOO...
phew
I have to prepare for my next lesson.
SHUFFLE SHUFFLE
Yeah, I should get to class.
UM...
WELL...
HOW ABOUT... THE ZOO?
If that's okay...
OEDO ZOO

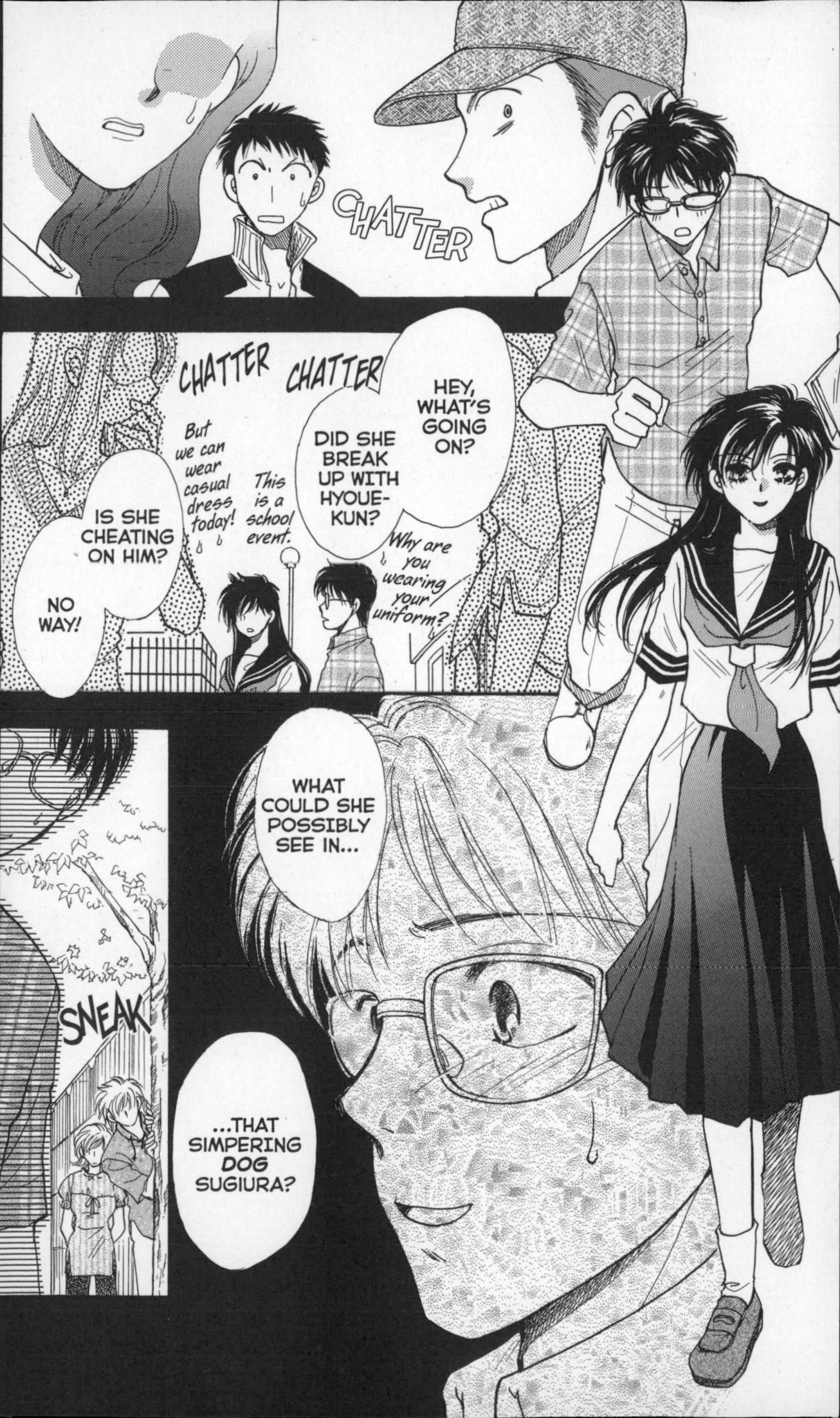
CHATTER
HEY, WHAT'S GOING ON?
CHATTER
DID SHE BREAK UP WITH HYOUE-KUN?
Why are you wearing your uniform?
This is a school event.
But we can wear casual dress today!
CHATTER
IS SHE CHEATING ON HIM?
NO WAY!
WHAT COULD SHE POSSIBLY SEE IN...
...THAT SIMPERING *DOG* SUGIURA?
SNEAK

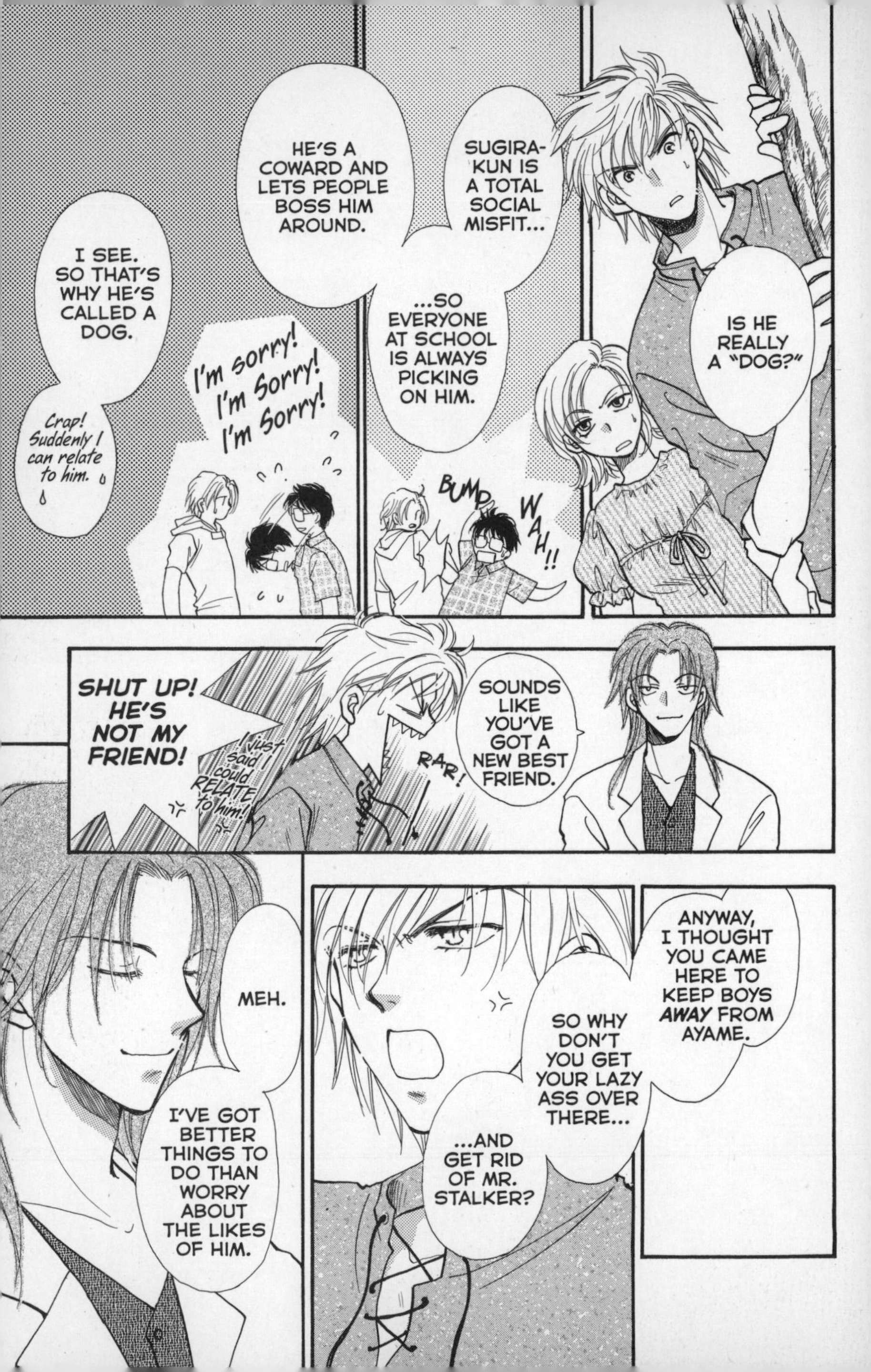
IS HE REALLY A "DOG?"
SUGIRA-KUN IS A TOTAL SOCIAL MISFIT...
HE'S A COWARD AND LETS PEOPLE BOSS HIM AROUND.
...SO EVERYONE AT SCHOOL IS ALWAYS PICKING ON HIM.
BUMP
WAH!!
I SEE. SO THAT'S WHY HE'S CALLED A DOG.
I'm sorry! I'm Sorry! I'm Sorry!
Crap! Suddenly I can relate to him.
SOUNDS LIKE YOU'VE GOT A NEW BEST FRIEND.
RAR!
SHUT UP! HE'S NOT MY FRIEND!
I just said I could RELATE to him!
ANYWAY, I THOUGHT YOU CAME HERE TO KEEP BOYS *AWAY* FROM AYAME.
SO WHY DON'T YOU GET YOUR LAZY ASS OVER THERE...
...AND GET RID OF MR. STALKER?
MEH.
I'VE GOT BETTER THINGS TO DO THAN WORRY ABOUT THE LIKES OF HIM.

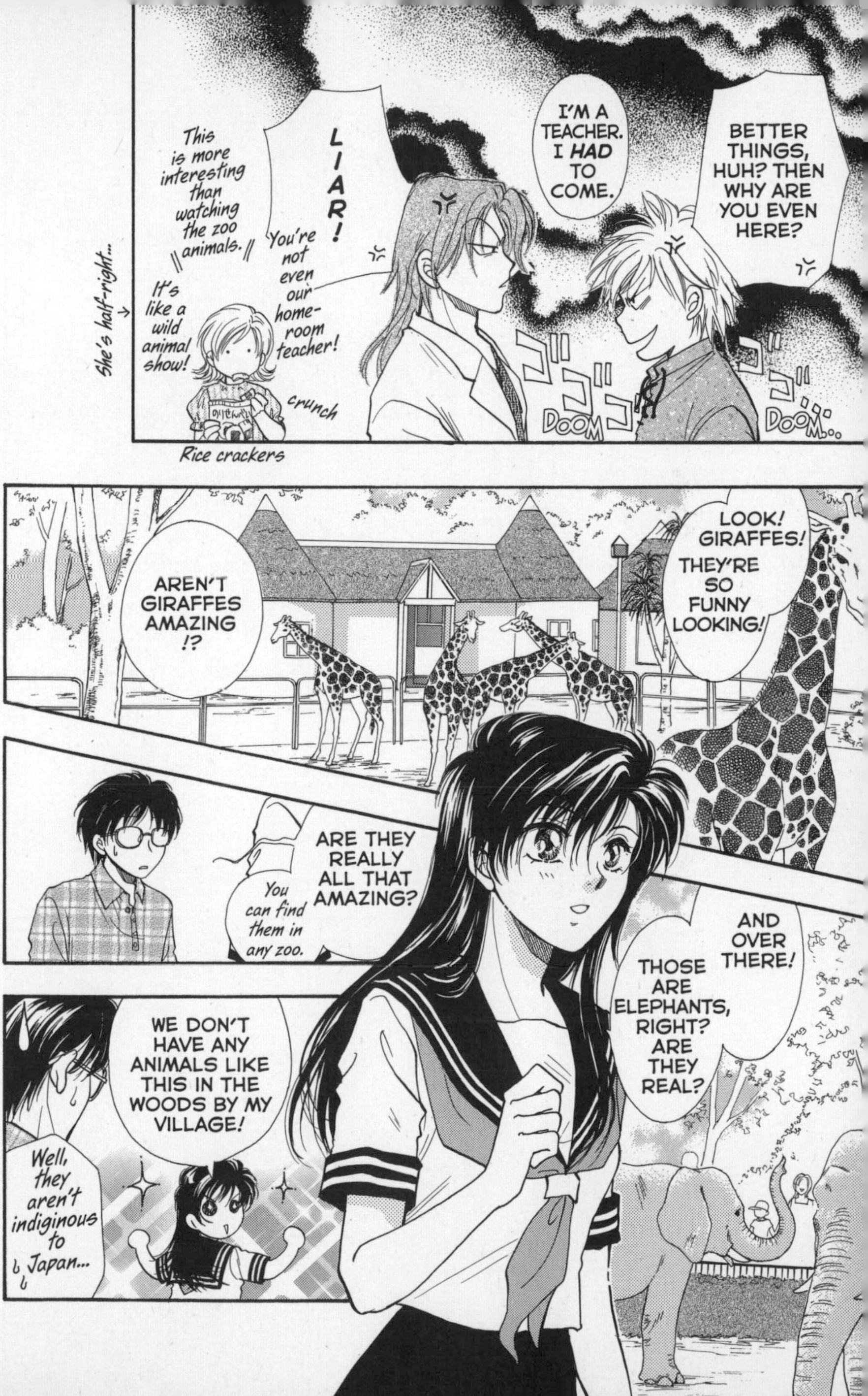
BETTER THINGS, HUH? THEN WHY ARE YOU EVEN HERE?
I'M A TEACHER. I *HAD* TO COME.
LIAR!
You're not even our home-room teacher!
This is more interesting than watching the zoo animals.
It's like a wild animal show!
crunch
Rice crackers
She's half-right...
DOOM
DOOM...
LOOK! GIRAFFES!
THEY'RE SO FUNNY LOOKING!
AREN'T GIRAFFES AMAZING!?
AND OVER THERE!
THOSE ARE ELEPHANTS, RIGHT? ARE THEY REAL?
ARE THEY REALLY ALL THAT AMAZING?
You can find them in any zoo.
WE DON'T HAVE ANY ANIMALS LIKE THIS IN THE WOODS BY MY VILLAGE!
Well, they aren't indiginous to Japan...

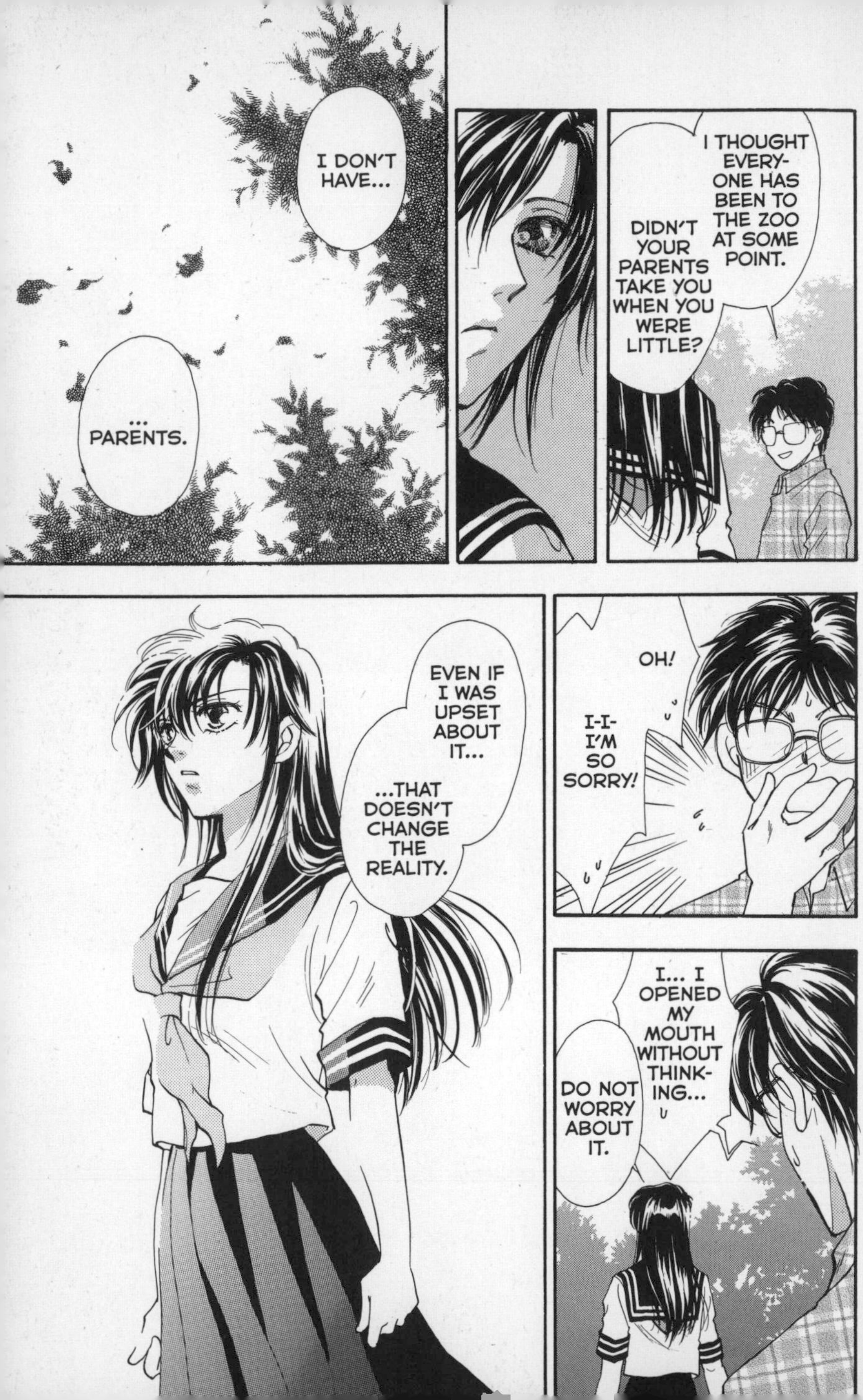
I THOUGHT EVERY-ONE HAS BEEN TO THE ZOO AT SOME POINT.
DIDN'T YOUR PARENTS TAKE YOU WHEN YOU WERE LITTLE?
I DON'T HAVE...
... PARENTS.
OH!
I-I-I'M SO SORRY!
I... I OPENED MY MOUTH WITHOUT THINKING...
DO NOT WORRY ABOUT IT.
EVEN IF I WAS UPSET ABOUT IT...
...THAT DOESN'T CHANGE THE REALITY.

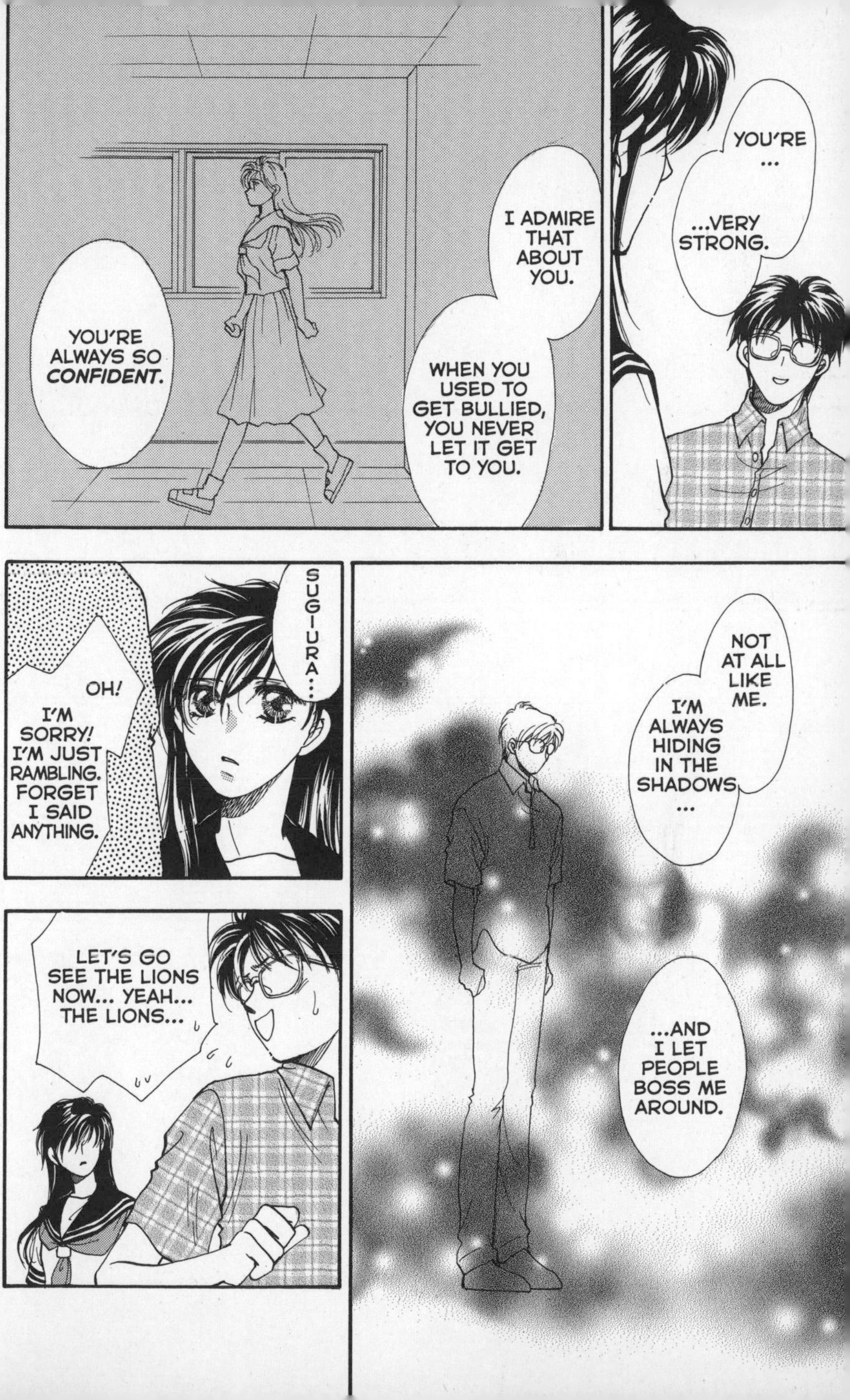
YOU'RE ...
...VERY STRONG.
I ADMIRE THAT ABOUT YOU.
WHEN YOU USED TO GET BULLIED, YOU NEVER LET IT GET TO YOU.
YOU'RE ALWAYS SO *CONFIDENT*.
NOT AT ALL LIKE ME.
I'M ALWAYS HIDING IN THE SHADOWS ...
...AND I LET PEOPLE BOSS ME AROUND.
SUGIURA...
OH!
I'M SORRY! I'M JUST RAMBLING. FORGET I SAID ANYTHING.
LET'S GO SEE THE LIONS NOW... YEAH... THE LIONS...

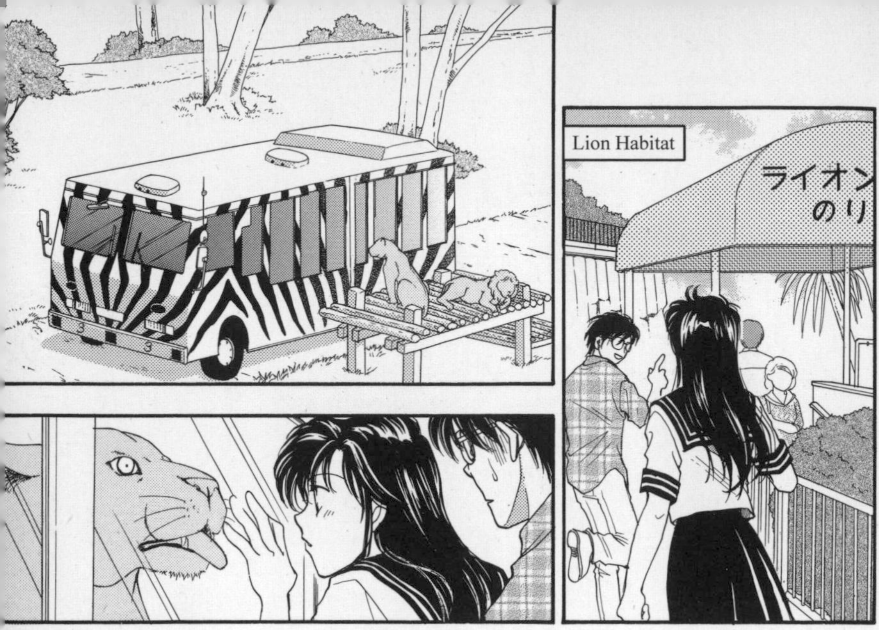
Lion Habitat
ライオン
のり

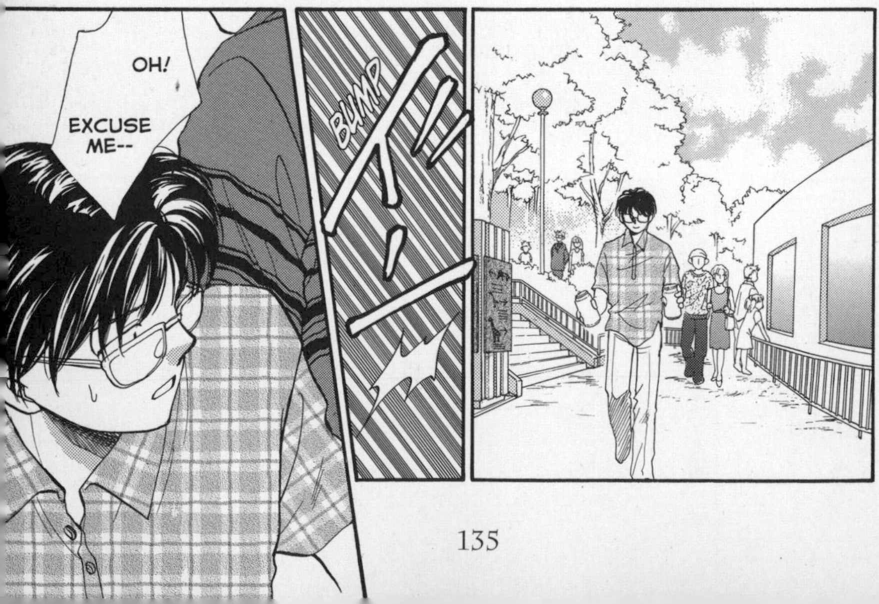
BUMP
OH!
EXCUSE ME--

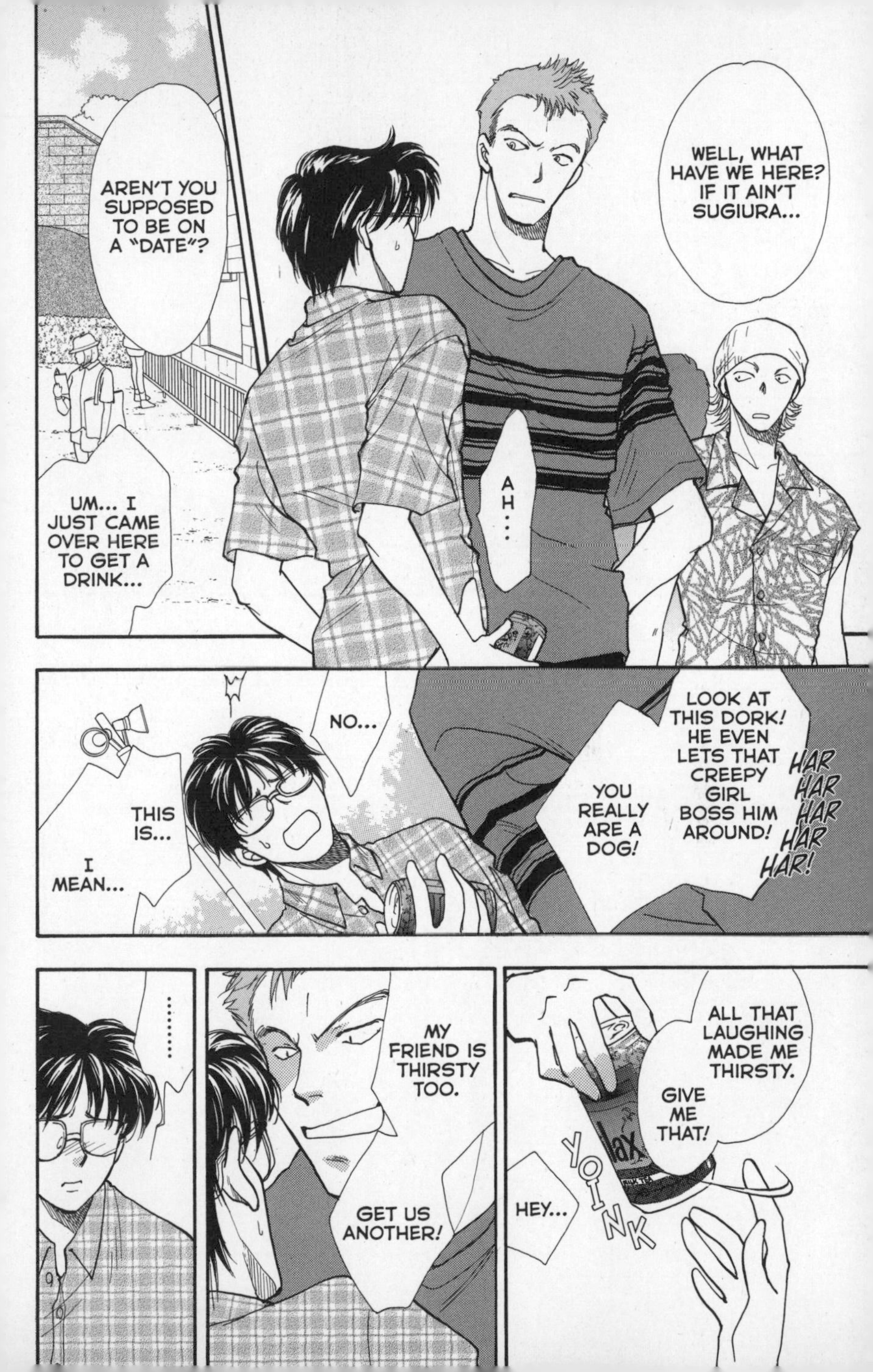
WELL, WHAT HAVE WE HERE? IF IT AIN'T SUGIURA...
AREN'T YOU SUPPOSED TO BE ON A "DATE"?
AH...
UM... I JUST CAME OVER HERE TO GET A DRINK...
LOOK AT THIS DORK! HE EVEN LETS THAT CREEPY GIRL BOSS HIM AROUND!
HAR HAR HAR HAR HAR!
YOU REALLY ARE A DOG!
NO...
THIS IS...
I MEAN...
ALL THAT LAUGHING MADE ME THIRSTY.
GIVE ME THAT!
YOINK
HEY...
MY FRIEND IS THIRSTY TOO.
GET US ANOTHER!
......

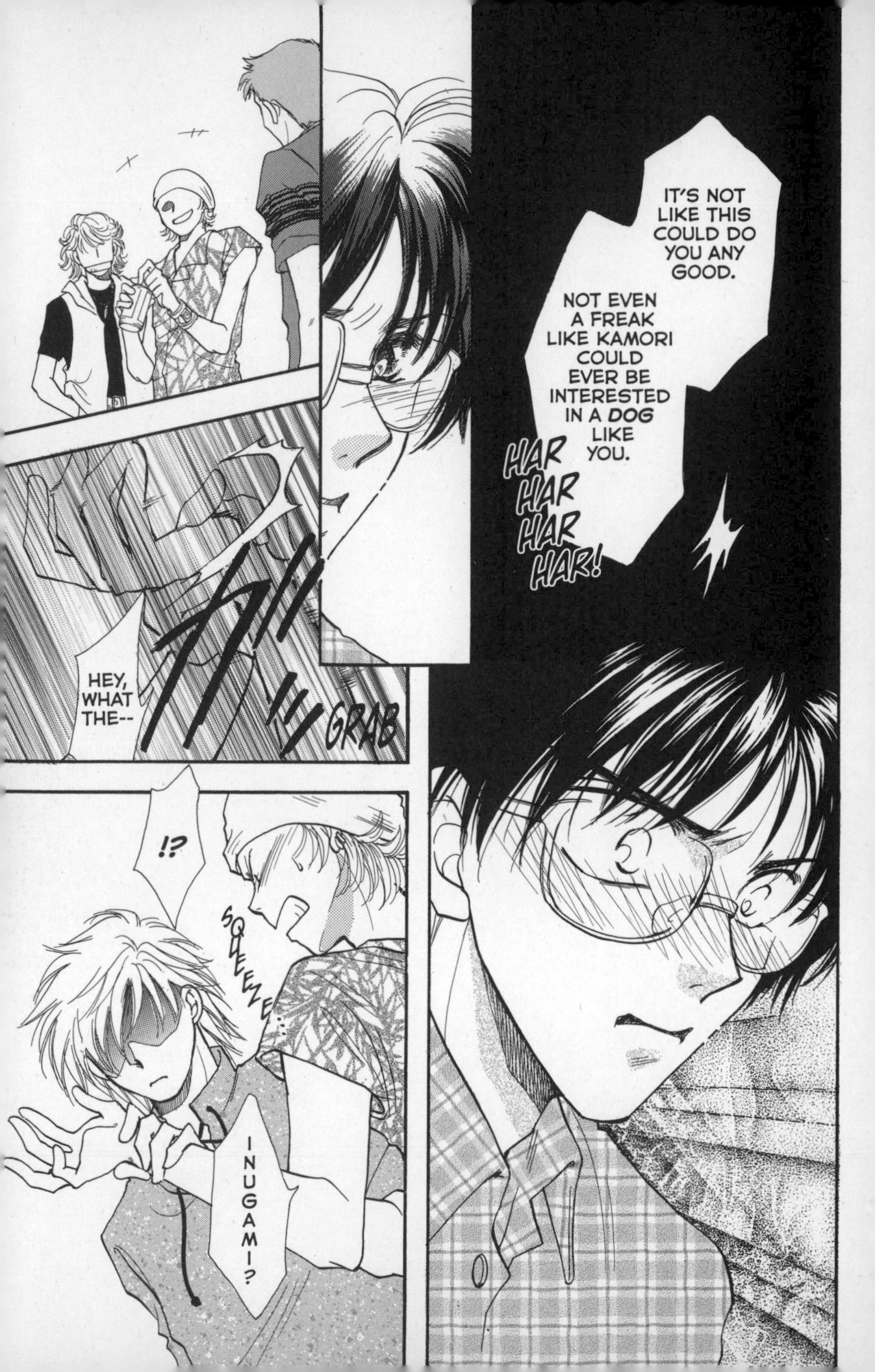
IT'S NOT LIKE THIS COULD DO YOU ANY GOOD.
NOT EVEN A FREAK LIKE KAMORI COULD EVER BE INTERESTED IN A *DOG* LIKE YOU.
HAR HAR HAR HAR!
HEY, WHAT THE--
GRAB
!?
SQUEEZE...
INUGAMI!?

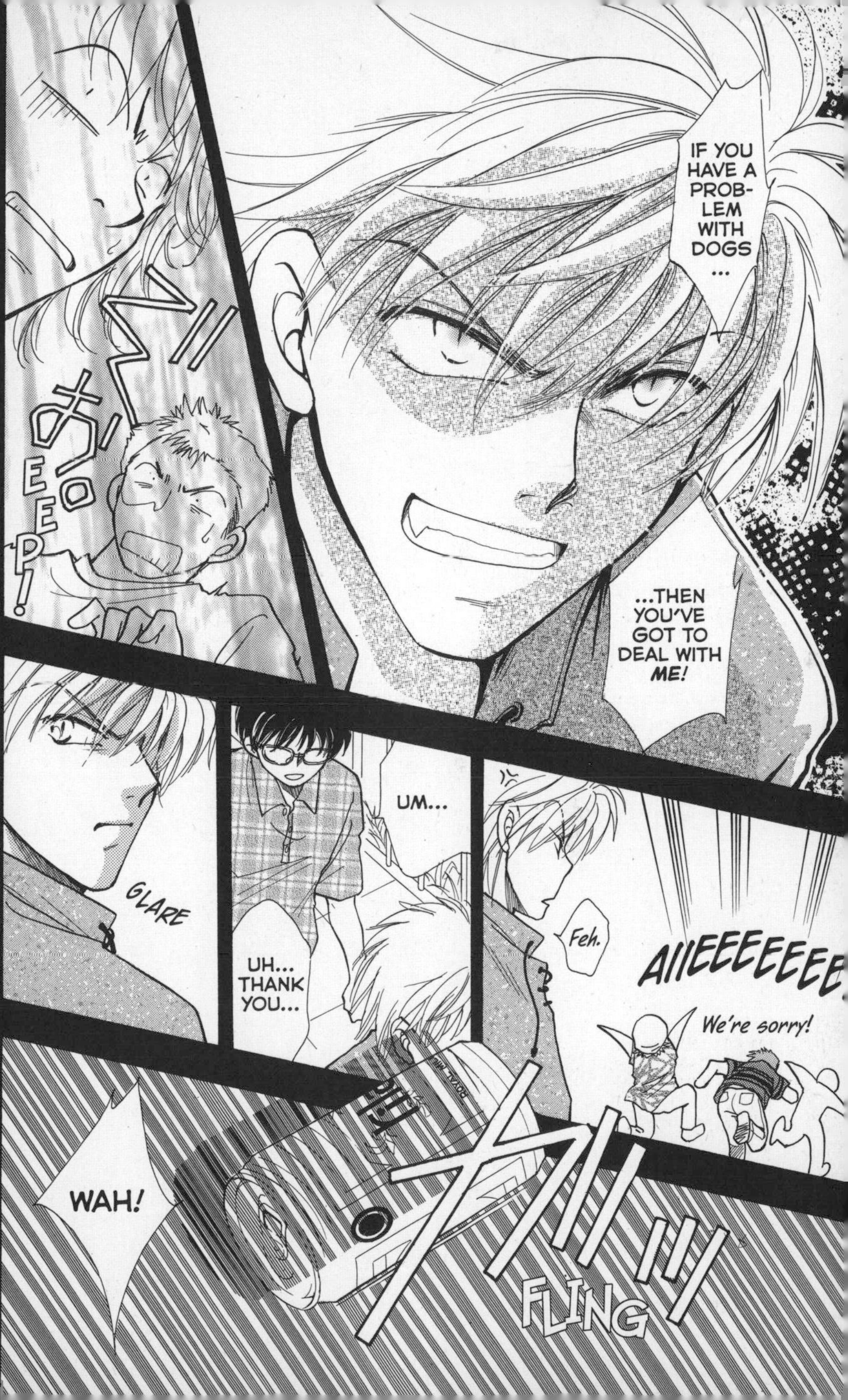
IF YOU HAVE A PROB-LEM WITH DOGS...
...THEN YOU'VE GOT TO DEAL WITH *ME!*
EEP!
Feh.
AIIEEEEEEEE
We're sorry!
UM...
UH... THANK YOU...
GLARE
WAH!
FLING

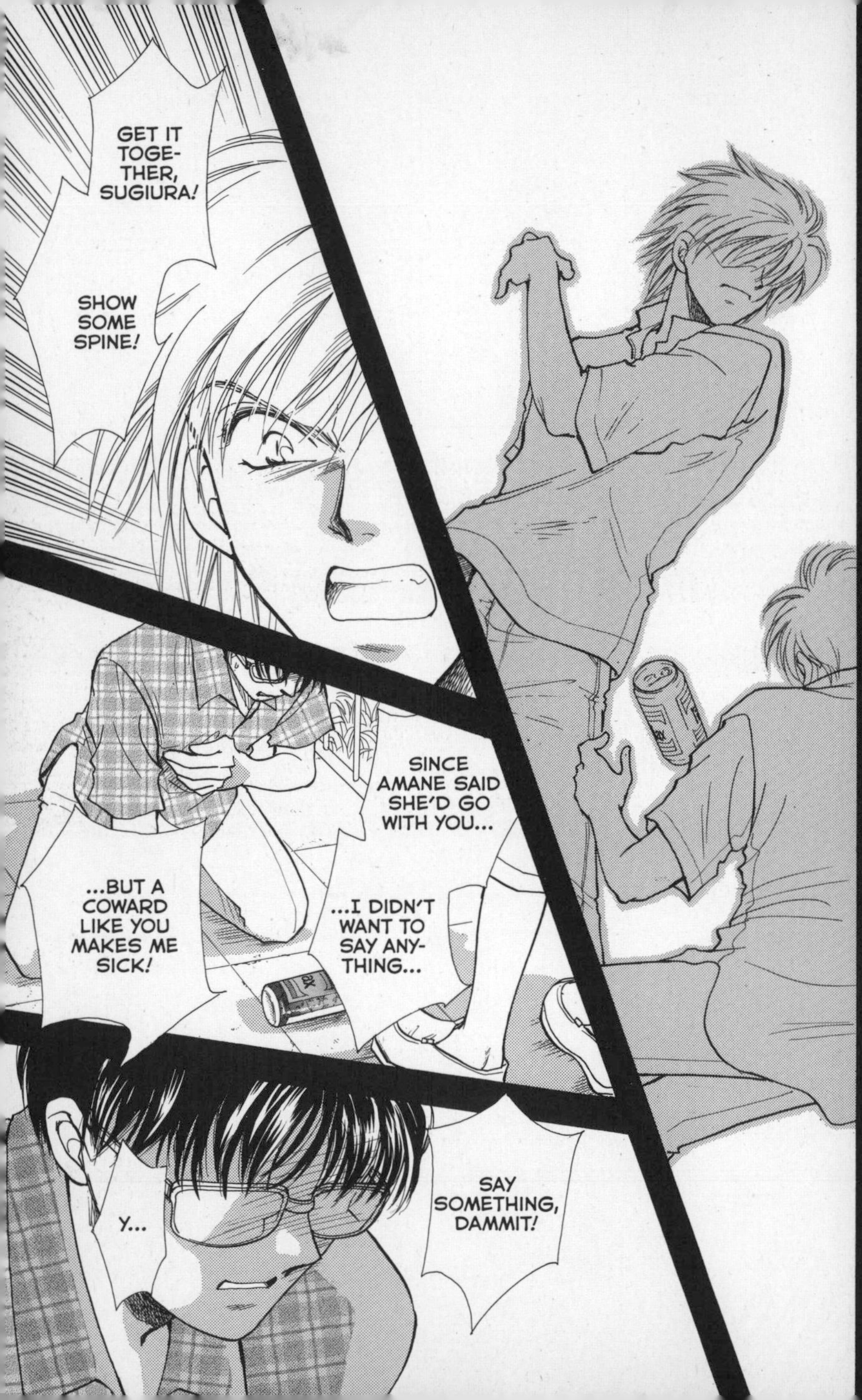
GET IT TOGE- THER, SUGIURA!
SHOW SOME SPINE!
SINCE AMANE SAID SHE'D GO WITH YOU...
...I DIDN'T WANT TO SAY ANY- THING...
...BUT A COWARD LIKE YOU MAKES ME SICK!
SAY SOMETHING, DAMMIT!
Y...

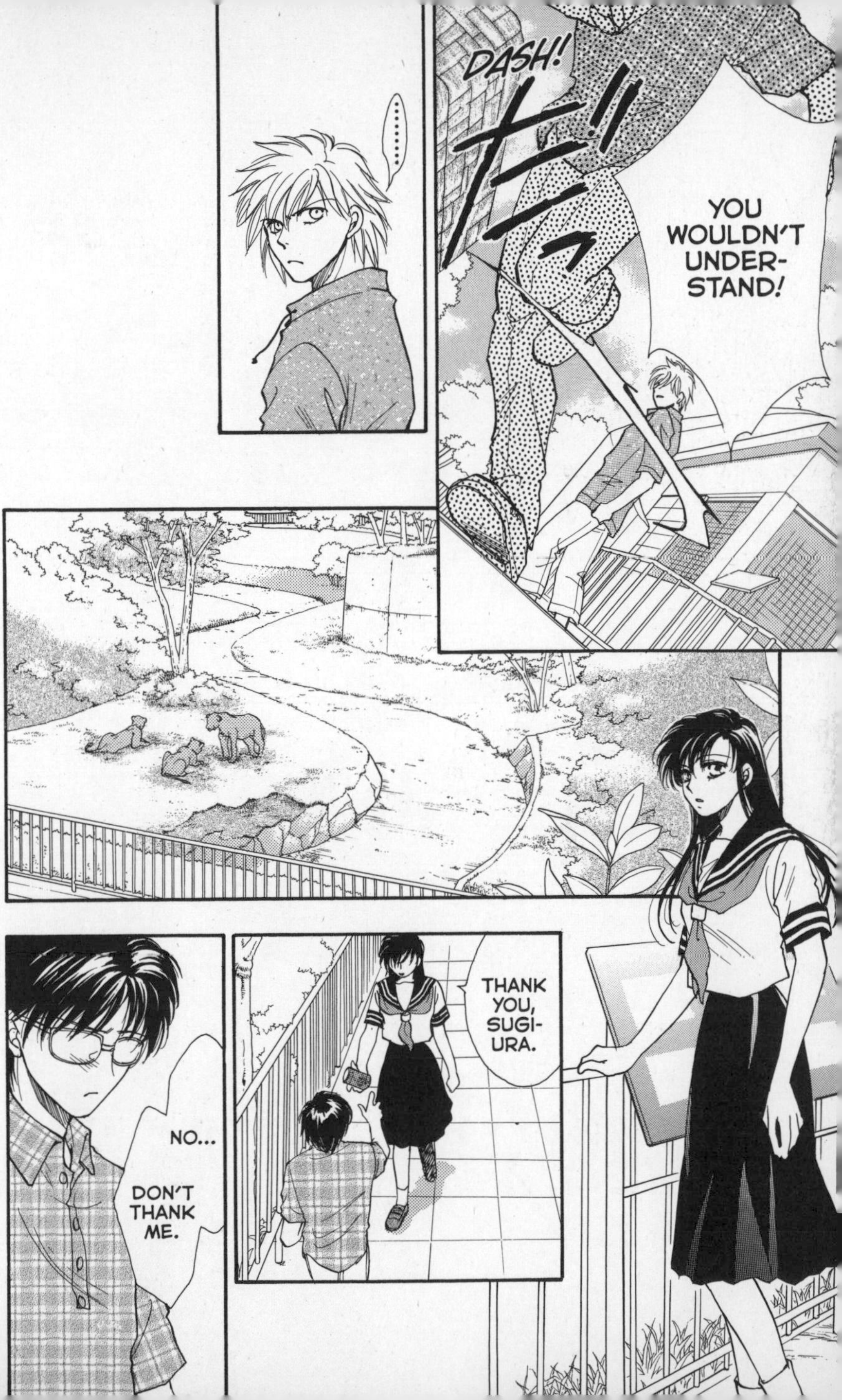
DASH!
YOU WOULDN'T UNDER-STAND!
......
THANK YOU, SUGI-URA.
NO...
DON'T THANK ME.

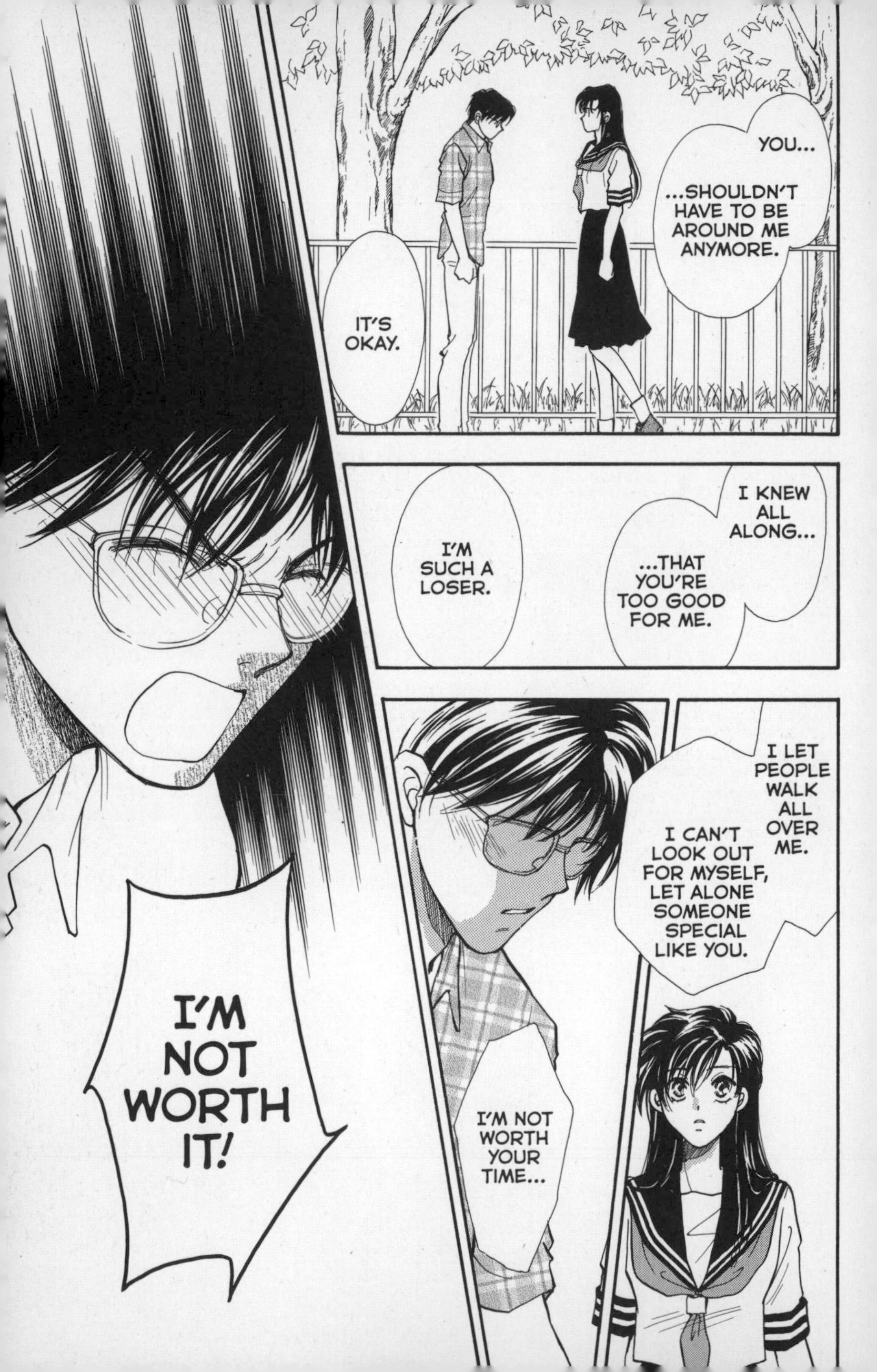
YOU...
...SHOULDN'T HAVE TO BE AROUND ME ANYMORE.
IT'S OKAY.
I KNEW ALL ALONG...
...THAT YOU'RE TOO GOOD FOR ME.
I'M SUCH A LOSER.
I LET PEOPLE WALK ALL OVER ME.
I CAN'T LOOK OUT FOR MYSELF, LET ALONE SOMEONE SPECIAL LIKE YOU.
I'M NOT WORTH YOUR TIME...
I'M NOT WORTH IT!

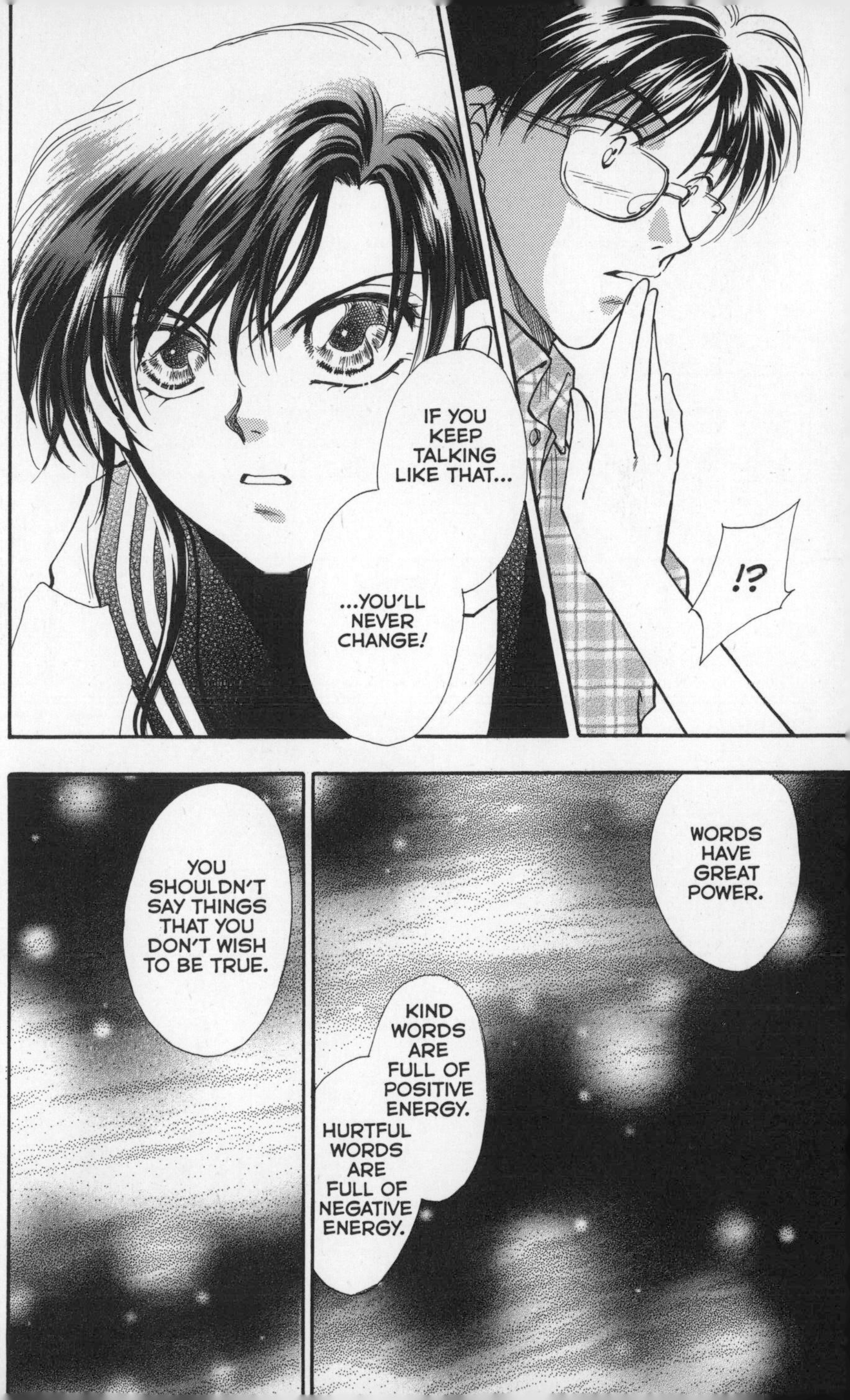
IF YOU KEEP TALKING LIKE THAT...
...YOU'LL NEVER CHANGE!
!?
WORDS HAVE GREAT POWER.
KIND WORDS ARE FULL OF POSITIVE ENERGY.
HURTFUL WORDS ARE FULL OF NEGATIVE ENERGY.
YOU SHOULDN'T SAY THINGS THAT YOU DON'T WISH TO BE TRUE.

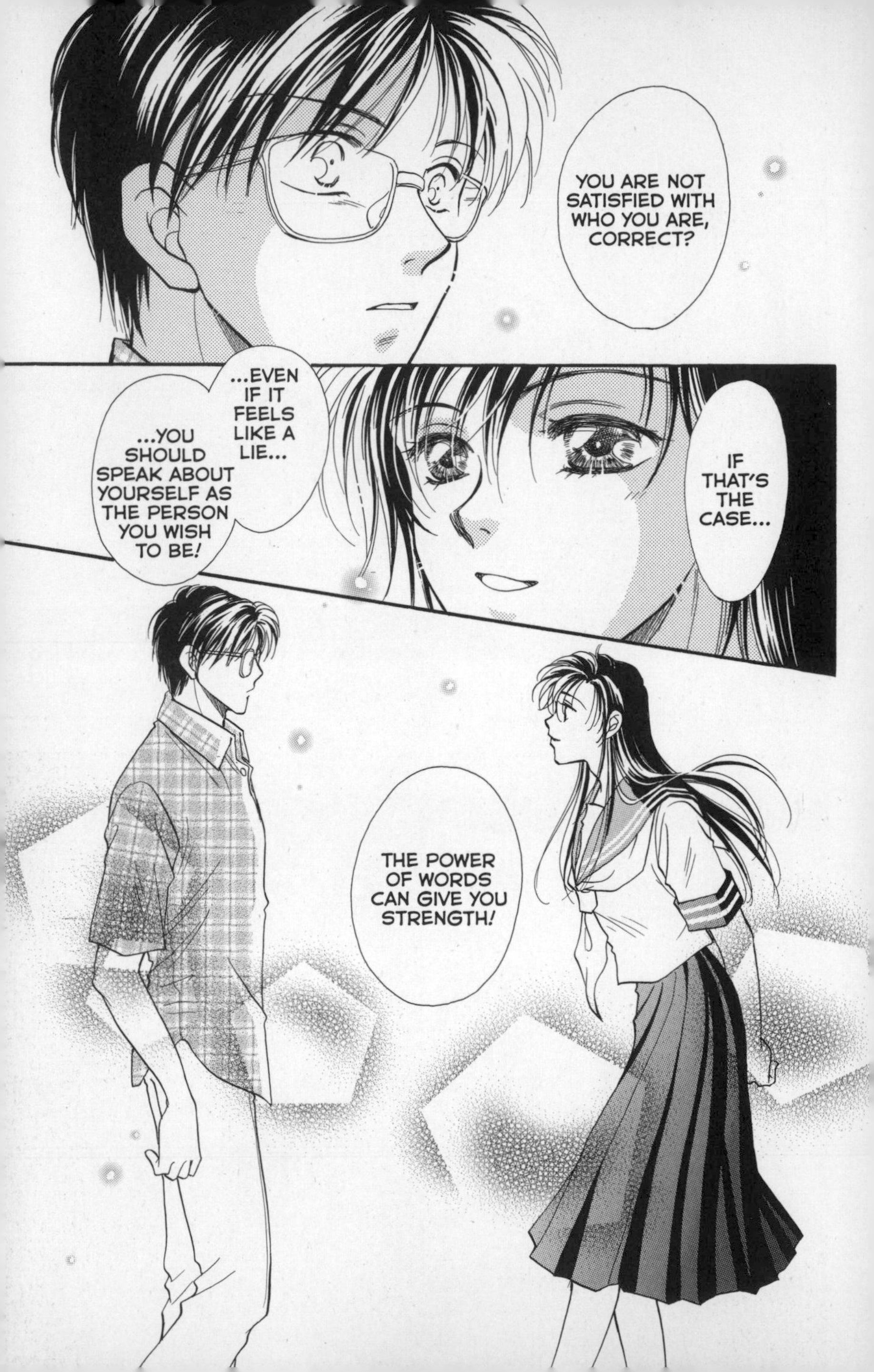
YOU ARE NOT SATISFIED WITH WHO YOU ARE, CORRECT?
IF THAT'S THE CASE...
...EVEN IF IT FEELS LIKE A LIE...
...YOU SHOULD SPEAK ABOUT YOURSELF AS THE PERSON YOU WISH TO BE!
THE POWER OF WORDS CAN GIVE YOU STRENGTH!

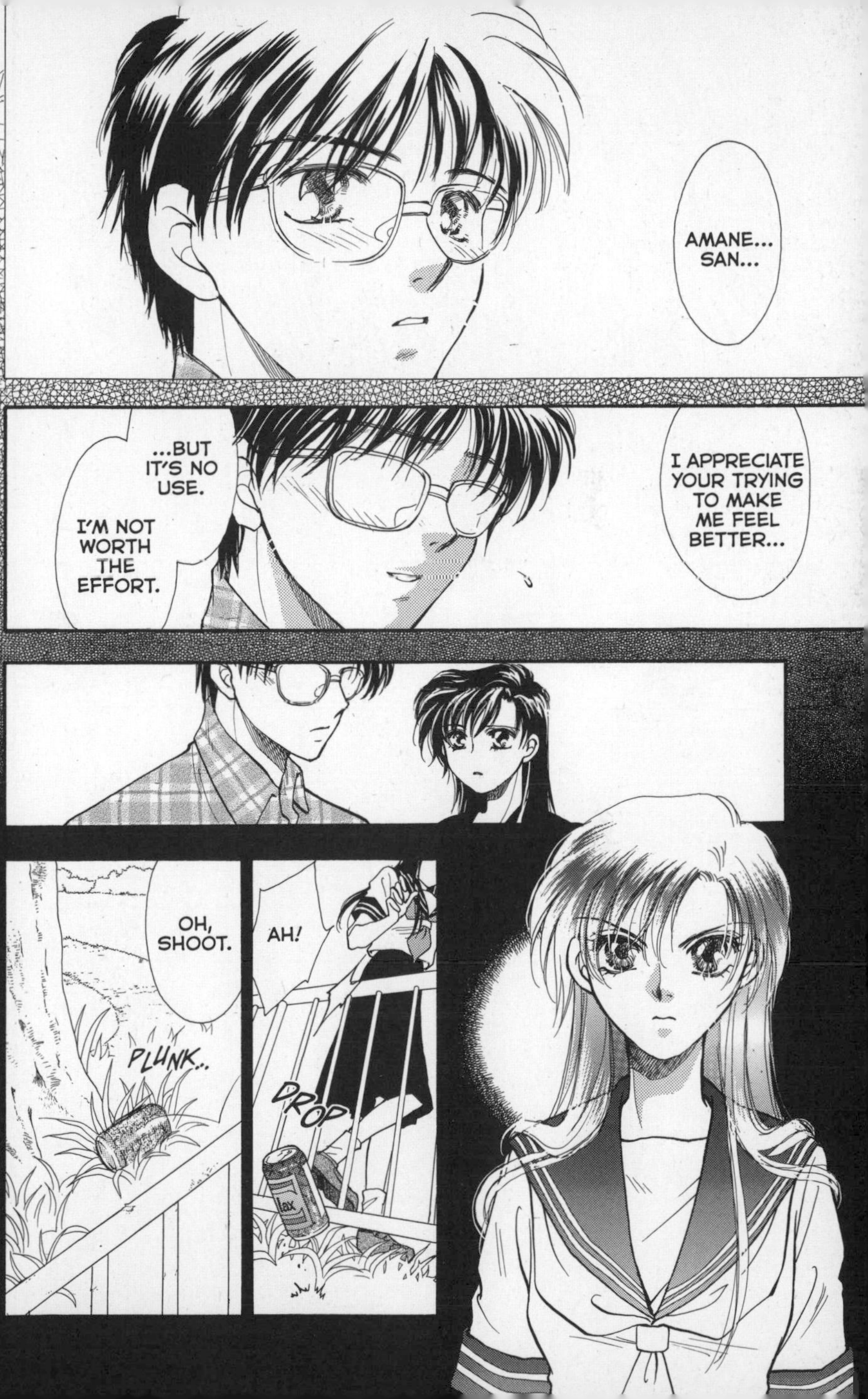
AMANE... SAN...
I APPRECIATE YOUR TRYING TO MAKE ME FEEL BETTER...
...BUT IT'S NO USE.
I'M NOT WORTH THE EFFORT.
AH!
DROP
OH, SHOOT.
PLUNK..

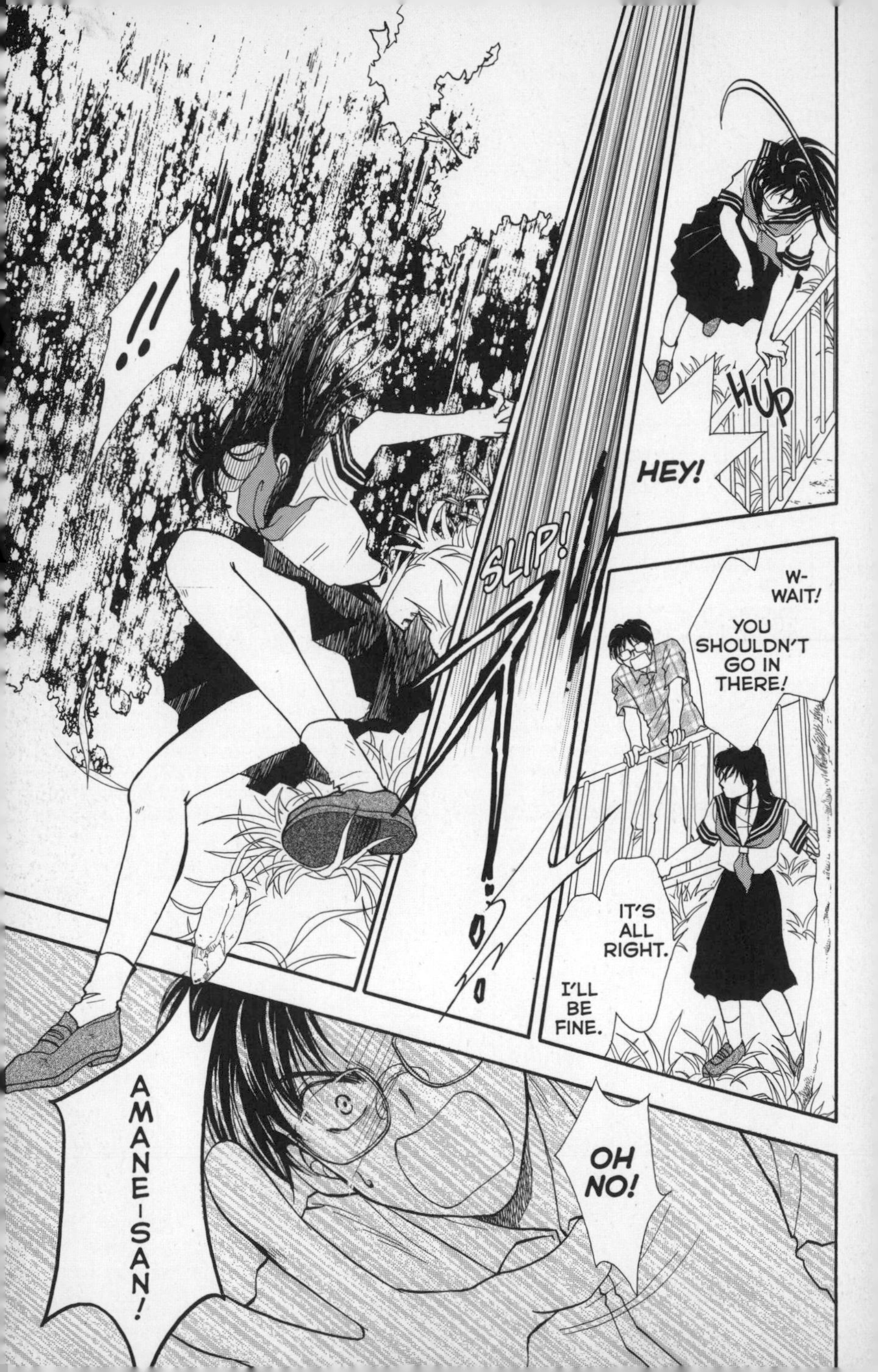
HUP
HEY!
W-WAIT! YOU SHOULDN'T GO IN THERE!
IT'S ALL RIGHT.
I'LL BE FINE.
SLIP!
!!
OH NO!
AMANE-SAN!

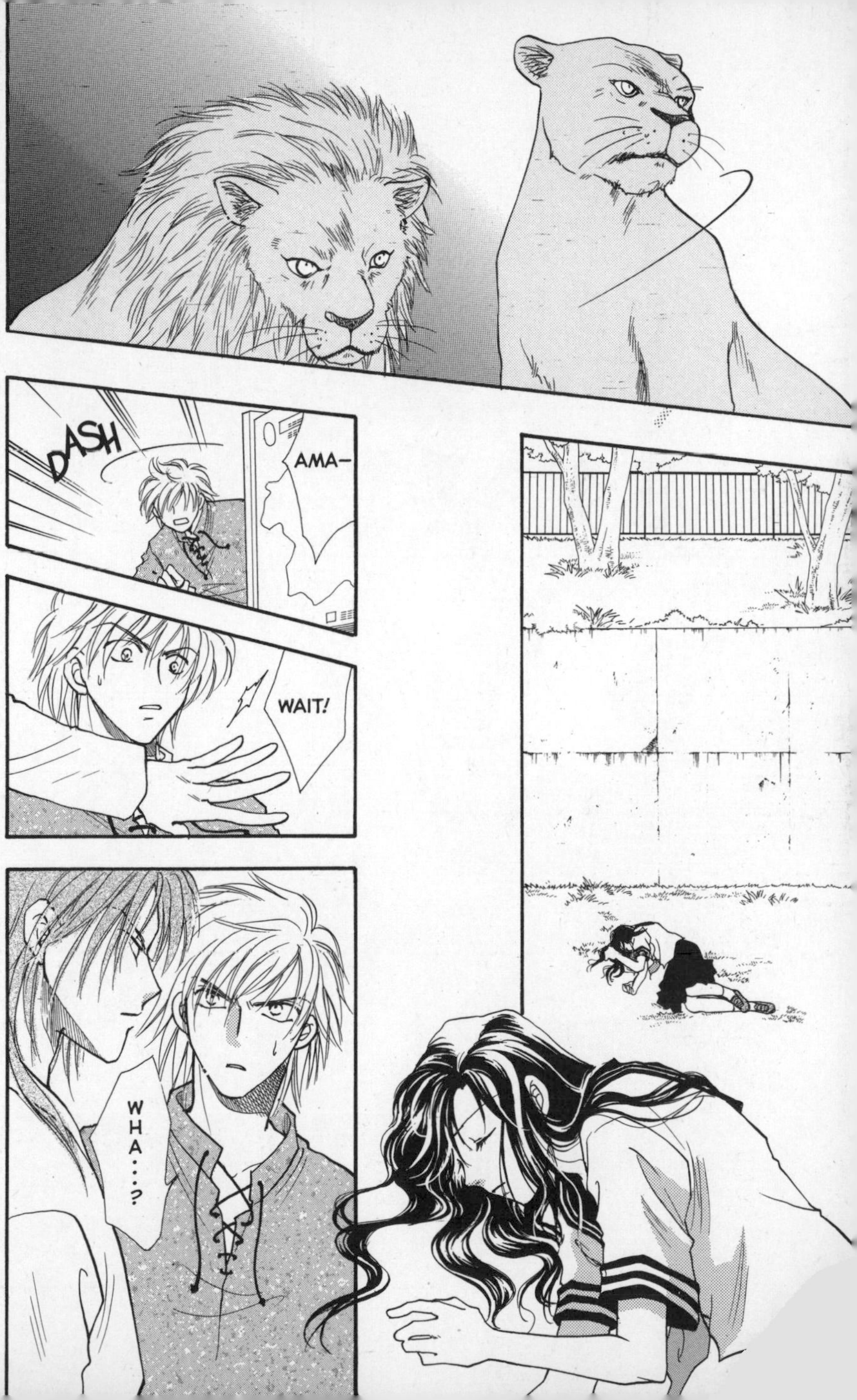
DASH
AMA–
WAIT!
WHA...?

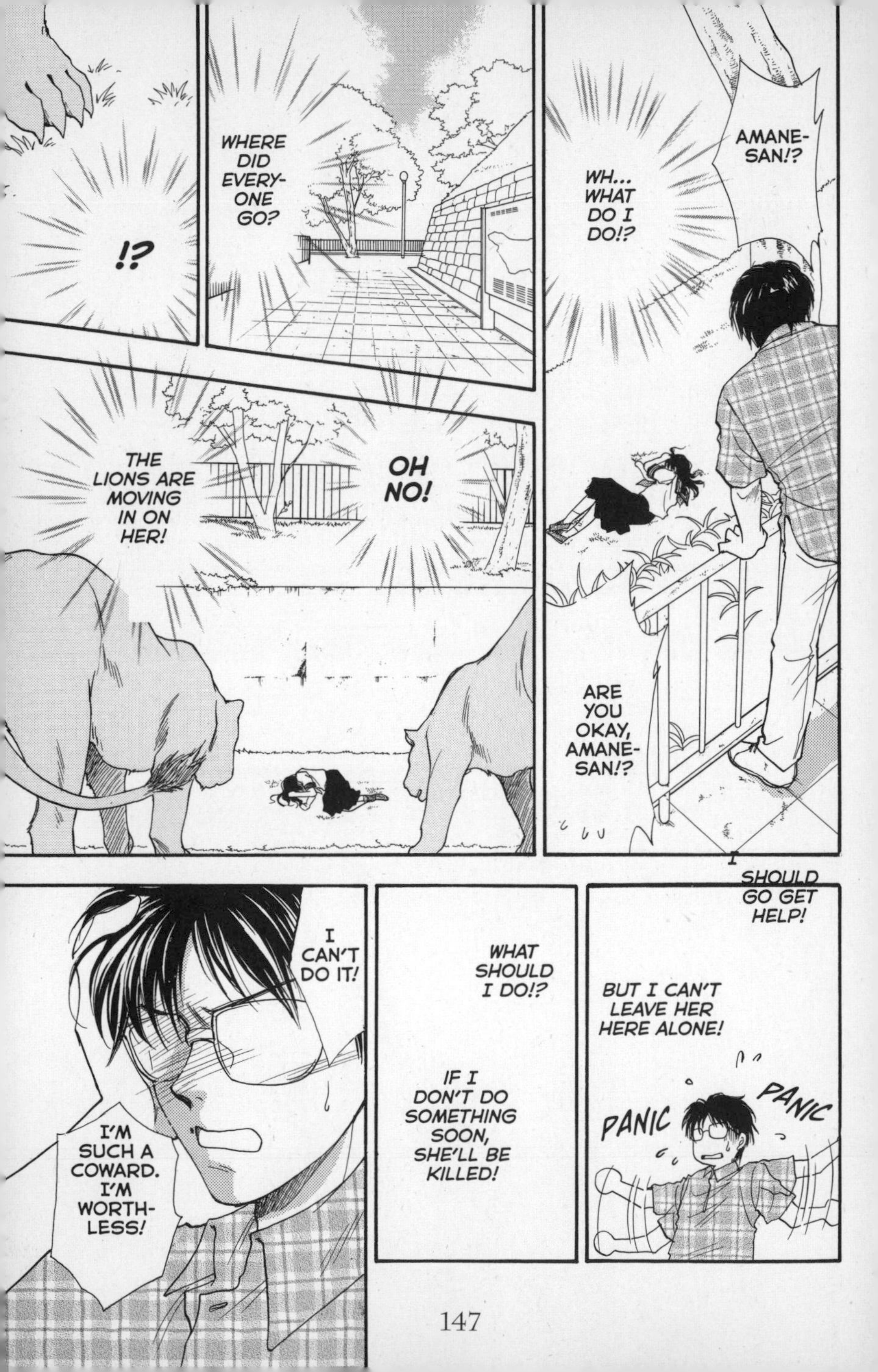
AMANE-SAN!?
WH... WHAT DO I DO!?
ARE YOU OKAY, AMANE-SAN!?
WHERE DID EVERY-ONE GO?
!?
OH NO!
THE LIONS ARE MOVING IN ON HER!
I SHOULD GO GET HELP!
BUT I CAN'T LEAVE HER HERE ALONE!
PANIC
PANIC
WHAT SHOULD I DO!?
IF I DON'T DO SOMETHING SOON, SHE'LL BE KILLED!
I CAN'T DO IT!
I'M SUCH A COWARD. I'M WORTH-LESS!

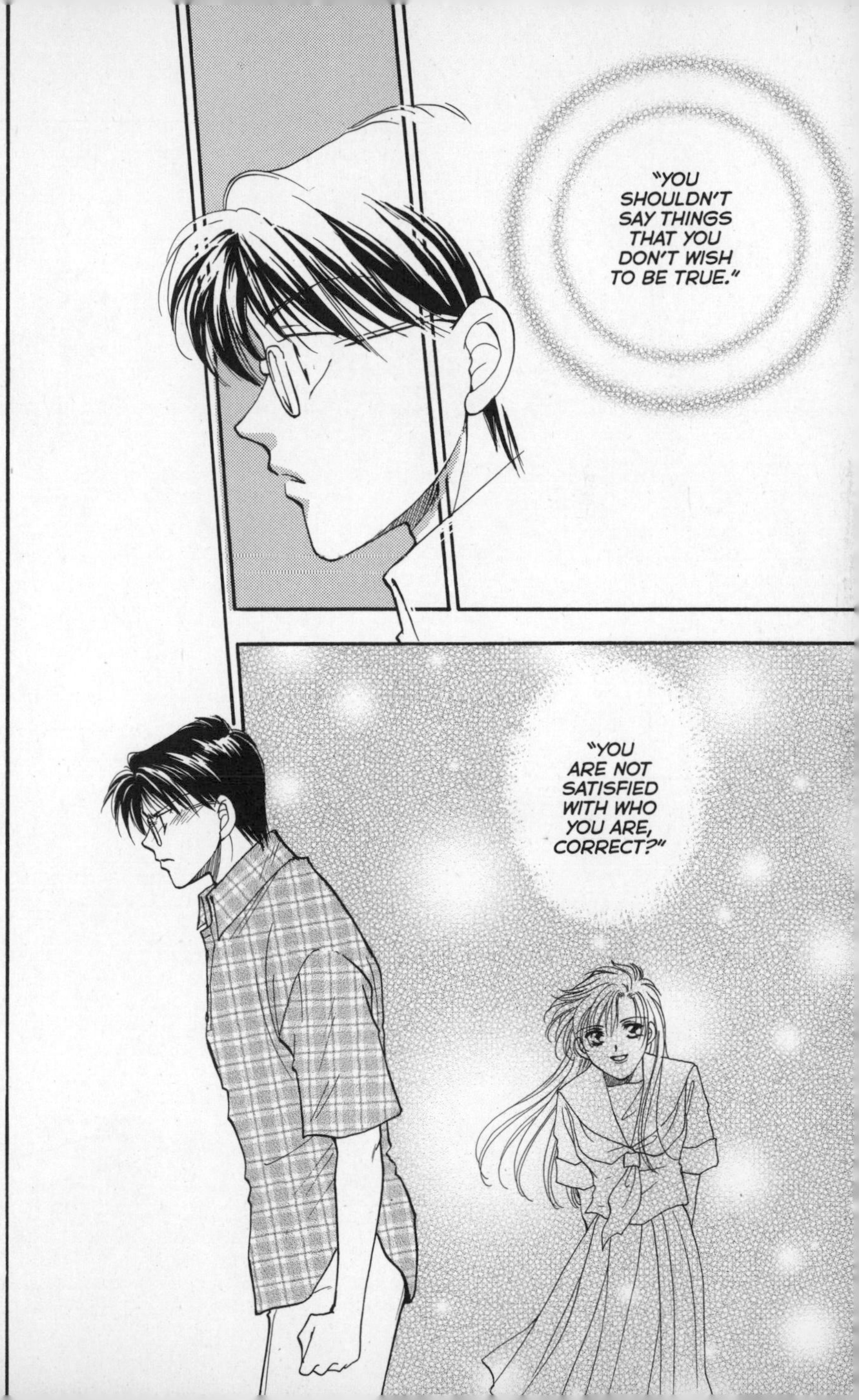
"YOU SHOULDN'T SAY THINGS THAT YOU DON'T WISH TO BE TRUE."
"YOU ARE NOT SATISFIED WITH WHO YOU ARE, CORRECT?"

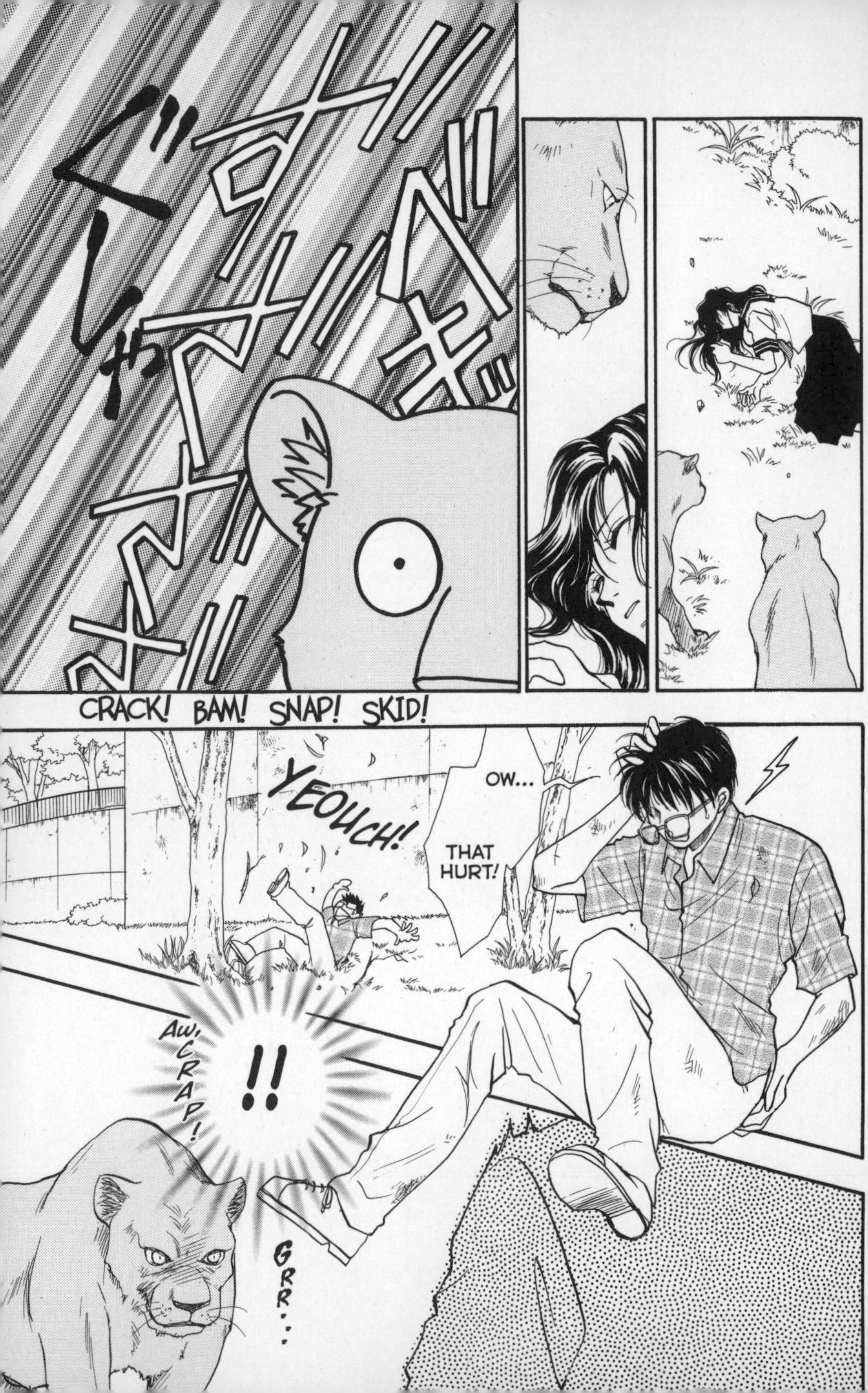
CRACK! BAM! SNAP! SKID!
OW...
THAT HURT!
YEOUCH!
!!
AW, CRAP!
GRR...

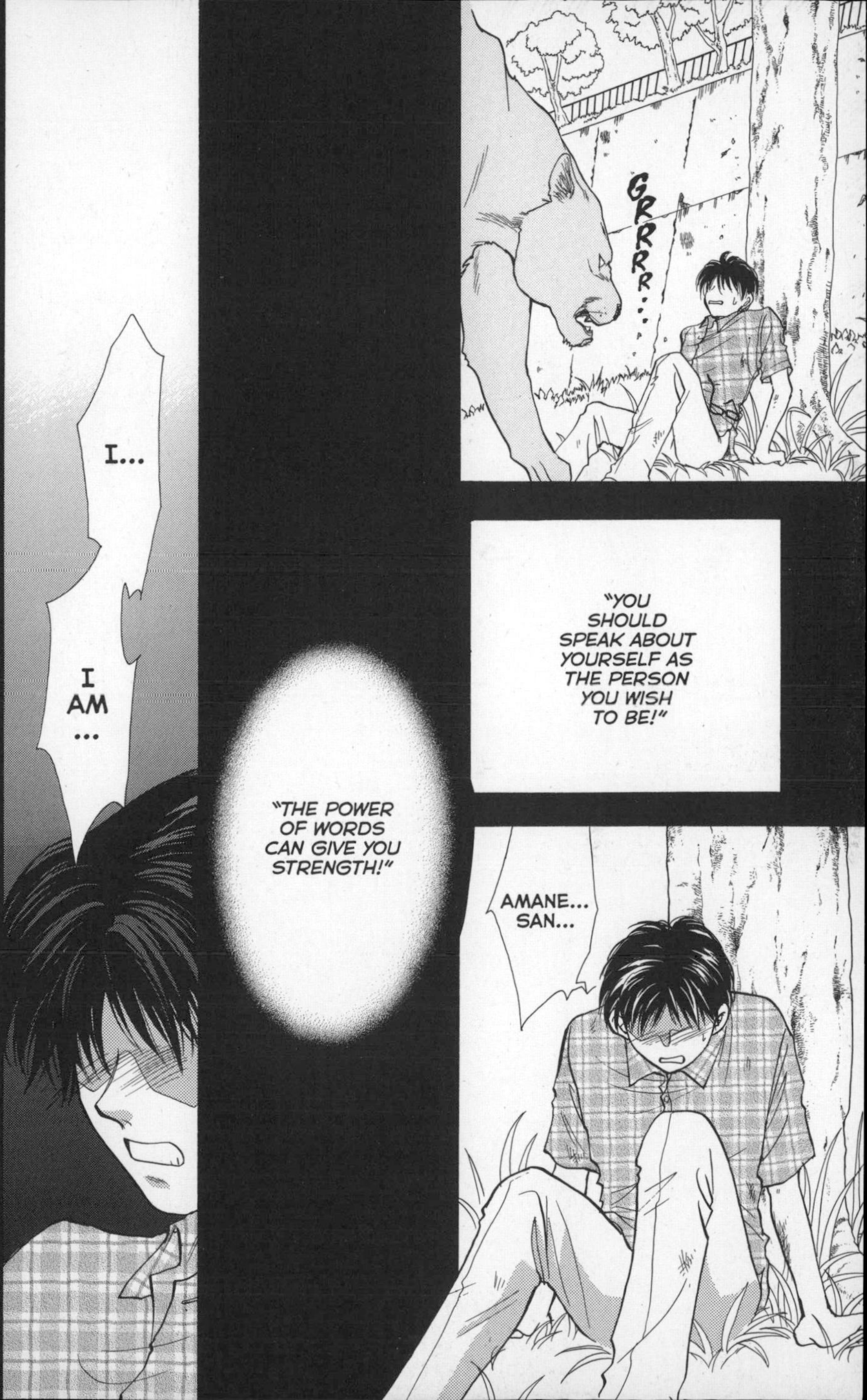
GRRRR...
"YOU SHOULD SPEAK ABOUT YOURSELF AS THE PERSON YOU WISH TO BE!"
AMANE... SAN...
"THE POWER OF WORDS CAN GIVE YOU STRENGTH!"
I...
I AM ...

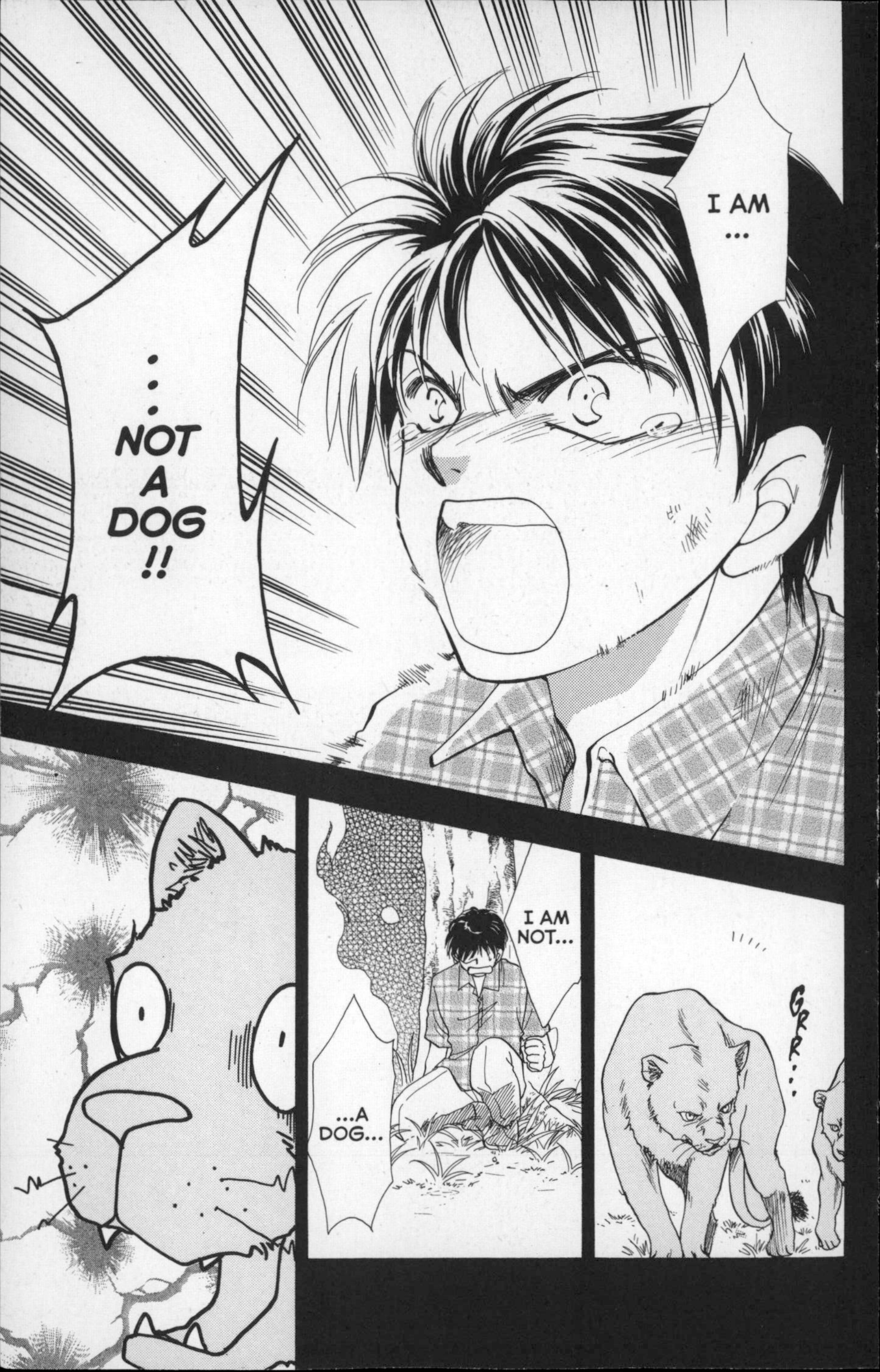
I AM ...
...NOT A DOG!!
GRRR...
I AM NOT...
...A DOG...

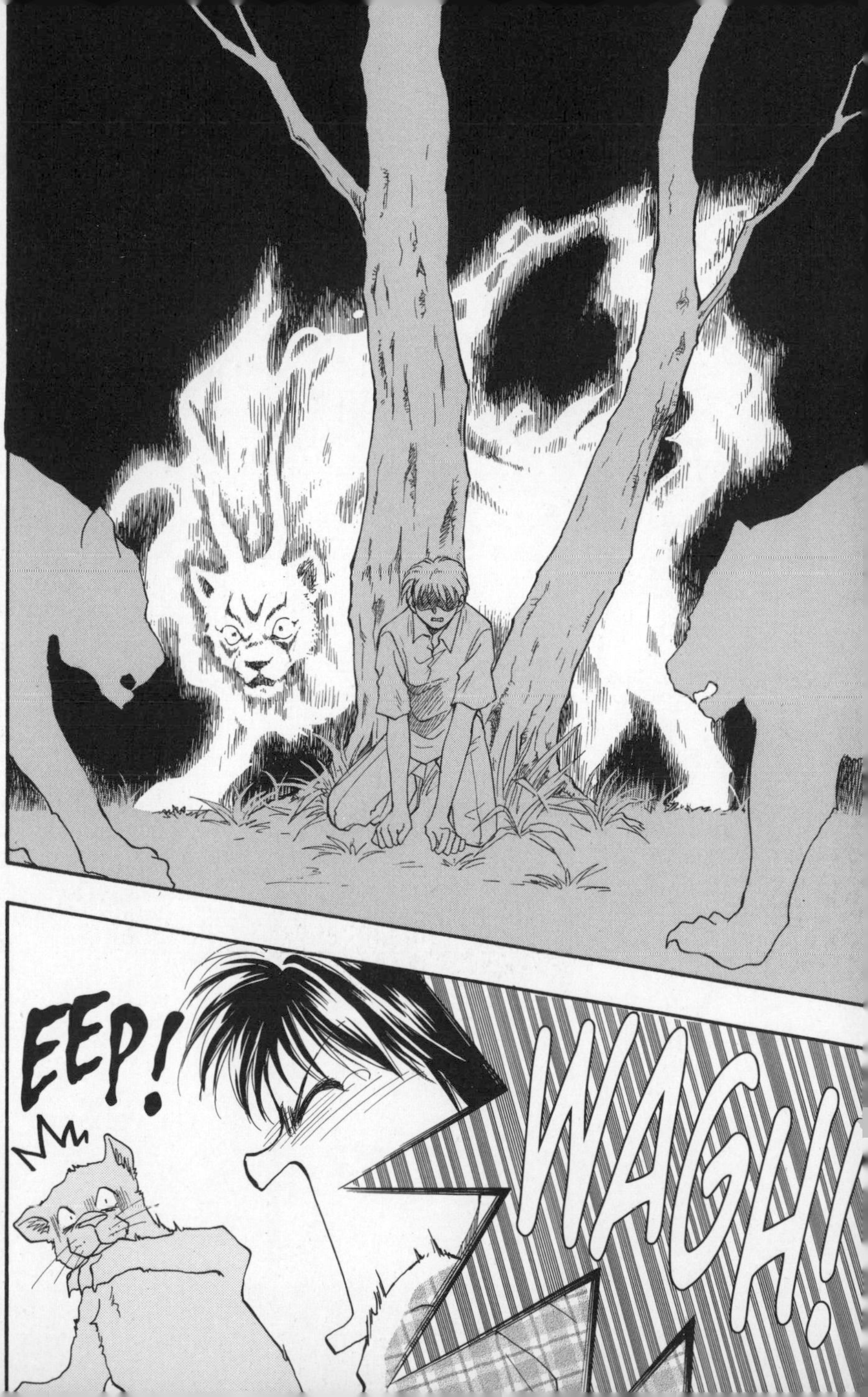
WAGH!!
EEP!

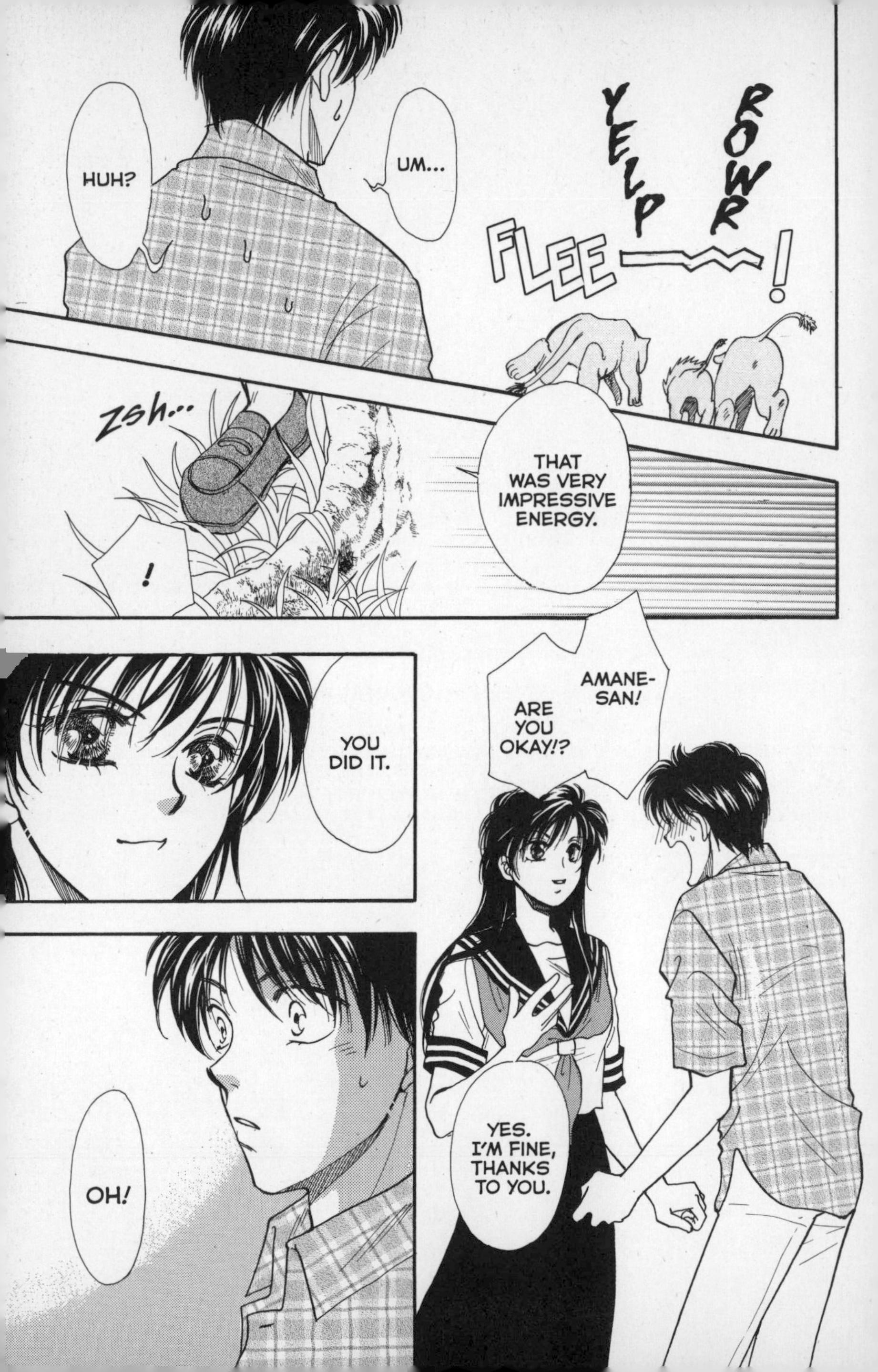
ROWR
YELP
FLEE—!
UM...
HUH?
THAT WAS VERY IMPRESSIVE ENERGY.
Zsh...
!
AMANE-SAN! ARE YOU OKAY!?
YES. I'M FINE, THANKS TO YOU.
YOU DID IT.
OH!

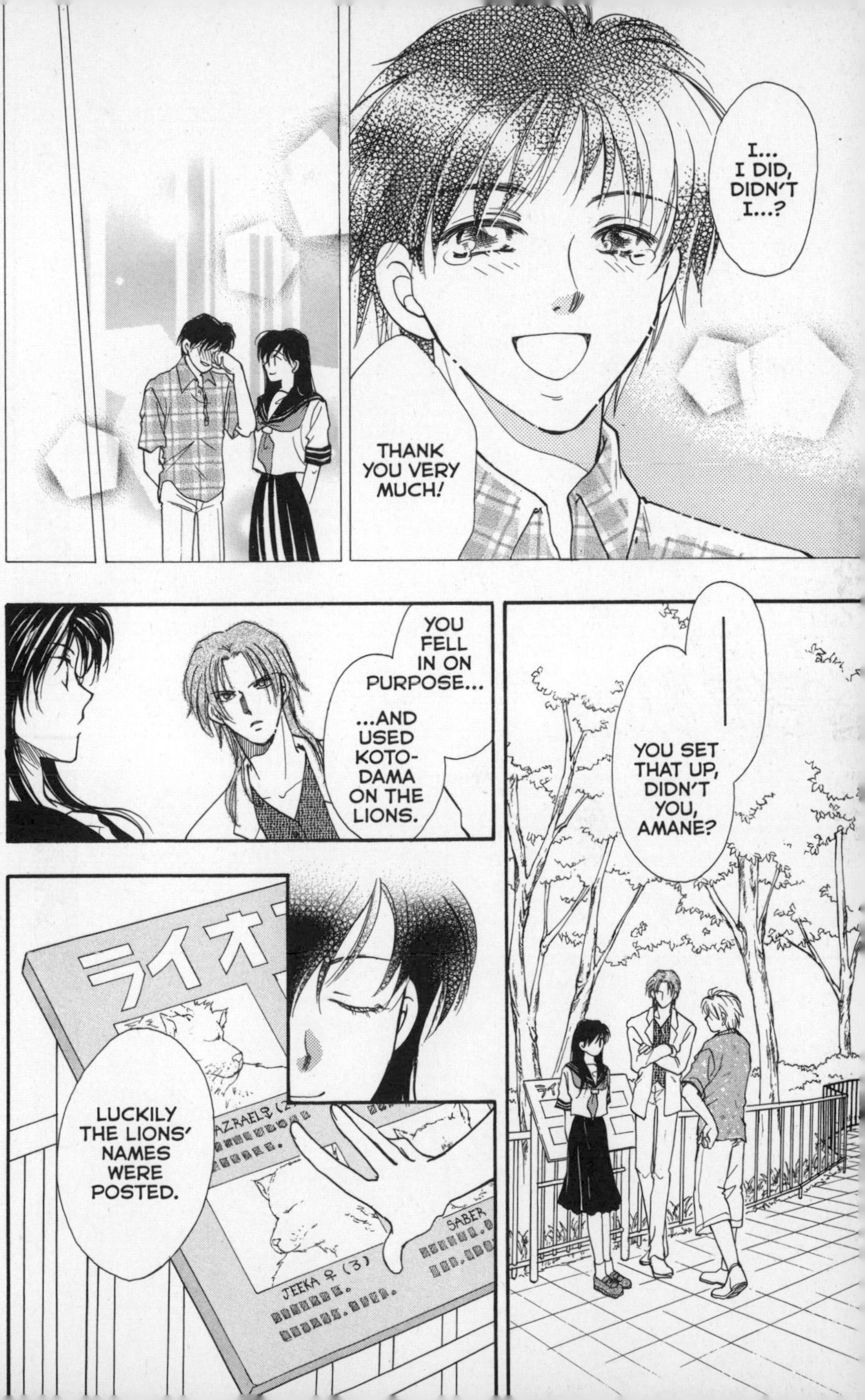
I... I DID, DIDN'T I...?
THANK YOU VERY MUCH!
—
YOU SET THAT UP, DIDN'T YOU, AMANE?
YOU FELL IN ON PURPOSE...
...AND USED KOTO-DAMA ON THE LIONS.
ライオ
AZRAEL♀
LUCKILY THE LIONS' NAMES WERE POSTED.
SABER
JEEKA ♀ (3)

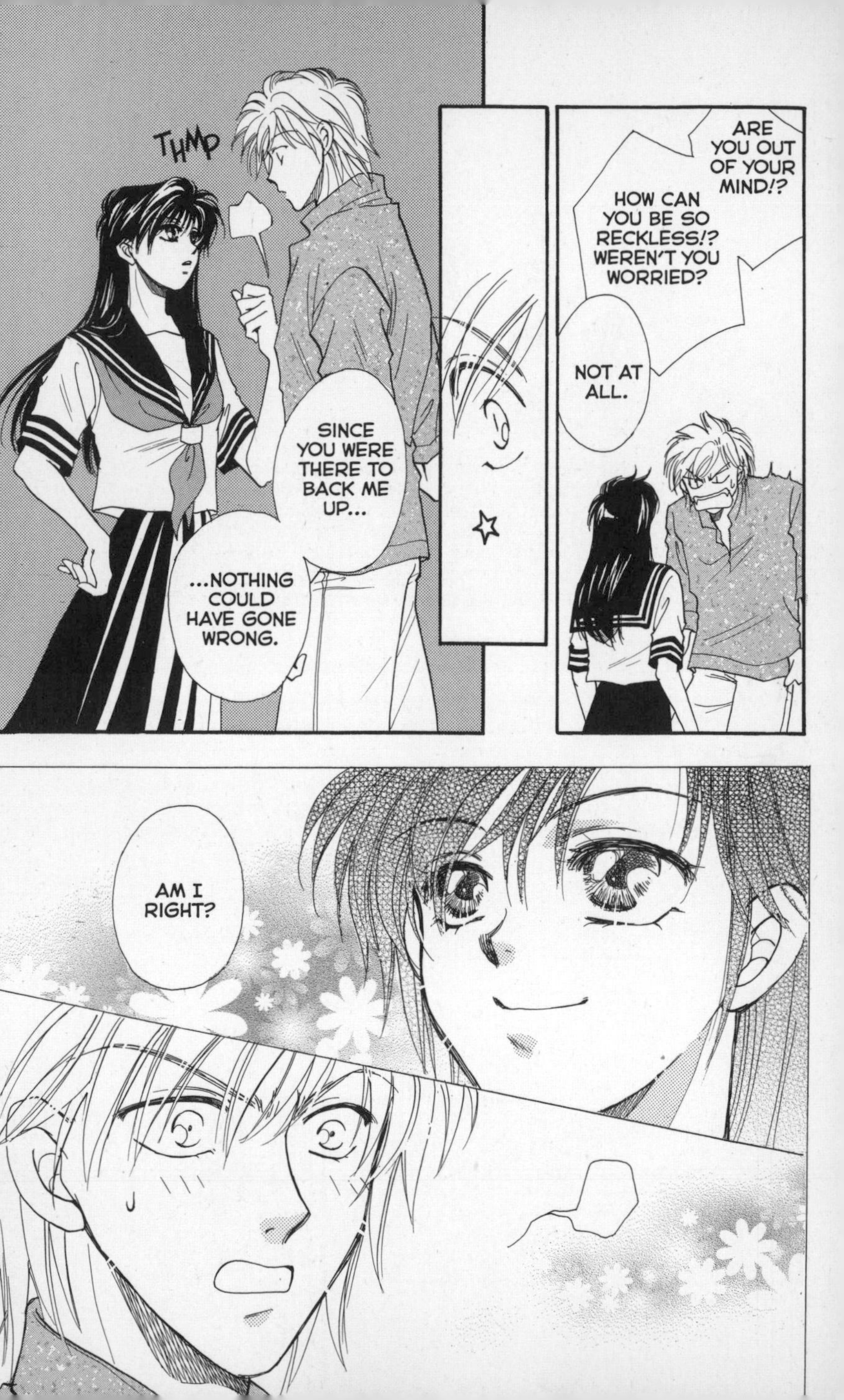
ARE YOU OUT OF YOUR MIND!?
HOW CAN YOU BE SO RECKLESS!? WEREN'T YOU WORRIED?
NOT AT ALL.
THMP
SINCE YOU WERE THERE TO BACK ME UP...
...NOTHING COULD HAVE GONE WRONG.
AM I RIGHT?

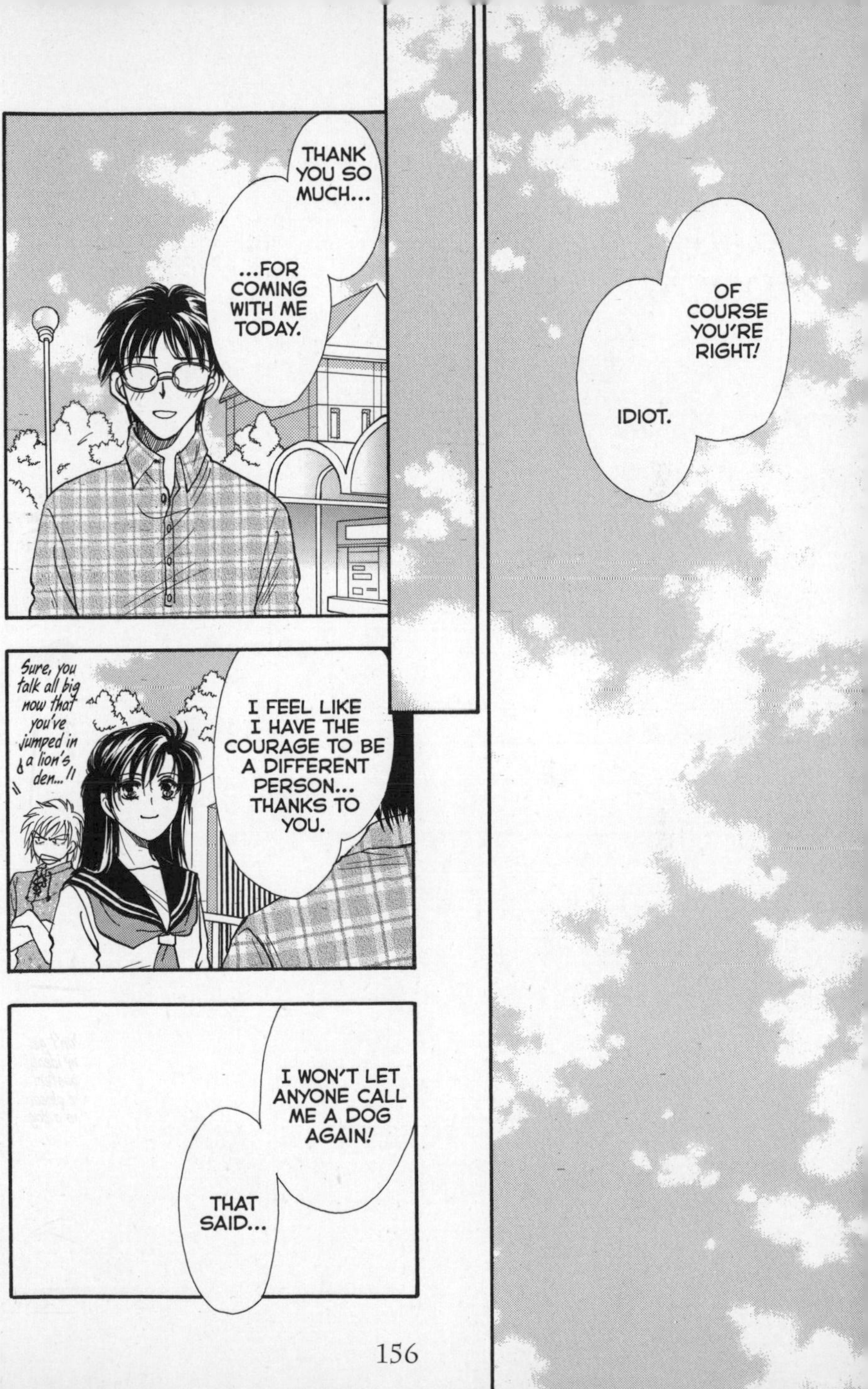
OF COURSE YOU'RE RIGHT!
IDIOT.
THANK YOU SO MUCH...
...FOR COMING WITH ME TODAY.
I FEEL LIKE I HAVE THE COURAGE TO BE A DIFFERENT PERSON... THANKS TO YOU.
Sure, you talk all big now that you've jumped in a lion's den...
I WON'T LET ANYONE CALL ME A DOG AGAIN!
THAT SAID...

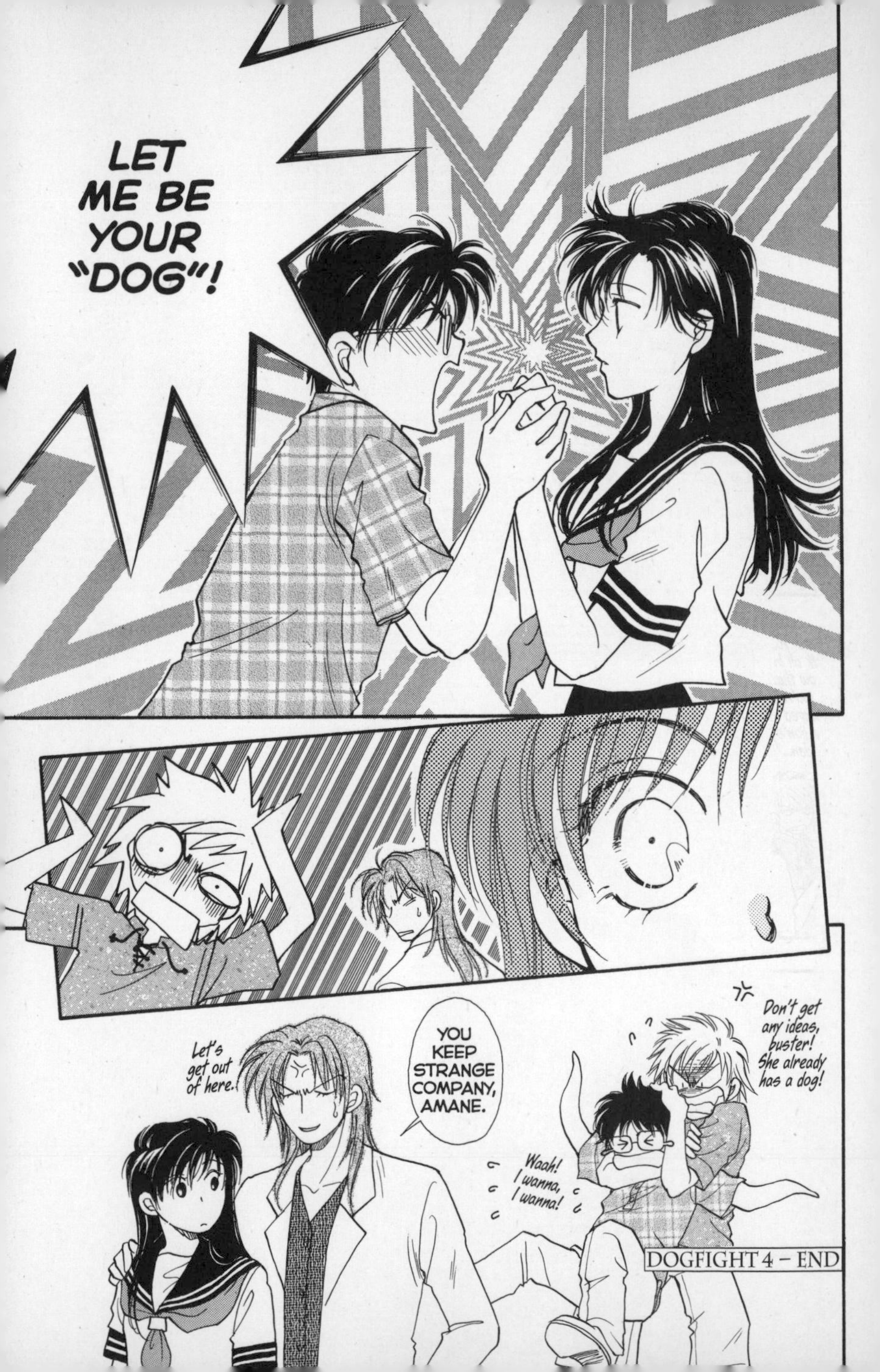
LET ME BE YOUR "DOG"!
Don't get any ideas, buster! She already has a dog!
Waah! I wanna, I wanna!
YOU KEEP STRANGE COMPANY, AMANE.
Let's get out of here.
DOGFIGHT 4 – END

KONNICHIWA!

THANK YOU VERY MUCH FOR PICKING UP HER MAJESTY'S DOG.

WHEN I THINK BACK, THIS STORY GOT ITS START BECAUSE OF AN IDEA MY EDITOR HAD. "IT'S SUMMER TIME," SHE SAID, "SO LET'S TRY SOMETHING IN THE HORROR VEIN. YOU'RE GOOD AT THAT SPOOKY STUFF, AREN'T YOU?"

THE FACT THAT THE SERIES ENDED UP BECOMING THIS POPULAR IS SOMEWHAT SURPRISING TO ME. I'M VERY GRATEFUL THAT THIS SERIES EVEN GOT COLLECTED INTO A TANKOBON (GRAPHIC NOVEL). FOR THAT, I REALLY MUST THANK MY RESPECTFUL EDITOR, MY STAFF AND MY FANS... OH I AM DEEPLY GRATEFUL.

(TO BE HONEST, EDITOR-SAN, I'M NOT PARTICULARLY GOOD AT HORROR STORIES! HA HA!)

BECAUSE IT HAPPENED SO FAST, THE CHARACTERS WERE ALL MADE UP AT THE VERY LAST MINUTE. BUT I FIGURED IF I'M GOING TO DO THIS AT ALL, I'VE GOT TO MAKE THEM CHARACTERS THAT I REALLY CARE ABOUT! (LAUGH). MAYBE THAT'S WHAT HELPED THE POPULARITY? I'M SURPRISED HOW MANY PEOPLE WROTE IN SAYING THAT THEY COULD RELATE TO MY CHARACTERS. IT SEEMS LIKE MANY PEOPLE ARE ENJOYING IT, AND FOR THAT REASON, I'M VERY HAPPY! SINCE THIS VOLUME WAS PUBLISHED AS VOLUME 1, IT LOOKS LIKE I'LL BE ABLE TO CONTINUE THE SERIES FOR A WHILE. I WILL WORK HARDER TO MAKE IT LOVABLE SO THAT YOU AND I WILL CARE ABOUT ALL THE CHARACTERS! I DON'T THINK THAT CAME OUT RIGHT... (LAUGH). I WILL DO MY BEST! PLEASE LOOK FORWARD TO THE NEXT VOLUME!! PRETTY PLEASE...?

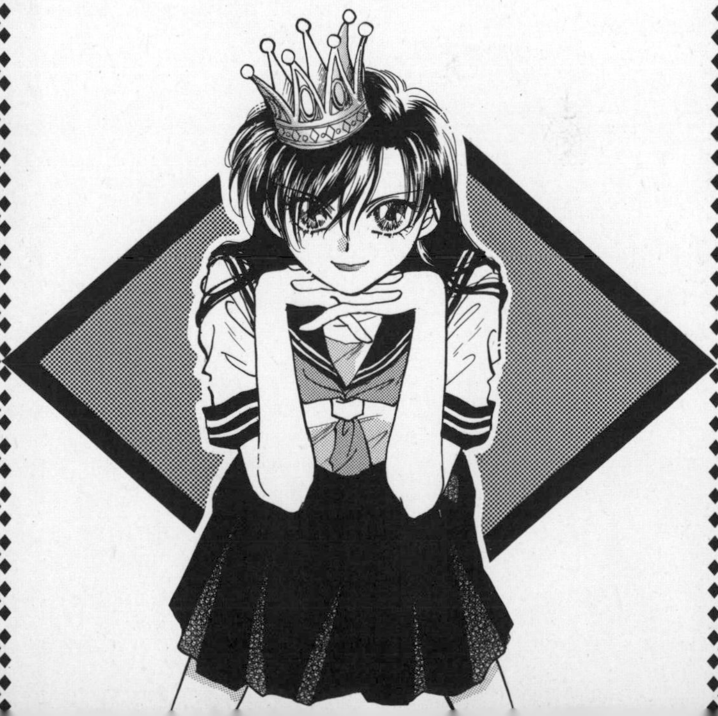

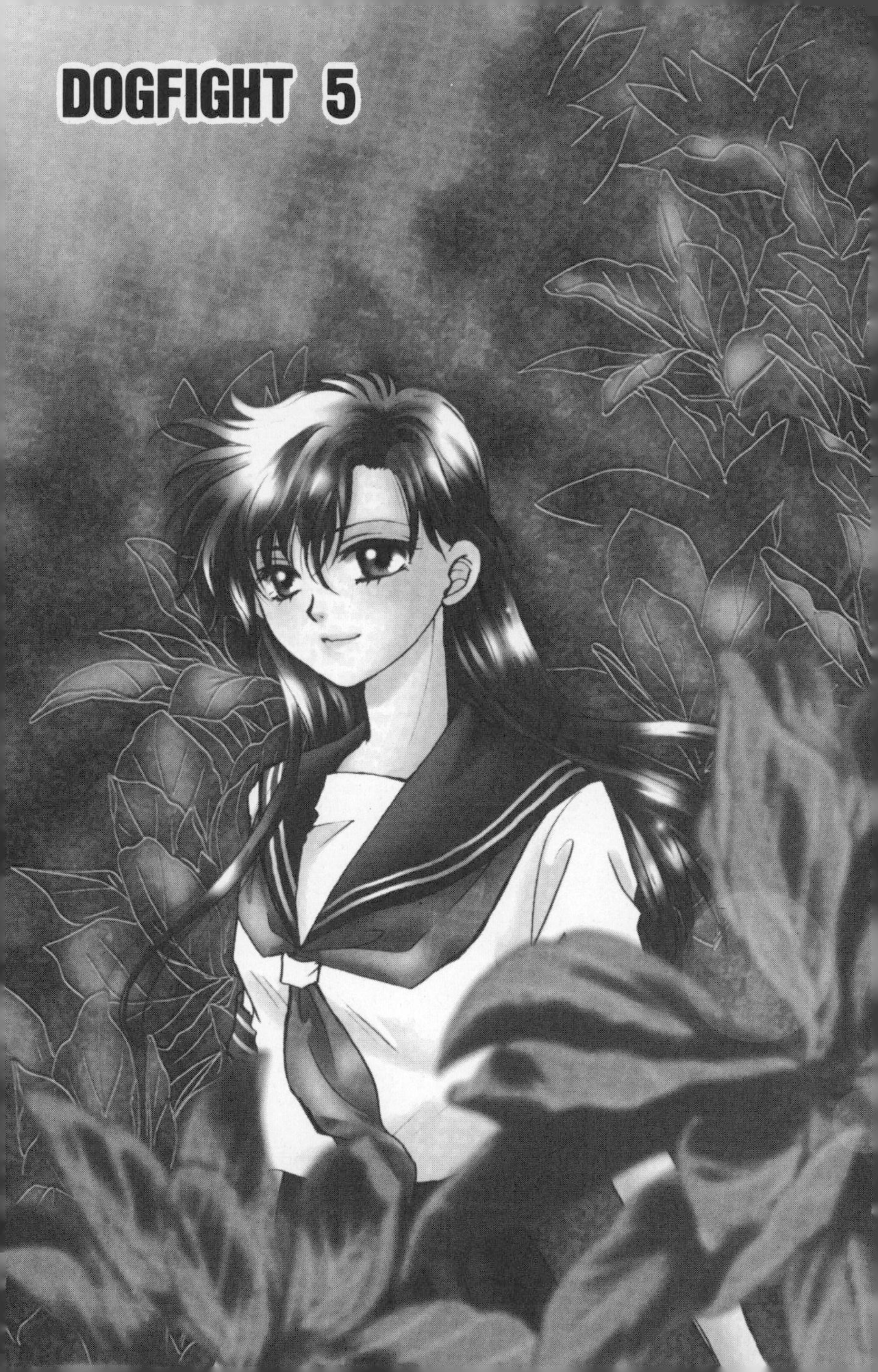
DOGFIGHT 5

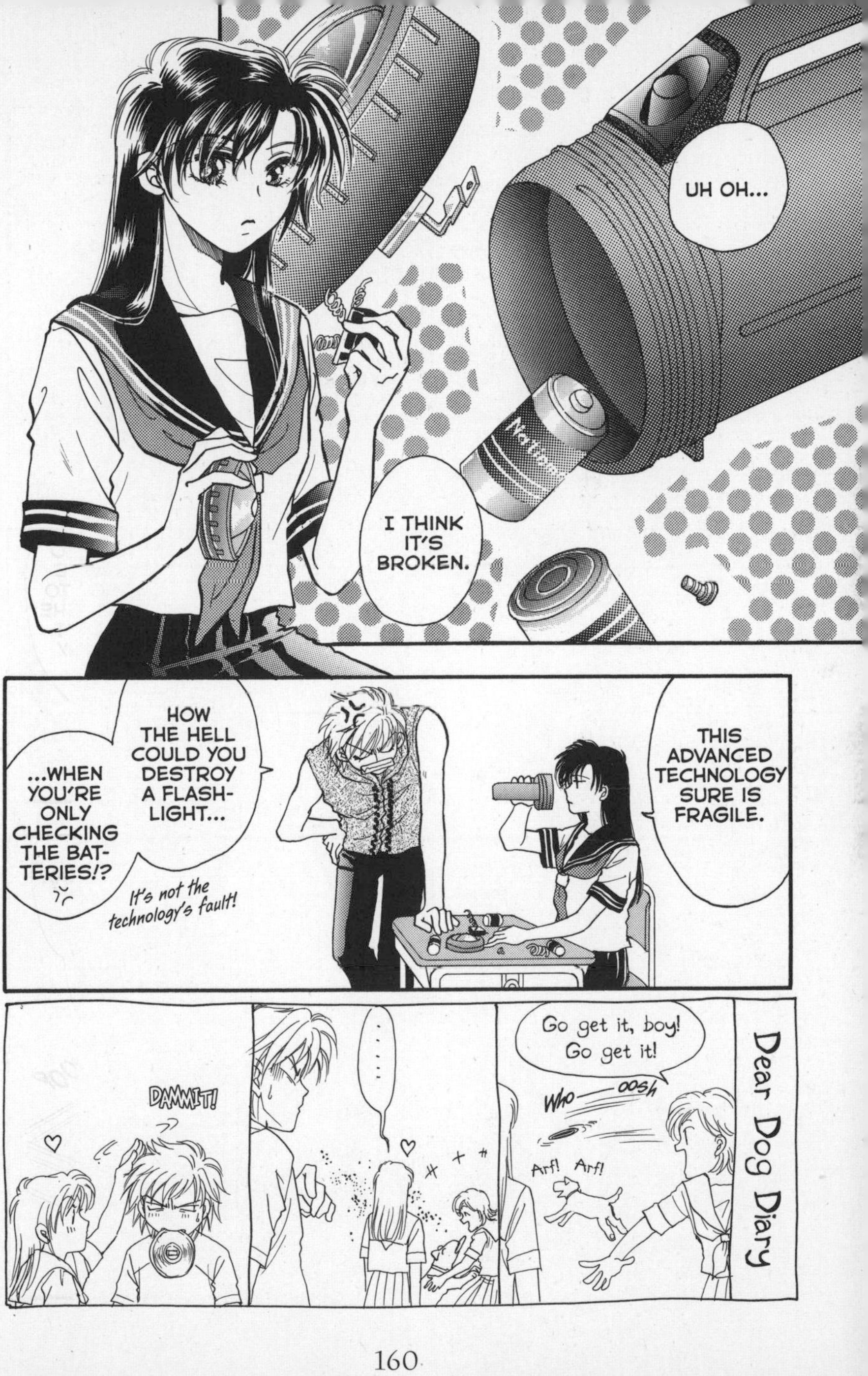
UH OH...
I THINK IT'S BROKEN.
THIS ADVANCED TECHNOLOGY SURE IS FRAGILE.
HOW THE HELL COULD YOU DESTROY A FLASH-LIGHT...
...WHEN YOU'RE ONLY CHECKING THE BAT-TERIES!?
It's not the technology's fault!
Dear Dog Diary
Go get it, boy! Go get it!
Who——oosh
Arf! Arf!
......
DAMMIT!

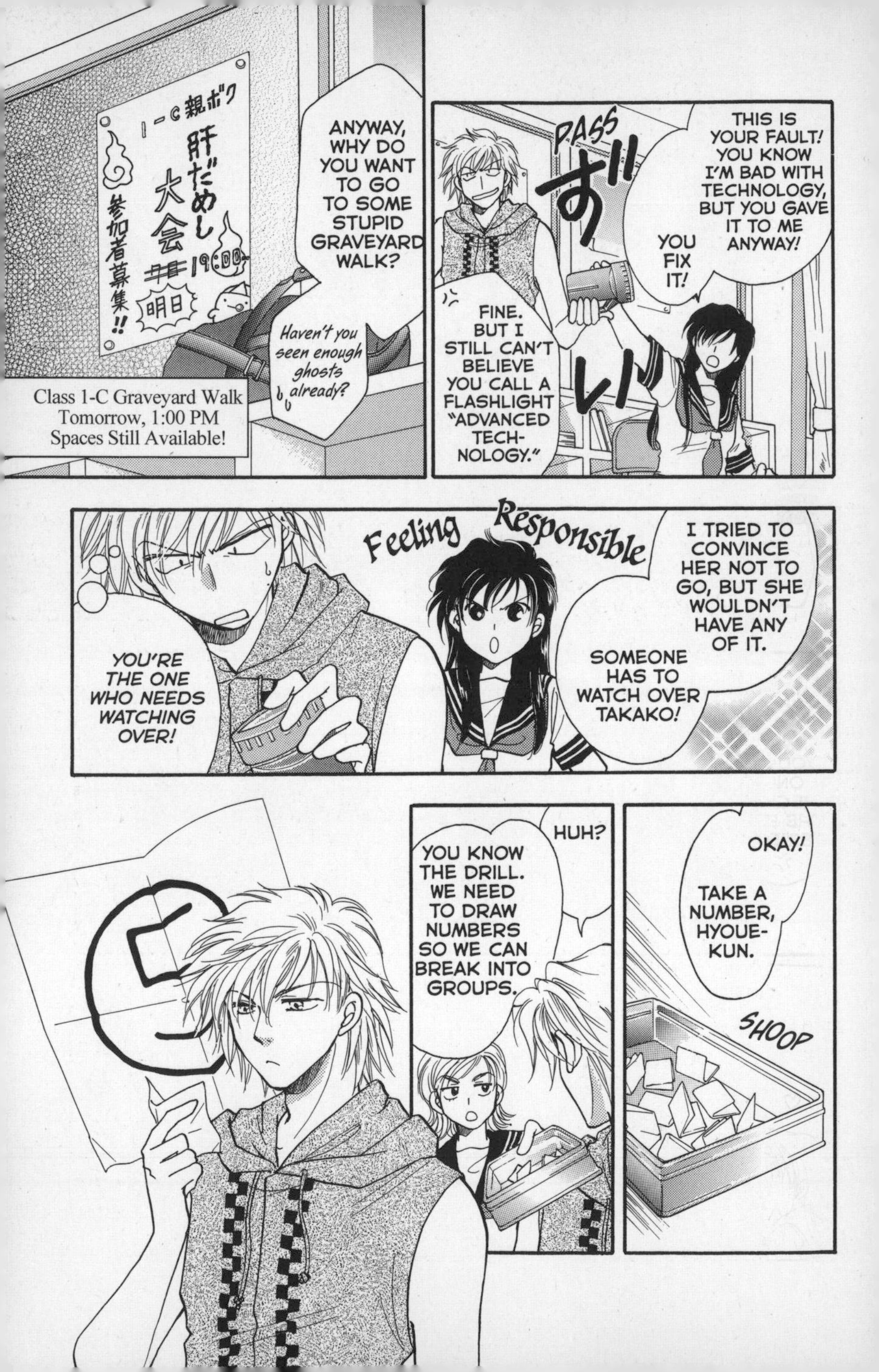

THIS IS YOUR FAULT! YOU KNOW I'M BAD WITH TECHNOLOGY, BUT YOU GAVE IT TO ME ANYWAY!
YOU FIX IT!
PASS
FINE. BUT I STILL CAN'T BELIEVE YOU CALL A FLASHLIGHT "ADVANCED TECH-NOLOGY."
ANYWAY, WHY DO YOU WANT TO GO TO SOME STUPID GRAVEYARD WALK?
Haven't you seen enough ghosts already?
1ーC親ボク
肝だめし大会
19:00
参加者募集!!
明日
Class 1-C Graveyard Walk
Tomorrow, 1:00 PM
Spaces Still Available!
I TRIED TO CONVINCE HER NOT TO GO, BUT SHE WOULDN'T HAVE ANY OF IT.
SOMEONE HAS TO WATCH OVER TAKAKO!
Feeling Responsible
YOU'RE THE ONE WHO NEEDS WATCHING OVER!
OKAY!
TAKE A NUMBER, HYOUE-KUN.
SHOOP
HUH?
YOU KNOW THE DRILL. WE NEED TO DRAW NUMBERS SO WE CAN BREAK INTO GROUPS.

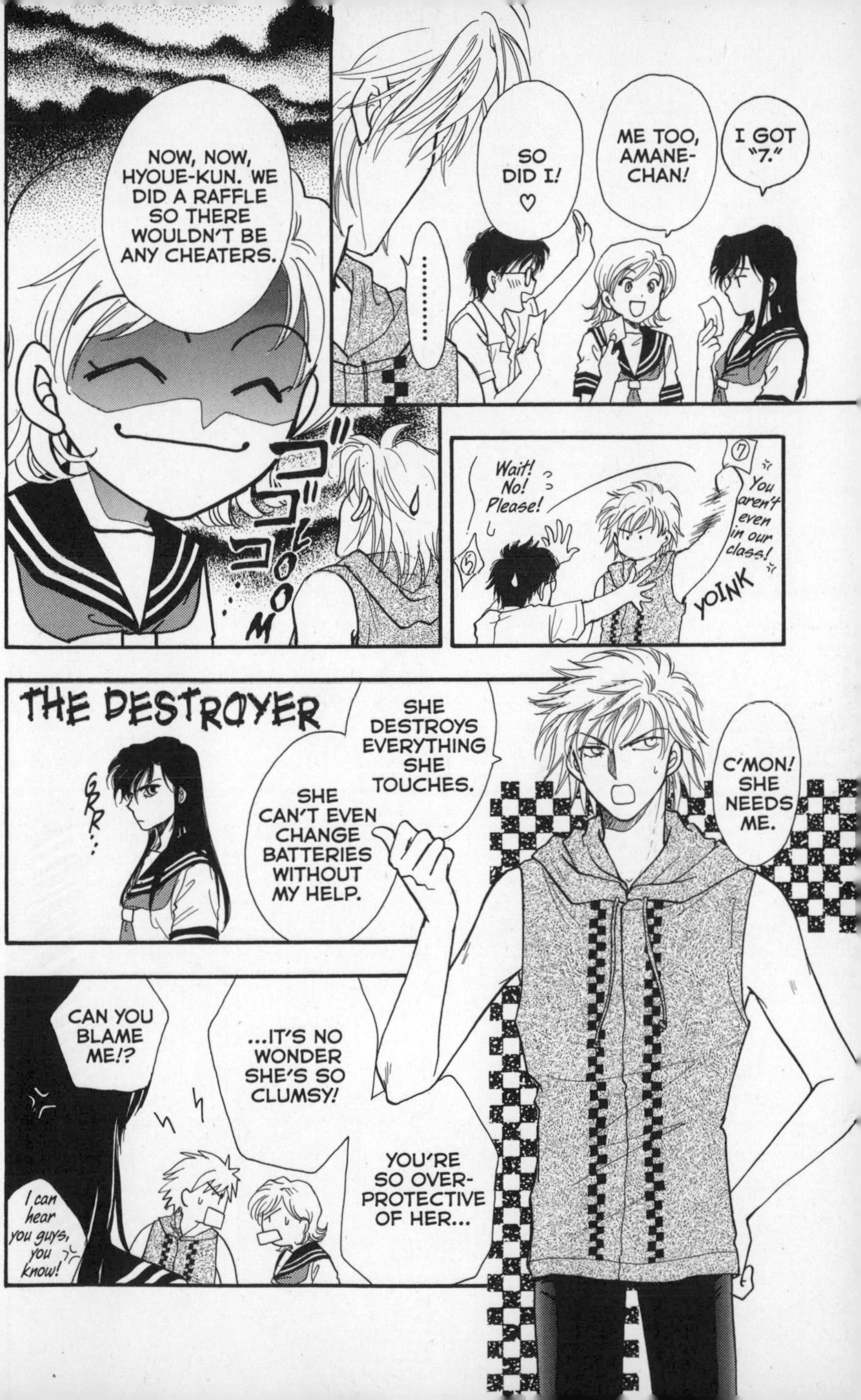
I GOT "7."
ME TOO, AMANE-CHAN!
SO DID I! ♡
......
You aren't even in our class!
Wait! No! Please!
YOINK
NOW, NOW, HYOUE-KUN. WE DID A RAFFLE SO THERE WOULDN'T BE ANY CHEATERS.
C'MON! SHE NEEDS ME.
SHE DESTROYS EVERYTHING SHE TOUCHES.
SHE CAN'T EVEN CHANGE BATTERIES WITHOUT MY HELP.
THE DESTROYER
GRR...
YOU'RE SO OVER-PROTECTIVE OF HER...
...IT'S NO WONDER SHE'S SO CLUMSY!
CAN YOU BLAME ME!?
I can hear you guys, you know!

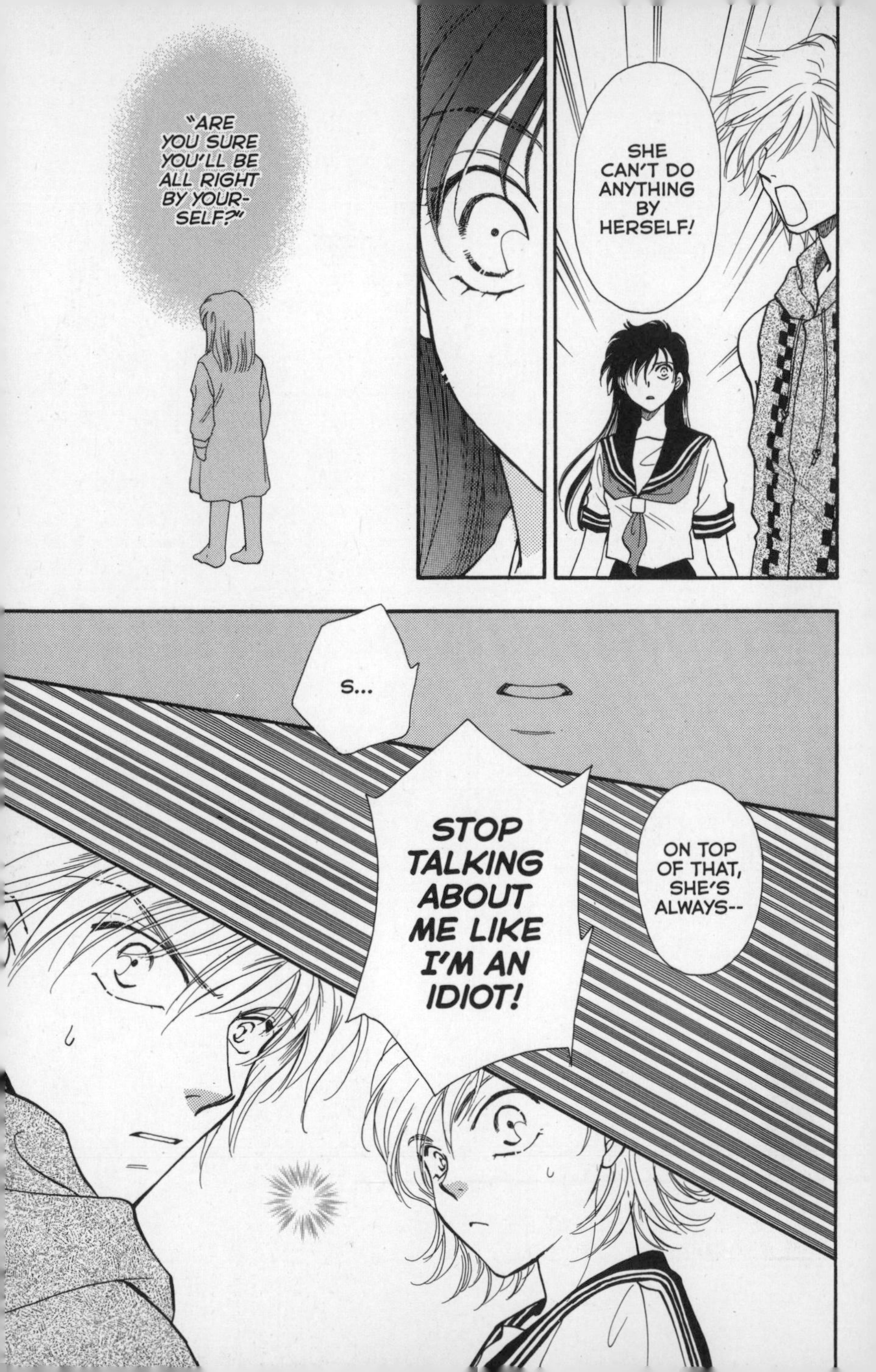
SHE CAN'T DO ANYTHING BY HERSELF!
"ARE YOU SURE YOU'LL BE ALL RIGHT BY YOUR-SELF?"
ON TOP OF THAT, SHE'S ALWAYS--
S...
STOP TALKING ABOUT ME LIKE I'M AN IDIOT!

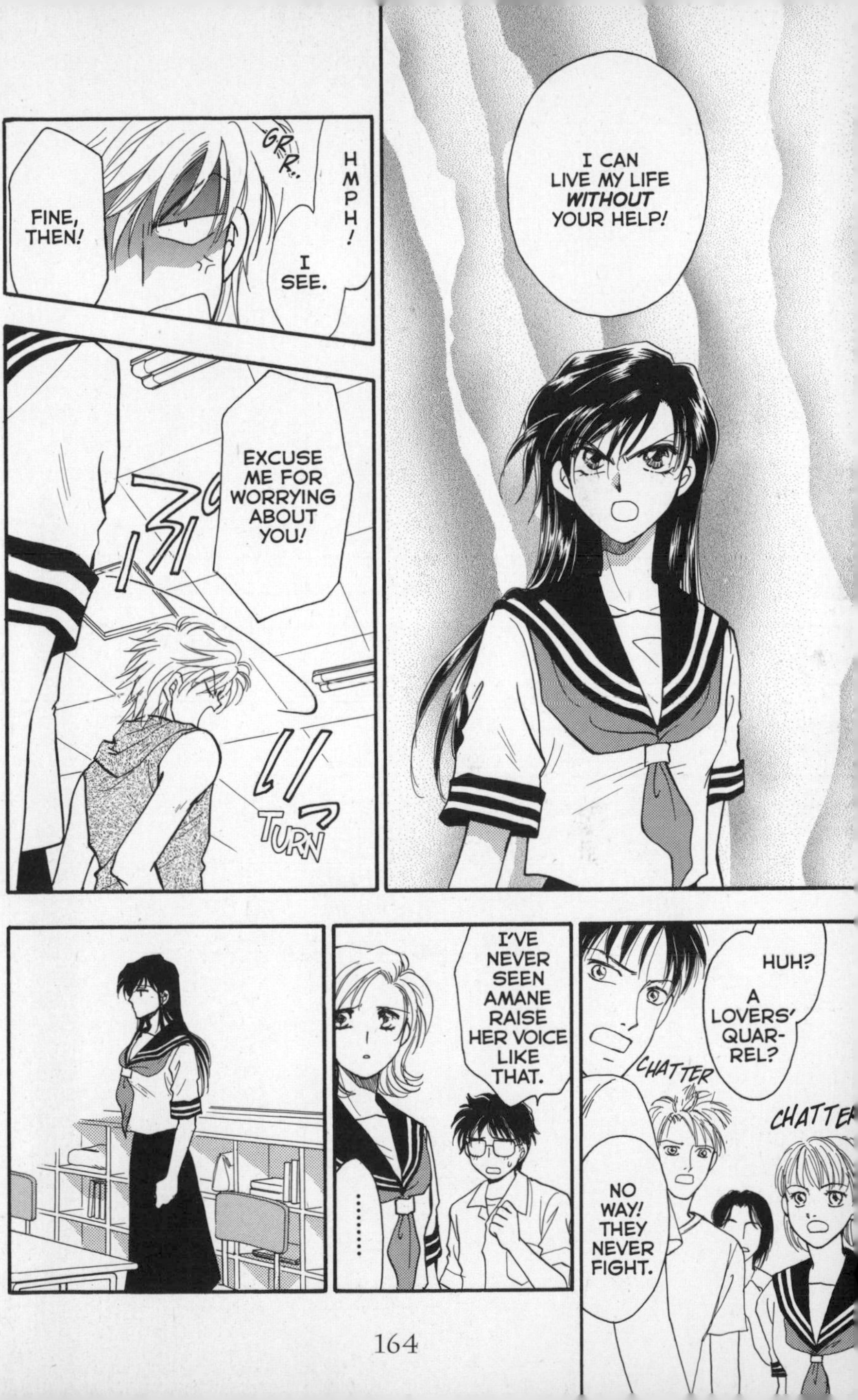
I CAN LIVE MY LIFE *WITHOUT* YOUR HELP!
HMPH!
I SEE.
GRR..
FINE, THEN!
EXCUSE ME FOR WORRYING ABOUT YOU!
TURN
HUH? A LOVERS' QUARREL?
CHATTER
NO WAY! THEY NEVER FIGHT.
CHATTER
I'VE NEVER SEEN AMANE RAISE HER VOICE LIKE THAT.
....

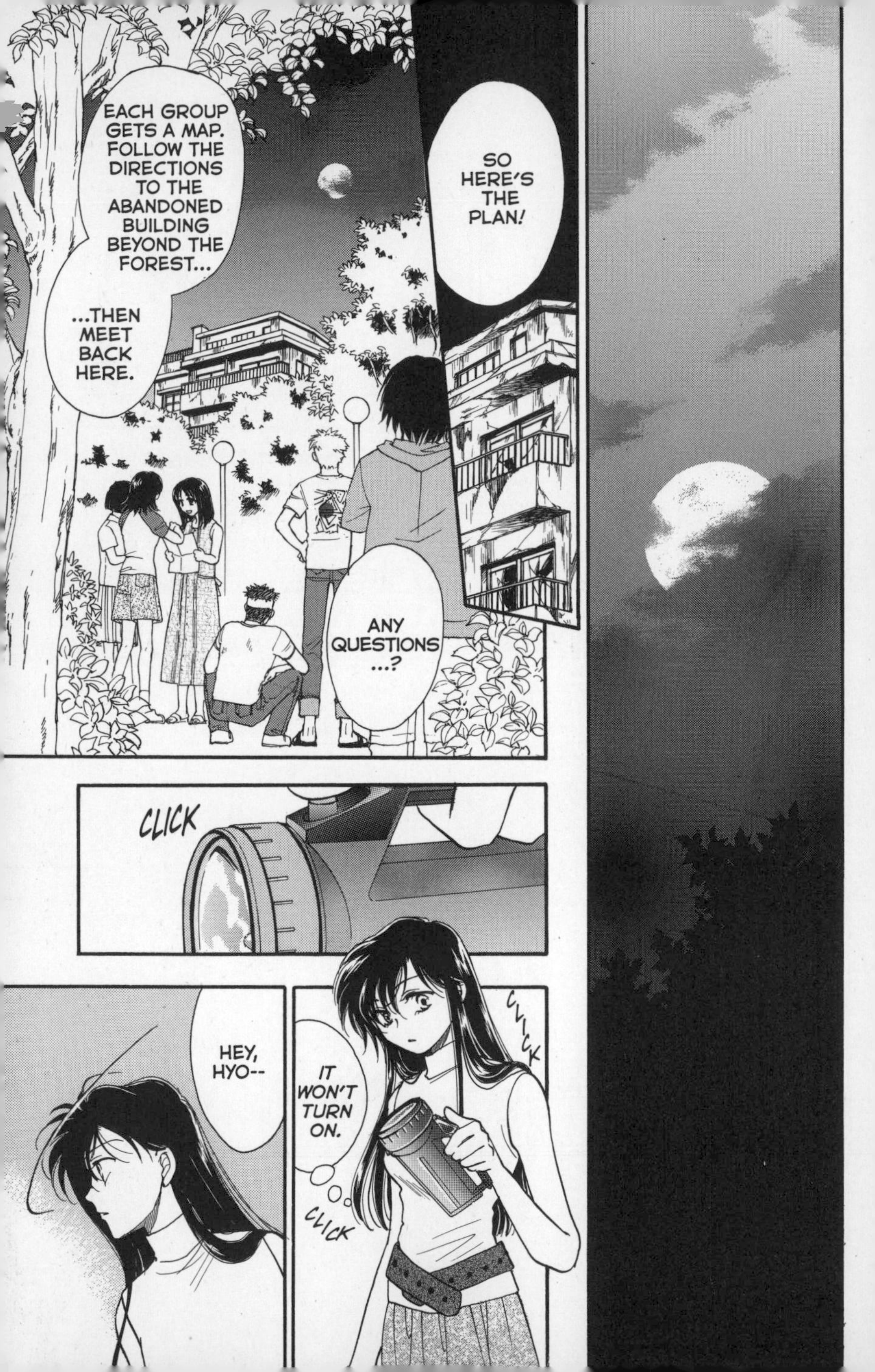
SO HERE'S THE PLAN!
EACH GROUP GETS A MAP. FOLLOW THE DIRECTIONS TO THE ABANDONED BUILDING BEYOND THE FOREST...
...THEN MEET BACK HERE.
ANY QUESTIONS ...?
CLICK
CLICK
IT WON'T TURN ON.
CLICK
HEY, HYO--

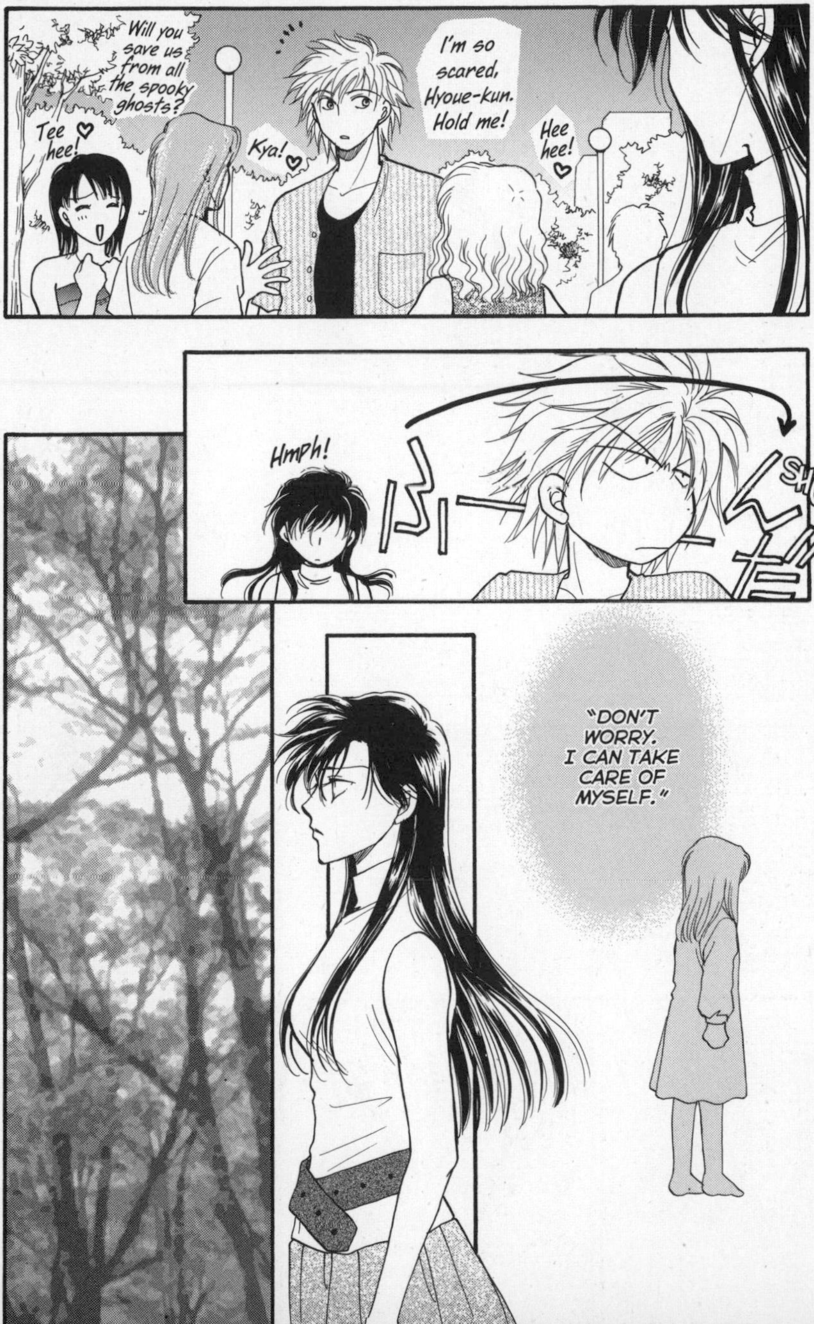
Hee hee! ♡
I'm so scared, Hyoue-kun. Hold me!
Kya! ♡
Will you save us from all the spooky ghosts?
Tee hee! ♡
SHUN
Hmph!
"DON'T WORRY. I CAN TAKE CARE OF MYSELF."

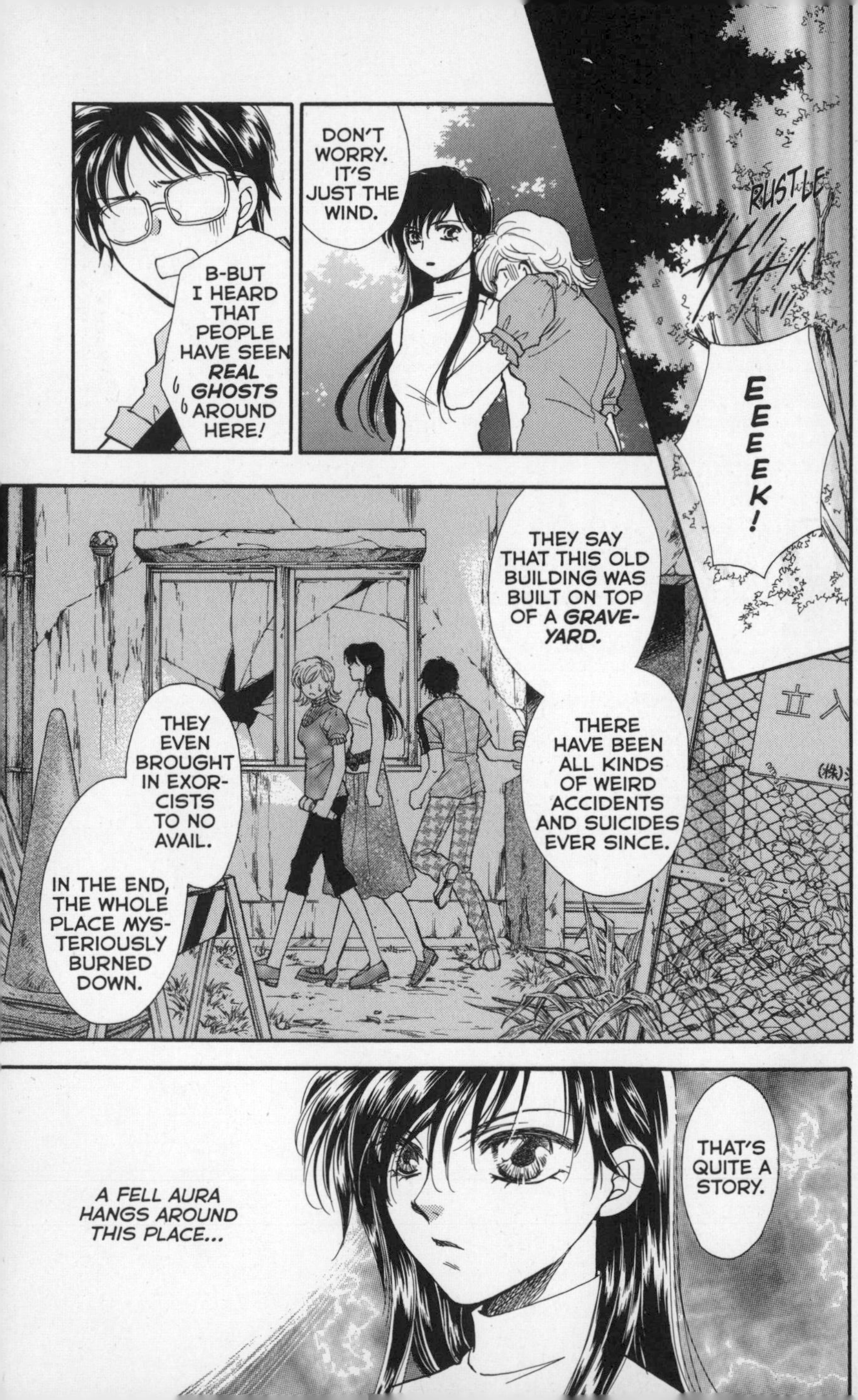
RUSTLE
EEEEK!
DON'T WORRY. IT'S JUST THE WIND.
B-BUT I HEARD THAT PEOPLE HAVE SEEN *REAL GHOSTS* AROUND HERE!
THEY SAY THAT THIS OLD BUILDING WAS BUILT ON TOP OF A *GRAVE-YARD.*
THERE HAVE BEEN ALL KINDS OF WEIRD ACCIDENTS AND SUICIDES EVER SINCE.
THEY EVEN BROUGHT IN EXOR-CISTS TO NO AVAIL.
IN THE END, THE WHOLE PLACE MYS-TERIOUSLY BURNED DOWN.
THAT'S QUITE A STORY.
A FELL AURA HANGS AROUND THIS PLACE...

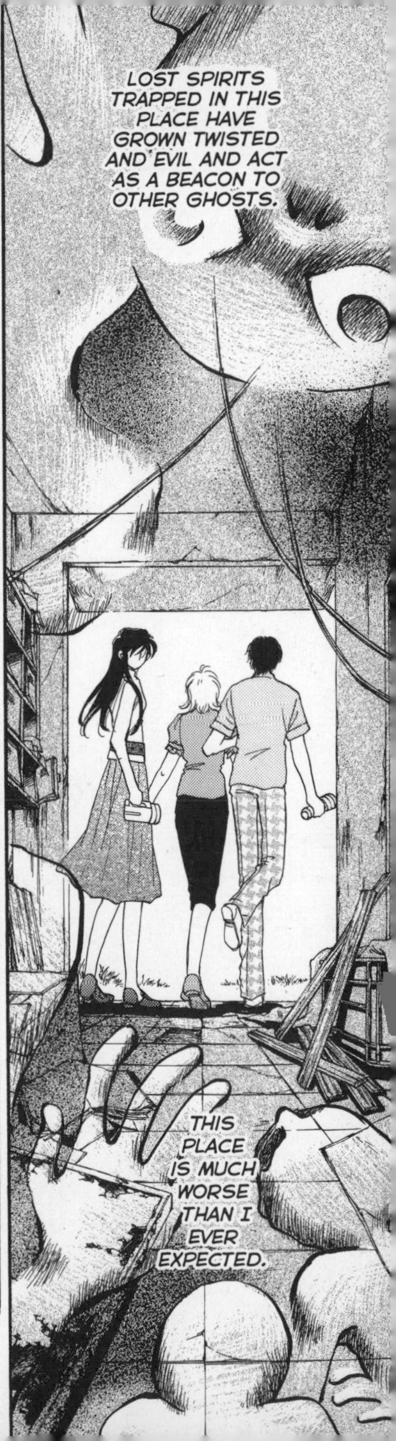
LOST SPIRITS TRAPPED IN THIS PLACE HAVE GROWN TWISTED AND EVIL AND ACT AS A BEACON TO OTHER GHOSTS.
THIS PLACE IS MUCH WORSE THAN I EVER EXPECTED.

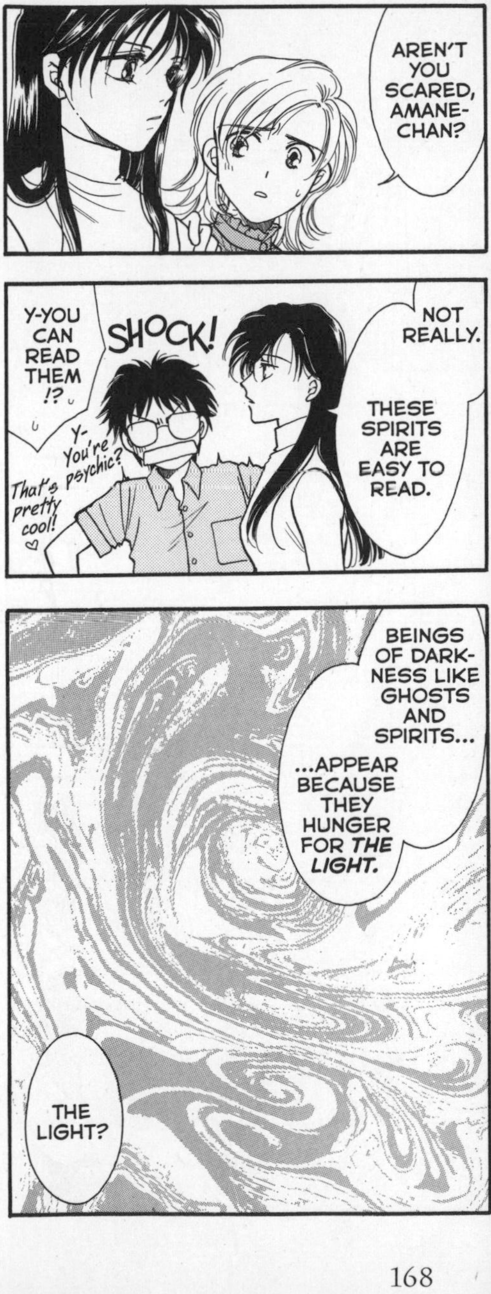
AREN'T YOU SCARED, AMANE-CHAN?
NOT REALLY.
THESE SPIRITS ARE EASY TO READ.
SHOCK!
Y-YOU CAN READ THEM !?
Y-You're psychic? That's pretty cool! ♡
BEINGS OF DARKNESS LIKE GHOSTS AND SPIRITS...
...APPEAR BECAUSE THEY HUNGER FOR *THE LIGHT.*
THE LIGHT?

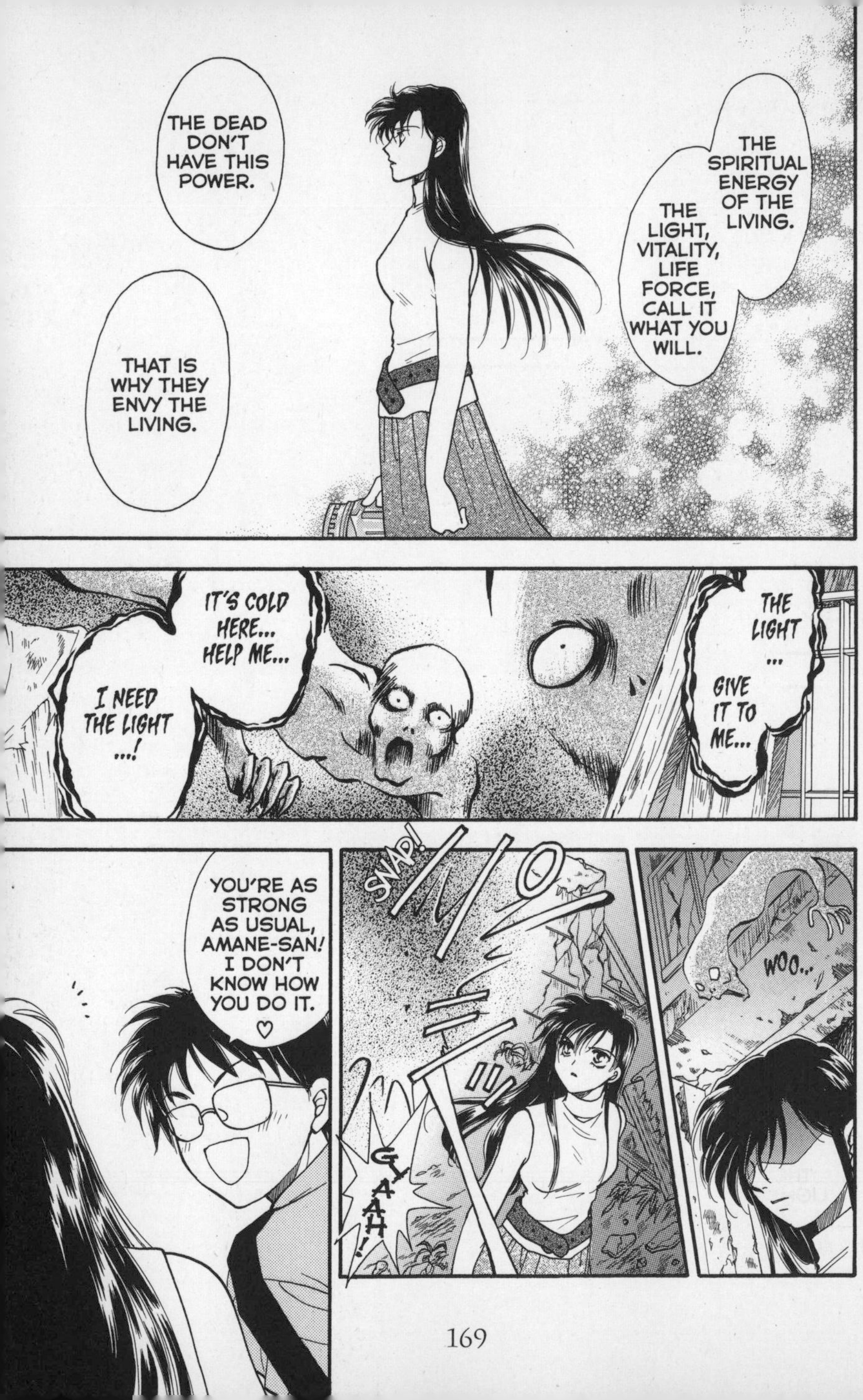
THE SPIRITUAL ENERGY OF THE LIVING.
THE LIGHT, VITALITY, LIFE FORCE, CALL IT WHAT YOU WILL.
THE DEAD DON'T HAVE THIS POWER.
THAT IS WHY THEY ENVY THE LIVING.
THE LIGHT ... GIVE IT TO ME...
IT'S COLD HERE... HELP ME...
I NEED THE LIGHT ...!
WOO..
SNAP!
GYAAH!
YOU'RE AS STRONG AS USUAL, AMANE-SAN! I DON'T KNOW HOW YOU DO IT. ♡

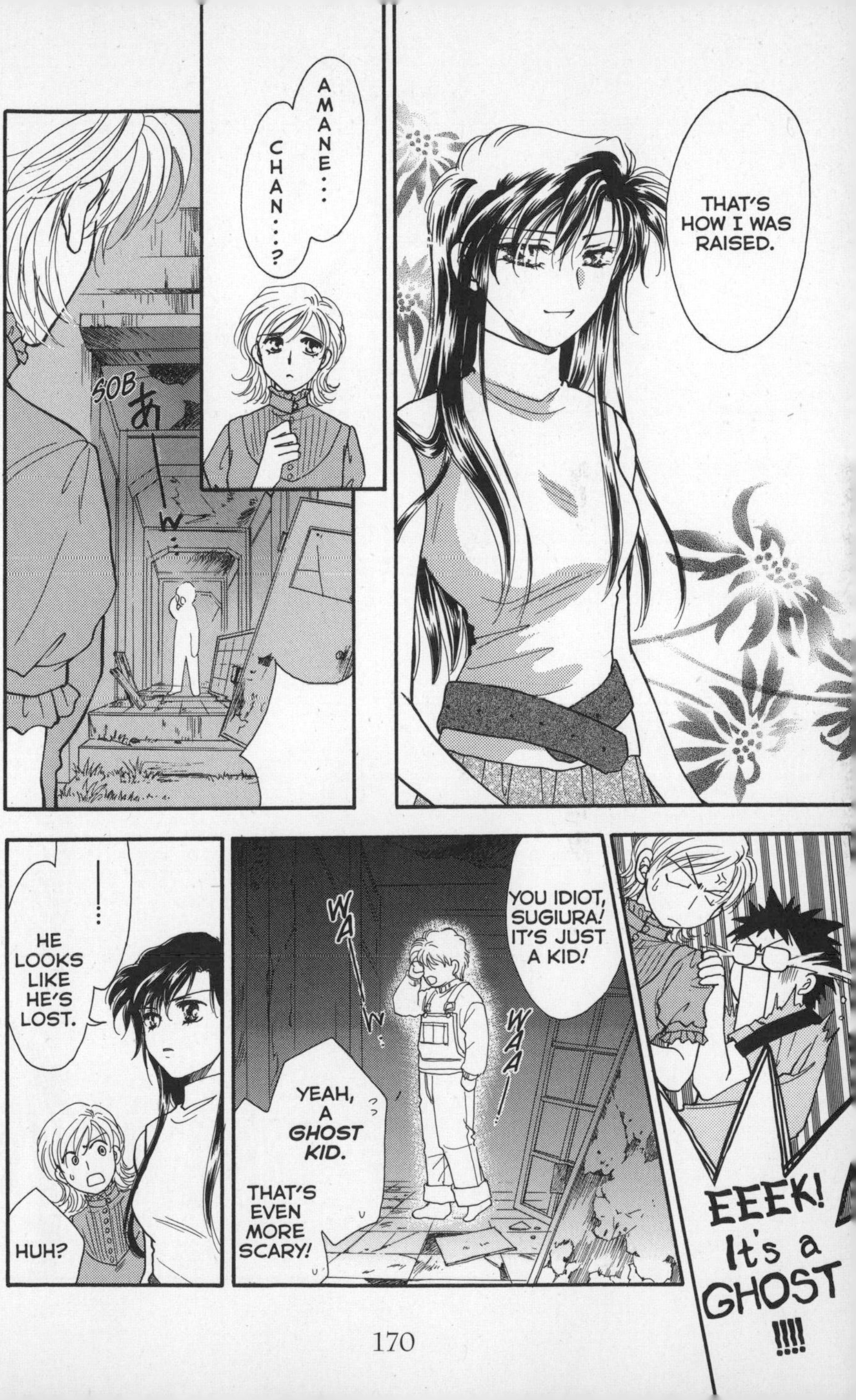
THAT'S HOW I WAS RAISED.
AMANE... CHAN...?
SOB
あ
W...
EEEK! It's a GHOST!!!!
YOU IDIOT, SUGIURA! IT'S JUST A KID!
WA...W...
WAA!
YEAH, A GHOST KID.
THAT'S EVEN MORE SCARY!
...!
HE LOOKS LIKE HE'S LOST.
HUH?

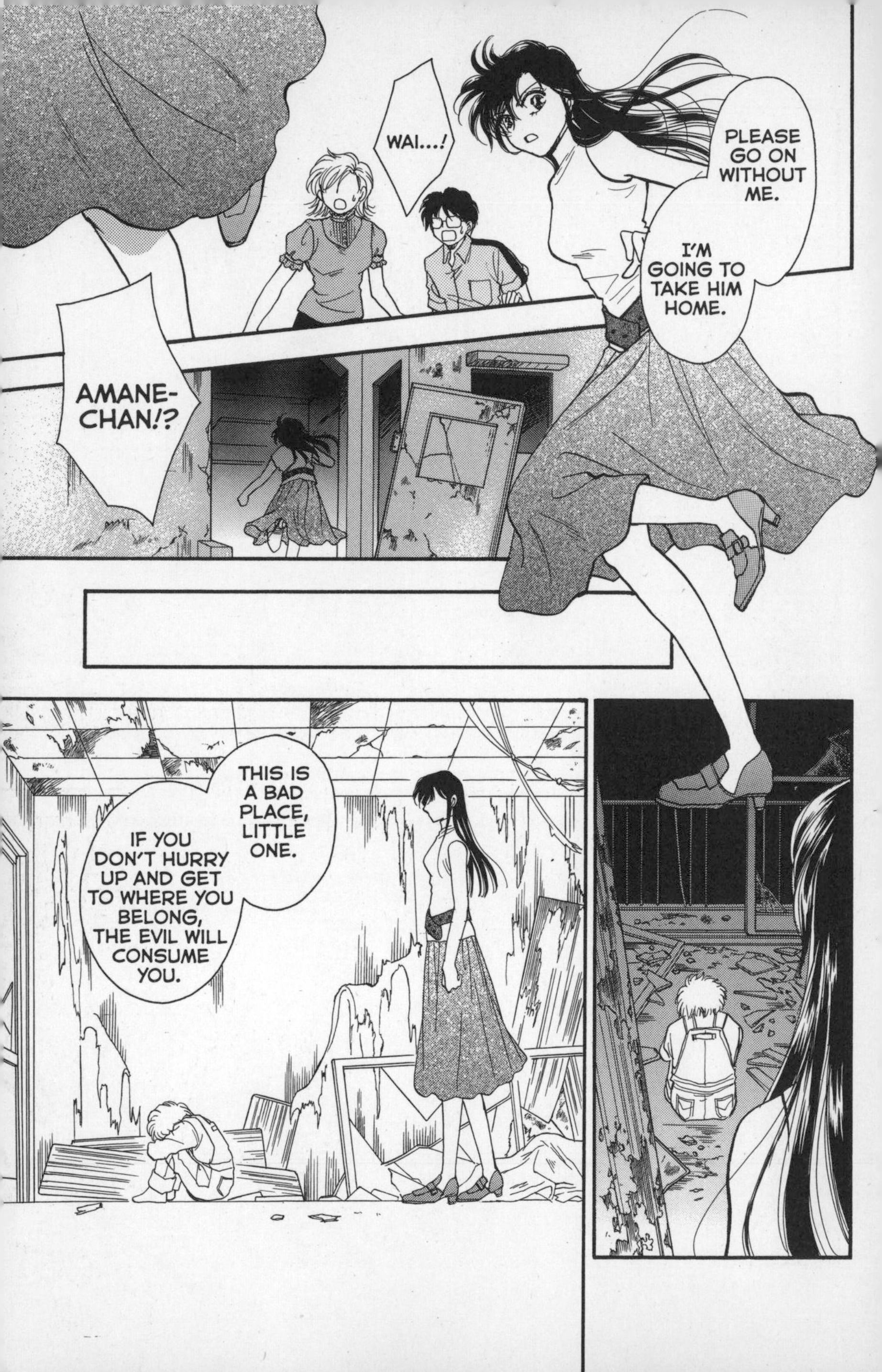
PLEASE GO ON WITHOUT ME.
I'M GOING TO TAKE HIM HOME.
WAI...!
AMANE-CHAN!?
THIS IS A BAD PLACE, LITTLE ONE.
IF YOU DON'T HURRY UP AND GET TO WHERE YOU BELONG, THE EVIL WILL CONSUME YOU.

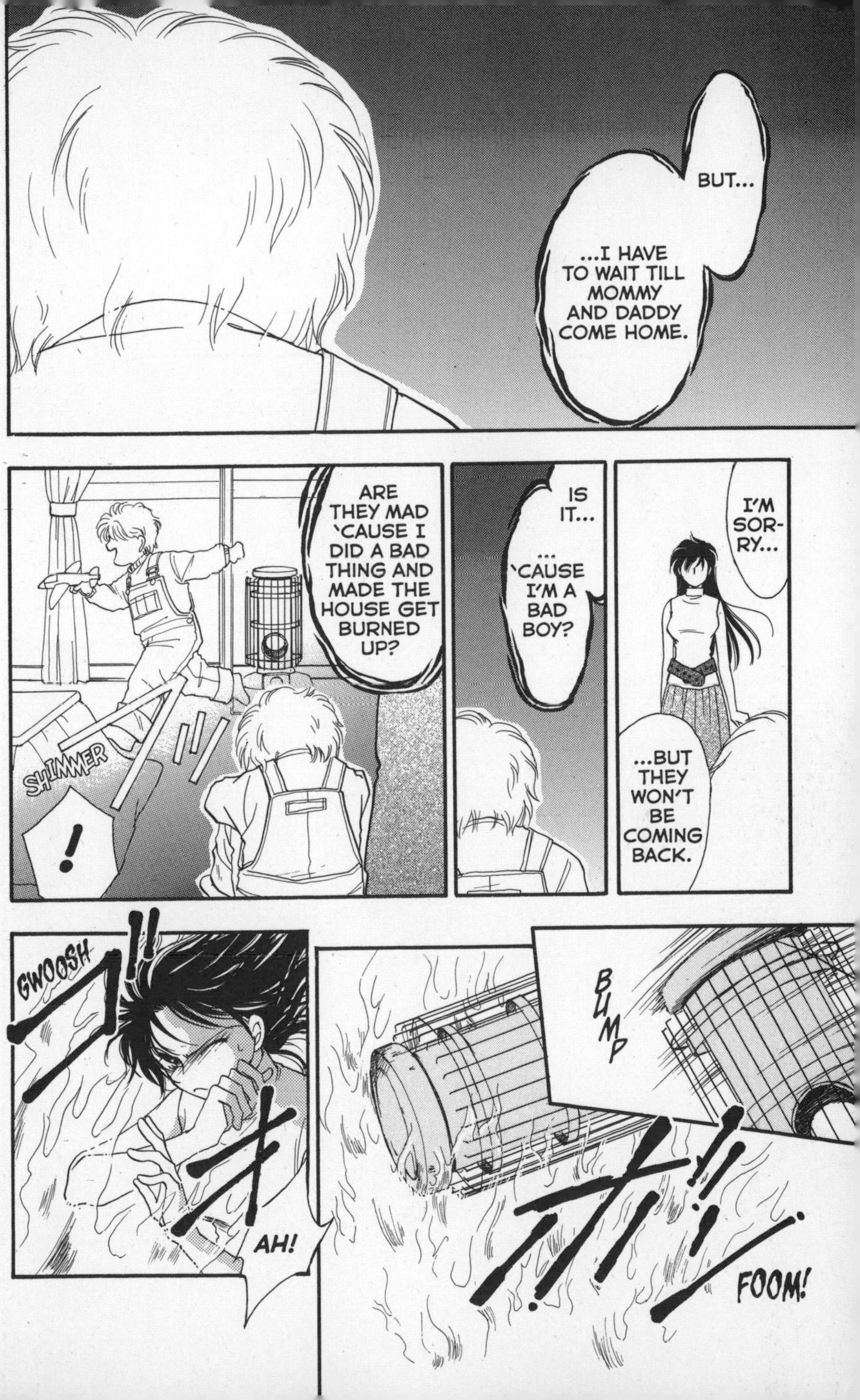

BUT...
...I HAVE TO WAIT TILL MOMMY AND DADDY COME HOME.
I'M SORRY...
...BUT THEY WON'T BE COMING BACK.
IS IT...
...'CAUSE I'M A BAD BOY?
ARE THEY MAD 'CAUSE I DID A BAD THING AND MADE THE HOUSE GET BURNED UP?
SHIMMER
!
BUMP
FOOM!
GWOOSH
AH!

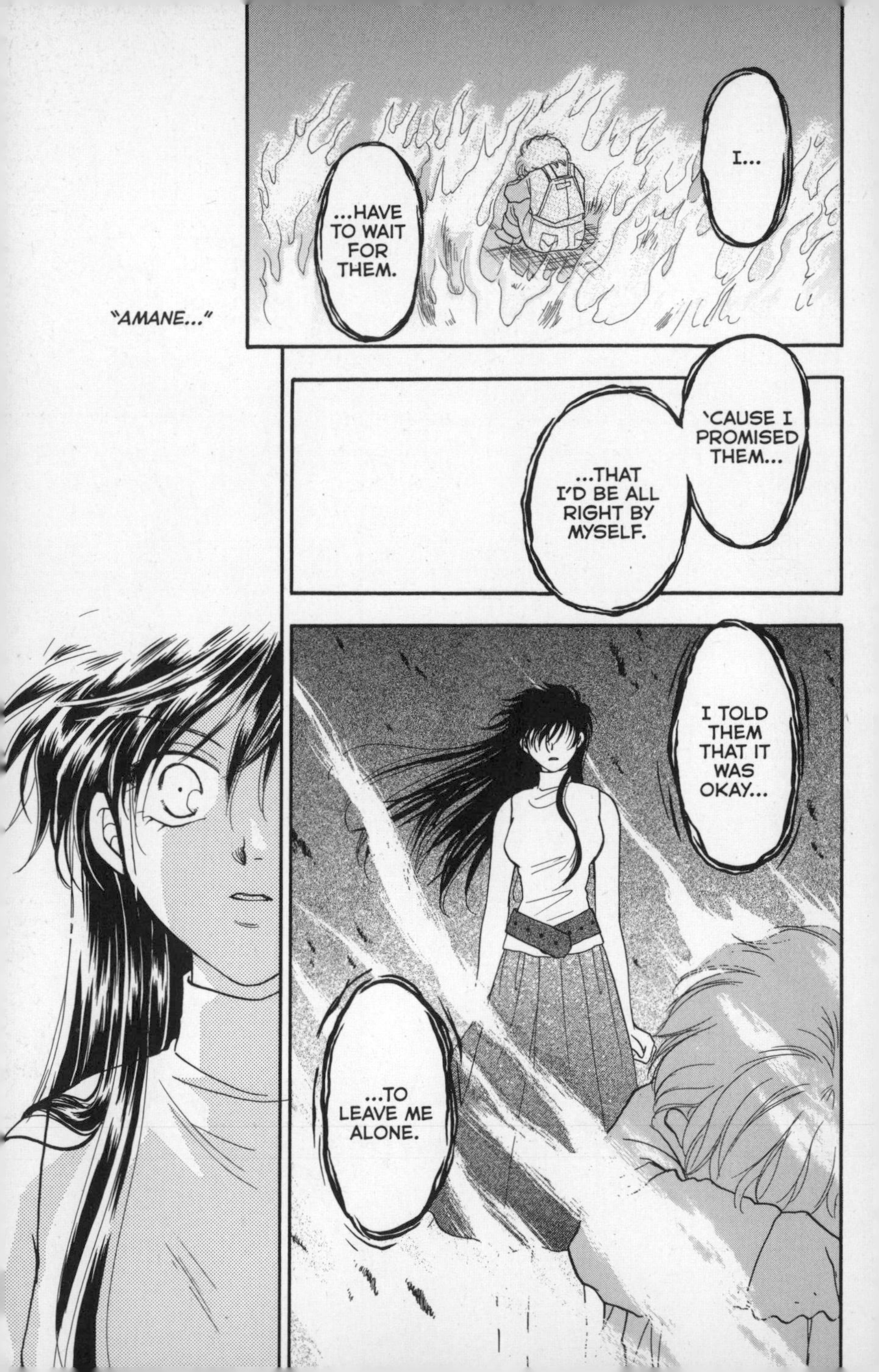
I...
...HAVE TO WAIT FOR THEM.
"AMANE..."
'CAUSE I PROMISED THEM...
...THAT I'D BE ALL RIGHT BY MYSELF.
I TOLD THEM THAT IT WAS OKAY...
...TO LEAVE ME ALONE.

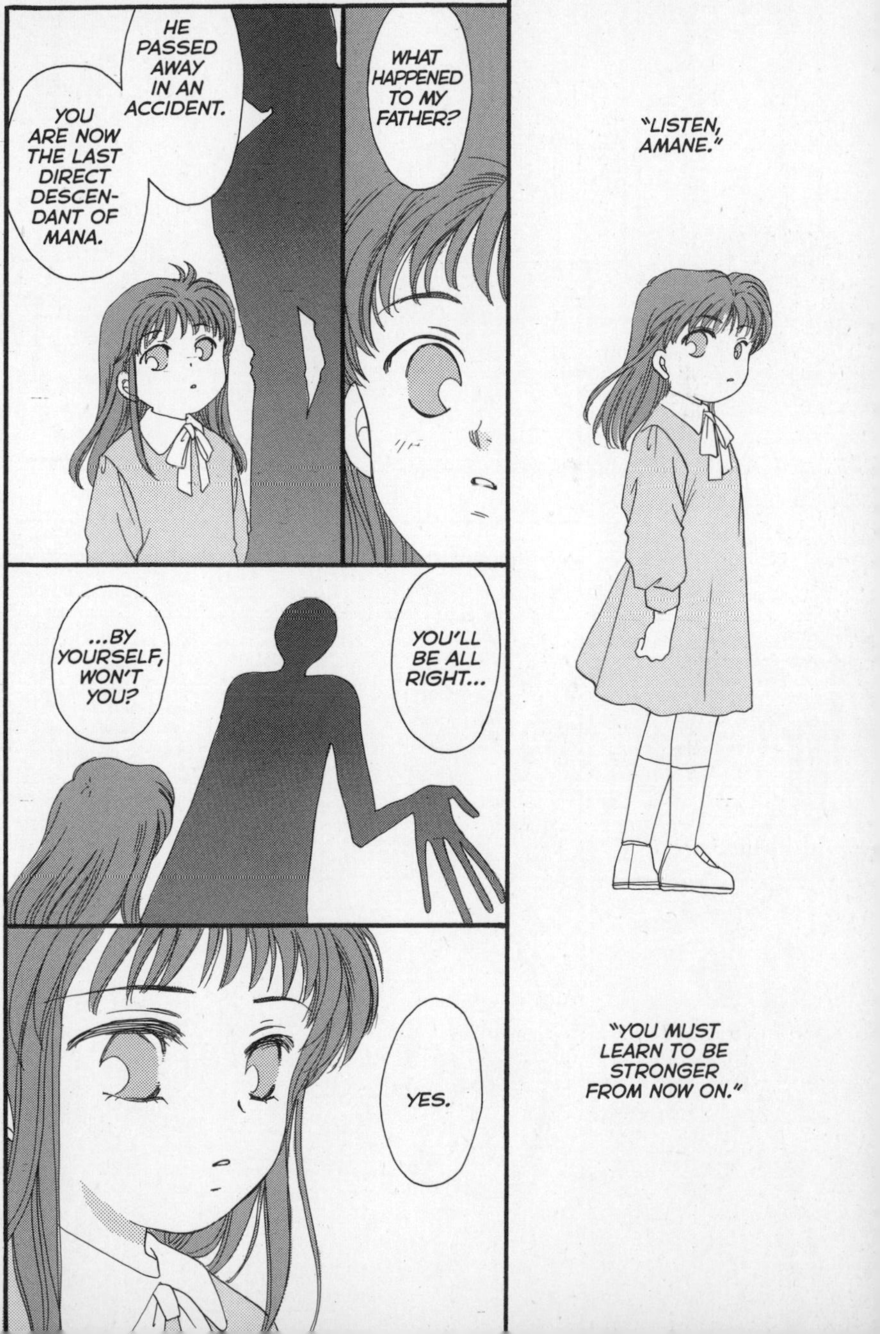
"LISTEN, AMANE."
"YOU MUST LEARN TO BE STRONGER FROM NOW ON."
WHAT HAPPENED TO MY FATHER?
HE PASSED AWAY IN AN ACCIDENT.
YOU ARE NOW THE LAST DIRECT DESCENDANT OF MANA.
YOU'LL BE ALL RIGHT...
...BY YOURSELF, WON'T YOU?
YES.

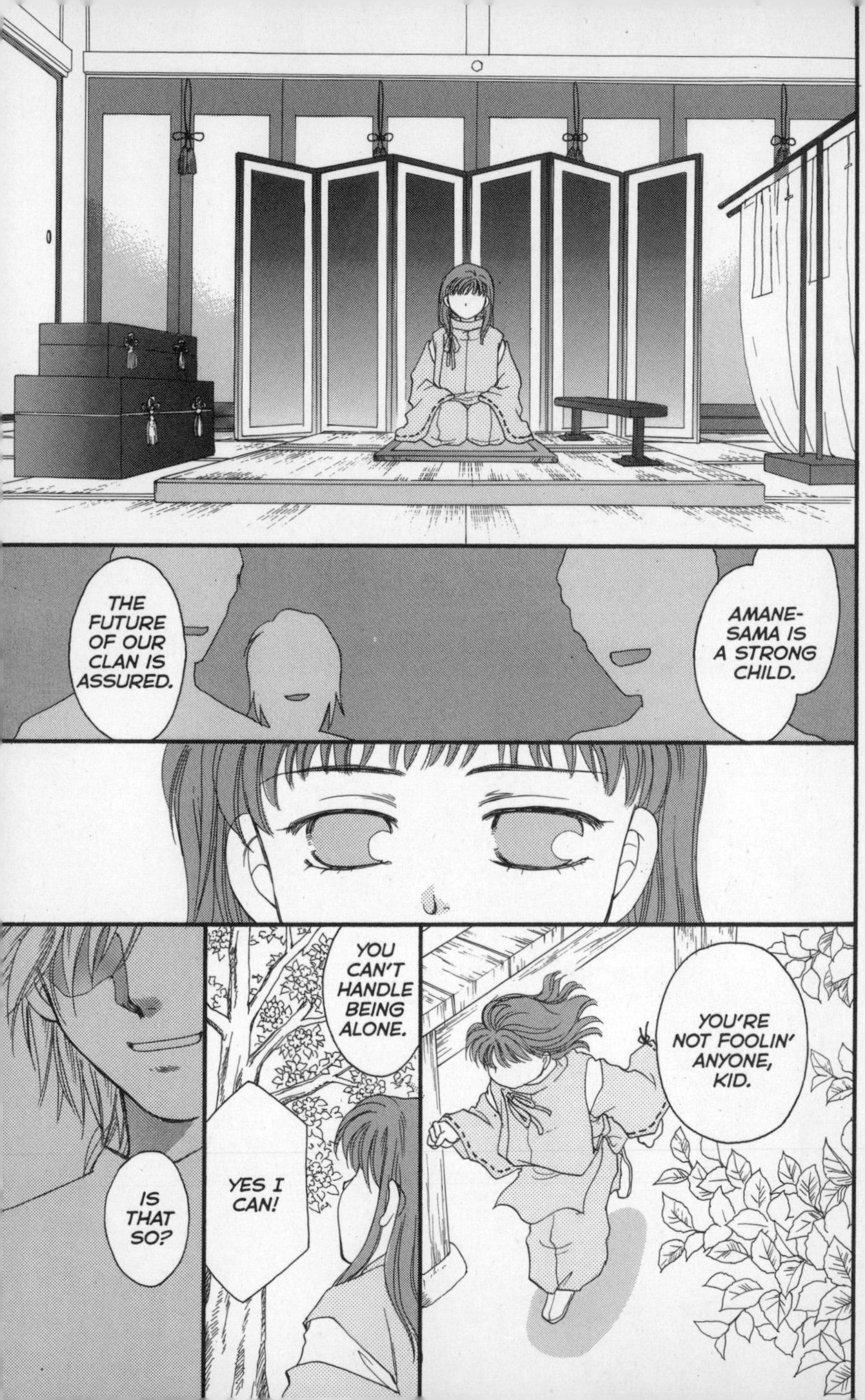
AMANE-SAMA IS A STRONG CHILD.
THE FUTURE OF OUR CLAN IS ASSURED.
YOU'RE NOT FOOLIN' ANYONE, KID.
YOU CAN'T HANDLE BEING ALONE.
YES I CAN!
IS THAT SO?

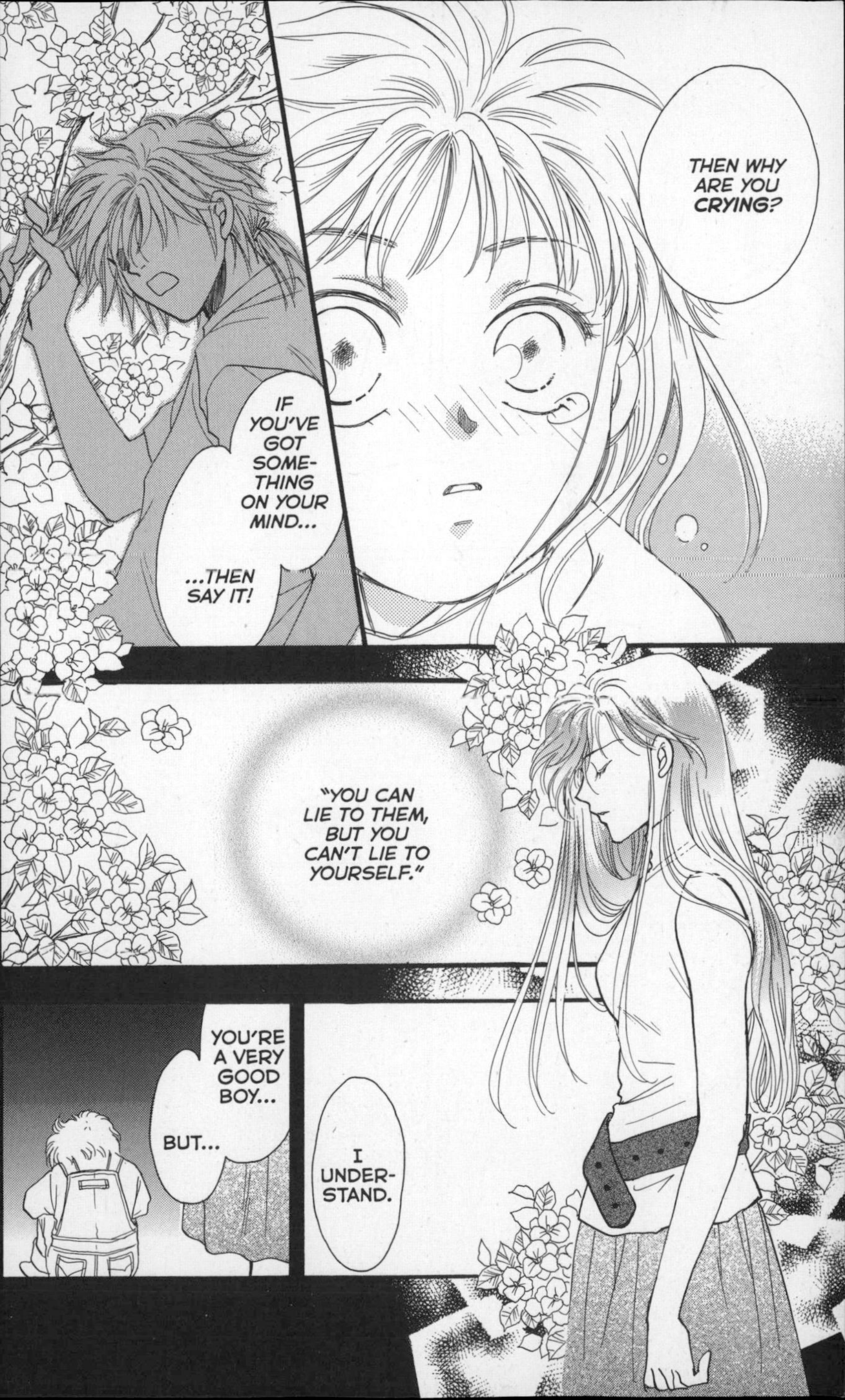
THEN WHY ARE YOU CRYING?
IF YOU'VE GOT SOME-THING ON YOUR MIND...
...THEN SAY IT!
"YOU CAN LIE TO THEM, BUT YOU CAN'T LIE TO YOURSELF."
I UNDER-STAND.
YOU'RE A VERY GOOD BOY...
BUT...

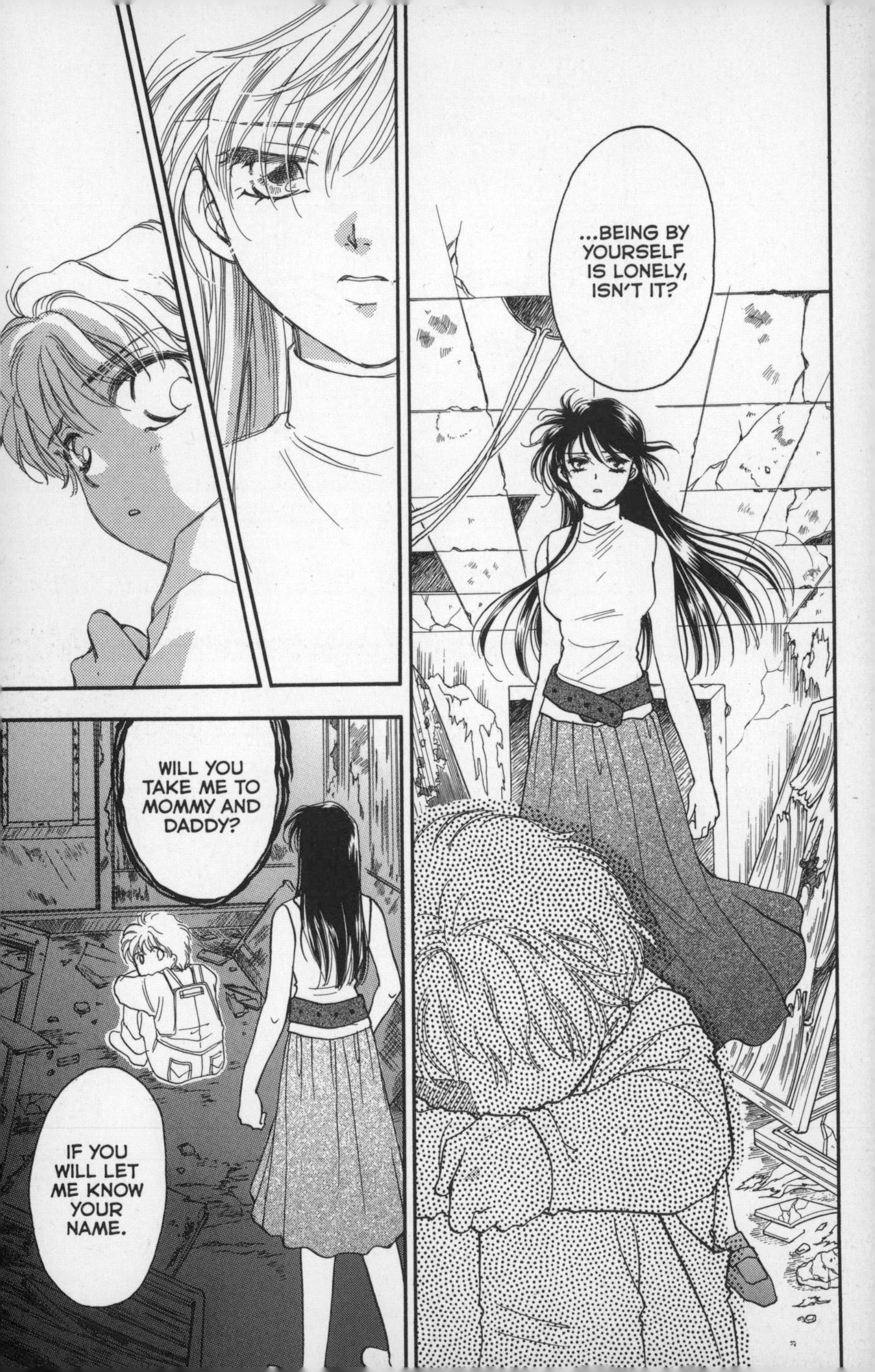
...BEING BY YOURSELF IS LONELY, ISN'T IT?
WILL YOU TAKE ME TO MOMMY AND DADDY?
IF YOU WILL LET ME KNOW YOUR NAME.

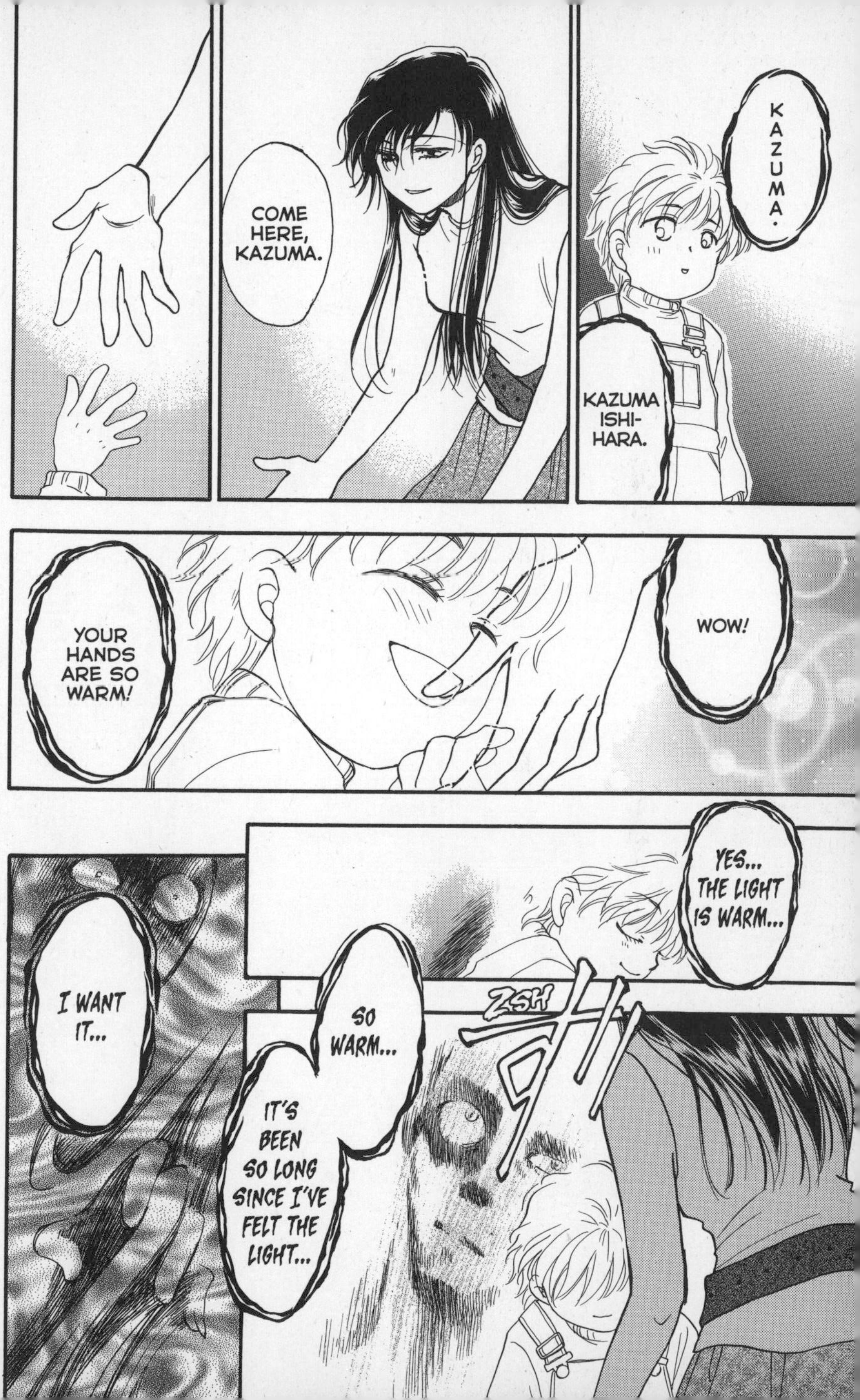
KAZUMA.
KAZUMA ISHI-HARA.
COME HERE, KAZUMA.
WOW!
YOUR HANDS ARE SO WARM!
YES... THE LIGHT IS WARM...
ZSH
SO WARM...
IT'S BEEN SO LONG SINCE I'VE FELT THE LIGHT...
I WANT IT...

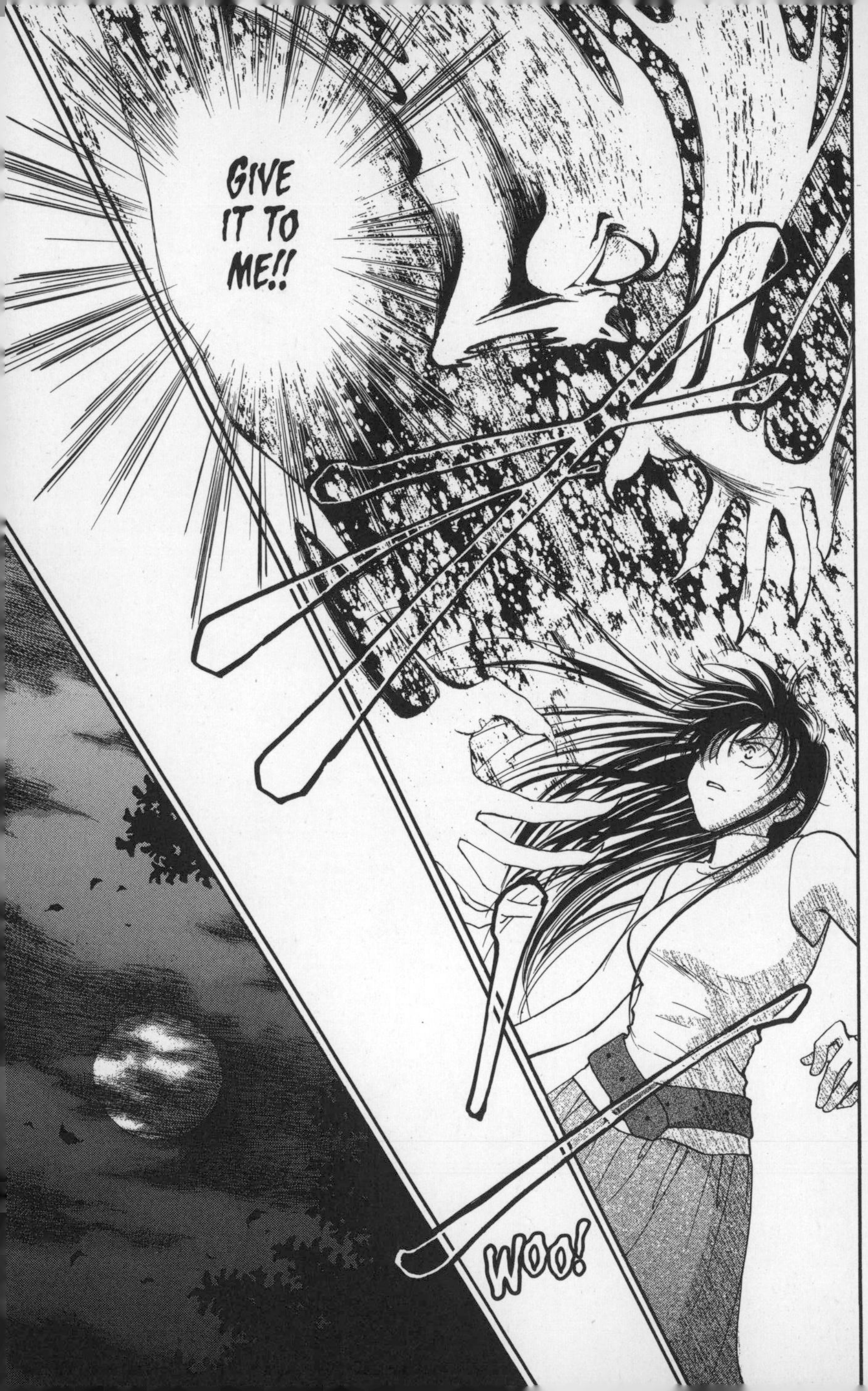
GIVE IT TO ME!!
WOO!

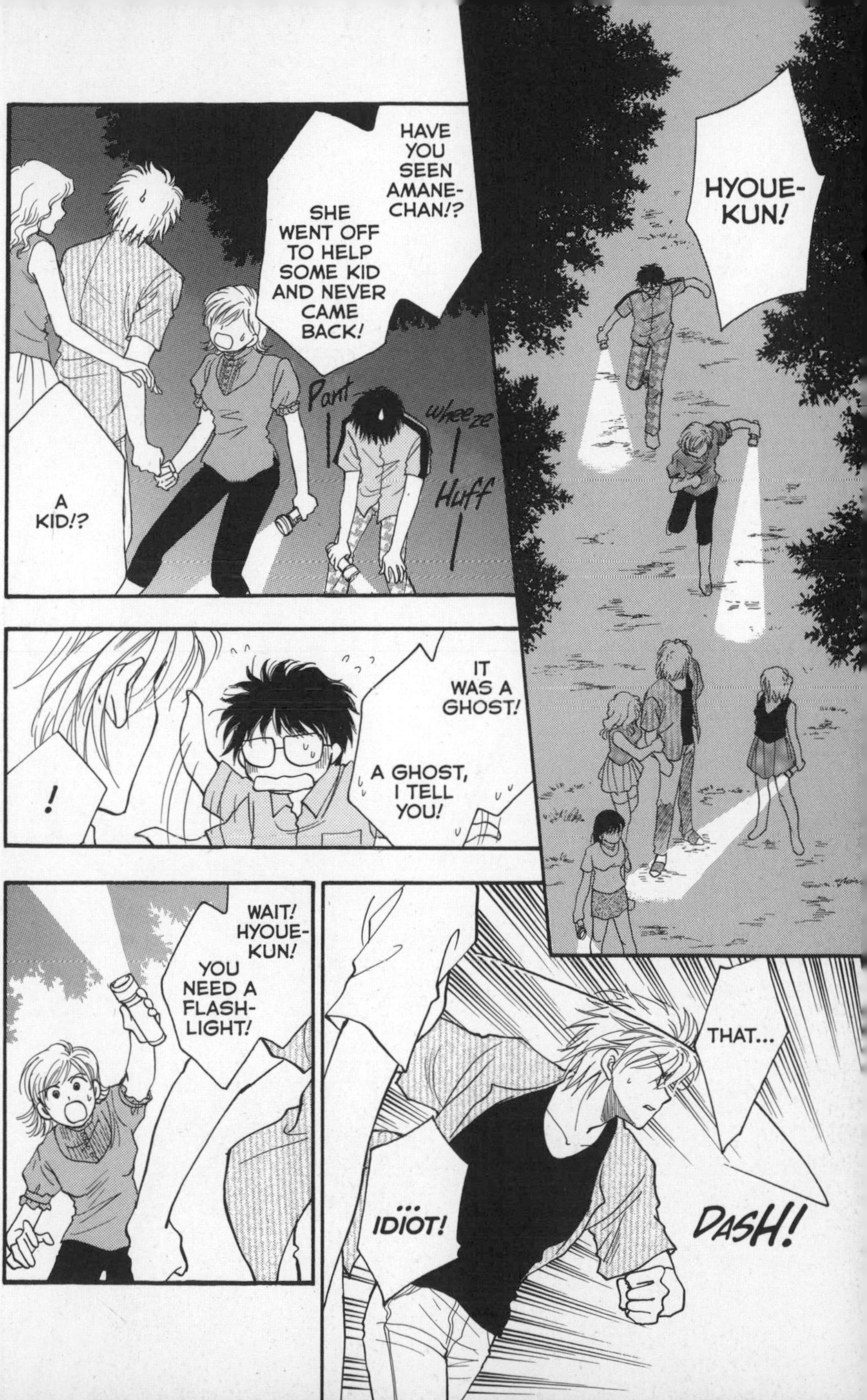
HYOUE-KUN!
HAVE YOU SEEN AMANE-CHAN!?
SHE WENT OFF TO HELP SOME KID AND NEVER CAME BACK!
Pant
wheeze
Huff
A KID!?
IT WAS A GHOST!
A GHOST, I TELL YOU!
!
THAT...
...IDIOT!
DASH!
WAIT! HYOUE-KUN!
YOU NEED A FLASHLIGHT!

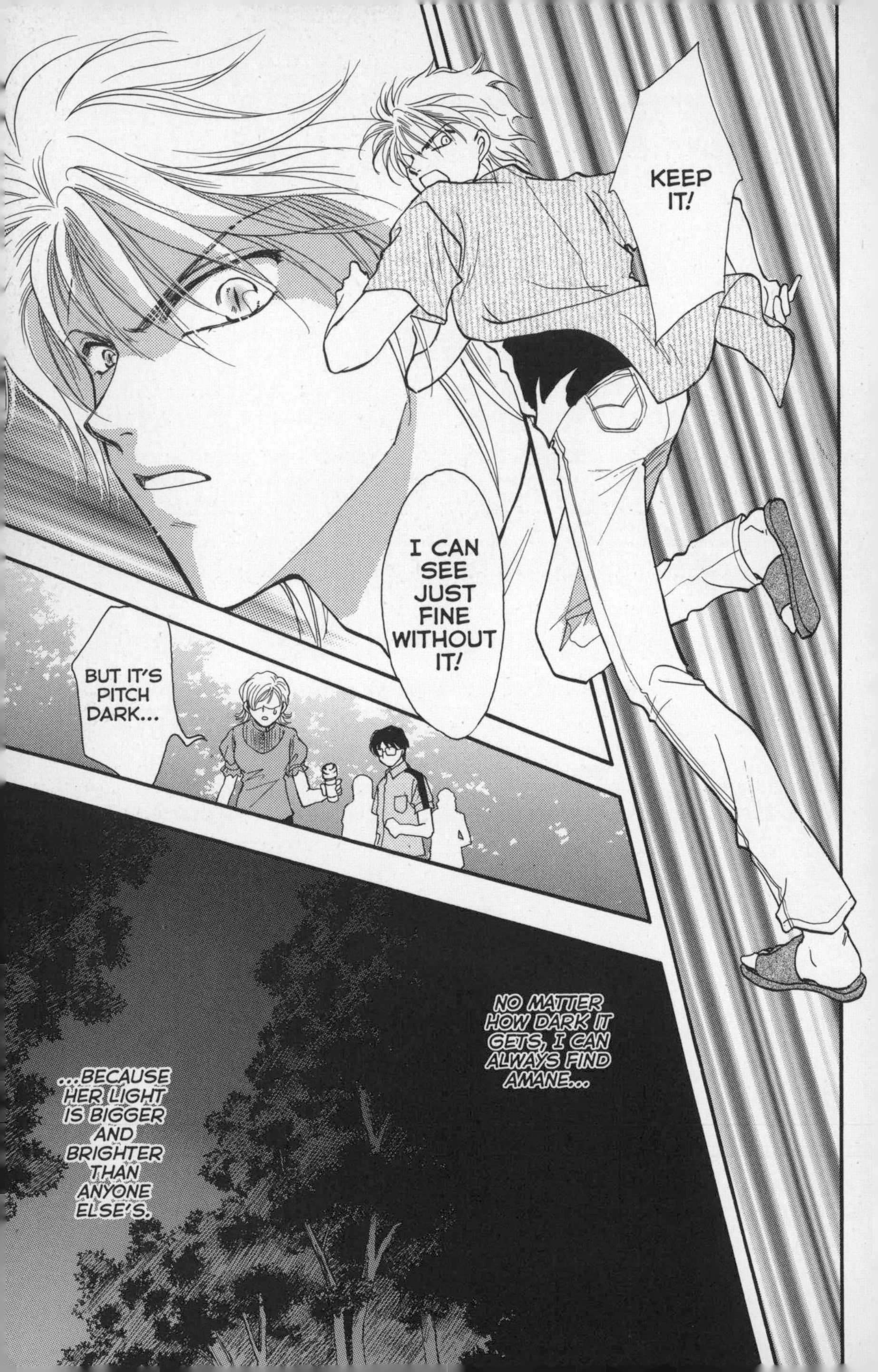
KEEP IT!
I CAN SEE JUST FINE WITHOUT IT!
BUT IT'S PITCH DARK...
NO MATTER HOW DARK IT GETS, I CAN ALWAYS FIND AMANE...
...BECAUSE HER LIGHT IS BIGGER AND BRIGHTER THAN ANYONE ELSE'S.

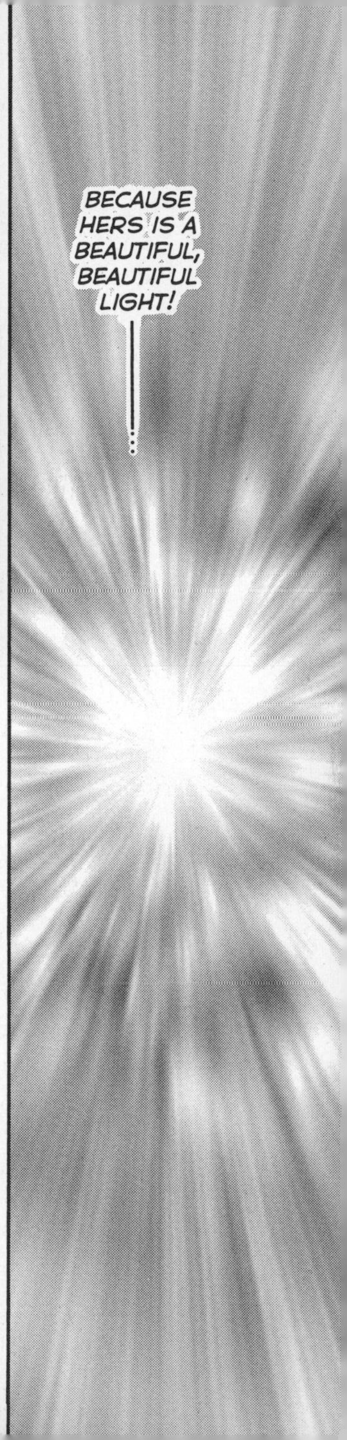
BECAUSE HERS IS A BEAUTIFUL, BEAUTIFUL LIGHT!

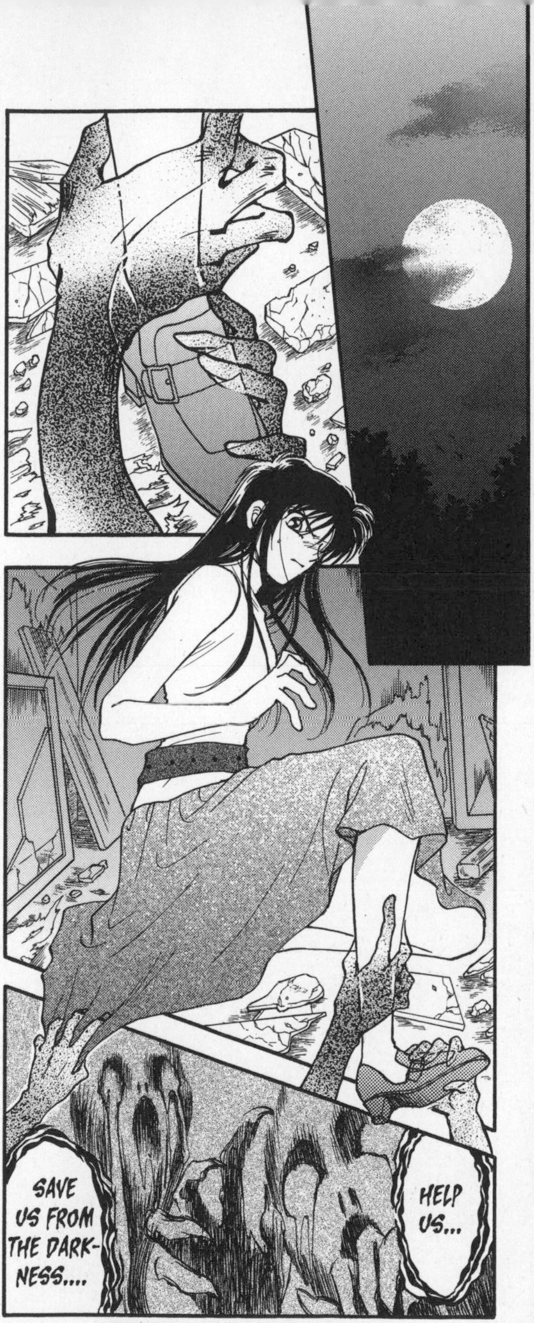
HELP US...
SAVE US FROM THE DARK-NESS....

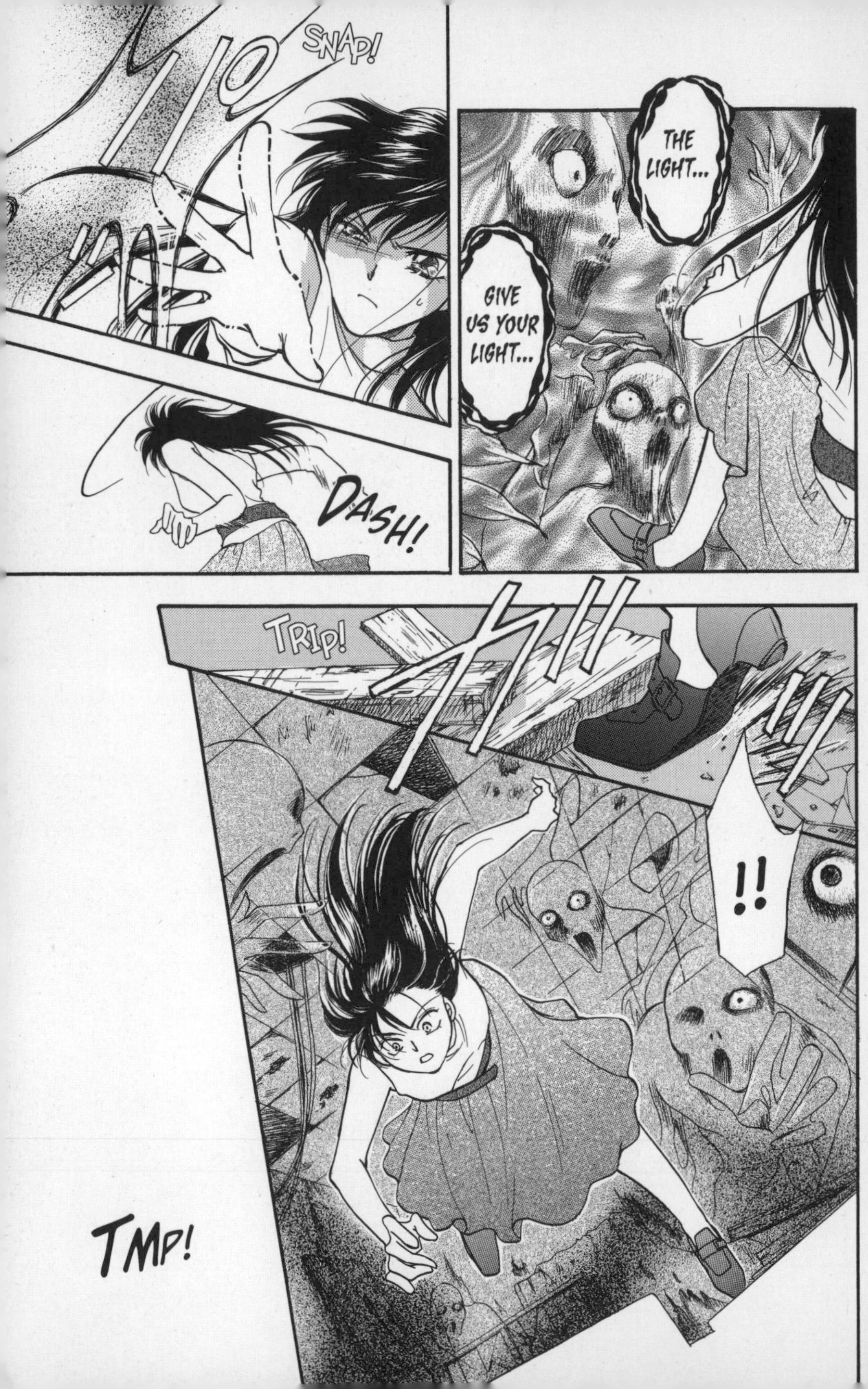
THE LIGHT...
GIVE US YOUR LIGHT...
SNAP!
DASH!
TRIP!
!!
TMP!

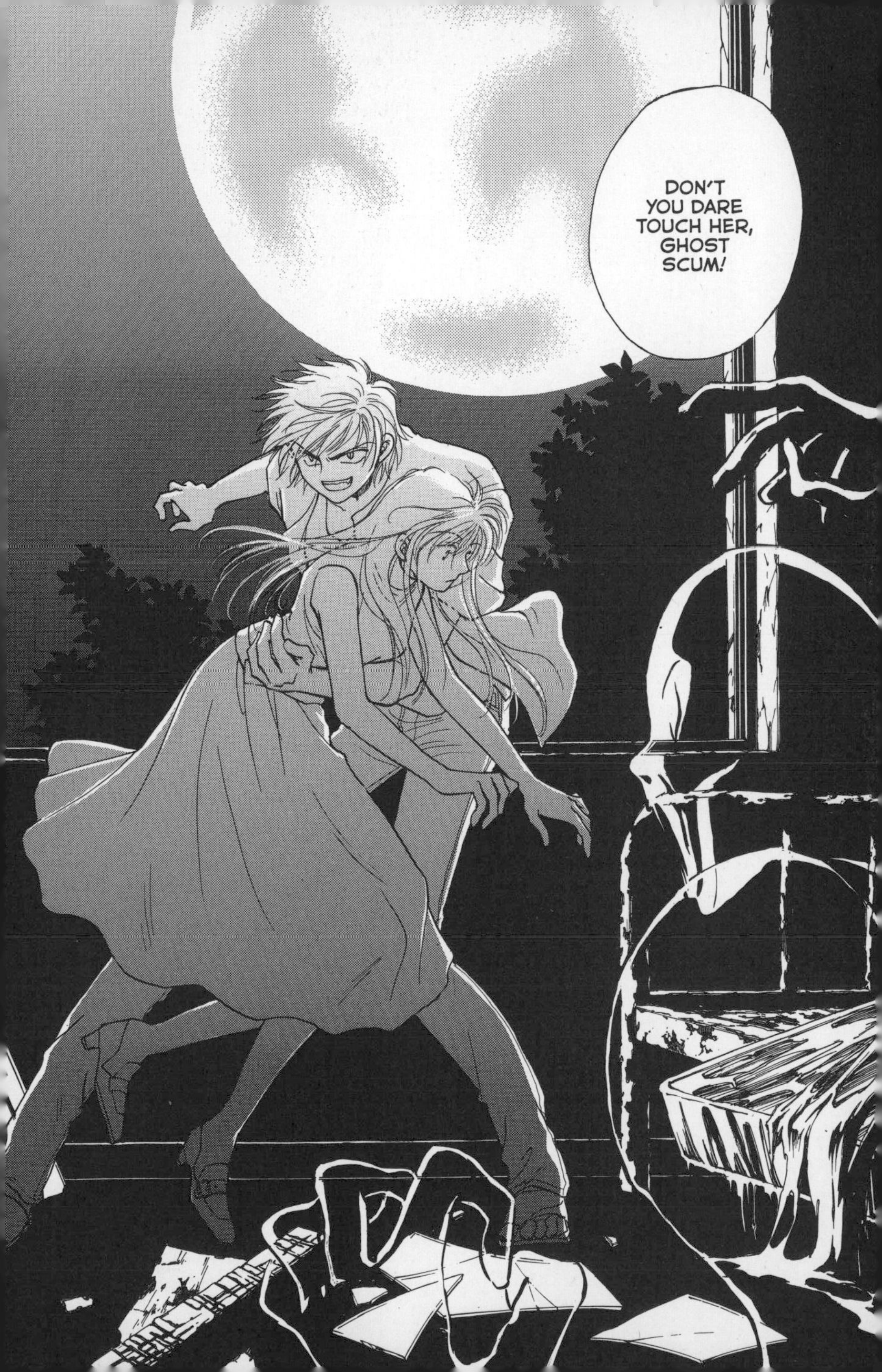
DON'T YOU DARE TOUCH HER, GHOST SCUM!

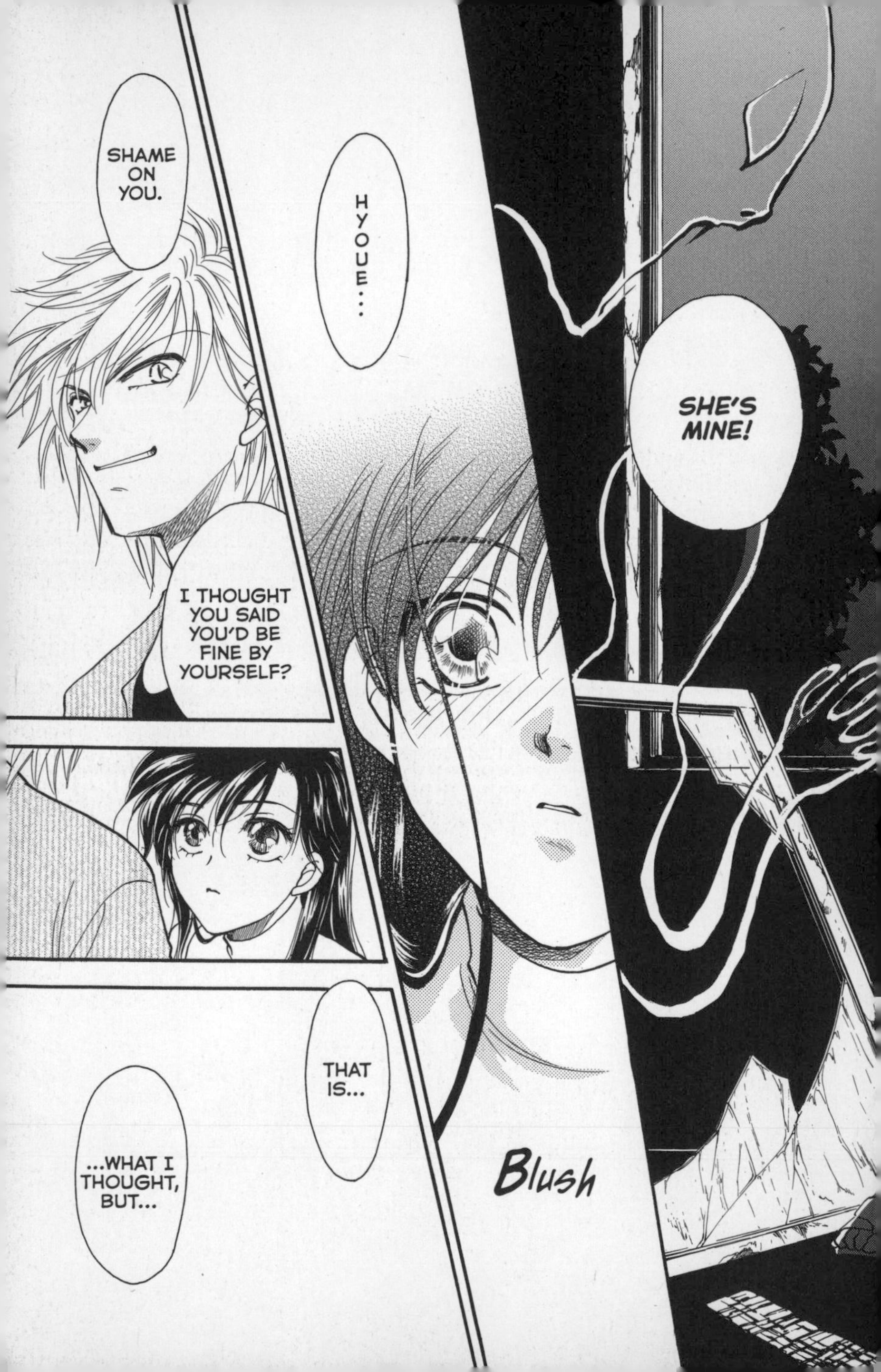
SHE'S MINE!
HYOUE...
Blush
SHAME ON YOU.
I THOUGHT YOU SAID YOU'D BE FINE BY YOURSELF?
THAT IS...
...WHAT I THOUGHT, BUT...

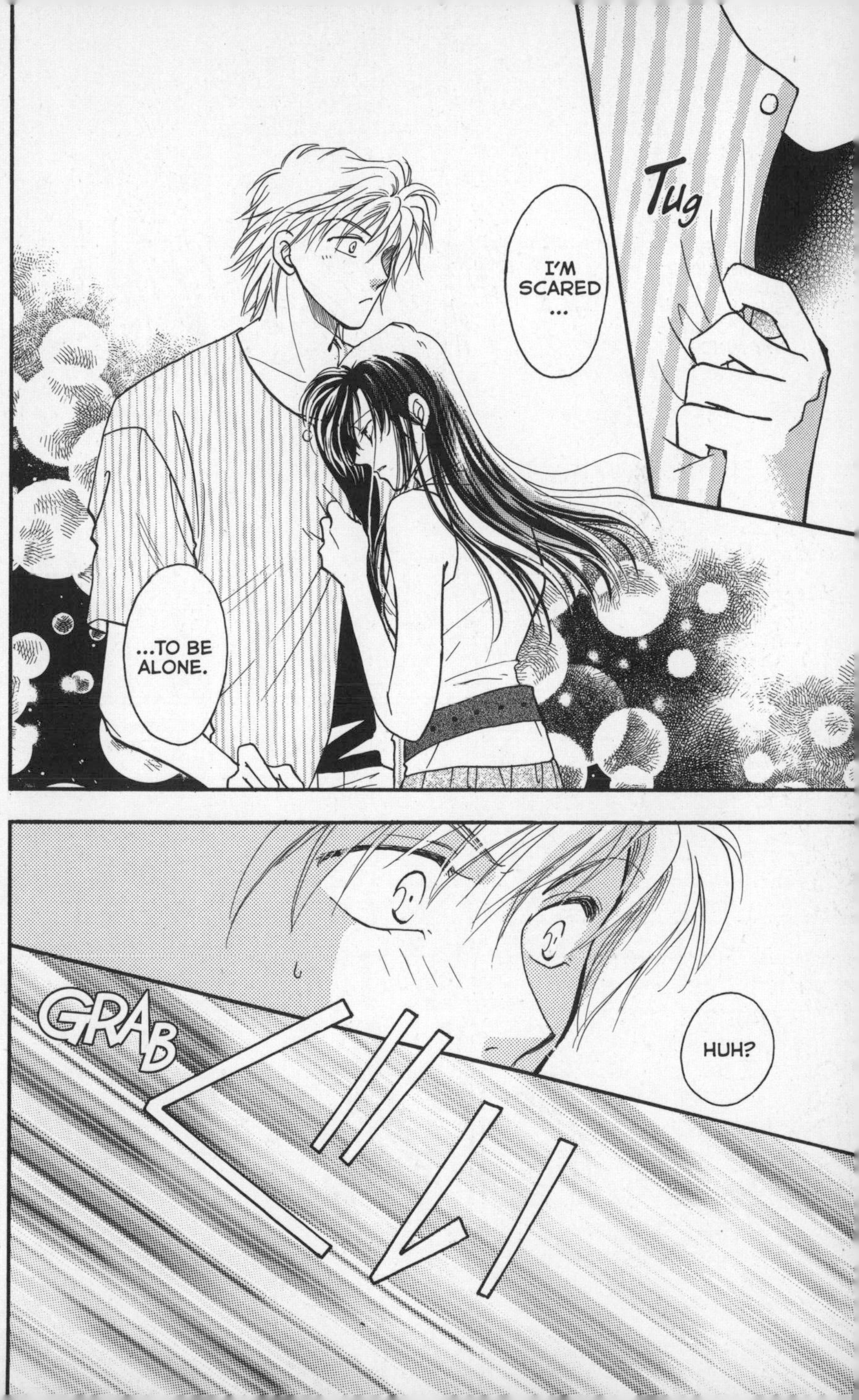
Tug
I'M SCARED ...
...TO BE ALONE.
HUH?
GRAB

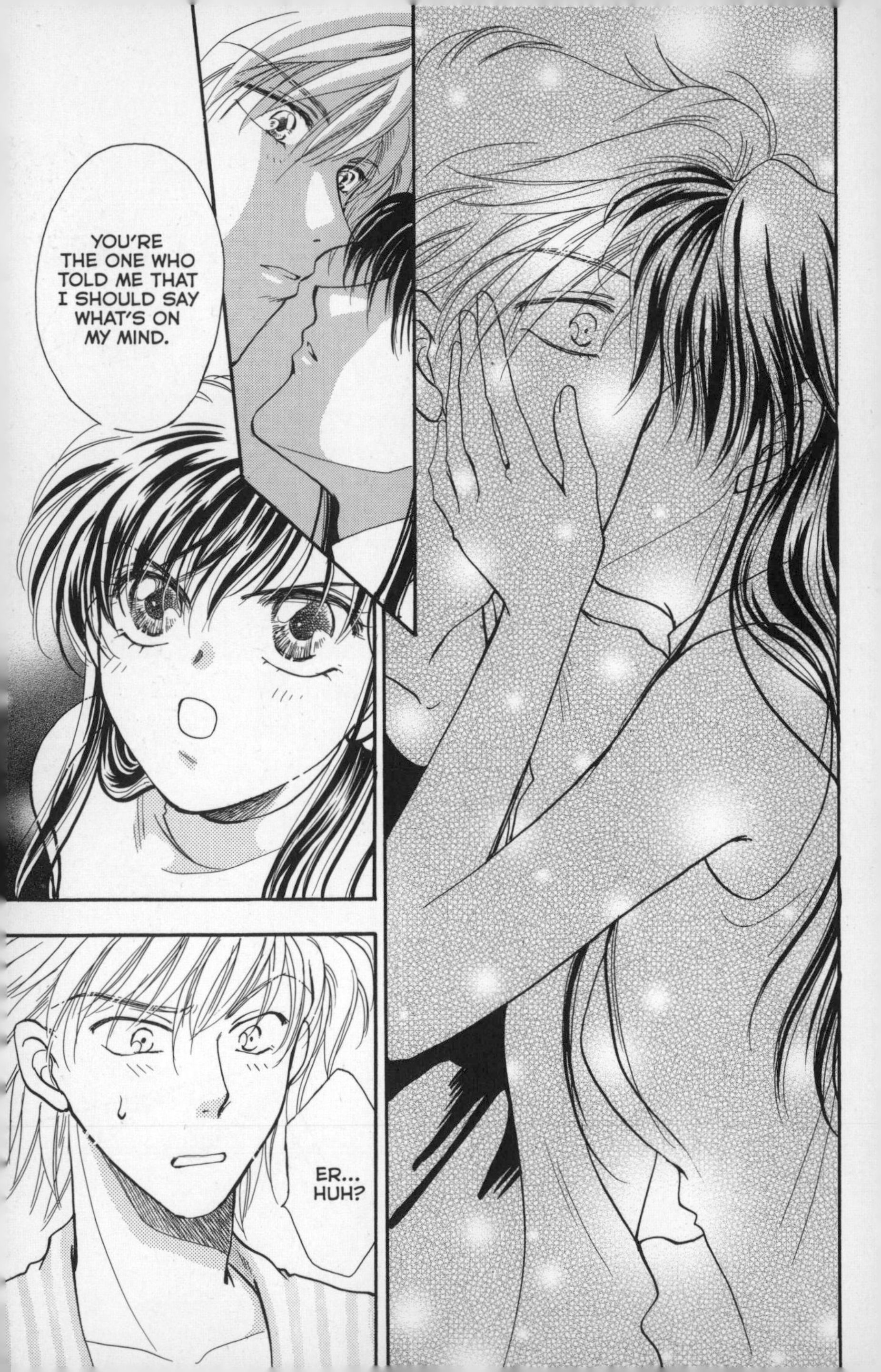
YOU'RE THE ONE WHO TOLD ME THAT I SHOULD SAY WHAT'S ON MY MIND.
ER... HUH?

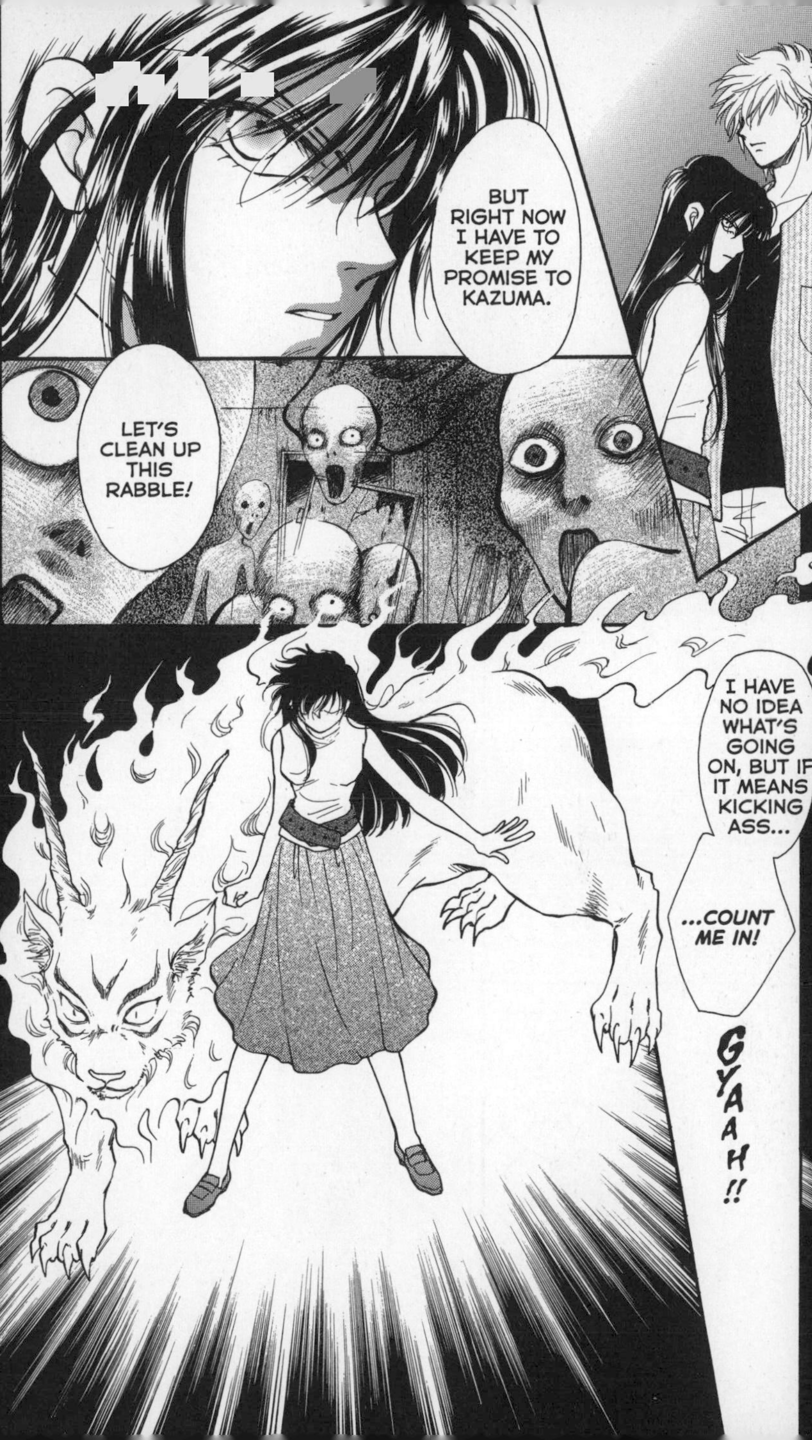
BUT RIGHT NOW I HAVE TO KEEP MY PROMISE TO KAZUMA.
LET'S CLEAN UP THIS RABBLE!
I HAVE NO IDEA WHAT'S GOING ON, BUT IF IT MEANS KICKING ASS...
...COUNT ME IN!
GYAAH!!

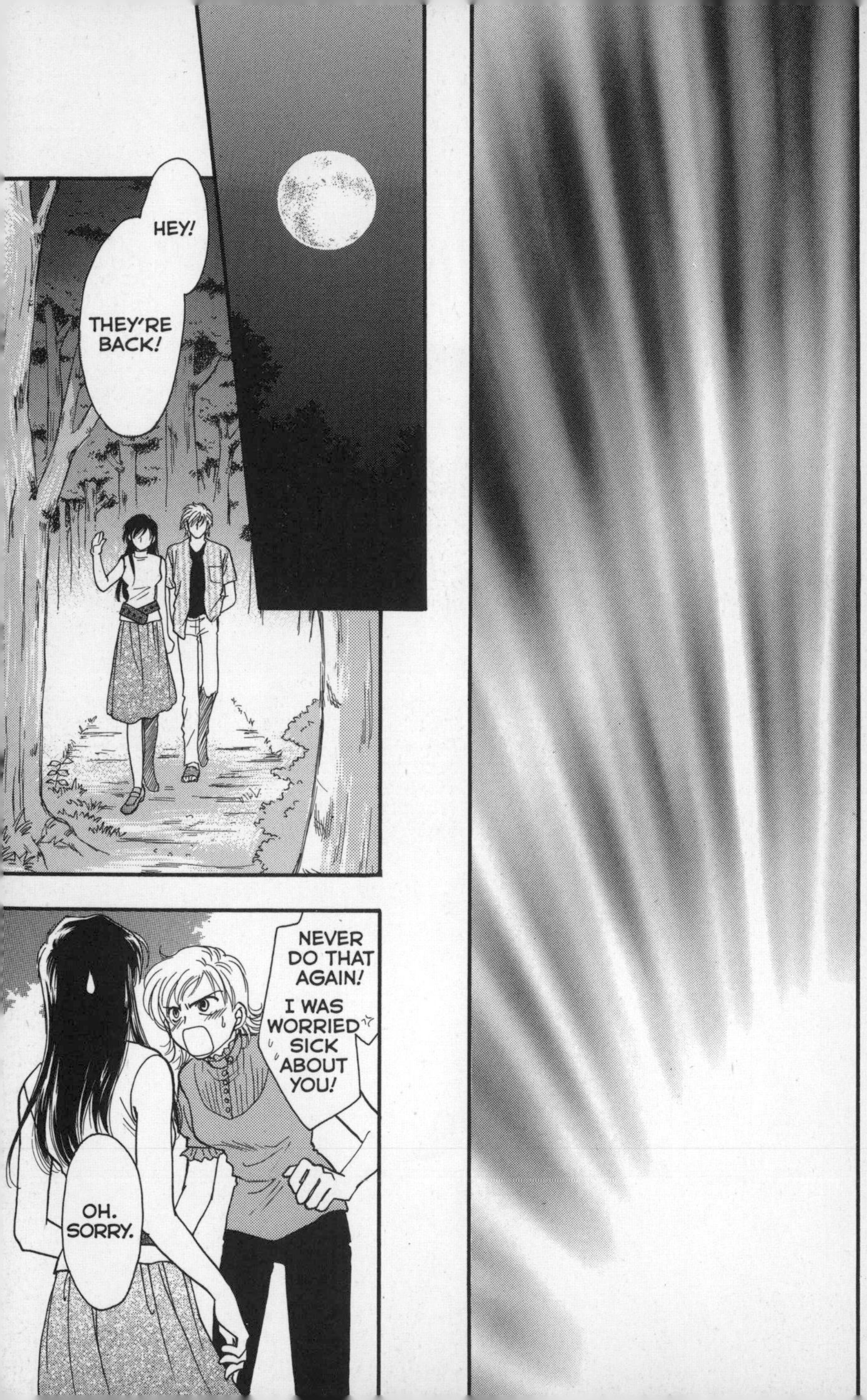
HEY!
THEY'RE BACK!
NEVER DO THAT AGAIN!
I WAS WORRIED SICK ABOUT YOU!
OH. SORRY.

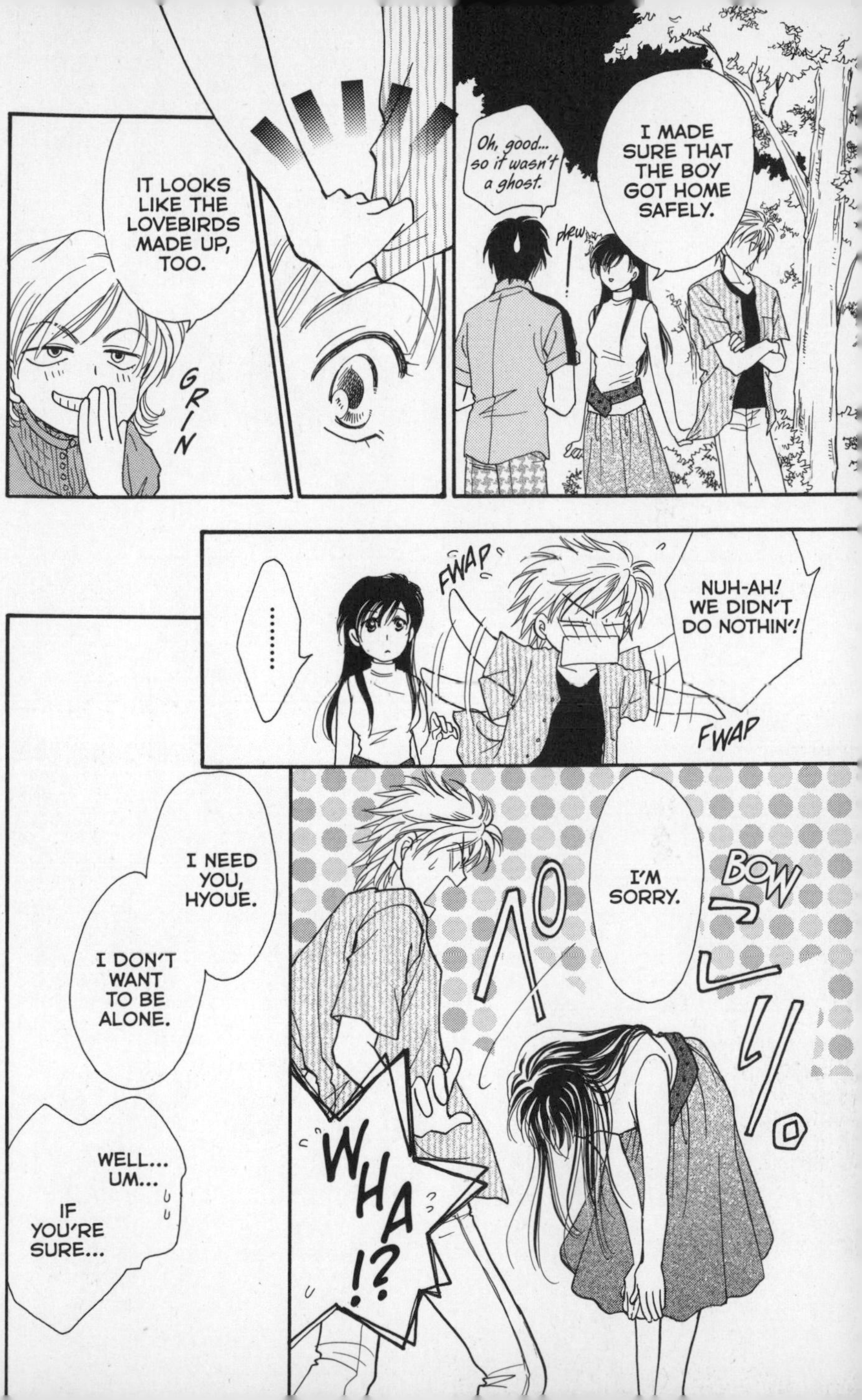
I MADE SURE THAT THE BOY GOT HOME SAFELY.
Oh, good... so it wasn't a ghost.
phew
IT LOOKS LIKE THE LOVEBIRDS MADE UP, TOO.
GRIN
NUH-AH! WE DIDN'T DO NOTHIN'!
FWAP
FWAP
......
I'M SORRY.
BOW
WHA!?
I NEED YOU, HYOUE.
I DON'T WANT TO BE ALONE.
WELL... UM...
IF YOU'RE SURE...

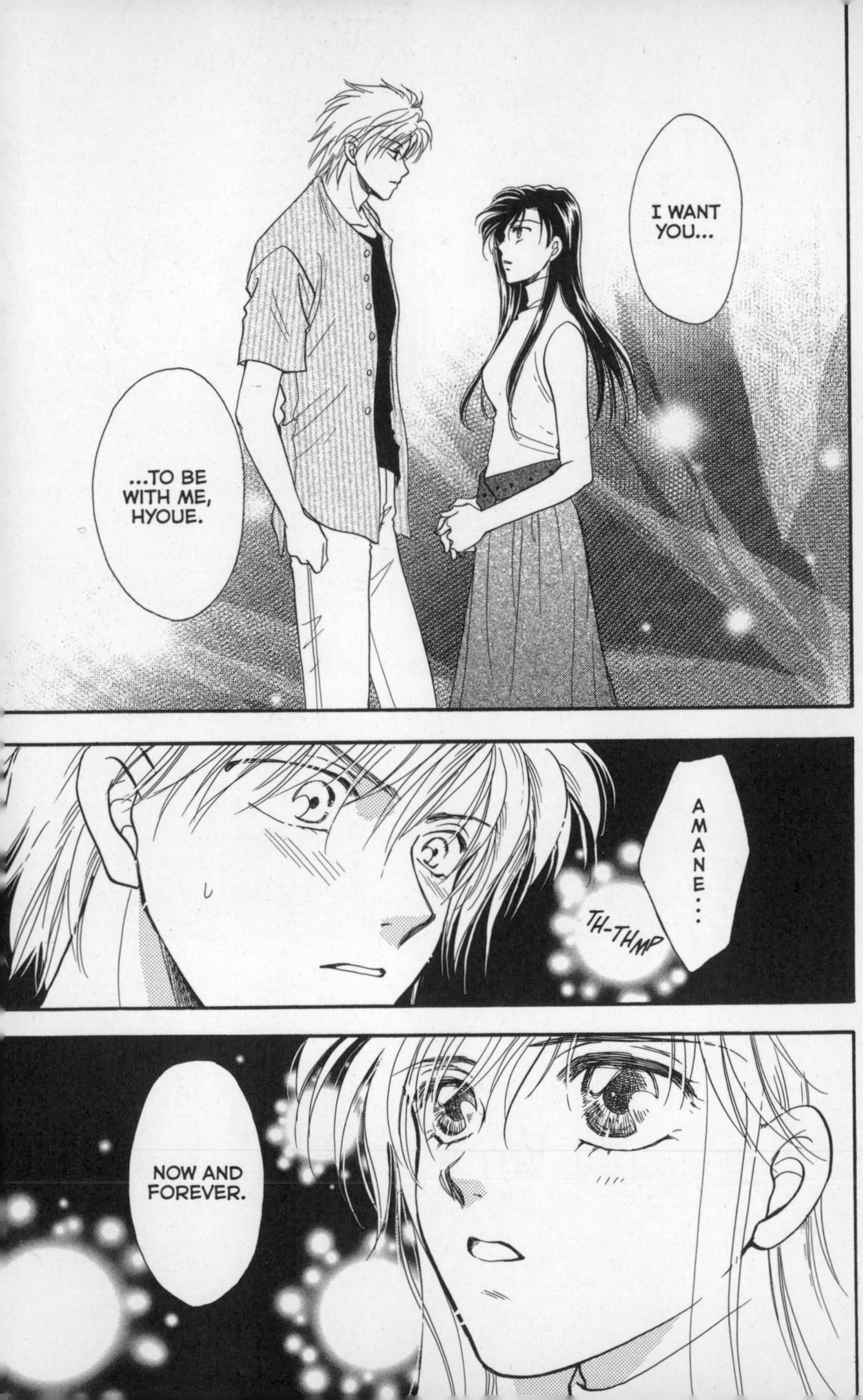
I WANT YOU...
...TO BE WITH ME, HYOUE.
AMANE...
TH-THMP
NOW AND FOREVER.

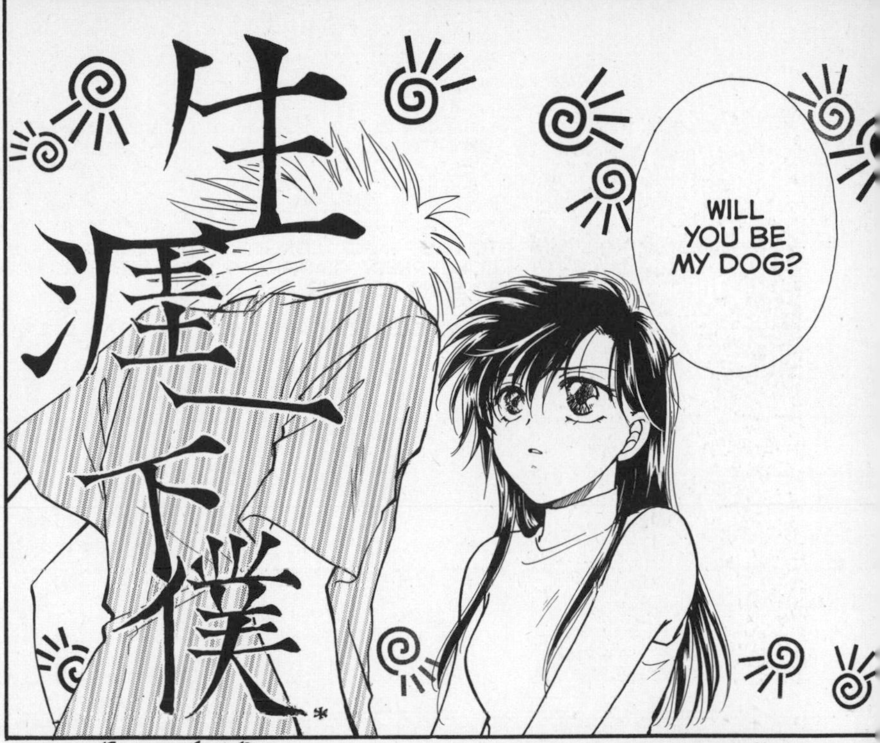
WILL YOU BE MY DOG?
生涯下僕*

*Forever her Dog

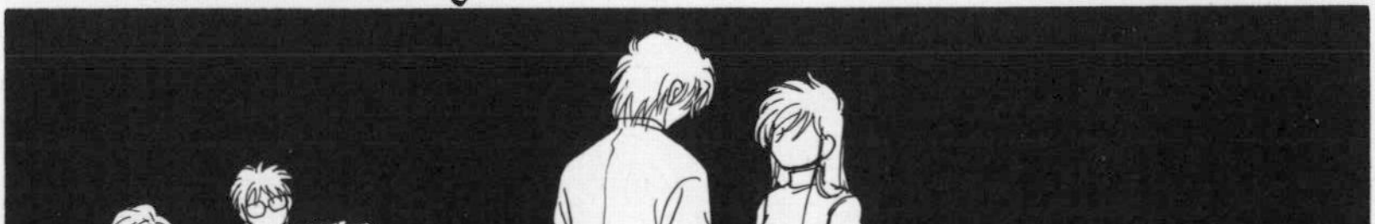

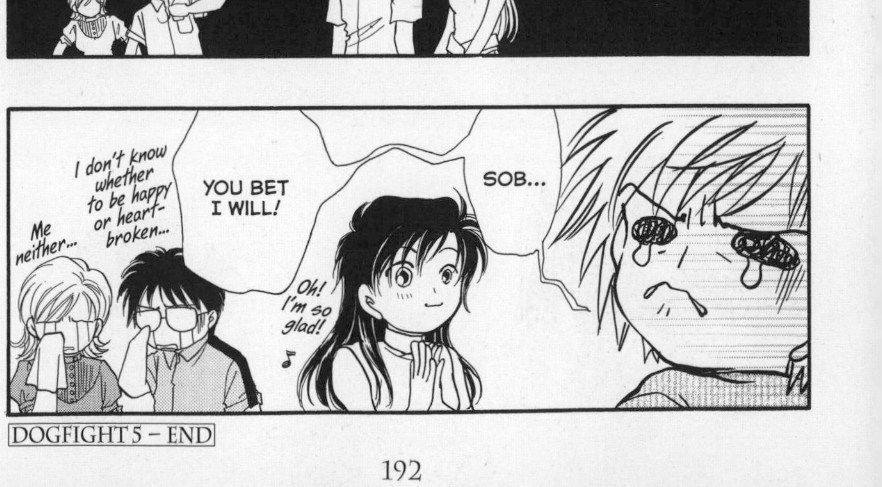
SOB...
YOU BET I WILL!
Oh! I'm so glad!
I don't know whether to be happy or heart-broken...
Me neither...

DOGFIGHT 5 – END

SPECIAL ♡ THANKS
Ao.S
Takumi.A
Yukako.T
Emu.K
Harumi.M
Riu.A
Shiori.A
Reiko.O
Akira.K
Yui.M
Hana.U
Miyuki.N
Tohru.K
Hitoyo.S
Y.Iwahashi
&
My family

SO...HOW DID YOU LIKE IT? I'M SO NERVOUS! -;SWEAT;- WHAT STARTED AS A HORROR MANGA HAS PRETTY MUCH TRANSFORMED INTO MY FAVORITE KIND OF STORY. BUT JUST BECAUSE I LIKE IT DOESN'T MEAN OTHER PEOPLE WILL BE ABLE TO ENJOY IT. THE SERIES MAY NOT BE ABLE TO LAST MUCH LONGER... (NO, SERIOUSLY I'M CONCERNED! -;LAUGH;-) SO, PLEASE FEEL FREE TO SEND ME YOUR FEEDBACK!!

IN ANY CASE, I HOPE TO SEE YOU AGAIN SOON! ♡

2001. 8. MICK

Are you caught under Amane's spell? Does Hyoue have you on a leash? Well now's your chance to share the love with other HMD fans. Go! Comi is now accepting fan art for future volumes of *Her Majesty's Dog*! Send your fan art and letters to:

Go! Media Entertainment
5737 Kanan Rd. #591
Agoura Hills CA 91301

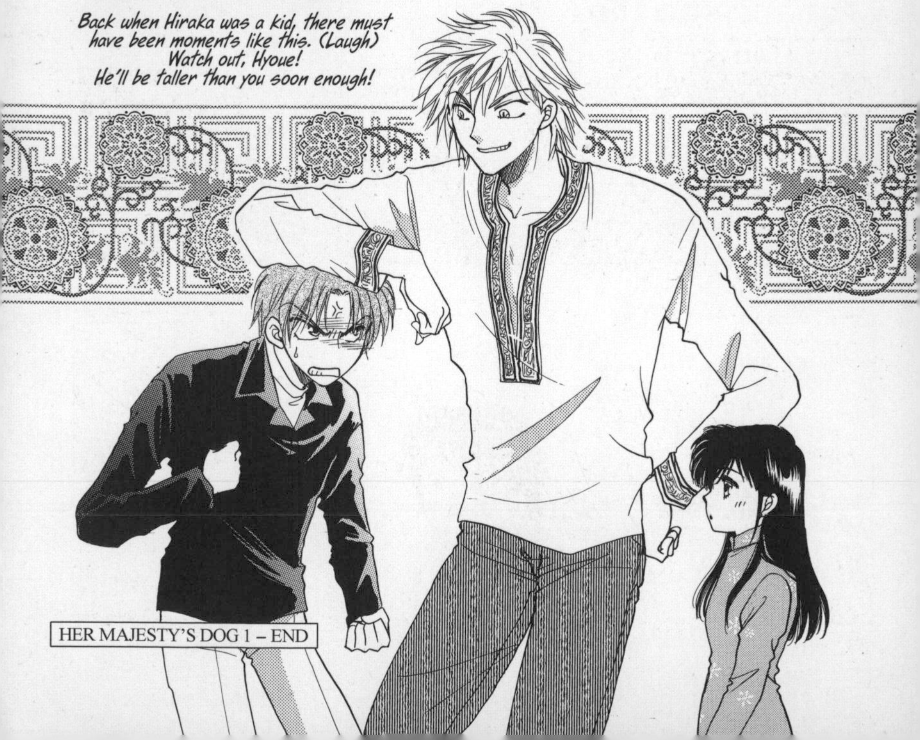
Back when Hiraka was a kid, there must have been moments like this. (Laugh)
Watch out, Hyoue!
He'll be taller than you soon enough!

HER MAJESTY'S DOG 1 – END

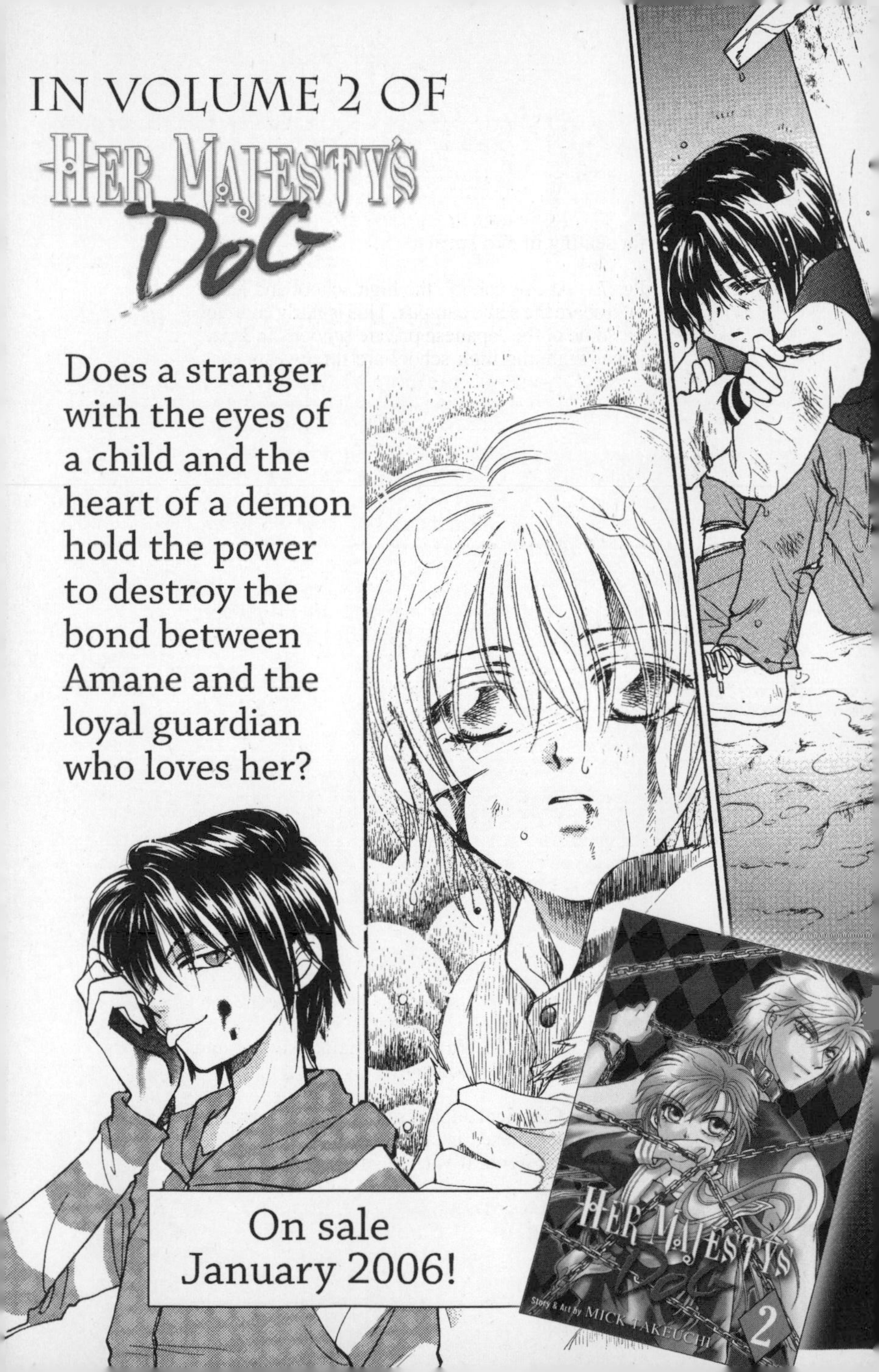
IN VOLUME 2 OF
HER MAJESTY'S DOG
Does a stranger with the eyes of a child and the heart of a demon hold the power to destroy the bond between Amane and the loyal guardian who loves her?
On sale January 2006!
HER MAJESTY'S DOG
Story & Art by MICK TAKEUCHI
2

TRANSLATOR'S NOTES

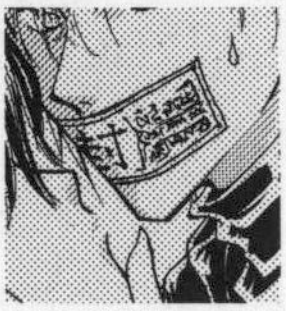

Pg. 1 – The paper in Hyoue's mouth is a charm for sealing in evil spirits.

Pg. 7 – At this school, the high school and junior high share the same campus. This is fairly common for some of the Japanese private schools. In Japan, junior high and high school are three years each. Amane, Hyoue and Takako are 1st year high school students.

真 MA
名 NA
使 TSU KA
い I

Pg. 36 – The kanji characters in "manatsukai" literally mean "True Name Controller."

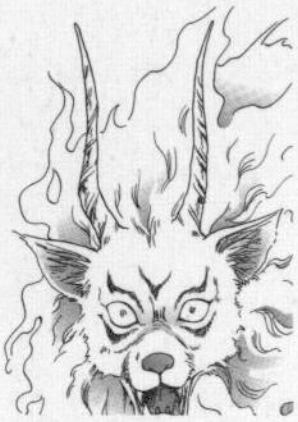

Pg. 36 – Koma-oni is based on the mythological Komainu (Korean Dog). Pairs of the lion-like statues were placed on the sides of a shrine or temple entrance to ward of spirits. Komainu entered Japan via China or Korea. Hyoue's true form is based on a Komainu.

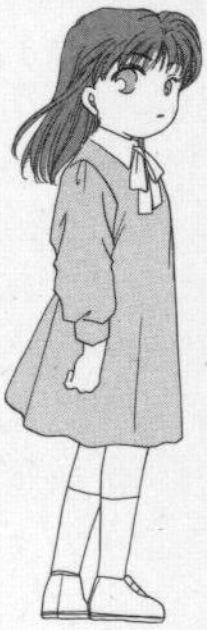

Pg. 47 – A Lolita Complex (called "loli-com" or "rori-com" in Japan) refers to an adult male who is fixated on an underage girl.

Pg. 55 – The Japanese phrase for jealousy is "yakimochi o yaku," which also means "to cook rice cakes." It's a Japanese tradition to cook rice cakes during celebration of New Year's. Amane is so naïve that she thought Takako was referring to Hyoue cooking rice cakes, as opposed to him being jealous of Takako.

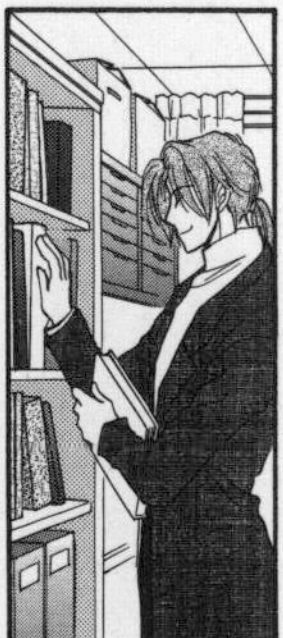

Pg. 83 – In Japan, classes are divided by Homeroom. A group of around 40 students take the same coursework together. Most courses are taught in the same room, with teachers rotating in and out while students remain. Amane and crew are in Homeroom 1-C.

Pg. 86 – Classical Japanese, also known as Traditional Japanese, is an old style of Japanese writing not generally used in modern day. It's particularly important to study in order to read classic Japanese poetry and texts.

Kotodama: From the Mouths of the Gods

The concept of Kotodama originated in ancient Japan, in a time when people believed that words themselves possessed a power that could control the lives and futures of human beings. In a time before written language, words were perceived as potent, even dangerous, and were thus used only when necessary. Language itself was treated as if it were a living thing imbued with its own spirit, making it something to both respect and fear.

This belief was hardly exclusive to Japan. Almost every ancient culture on Earth had a spiritual belief or theory about the power of words. Some religions even went so far as to forbid the use of certain words -- the name of a god, for example -- that were believed to have a power so great that they could destroy mankind. In Egypt, there were certain words reserved strictly for use by the gods, words that could allow their speaker the power to forge and rule over the world.

But the belief that even small words can effect the outcome of one's life on a daily basis still lingers on even today. There are countless books and theories about positive thinking and the power of changing one's life through how one speaks. It's not inconceivable that there might be individuals out there who were raised with an understanding of the power of language and can use it as Amane does, to heal the pain of old wounds, and call to rest the restless spirits who have nothing left to them but words of grief.

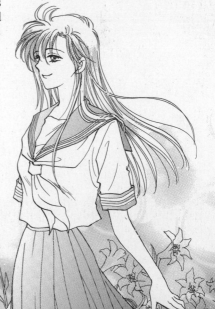

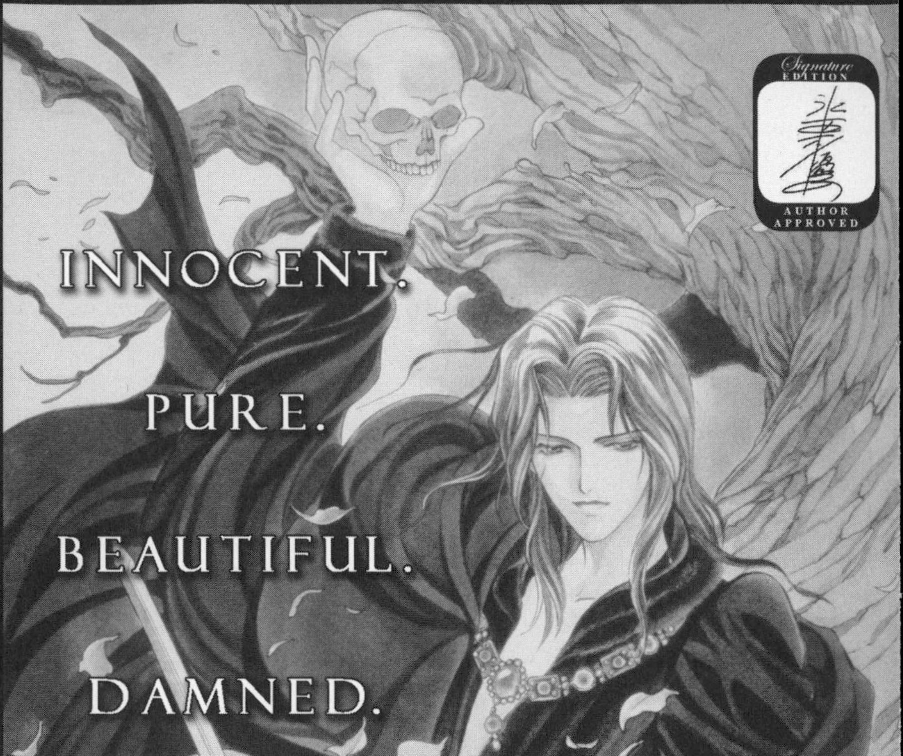
Signature EDITION
AUTHOR APPROVED
INNOCENT.
PURE.
BEAUTIFUL.
DAMNED.
Cantarella
© 2001 You Higuri/Akitashoten

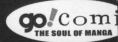

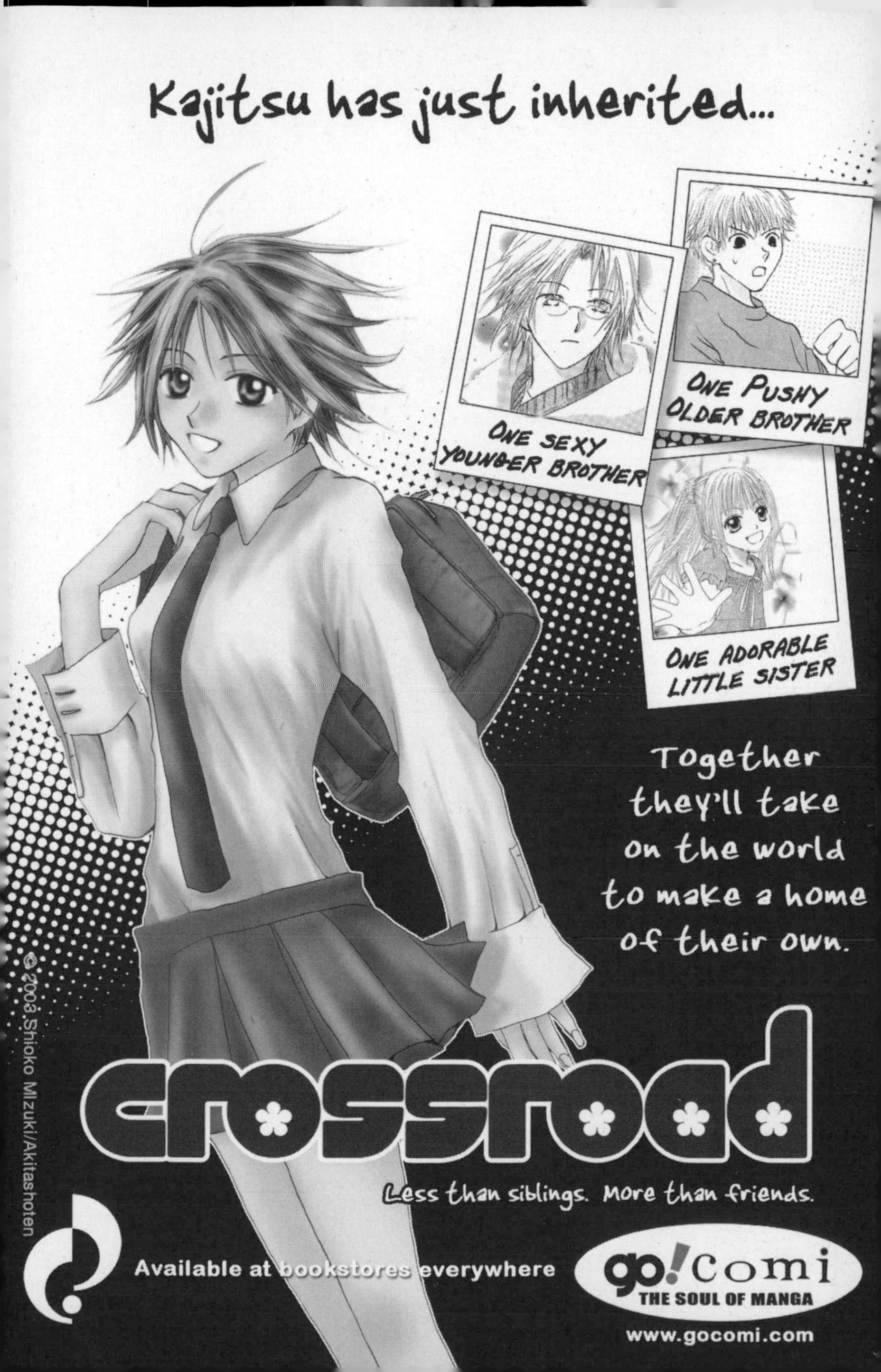
Kajitsu has just inherited...
One sexy younger brother
One pushy older brother
One adorable little sister
Together they'll take on the world to make a home of their own.
© 2003 Shioko Mizuki/Akitashoten
crossroad
Less than siblings. More than friends.
Available at bookstores everywhere
go!comi
THE SOUL OF MANGA
www.gocomi.com

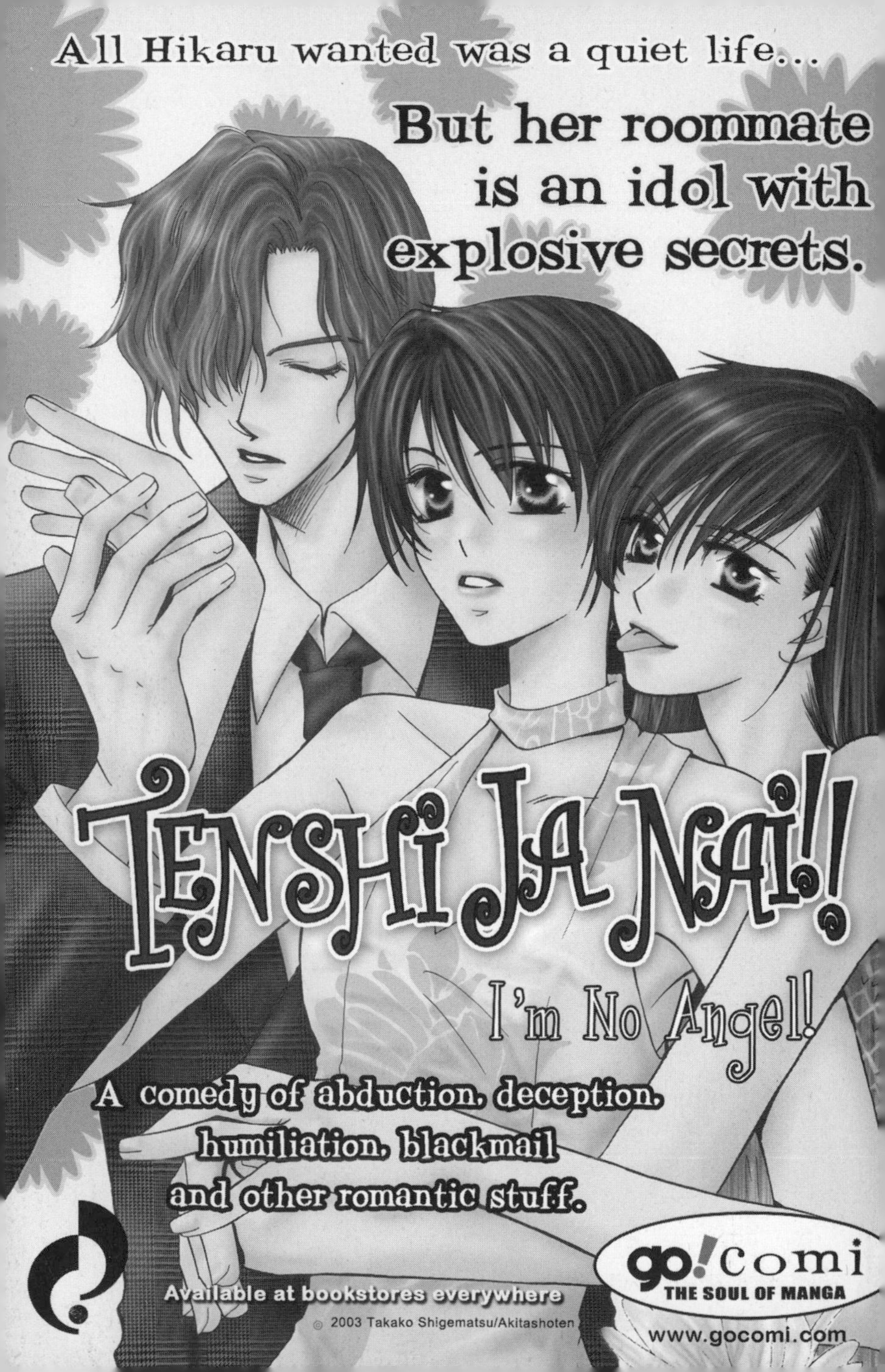
All Hikaru wanted was a quiet life...
But her roommate is an idol with explosive secrets.
TENSHI JA NAI!!
I'm No Angel!
A comedy of abduction, deception, humiliation, blackmail and other romantic stuff.
Available at bookstores everywhere
© 2003 Takako Shigematsu/Akitashoten
go!comi
THE SOUL OF MANGA
www.gocomi.com

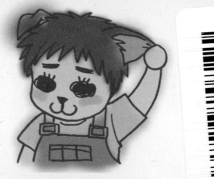

MICK TAKEUCHI

"Those things on top of my self-portrait are supposed to be dog ears. Back when I worked as an assistant to another manga artist, my sensei once told me, "Mick, the way your one ear droops, you look like a puppy." Ever since then I've liked to imagine that once I become a respected manga artist, both of my ears will stand up straight!"

ABOUT THE MANGA-KA

Mick Takeuchi has been creating manga since 1994. Her early works include *Miharu Shinjou Jewelry File*, *A Wise Man Sleeps,* and *Ayakashi Hime Kurenai*. In October 2000, she began *Her Majesty's Dog* (*Jousama no Inu*), her longest and most popular work. It started out as a part-time project, with quarterly chapters, but was so popular that since 2002, it's been running monthly and has become her sole project. When she's not busy working, she enjoys wandering around the city. Her birthday is July 4th. *Her Majesty's Dog* is her first book to be translated into English.